DEMOCRATIC RENEWAL
AND THE MUTUAL AID
LEGACY OF US MEXICANS

▼ ▼

Democratic Renewal
AND Mutual Aid Legacy
THE
of US Mexicans

▲ ▲ ▲ ▲ ▲ ▲ ▲ ▲ ▲ ▲ ▲ ▲ ▲ ▲ ▲ ▲ ▲ ▲ ▲

JULIE LEININGER PYCIOR

*For June,
With much affection
& gratitude,
Julie*

Texas A&M University Press
College Station

Manufactured in the United States of America
This paper meets the requirements of ANSI/NISO Z39.48–1992
(Permanence of Paper).
Binding materials have been chosen for durability.

LIBRARY OF CONGRESS CATALOGING-IN-PUBLICATION DATA

Pycior, Julie Leininger, author.
Democratic renewal and the mutual aid legacy of US Mexicans /
Julie Leininger Pycior.—First edition.
pages cm
Includes bibliographical references and index.
ISBN 978–1-62349-128-4 (cloth : alk. paper)—
ISBN 978-1-62349-165-9 (e-book)
1. Mexican Americans—Social networks—Southwest, New—History—20th century.
2. Mexican Americans—Southwest, New—Societies, etc.—History—20th century.
3. Fraternal organizations—Southwest, New—History—20th century.
4. Mexican Americans—Southwest, New—Social conditions—20th century.
5. Mexican Americans—Southwest, New—Ethnic identity. 6. Southwest,
New—Emigration and immigration. 7. Mexico—Emigration and
immigration. 8. Solidarity. 9. Mutualism. I. Title.
E184.M5P93   2014
973.046872—dc23
2013043595

To Arnoldo De León—and to Mom
and
To the memory of Julian Samora

Contents

Acknowledgments

This long, on-again/off-again project stands on so many shoulders! Almost forty years ago, when first investigating the patterns and significance of mutual aid among US Mexicans, I was aided enormously by *mutualista* members who shared their organizational records, including Jesús Gamboa of Mutual Monte de las Cruces and, in particular, Lucas Garza of Sociedad de la Unión, both in San Antonio. Pulling down ledger books from a shelf above the bathroom of La Unión's headquarters, Garza said, "These minutes almost got thrown out when our old hall was destroyed to make way for the new highway." Dating back to the 1880s, these records offered a window on the workings of the largest *mutualista* society in San Antonio, the city with the largest Mexican population in the first half of the twentieth century.

Work on this dissertation greatly benefited from the insights of my co-directors, Philip Gleason and Julian Samora. A distinguished historian of immigration/ethnicity and so much more, Philip Gleason offered consistent, encouraging guidance. For his part, the trailblazing Chicano sociologist Julian Samora provided a model of research that resonates in the public sphere, while his ongoing Mexican American studies interdisciplinary seminar created the best kind of academic community. As I went on to other research projects, the idea of this book endured, thanks in part to the wonderful encouragement of Arnoldo De León, the dean of Tejano historians. When I was on the periphery of my field (teaching the odd adjunct course and endeavoring to pursue Mexican American history from a bungalow in Flushing, Queens), he facilitated the first scholarly publication of my *mutualista* findings, and later he touted the project to the distinguished editor-in-chief of Texas A&M Press, Mary Lenn Dixon, who stayed the long course (ably assisted, most recently, by Katie Cowart). Thanks also to associate editor Patricia Clabaugh for skillfully shepherding the manuscript through the production process and to the fine copyediting team, notably Amy Peterson and, especially, Marsha Hall.

On viewing the momentous mass immigration marches of 2006, it struck me that they were animated to a large degree by barrio mutual aid that harkens back to historical *mutualista* organizing. In updating the research, I took the bold step—bold for a historian, at least—of recasting the findings thematically from present to past. The idea of a reverse-chronological approach stemmed in part from my experience of having worked with a journalist in recent years, the legendary public broadcaster Bill Moyers (notably in editing his best-selling collection of writings and speeches, *Moyers on America: A Journalist and His Times*[1]). I am also grateful to the two anonymous readers of the manuscript for their endorsement, as historians, of recasting the material chronologically.

Archivists have illumined the way as well, led by Margo Gutiérrez of the Benson Latin American Collection at the University of Texas, who in the process became a treasured friend. Others who have become dear colleagues include Thomas Kreneck and Christine Marín, who were the long-time heads of their respective Special Collections: his at Texas A&M Corpus Christi, hers at Arizona State University. This study also has benefited enormously from archivist Grace Charles at Texas A&M Corpus Christi and the staffs at the Archivo General de la Nación (Mexico City); the Archivo de la Secretaría de Relaciones Exteriores "Génaro Estrada" (Mexico City); the Bancroft Library, University of California, Berkeley; the Briscoe Center for American History, University of Texas; the Institute for Texas Cultures (San Antonio); the National Archives (Department of State Papers); the New-York Historical Society; the New York Public Library; the Sonnichsen Special Collections Department, University of Texas at El Paso; the Stanford University Department of Special Collections; the Texas State Library and Archives; the University of Arizona Special Collections; the University of New Mexico Special Collections; the University of Notre Dame Archives; the Victoria History Center, University of Houston-Victoria/Victoria College; the Walter Reuther Labor History Archives, Wayne State University; and the Webb County (Texas) Heritage Foundation. The library staff at Manhattan College has also been very helpful.

Crucial to this story have been oral history interviews with grassroots organizers and other history makers, all of whom made time amid competing demands to share their insights and recollections. These include Soledad Alatorre; Luis Benítez; Sr. Gertrude Cook; Ernesto Cortés Jr.; Dr. Efraín Domínguez; Herman Gallegos; Clara Gamboa; Jesús Gamboa; Lucas Garza; Gustavo Gutiérrez; Antonia Hernández; Enrique Hernández; Elena Hernández; Ed Idar Jr.; Rubén Navarrette; María Varela, Baldemar Velásquez, and Raúl Yzaguirre.

This book also benefits from some revelatory photographs. Especially generous in sharing their work with me were Juan Alaniz, Rubén Archuleta, James Evangelista, María Gregorio-Oviedo, and Pam Stephenson. I also am most grateful for research grants that supported this project at various points along the way, from a Phelan fellowship at the dissertation stage to a Manhattan College summer grant at the research stage to a Schumann Center grant during the recent recasting of the manuscript material.

Colleagues who have served as informed sounding boards include, at Manhattan College, Joan Cammarata, Ricardo Della Buono, Winsome Downey, June Dwyer, Joseph Fahey, Jeff Horn, George Kirsch, Luis Loyola, Claire Nolte, Michele Saracino, and Margaret Toth. Also extremely helpful while at the college was sociologist Kevin Dougherty, now at Teachers College, Columbia University. The Institute of Mexican Studies of the City University of New York has been a wonderful resource for this project, from the research findings of faculty members Alyshia Gálvez, Robert Smith, and David Badillo to the Institute's Virtual Seminar on Mexican Migration conducted with the Benemérita Universidad Autónoma de Puebla.

Over the years, so many friends have supported my activities that it is impossible to mention them all—they are like the stars in the sky—but I will try to signal those that stand out for their deep constancy. In Texas I must start with my verdadera comadre, Jackie Kerr, M.D., and her husband, political scientist Gary Keith, as well as Jim Harrington, founding director of the Texas Civil Rights Project. Betty Sue Flowers, former director of the LBJ Library, has also provided treasured support. Luckily for me, she now makes New York the base of her increasingly global activities. Others in New York have long encouraged this project, notably Barbara Abrash; Father John P. Duffell; Mary Jane Lilly; Eileen O'Neill (for many years at Random House), and Vanessa Merton, director of the Immigrant Justice Clinic at the Pace University School of Law.

Then there's my family. When I floated this project by my brother, his enthusiasm warmed my heart, while my mom's friendly, interested, but persistent questions about the book's progress encouraged me to stay on track (as did her beloved late partner, Dr. Bernard Brock of Wayne State University, an expert in grassroots political communication). My dear late father, my step-mom, and my sister were wonderfully supportive as well, while my own children have been great. During the course of this project, my Anna and Bob have become fine young adults who care deeply about the world, including the questions raised in this study (as does Bob's dear wife, Celine George). As for my life partner, Stan: twice before in book acknowledgements I referred to him as "my rock." How true that remains— my rock, my ballast, and my love.

Introduction

For all its importance, at first glance nothing seems more peripheral or passé than *mutualista*-style organizing. Few national observers recognize the *mutualista* influence on policy issues today, and no wonder: groups that labeled themselves "*mutualista*" were already in decline by the 1930s and even in their heyday typically operated far from the national stage, in barrios where US Mexicans struggled to survive. In fact, however, the long tradition of barrio mutual aid continues to resonate widely, influencing such important contemporary issues as immigration and the role of organized labor in a global economy.

The mass marches that have brought the immigration issue center stage "constitute a form of *resistance* [*sic*] to racialization, reminiscent of the *mutualistas* in the early 20th century," in the words of social scientist Jonathan Fox.[1] Thus, Part One of the book leads off with "Mutual Aid and Mexican Immigrant Organizing." Mexicans famously constitute the largest US immigrant group today, and they have held that position for more than half a century, while mutual aid organizations themselves are most commonly associated with immigrants. In particular we think of the European immigrants from a century ago, but many activities carried out by Jewish, Italian, and such mutual benefit societies also can be seen in Mexican immigrant mutual aid, then and now, from burial funds to celebrations of homeland traditions.

Mexican immigrant mutual aid often demonstrated more active transnational organizing, however, given the proximity of the mother country. Some of the first Mexican immigrants to the United States had traveled that very same route a few years earlier when the journey had been totally within Mexico; no wonder they tended to disregard the new border laid down in their midst. The Tucson-based Alianza Hispano Americana, for instance, established chapters in Mexico, and its US chapters, stretching from California to New York by the 1920s, made the Alianza the first national Latino organization in the nation. Efforts at mutual aid among today's Mexican immigrants are deeply transnational as well. Known as "hometown associations," or "asociaciones de oriundos," these groups support projects in their towns of origin. This, as the Alianza has been characterized as a hometown association by a historian who rightly notes that a large portion of its leaders hailed from one Mexican state: Sonora.[2]

Many of these Sonorans themselves were transnational, for they had not relocated at all, with their strip of Sonora having been annexed by the United States in 1853. The first *mutualista* activities in the United States—initiated in the second half of the nineteenth century—often were efforts at mutual protection on the part of Mexicans who now found themselves in a minority position. This impetus was reinforced as segregation and discrimination escalated in the first decades of the twentieth century, particularly in the rural Southwest. Thus, even as Mexican mutual aid resembled that of Ellis Island immigrants, it also echoed the venerable, historic African American mutual benefit associations, with "*Mutualismo* and Civil Rights Organizing" constituting Part Two of the book.[3]

At a White House civil rights conference, Raúl Yzaguirre of National Council of La Raza (NCLR) put it this way: "It's a largely unknown, untold story. My organization had its roots with the *Mutualista Movements*, the Mutual Aid Society movement in the 1800's. This was a struggle to protect ourselves against a lot of injustices." In fact, as the leading Latino civil rights organization, NCLR constitutes the largest civil rights organization in the nation overall, in the sense that Latinos constitute the nation's largest minority—and with Mexicans the largest cohort of that minority. And NCLR is among the main actors in immigrant rights as civil rights. In many ways, the *mutualista* civil rights story is an important, overlooked chapter in the civil rights saga of the nation's largest minority group and immigrant group.[4]

The *mutualista* organizing approach also informs two major issues of concern to the general public: job insecurity and the increasing role of money in politics. These are addressed, respectively, in Part Three, "*Mutualista*-Style Labor Organizing" and Part Four, "Barrio Community Organizing."

Part Three begins with a chapter showcasing innovative strategies for a labor movement increasingly on the ropes—strategies that draw on the creative, *mutualista*-style membership drives in the 1950s and 1960s by farm labor organizer Ernesto Galarza and his protégé César Chávez. The importance of the Mexican mutual aid approach is underscored in the second chapter of the labor section, "Trans-Border Organizing." This chapter outlines ways in which some of today's cutting-edge transnational organizing in fact echoes *mutualista* labor activities of a century ago. In 2005, the Farm Labor Organizing Committee (FLOC) extended its labor organizing efforts to Mexico itself, setting up an office in Monterrey. This, even as Galarza in the 1950s had tried to recruit in Mexico, while a century ago, a major US *mutualista* group had established branches in some of the same Mexican cities where FLOC would set up offices years later.

The fact that transnational unionizing dates back a hundred years can buttress the case for a stronger labor role in transnational trade agreements. Ethnic Mexican labor organizing might even resonate with those in the white working class who resent trade agreements that they see as favoring corporate interests: workers whose economic resentment historically has fed into anti-Mexican tendencies. Meanwhile, FLOC is an active member of the institution most commonly associated with the white working class, the American Federation of Labor-Congress of Industrial Organizations (AFL-CIO). Indeed, Latino/a-dominated labor organizations played the main role in persuading the AFL-CIO to officially reverse its restrictionist stance in 2000.[5]

Along with worries over job security, polls show widespread public concern regarding the outsized role in the political process of large financial contributions. "The only answer to organized money is organized people," the legendary community organizer Ernesto Cortés Jr. famously noted.[6] Part Four, "Barrio Community Organizing," traces the vibrant community organizing in many barrios of the Southwest and teases out the links to the *mutualistas* that once empowered people in those very same neighborhoods, from legal aid services to leadership training and experience.

In the opening chapter of Part Four, we meet veteran activist Soledad "Chole" Alatorre and some of her neighbors in the venerable Mexican community in Los Angeles known as Pacoima. All of them are active in the community organization OneLA, even as Alatorre organized in Pacoima half a century ago. Mobilizing immigrant workers, she utilized the *mutualista* approach, working below the radar, at the barrio level, organizing without regard to a person's immigration status. For its part, OneLA depends on neighborhood house meetings, where everyone is welcome, and folks hone their priorities. Then OneLA members by the hundreds assemble from all across Los Angeles to ask pointed questions of leading politicians and business leaders regarding the issues that have emerged as being of paramount concern to them: in this case, mortgage refinancing. This amazing convention of ordinary Angelenos—mostly minority, especially Mexicans—serves as a window into one of the principal bright spots for democratic engagement at a time when powerful financial interests increasingly exercise disproportionate influence on the political process.[7]

On the other hand, the sophisticated policy presentations to top officials—not to mention the diverse ethnic and racial backgrounds of OneLA members—contrast with the historic *mutualista* societies, which emphasized an ethnic Mexican identity and often devoted much of their time to burial insurance. Modern community organizing thus illustrates some of the limits of *mutualista* organizational influence, serving as a reminder that the national attention garnered by US Mexicans today contrasts with the marginal status of most traditional *mutualista* groups, at least officially. Then there is the fact that women hold top leadership posts in today's groups. Thus, NCLR's current president is Janet Murguía, but while women sometimes founded their own *mutualistas,* and not infrequently served as officers in mixed-gender ones, they almost never were elected president. (Such was the case, of course, with most voluntary associations a century ago, including those of Anglo-Americans).[8]

Such disjunctions remind us of the extent to which the past is a different place, as with the *mutualista* ethos having waxed and waned over the course of 150 years. The dominant organizational model in Mexican barrios all across the country by the early decades of the twentieth century, this movement was decimated in the 1930s by the Depression and by mass immigration roundups carried out by public officials. *Mutualismo* was further eclipsed by the rising civil rights movement of the postwar era. World War II veterans, building on the work begun in the 1930s by the League of United Latin American Citizens (LULAC), emphasized equal rights for US citizens of Mexican descent, implicitly defining themselves against the seemingly old-fashioned Spanish-language world of the *mutualista* societies. Take the case of Raúl Yzaguirre: while *mutualista* organizations were important—indeed crucial—to his family's survival and to his ability to further his education, Yzaguirre learned to challenge discriminatory laws through his participation in the principal Mexican American civil rights group founded in the postwar period, the American GI Forum.[9]

This does not mean that the *mutualista* approach disappeared. The main people organizing immigrant workers in the postwar era—many of them targets of the Red Scare, many of them women, such as Chole Alatorre—embraced Mexican mutual aid's transnational perspective and its deep roots in the barrios. The *mutualista* emphasis on recruiting and welcoming members regardless of their immigration status was more relevant than ever, in that the conventional liberal line of the time—including for LULAC and the GI Forum—in fact emphasized restriction, as with liberals' support of Operation Wetback in 1954. Immigrant organizers also were more comfortable with mutual aid's cooperative culture, including an absence of the male military, "patriotic" ethos.

Besides, "men are the flesh but women are the bones" of organizing, according to award-winning community organizer María Varela, and the chapter on women's central leadership role is called "The Bones of Community Organizing." Varela, who came of age in the civil rights and Chicano/a movements of the 1960s and 1970s, was instrumental in the founding of cooperatives among people who had raised sheep in northern New Mexico for centuries, bringing this economic model, in her words, "Into a different environment that still had its fundamental roots in the sort of mutual help and self-sufficiency model of early *mutualistas.*"[10]

Varela's generation, which drew on the example of people such as Chole Alatorre, now is ceding leadership to the rising millennial generation. The challenges and opportunities barrio organizers face today, from global media and the Internet to the increasingly important role of corporate foundations, would seem to be a world away from the barrio-based *mutualistas* of yore, but in fact the *mutualista* approach powerfully addresses both issues. With regard to the media, these groups employed trans-border communication networks that, although modest, anticipated the transnational Web activity of the Mexican immigrant hometown associations, or asociaciones oriundos. As for today's elite philanthropies, although the barrio groups of a century ago seem a world away from these boardrooms, in fact the *mutualista* model is explicitly invoked by major foundations as a cutting-edge template for diversifying their donor base in an increasingly multicultural society. These important, complex findings are explored in the last section of the book, Part Five: "Big Media, Big Money, and *Mutualista* Organizing."

Media coverage of mutual aid organizing among US Mexicans has long been relegated mainly to Spanish-language outlets, with even PBS and NPR, despite their "public" missions, seldom reporting on barrio organizing. (And of course the reactionary media outlets that sometimes vilify Mexicans evidence no interest in reporting on barrio efforts at mutual aid organizing.[11]) In contrast, *La Opinión* newspaper of Los Angeles, for instance, "Does an excellent job of covering our community . . . plays a critical role in getting the word out" to the greater Latino/Latina community, according to Los Angeles attorney Antonia Hernández, director of the California Community Foundation. Nearly a century ago, the grandfather of publisher Mónica Lozano founded *La Opinión* as well as *La Prensa* of San Antonio as independent daily newspapers for Mexican immigrants. By the 1920s, some thirty Spanish-language newspapers were circulating in San Antonio alone, with others being published in Mexican communities large and small all across the United States. These newspapers assiduously reported *mutualista* activities far and wide—and in some cases encouraged locals to found their own groups.[12]

By the 1930s, however, radio began to overshadow the press as the communication partner with grassroots organizing by US Mexicans. Pedro González of Los Angeles, for example, reported on air that mass immigrant roundups were forcing some US citizens to leave the country, and when he was hounded by the authorities and convicted on a highly questionable rape charge, *mutualista* groups were among those who pressured successfully for his early release. Today, meanwhile, nationally ranked radio shows such as *Piolín por la Mañana* have helped fuel the mass immigration protests.

For its part, Univisión sometimes outpaces the major networks in the Neilson ratings, and now the media are enhanced and augmented by the global reach of the Internet. Even those humble immigrant hometown associations boast far-reaching websites. It would seem that ethnic Mexicans, and Latinos in general, are poised to take their place on the main media stage, with barrio-based organizations experiencing media exposure beyond the wildest dreams of those *mutualista* leaders of yore.[13] Even so, a problematic factor has arisen: increasing control of the Spanish-language media by powerful outside financial interests, as with Univisión's takeover by a hedge fund. Of course, the Internet offers a powerful alternative media outlet but itself may be headed in a direction that favors privileged access for corporations. A few Latinos have joined the media reform activists who are calling for "net neutrality," but such liaisons are embryonic. On the other hand, just as *mutualista* organizers a century ago got the word out in a variety of self-supporting ways, today some leaders in self-help/mutual aid are thinking creatively with regard to media outreach.[14]

Meanwhile, barrio-based mutual aid seems remote from today's corporate foundations. In fact, however, major players in the foundation world, such as the Global Business Network's Monitor Institute, argue that the *mutualista* model is essential for the future of philanthropy itself. "Mutualismo Not Filantropía," trumpeted a recent Monitor Institute annual report. At the same time, the Monitor Institute embodies the priorities of the corporate sector in a number of ways, such as with the organization having been acquired recently by a firm that provides legal representation for corporations dealing with labor unions.[15]

NCLR, for its part, has a corporate board of advisors, but in contrast to corporations, it also has a board of advisors from the world of nonprofits and is not opposed to union organizing. In fact, in something of a breakthrough, recently the president of NCLR appeared together with the head of the AFL-CIO at a major news conference on immigration reform. Evidently both NLCR and the labor movement want to work toward democratic revitalization on a number of fronts.[16]

Like NCLR, the *mutualista* movement evidenced links to both business and labor, as does today's barrio community organizing, but in contrast to NCLR, barrio mutual aid has always been characterized by stronger ties to labor than to business. Historically, more than a few Mexican mutual aid officers owned small businesses, but *mutualista* societies seldom partnered with corporations: this, even as *mutualista* labor organizing was not uncommon, as we have seen. And while today organizations such as OneLA occasionally work with businesses, it is organized labor that OneLA lead organizer Ernie Cortés has cited as integral to successful civic empowerment, saying, "If we are interested in restoring broadly shared prosperity to the United States, we must take action to reverse the deterioration . . . of those community-based institutions (i.e., labor unions, schools, churches, and other voluntary associations) that were the foundation of civic culture and historically have buffered working families from the worst effects of a changing economy." Calling for a system that enables each and every one of society's stakeholders to have a place at the table, Cortés speaks of "that reciprocity that makes us human." Indeed, this phrase—"that reciprocity that make us human"—serves as the title for the concluding chapter of the book.[17]

This is the story of cutting-edge organizing with deep historic roots and highly sophisticated tactics on the part of people commonly viewed as marginal—"alien." Such paradoxes were first explored in my book *LBJ and Mexican Americans: The Paradox of Power*.[18] In that 1997 study, I noted that only a few, trailblazing historical works about Mexican Americans had been published. Since then there has been an explosion of such studies, including a number focused on one aspect or another of US Mexican organizing. One important work, among many, is Stephen Pitti's *The Devil in the Silicon Valley: Northern California, Race and Mexican Americans* (2003), which, in its analysis of power relations in Northern California, reveals a vibrant *mutualista* subtext.[19]

With regard to *mutualista* labor organizing, my work has been aided by books such as Roberto R. Calderón's study of the Texas/Coahuila mining region and Rodolfo Acuña's *Corridors of Migration*, on Arizona, California, and the adjacent states in Mexico. One of the most useful sources for both immigrant and civil rights *mutualista* activism is *Catarino Garza's Revolution on the Texas-Mexican Border* by Elliot Young. Garza operated as a *mutualista* leader at the same time that he was campaigning against the Texas Rangers and the Mexican dictatorship of Porfirio Díaz, and this book serves as a reminder that the chronicle of a single life can add depth to our understanding of historical events—even as biographies of US Mexicans remain scandalously rare.[20]

The lingering *mutualista* influence is seldom noted in studies of current US Mexican activism today. Important exceptions include a study on Latino civic engagement by the Woodrow Wilson Center and political scientist Immanuel Ness's analysis of the intersection between immigrant organizing and labor organizing.[21] Situating *mutualista* activities in the context of US mutual aid groups in general was facilitated by David Beito's findings in *From Mutual Aid to the Welfare State* and Theda Skocpol's *Diminished Democracy: From Membership to Management in American Civic Life*.[22]

"There are writings on mutualistas, on labor, on various other types of organizations, but this is the first work that attempts to provide a synthesis of the relationship between these groups over a long period of time," wrote an anonymous reviewer of this manuscript. This historian also pointed out that "although clearly a work of history, it is written with a clear eye toward contemporary relevance."[23] Indeed, each chapter begins with an account of the *mutualista* influence on a social movement today and then traces that story back through time.

The book's contemporary framework reflects the fact that in the new millennium, US Mexicans have moved from the perceived periphery of the national discourse to its center, with both the general public and elite opinion makers curious but confused and sometimes wary about such a turn of events. Now is the time for this story of democratic engagement, at once cutting-edge and deeply historical, with important lessons at both the grassroots and transnational levels.

PART I

Mutual Aid and Mexican Immigrant Organizing

Banding Together for Survival

The phone rang at the California immigration organization, and the message was urgent: a man was on the verge of death. Rushing to the site, the staffers discovered to their horror a person reduced to "skin and bones, almost like a cadaver, or like the people found after World War II at the gas chambers. The people that brought him abandoned him in the desert," according to one of the rescuers, Soledad "Chole" Alatorre.[1]

This was but the latest outrage that she and her colleague Bert Corona had encountered. When some growers detained workers in empty gasoline barrels, Alatorre likened this "hateful and underhanded" treatment to slavery. Similar incidents in Florida resulted in the Coalition of Immokalee Workers (CIW) mounting a photo exhibition about contemporary slavery in the fields. "When CIW co-director Lucas Benitez speaks of ending chattel slavery, he's hardly exaggerating," reported *The Nation*. "His organization has pushed the Department of Justice to prosecute five agricultural slavery rings in the South. In one case, undocumented workers had been bought from smugglers and kept under armed watch, their wages garnished to pay for their housing and other 'debts.'"[2]

Simmering resentment over such horrors helped lay the groundwork for the mass immigration marches of 2006 (with the spark provided by a congressional bill that, if enacted, would have made it a felony to violate immigration regulations or even to assist an undocumented immigrant). In the history of the United States, never had so many demonstrators turned out. From Chicago to the Deep South, they marched in 140 cities, with more than a million demonstrators in Los Angeles alone. Incredibly, the mass movement took place virtually without incident, with people mostly wearing white shirts and carrying American flags. Almost universally, they cast their message in terms of sober civic engagement, as if to give lie to those characterizing immigrants in general and Mexicans in particular as ignorant aliens lurking in the shadows. By demanding legislation to regularize the legal status of millions of people residing in the United States, the activism served notice to policy makers that immigrants were not some sort of disembodied "problem."

Despite the banner headlines, however, one major aspect went virtually unreported: the self-help/mutual aid organizations so instrumental in this mobilization. Called hometown associations (HTAs) (*Clubes de Oriundos* in Spanish), each HTA is comprised of people from the same hometown in Mexico. It was not media outlets but rather three Latina social scientists who noted that "the three states that experienced the largest turnouts in the spring, 2006 marches, by far—California, Texas, and Illinois—are also the three states that together account for the vast majority of Mexican HTAs." Indeed, although the US immigrant population is diverse, Mexicans famously constitute the largest cohort, as has been the case for decades. Thus, the second-most prominent flag, after the Stars and Stripes, was that of Mexico.

As a report by the Russell Sage Foundation noted, "Due in part to sheer numbers and new destinations, the most recent waves of Mexican immigration are leading to fundamental yet energizing social change in American society." After all, as they noted, "Mexico shares a 2,000-mile border with the United States and has become the country's second most important trading partner," even as "Mexican-origin communities in the Southwest . . . predate the arrival of Euro-Americans, as the names of streets, rivers, cities and states attest."[3]

Certainly this is true of the marches' epicenter, Los Angeles, with Mexicans the largest group of new residents—and also the largest population group when the city was part of Mexico. At the Los Angeles marches of 2006 and 2010, many of the placards featured Bert Corona. He passed away in 2001, and the rescue by Corona and Alatorre of the skeletal immigrant in the desert in fact took place some forty years ago. In the words of Alatorre, "We saw what would happen in the future."[4] Yes, Corona and Alatorre's Hermandad Mexicana Nacional (HMN) anticipated today's immigrant organizing. Their trailblazing organization at the same time drew on an even older tradition, the *mutualista* movement of the early 1900s. HMN constituted "a mutualista organization, a self-help social service agency that was also utilized as an organizing strategy," according to one researcher.[5]

Alatorre herself puts it this way: "We said, 'This we're not going to be able to do by ourselves,' for there were so very many people. Our solution was mutual aid. . . . The first order of business was to answer the needs of the undocumented—to teach the workers how to organize, how to do what was mutually necessary for them, and it was done under the obligation of *mutual aid* [her emphasis]: the one that knows, teaches the other one. He who has gone to obtain his unemployment insurance teaches the one going for the first time—and with Social Security . . . immigration forms. . . . This happened daily."[6]

Or as Bert Corona explained in his memoirs: "We needed and wanted

Figure 1. Many US flags and some Mexican ones in the mass immigration protests, 2006. (Courtesy Visions of America, Universal Images Group, Getty Images)

the participation of our members. We needed voluntary services in maintaining our headquarters, gathering food and clothing, and in our public demonstrations against the [immigration service] and the Border Patrol. We were an extended family, which looked after the needs of all of its members. All of this kind of assistance we got from our members."[7]

The early members also contributed their own *mutualista* organizational knowledge. Some immigrants brought information about such groups in Mexico, but, some also had relatives long resident in California who said that barrio mutual aid had a long history in the state. In noting the lingering *mutualista* influence, Chole Alatorre cited the example of La Beneficencia Mexicana. At the same time that Alatorre and Corona were founding their group along *mutualista* lines, La Beneficencia was advising several clubs formed by immigrants from Zacatecas. These Zacatecan groups, in turn, constituted some of the very first HTAs and in 1972 formed the first HTA federation, La Federación de Clubes Zacatecanos del Sur de California, which remains an important immigrant alliance.

Unlike HTAs, traditional *mutualistas* were not officially organized by or for people from the same hometown, although rural *mutualista* aid groups often were comprised of people from the same Mexican town. A few HTA federations active today even call themselves *mutualistas,* including a group in Houston from San Luis Potosí (Sociedad Mutualista Potosinos Unidos), and immigrants from a town in Guanajuato who now live in Ketchum, Idaho (Club Mutualista Amigos de Gervacio Mendoza). More importantly, much the same motive animated early organizing in both HTAs and *mutualistas:* how to respond to the crisis posed by the death of a loved one in a strange land. Many of the HTAs initially formed to provide funds for flying home the body of the deceased.[8] And although historic *mutualista* groups did not send the body back to the Mexican interior in that pre-jet era, they worked to assure that the dearly departed would receive a respectful burial and not end up in a potter's field.

Typically when a person passed away, the association's president convened a special meeting to plan the funeral. Members took turns representing the society at the wake, and someone who neglected this assignment could be fined. The association also sent its condolences to the family, as when the member of a San Antonio *mutualista* group thanked the society for its sympathy on the death of his mother, who, he proudly noted, was a descendant of a Mexican general who had fought the French invaders in the battle commemorated on Cinco de Mayo.[9]

Burial policies led to illness insurance, with benefits like those of mutual aid organizations for Europeans, Asians, and Puerto Ricans. In line with standard insurance principles, these grassroots mutual aid groups aimed to ensure that only some 10 percent of the membership would claim benefits at any one time. The typical *mutualista* constitution specified that each new member be healthy, under a certain age, able to prove good character by having no criminal record, and be sponsored by two active members. Proof of steady employment was also required, but not skilled or professional work, and some members listed themselves as "common laborers." On presentation of an illness certificate signed by a physician, the member would receive between fifty cents and two dollars per day, depending on the society.

Indeed, the exigencies of establishing a financial fund meant that the regulations were, if anything, more detailed and formalized than the rules governing the typical Mexican immigrant association today. A century ago most of the groups published booklets containing the constitution and the rules spelled out in formal (Spanish) language. As stated by a typical constitution, the organization was obligated "to aid members in time of sorrow . . . to hear all their petitions or complaints," to pay a weekly sum to bedridden members, to pay for funeral expenses, and to aid bereaved family members financially. The documents also spelled out the members' rights with regard to voting, holding office, and private use of group facilities such as libraries and meeting halls.[10]

Some groups even tried to anticipate the best response in the event of the demise of the organization, with one association providing that if the society disbanded, the members would divide the funds equally, while another decreed that a vote would determine the allocation of the remaining assets. In other words, the constitutions tried to provide a workable procedure for every contingency, from the organization's establishment to its possible dissolution. In flush periods, many groups offered enhanced benefits, from legal aid to continuing education to lectures and cultural events.[11]

The more successful associations issued death benefits amounting to as much as six hundred dollars—nearly what a common laborer or farmworker might earn in a year. In the San Antonio barrios of that time, in neighborhoods with little indoor plumbing and more than a few tin shacks, a family of six lived in an average of two rooms, amid rail yards and factories creating noise and pollution. Some of the societies even managed to continue issuing payments despite major natural catastrophes. In the horrific influenza outbreak after World War I, when forced to cancel two meetings due to the illness of its officers, Sociedad de la Unión of San Antonio nevertheless made good on the benefits for many of the infirm.

So recalled a typical *mutualista* member, Lucas Garza, a young man who had found steady if humble employment. Even though more than a few members of Sociedad de la Unión were small shopkeepers and neighborhood professionals, the largest cohort tended to come from the working class. More than half a century later, Garza still recalled with pride the date of his admission: February 22, 1924. Born in the Mexican town of Villa Hidalgo in 1908, Garza came to Laredo at age 15 with his father and brother. There they toiled in the coal mines ten hours per day for a mere 75 cents, so they quit and headed for San Antonio. When young Lucas could not find work, he and a cousin left to lay track for the railroad.

They had come north from the Mexican interior via the rails, after all—on a rail system built by US interests. Now railroad employment took them to Houston, Galveston—where they witnessed the totemic 1915 hurricane—Fort Worth, and, finally, that great rail hub of Chicago. There, Garza married a Mexicana who also had come up from San Antonio. The couple began a family, and they very well might have settled in Chicago, where he had joined the American Federation of Labor. But when his father died in 1922, Lucas felt compelled to return to Texas.

He and his wife raised three more children, and he noted that all of them were baptized at the venerable San Fernando Cathedral. One of his older brothers had landed a position as a foreman for the city, and he told Garza of an opening as a municipal laborer. The brother also touted the benefits of Sociedad de La Unión. Indeed, he himself may well have heard

of the municipal job through "La Unión," which counted among its honorary members an important city operative, Jacobo "Jake" Rubiola. In addition to Garza's brother, a family friend also praised the group, and Lucas
signed on. Two years later his beloved brother died, and Sociedad de La
Unión gave him a solemn funeral that Lucas Garza would never forget,
with the members solemnly assembled in their *mutualista* regalia.

Garza was also a typical member in that he was male, like the majority of
the immigrants and *mutualista* associates. Today as well, most immigrants
and HTA members are male. At the same time, it is clear that women such
as Gloria Saucedo, a leader of the Los Angeles mass marches, are central to
today's immigrant organizing. In contrast, women seldom headed mixed-
gender *mutualista* groups, but some served as officers. Others founded
their own *mutualista* associations. Moreover, the activities run by women,
whether officers or not, were crucial to the success of those organizations,
from gathering important neighborhood news to organizing elaborate
fundraising.[12]

Like today's HTAs, some *mutualista* groups established networks of
chapters. Just as the Zapotecan HTAs formed a California federation in
the 1970s, the group that had first advised them, La Beneficencia, itself
had branches throughout Southern California. This was in the 1930s, when
thousands of people were being forced to suddenly leave the United States
for Mexico. Some left out of economic desperation. Many more were victims of the immigration roundups that caused panics from the Southwest
to Detroit, with the largest number of mass arrests occurring in Southern
California. Often the principal, and even the only, organizations these immigrants could turn to for help—that they could trust—were the mutual
aid associations operated by their neighbors and friends. *Mutualista* groups
raised money and did their best to advise panicky immigrants, sometimes along with the Mexican consulate. Unlike today, however, no protest
marches arose, for the anti-immigrant fever was at its most virulent in the
worst of economic times, and white Anglo-Saxon superiority was assumed
by many public officials in this pre-civil rights era. The barrio-based organizations and alliances did what they could, helped where they could, even as
their own membership ranks were decimated and their coffers rapidly depleted. Today this organizational legacy lingers in a kind of half-life through
the HTAs and in the grand former headquarters of La Beneficencia, which
now serves as the cultural center La Casa del Mexicano.[13]

Like La Beneficencia, a number of other California *mutualista* groups established federations. In 1917 the *Los Angeles Times* reported that a league
of *mutualista* organizations had been founded there, and by the 1920s a
second *mutualista* alliance included a very active branch in Santa Barbara,

Figure 2. La Casa del Mexicano—Comité de Beneficencia Mexicana. (Photo by Anne Cusack, Copyright © 2008 *Los Angeles Times*, reprinted with permission)

whose projects included a baseball team. Meanwhile, Santa Barbara–based *mutualista* associations banded together in a local Confederación de Sociedades Mutualistas, which sponsored celebrations that drew thousands of the city's residents. This local confederation also worked with Mexican patriotic groups and the Santa Barbara Mexican consul in planning major holiday events, including a commemoration of Mexican Independence that lasted for three days. According to the Santa Barbara *Morning Press,* the festivities attracted "practically every member of the Mexican colony." As one barrio resident recalled years later, "There was so much going on all the time . . . there was never a dull moment."[14]

From baseball teams to traditional festivals, *mutualista* associations helped immigrants navigate their new world while still honoring their own culture. In that sense, these organizations resembled the mutual benefit associations of the European immigrants who came through Ellis Island. For instance, Bert Corona noted that his organization resembled not just those of Mexicans but also the ones founded by European immigrants. A major study of today's Mexican HTAs likens them to immigrant organizations formed in earlier eras by Jewish and Japanese newcomers—even if the report more closely links these HTAs to the historic Mexican *mutualista* groups, characterizing them as "important in labor organizing, business development and local politics."[15]

A few venerable *mutualista* associations still manage to carry on today, such as Sociedad Mutualista Mexicana, the Mexican Society of Youngstown, Ohio. One longtime leader puts it this way: "Our parents came here years ago, to the Mahoning Valley, to find jobs. They discovered there were cultural problems and language barriers. They needed each other." The group was founded, in its words, "To preserve the honor and good name of our Mexican nationality." And today, according to a Youngstown journalist, the organization's leaders "point out that the stereotypes about Mexico and Mexicans need to be destroyed." The members reminded him that seven US states were once part of Mexico and "that Mexicans are a hard-working and resourceful people." One officer called for even more advocacy on behalf of immigrants, saying, "People who have served in the armed forces, people who have given so much, and are very much part of this community—I'd like them to speak up when they hear on the radio . . . 'Mexicans!' this, and 'Mexicans!' that . . . to pick up the phone and say, 'Wait a minute . . . that's my people—that's me!' And what are you saying about these people? Let me tell you something about my story, before you decide to paint us as—whatever—criminals."[16]

A Mutualista Mexicana officer who herself immigrated to Youngstown points to the importance of the soccer games sponsored today by the society. Operating within a safely innocuous "recreational" frame, they echo an organizing tactic long used by barrio mutual aid groups, whether hosting a dance or a boxing match at their headquarters or sponsoring a baseball team, as with that *mutualista* in 1920s Santa Barbara. Moreover, as Bert Corona pointed out, immigrants sorely lack recreational outlets.[17]

Today, soccer leagues constitute powerful organizational tools in Mexican immigrant communities from Texas to New York. One of the founders of a Mexican soccer club in California puts it this way: "It was from our link to these sports events that it occurred to us to form an association that would have more diverse goals. . . . One of our first goals was to buy an ambulance for our town." Similarly, a group of immigrants from Ocampo, Guanajuato, who came to Dallas and formed a soccer team went on to found an HTA with the motto "Solo Juntos Lo Lograremos" ("We Will Only Achieve Things Together"). In that spirit they participate in the national network Casas de Guanajuato.[18]

Or take the case of immigrants to New York City from the town of Ticuani, Puebla: "Ticuaneses create and reproduce a transnational political community, a Ticuanense 'we' that is understood in the zocalo in Ticuani as well as on the baseball and soccer fields of Brooklyn," notes a path-breaking study of Mexicans in New York.[19]

Such organizing offers mutual support for vulnerable people, many of whom have been unable to become legal residents, let alone citizens. For their part, historically Mexican barrio associations "flaunted their allegiance to Mexico at a time when such demonstrations were derided, discouraged, and suppressed by American society. They represented models of resistance and cultural identification that inspired subsequent generations of Mexicans," notes historian Juan Ramón García in his history of Mexicans in the US Midwest. For instance, in East Chicago, Indiana, a *mutualista* group founded in the 1920s by indigenous people from Michoacán was named after the Aztec prince Cuauhtémoc. As for Michoacán immigrants to the Chicago region today, many belong to the Federation of Illinois Michoacán Hometown Associations, *Federación de Clubes Michoacanos en Illinois*. This serves as a reminder that the Midwest has long been an important (if secondary) destination for Mexican immigrants.[20]

Although California has been the principal destination for Mexican immigrants since the 1930s, Texas held that title in earlier times. Take the case of Bert Corona, whose immigrant organizing was so important in the later decades of the twentieth century. He came to California from El Paso, where his parents were among the many immigrants who helped that border city grow tenfold between 1900 and 1910, and exponentially in the wake of the Mexican Revolution of 1910–20. Emigration was also fueled by US industrial recruitment during World War I, followed by laws in the 1920s restricting immigration from southern and eastern Europe. About one million Mexicans entered the United States between 1900 and 1930, especially through Texas, where they soon outnumbered the longstanding Mexican-heritage population.

In El Paso, a dozen *mutualista* organizations were active by 1919, with such groups springing up wherever Mexican immigrants were settling, from countless rural enclaves to Houston, where some of the associations soon owned their own headquarters and, in at least one case, a theater. Corpus Christi *mutualista* organizations, meanwhile, actually outnumbered all the Anglo American associations combined. Predictably, it was San Antonio that emerged as the unofficial capital of the *mutualista* movement. Not only did more Mexicans settle there than in any other city, but it also served as the railroad hub for immigrants headed elsewhere: to the steel mills and factories of the Midwest, or the sugar beet fields of the Great Plains. By the 1920s, countless *mutualista* groups were operating in San Antonio, including a few dating back to the 1870s and 1880s.[21] These groups "worked for the betterment and good name of *mexicanos*," reported San Antonio's *La Prensa* in 1925, the largest Spanish-language newspaper in the United States at the time.[22]

Then and now, Mexican immigrants have joined together for mutual aid and protection. Despite the daunting difficulties—and in response to those same challenges—US Mexicans have woven networks whose extensive reach is belied by their barrio origins.

Dealing with the Mexican Government

Few people in the United States recognize that Mexican immigrant hometown associations (HTAs) sponsor innumerable construction projects back in Mexico—let alone that US Mexicans have been engaged in trans-border mutual aid for generations.

Money sent back home by immigrants constitutes Mexico's second biggest revenue source, and while individual remittances account for most of this, the amount from HTAs is significant and growing. Impressed by this, the Mexican government in 2002 began offering to triple the HTA funding: the 3x1 program. Mexican president Vicente Fox himself touted this initiative on a swing through the United States in 2003. By 2008, over five hundred HTAs in thirty-five US states were sponsoring two thousand five hundred such projects in twenty-seven Mexican states. No wonder the president of the Inter-American Development Bank has characterized 3x1 as "a leading axis of economic and social development."[1]

At the same time, some analysts see the matching funds as something of a ploy—a safety valve to reduce pressure for increased tax rates on upper-income Mexicans—even as the government's contributions actually pale in comparison to those of the largely working class, often-undocumented HTA members. One Mexican journalist noted acerbically that the government funds devoted to the program barely exceeded the money allocated by the Mexican president for his own public relations and polling consultants. Indeed, projects sponsored independently by Mexican immigrant organizations have long been the main sources of aid—"0x1," Zacatecan immigrants have dubbed them.[2]

It was just such projects carried out by Zacatecas HTAs that prompted state officials in Zacatecas to suggest the first matching-fund initiative in 1993. Some of the very first HTAs were founded by California Zacatecans in the 1960s, and Zacatecans had been immigrating to the state for generations, dating back to the heyday of the *mutualistas*. These groups also provided aid to communities in Mexico—albeit more sporadically, as in 1943 when *mutualista* associations in Los Angeles spearheaded a relief effort after a hurricane struck the west coast of Mexico.

Today's aid dwarfs such initiatives, with the support so influential that the Mexican government in 2006 began allowing emigrants to vote in Mexican presidential elections. That year both of the main candidates spoke of the need to lobby Washington for immigration reform, but they differed sharply on the measures they proposed to improve the Mexican economic conditions that trigger much of the emigration in the first place. Andrés Manuel López-Obrador of the social democratic Partido de la Revolución Democrática (PRD)—"AMLO," as he was dubbed by his supporters—called for restoring the tariffs on agricultural imports (so as to protect small farmers from the competition with cheap crops from highly subsidized US agribusiness), restoration of land guarantees to small farmers and community farms as provided by the Constitution of 1917, government jobs programs, and enforcement of Mexican laws protecting the right of workers to organize. Felipe Calderón of the conservative Partido de Acción Nacional (PAN) emphasized deregulation, privatization, and international trade policies to encourage foreign investment and job creation. AMLO won most of the expatriate vote, which helped make the outcome exceedingly close, with Calderón declared the winner in a highly contested result.[3]

This influence of US Mexicans and their associations, while at historic heights, is not unprecedented. More than a century ago, *mutualista* organizers in the United States influenced Mexican national politics as well. Some even led rebellions against the longtime dictator Porfirio Díaz, notably *mutualista* leader Catarino Garza.

Born in 1859 just across the border from Texas, Garza immigrated to the United States in the 1870s. This was immigration in name only, however, for the international boundary had been established only a few years before his birth. Garza came north at a time when US companies were linking the two countries together, and at one point he was a traveling salesman for Singer Sewing Machine—in Mexico. Still, Garza emerged as a main critic of US business practices in Mexico, carried out with the encouragement of the corporatist Porfirian regime.[4]

By 1890 Garza had established an organizational network in South Texas consisting of several *mutualista* groups and a number of newspapers, including *El Mutualista*. The following year, when fellow anti-Porfirian activist Ignacio Martínez was gunned down on the streets of Laredo by agents of the regime, Garza led a raid on Mexican forces just across the border. After several skirmishes, his band returned to Texas, where news of the exploits swelled the ranks to five thousand. The US Army and Texas Rangers scoured South Texas for Garza enclaves. The Rangers were particularly aggressive in their pursuit, vandalizing several ranches. Garza decried attacks

Figure 3. Catarino Garza, c. 1894. (Courtesy The Daughters of the Republic of Texas Library, Rose Collection, #CN96.801)

on Texas Mexicans by "los rinches," as the Rangers were derisively known by Tejanos.

Garza fled to the Caribbean, then to Colombia. He met his demise in a firefight with forces of the Colombian dictatorship, supported by US Marines sent "to protect American interests there," according to *The San Francisco Examiner*.[5] Catarino Garza's revolutionary message lived on via one of his Texas cohorts, Paulino Martínez, who provided the launching pad for the Mexican Revolution of 1910. Out of Martínez's San Antonio print shop, Francisco Madero published the call that stirred Mexicans to overthrow the Díaz regime in this, the first major revolution of the twentieth century.[6]

Even as Garza was operating out of the Brownsville area in the 1890s, another *mutualista* leader and rebel, Víctor Ochoa, was organizing in El Paso. Like Garza, Ochoa was born in a Mexican border town: in this case Presidio, where his father worked as a customs official and was rumored to have helped supply the forces of Benito Juárez against the French invaders in the 1860s. Víctor Ochoa founded several *mutualista* organizations in Texas, including the Unión Occidental Mexicana, whose founding principles included open discussion and moral rectitude, along with mutual aid.

Calling Porfirio Díaz a "monarch," Ochoa raised troops on both sides of the border and raided a number of Mexican government installations. Arrested in 1893 in El Paso on charges of having smuggled arms to his forces in Mexico in violation of US neutrality law, Ochoa was tried in Fort Stockton, Texas. He managed an acquittal and continued to elude the Mexican secret police, but Texas Rangers captured him the following year, and this time he was convicted. Stripped of his US citizenship, Ochoa was sentenced to two years imprisonment at Kings County Penitentiary in Brooklyn, New York.

From this point on, however, Ochoa's story contrasts markedly with Garza's, for Ochoa left behind the world of *mutualista* organizing and rebellion to become a businessman entrepreneur, reinventing himself— through inventions. After his release, Ochoa remained in the New York area, where he developed a reversible gas motor and a pocket clip for pens and pencils, eventually selling that patent to the famed Waterman Pen Company. That same year, 1907, Ochoa sold the patent for an electric brake to the American Brake Company.

These inventions, utilized by millions of people, nonetheless were overshadowed by his most spectacular invention: a collapsible, transportable airplane, the "Ochoaplane." Within a few years he was the president of the International Airship Company, and as the head of his own business he presented himself as a member of the white elite, telling the New York– area press that his mother's family was of Scottish background and that his family had owned considerable land prior to its takeover by the Porfiristas. The reinvention worked. Ochoa's acceptance was such that his citizenship rights were reinstated by President Theodore Roosevelt himself. Ochoa married Amanda Cole, granddaughter of the celebrated artist Thomas Cole, founder of the Hudson River School of painting.[7]

Given that Ochoa was de-emphasizing his Mexican side, it is no surprise that he made no contact with the Sociedad Mutualista Mexicana of New York City. This, even as his shift from revolutionary to businessman would not have bothered this particular *mutualista* organization, which held an event at the Waldorf-Astoria Hotel, evidencing none of the revolutionary fervor that Ochoa and Garza had shown during their time as *mutualista* organizers.

While some barrio mutual aid groups were led by revolutionaries and/or championed radical goals—notably with regard to labor organizing—most avoided debates over Mexican politics. This reluctance increased once the various revolutionaries turned on one other after toppling the corrupt Díaz regime in 1911, with the internecine bloodshed fed by the new machines of war. Award-winning memoirist John Phillip Santos of San Antonio wrote that some of his Mexican family members "were never much taken with 'American-struckedness,' but they weren't Mexican nationalists either . . . didn't particularly care for any of the warring factions. In fact, politics seemed to them little more than chicanery in fancy trappings. . . ." Santos described the situation this way: "Abuelo Jacobo wasn't going to wait until he saw his adored sons fighting each other across barricades for the benefit of good-for-nothing *pelados* and *charlatans* in Monterrey and Mexico City . . . . The roads led north, and Mexico lost an entire generation to migration and war. Many went to San Antonio, joining the legions of Mexicanos who had already been there for so long."[8]

"Outposts of the 'pueblo Mexicano'" (as Santos calls them) also were established from Missouri to Pennsylvania. A seven-year-old girl who fled with her family from the central Mexican state of Guanajuato eventually ended up in Indiana. "I recalled many things," she recounted to the author some sixty years later. "I saw the soldiers, and since I was young, I wasn't afraid at all. . . . Only I walked through the streets getting whatever I was able to get, because after a while you couldn't get hardly anything . . . because the soldiers didn't leave a thing. They dumped over the small pails and fed their horses everything that had been harvested. Many people died of hunger. One of our aunts died of hunger, and she had four children, and one of them also died."[9]

By the 1920s, US Mexicans had founded *mutualista*-type associations in barrios all across the United States. Some of these groups established nationwide networks, as was the case with the Comisiones Honoríficos and Brigadas de la Cruz Azul. The honorific commissions, as their name implies, concerned themselves mainly with cultural and patriotic events, whereas the Cruz Azul (Blue Cross) focused on helping those in need—not unlike the Red Cross, although Cruz Azul's model likely was Cruz Blanca (White Cross), founded in Laredo by Leonor Villegas de Magnón, initially to aid injured members of Venustiano Carranza's revolutionary army.[10]

Soon after they were founded, Cruz Azul and Comisión Honorífica chapters were busy distributing model labor contracts in English and Spanish that had been drafted by the San Antonio consulate in response to what *La Prensa* of San Antonio called "the frequency . . . of complaints of Mexicans" over having been tricked into signing unfair labor agreements. Just two years after the first groups were founded in San Antonio, a convention was held there, with twenty-seven Comisiones and twelve Cruz Azul brigades sending 150 delegates. They voted to establish a legal aid fund "for the defense of those compatriots that have litigation in American tribunals," and a number of dignitaries addressed the conference, including an official from the Immigration Service and even the mayor of San Antonio himself.

These groups often gave honorary membership to important Texas officials while still maintaining close ties with the consulate, and at public events members sang both national anthems and displayed both flags.[11]

In navigating transnationally, these organizations were showing their barrio neighbors how to do so as well. "It wasn't just a matter of holding festivities," longtime immigrant organizer Chole Alatorre says, emphasizing that these "patriotic groups," as she called them, were early supporters of the Mexican immigrant community.[12] Such was the case all across the United States. In fact, the Cruz Azul was such a widespread instance of women's organizing that in less than five years it was operating in nearly every community with a Mexican consulate, including Minnesota, New York, and even Alaska. Cruz Azul Mexicana may well have been the first nationwide Latina organization in the history of the United States.

In Texas alone at least fifty brigades were operating just three years after *La Prensa* reported the organization's 1921 founding in San Antonio by "ladies of our colonia, to help the needy . . . to bring the counsel of charity to Mexican families struck by the blows of sorrow."[13] One such leader was Josefina Rosales Ypiña, who became active in Cruz Azul just a few years after immigrating with her family in 1918 to Houston. Aiding immigrant women and their babies, she instructed mothers in childcare, sanitation, and English. To this extent she resembled the WASP settlement house workers who sought to "improve" the immigrants, even as Ypiña stood in contrast to them personally, for she, like the women she served, was a Mexican immigrant.

The Cruz Azul launched numerous projects in San Antonio, notably a medical clinic that offered free services to hundreds of barrio residents, thanks in part to support from the large local *mutualista* network and contributions by the consulate. At the clinic's inauguration in 1925, the secretary of external relations, the Mexican equivalent of secretary of state, was among those in attendance. Other Cruz Azul chapters also founded medical centers. In fact, the first such clinic came not in San Antonio but in the much smaller Mexican community of San Francisco, with the San Antonio project delayed due to wrangling among local Cruz Azul leaders.

A number of Cruz Azul brigades founded libraries, and some even sponsored primary schools in Mexico, in that respect presaging the transnational projects of the HTAs. The Cruz Azul also aimed to lessen the suffering of Mexicans returning to their homeland. These organizational efforts dovetailed with the Mexican government's policy of trying to stem the depopulation of its countryside. In 1921 the San Antonio Cruz Azul helped one thousand people return to Mexico, and a few years later the El Paso Cruz Azul established Casa de Repatriado across the border in Ciudad Juárez.

This trans-border project provided sustenance for those setting out on the long, arduous trek back to their homes deep in the Mexican interior.[14]

But working with the consulate could be a two-edged sword. When the Los Angeles consul general saw that *mutualista* associations were organizing into confederations, he sponsored his own alliance. In 1925 he called a meeting of the many *mutualista* and related barrio organizations, which resulted in the founding of the Confederación de Sociedades Mexicanas (CSM), with the consul named honorary president. In that capacity he presided over grand Mexican holiday celebrations and sometimes asked the CSM to spearhead charity campaigns. Then, in 1927, according to historian Gilbert González, "The CSM made the momentous decision . . . to organize the first Mexican labor union in the United States," noting, however, that "initiative came directly from President Plutarco Elías Calles" in hopes that such a union would affiliate with the Mexican government's official union. The CSM approved the resolution "overwhelmingly," writes González, even as the Mexican government had "its fingerprints over the whole enterprise," with this meddling alienating many of the local organizers. In contrast, the independent CSM, with its active community involvement, continued operating, sponsoring events into the 1930s.[15]

At this time, a number of *mutualista* organizations in Mexico and the United States had long been in contact with each other, and a few US *mutualistas* even founded chapters in Mexico. Leading the way was the Arizona-based Alianza Hispano Americana (AHA), which had established 44 lodges in Mexico by the mid-1930s. The majority were in northern Mexico, particularly in the state of Sonora. To the extent that they constituted a kind of "Club Sonorense," they presaged today's HTA federations. The AHA also established two chapters in Mexico City.

The Mexican government evidenced keen interest, and no wonder, for by this time the AHA constituted not only the largest *mutualista* in the United States but also the largest Hispanic organization in the United States, period—and arguably the first national Hispanic association in US history. The attention from Mexican government officials, however, mostly proved problematic. Mexico demanded that the Alianzas invest in Mexican government securities rather than US bonds: yet another indication of the desire on the part of the post-revolutionary government to influence if not control the Mexican community abroad. As a result of these factors, along with difficulties in monitoring the increasing internal problems of the Mexican lodges, the AHA severed relations with its Mexican branch in 1936. This episode serves as an early illustration of problems that can arise with transnational organizing efforts. At any rate, the AHA's Mexican project constitutes a trailblazing instance of such activism.[16]

Today this trans-border legacy lives on. As Mexican scholar Cecilia Imaz notes, "Through organisations such as *mutualistas, Juntas Patrióticas, Comisiones Honoríficas,* union organisations, Hometown Associations and State Federations, the Mexican government, based on its extended consular network, has developed ties with the organised Mexican migrant population in the US." She points out that "this relationship between the Mexican government and the organised Mexican immigrant community is the core element of an evolving process of political transnational activities."[17] Particularly noteworthy was Mexico establishing an advisory council in 2003 consisting entirely of Mexican immigrants, the Consejo Consultivo del Instituto de Mexicanos en el Exterior (CCIME). CCIME representatives are elected in a process conducted by the forty-six individual consuls across the United States, making it extensive and grassroots while at the same time maintaining a connection with the highest level of the Mexican government.

Official links can also spell political manipulation, however, as when a CCIME member from Milwaukee was selected because of his ties to the local consul, according to the Milwaukee newspaper *El Conquistador,* which also accused this CCIME representative of selling phony US identification cards to Mexican immigrants. Even so, as Imaz notes, "With the formation of the IME [Institución de Mexicanos en el Extranjero/Institute of Mexicans Abroad] and the CCIME, the institutionalisation of this transnational relationship goes beyond any precedent in the history of the Mexican government's efforts to address the needs of the Mexican immigrant community *from both sides* [sic] of the border."[18]

This path-breaking civic engagement means that Mexican immigrants can directly address the president of Mexico on policy issues of concern to their community. Thus, CCIME representative Rita Méndez gave a speech before Mexican president Felipe Calderón in 2009. After praising his administration's "promotion of diverse educational programs" both in Mexico and among Mexicans in the United States, this Mexican immigrant woman presented the president of Mexico with a transnational challenge: to lobby the White House to end the legal limbo faced by college-age Mexican immigrants to the United States.

"Mr. President," Rita Méndez began, "we are confronting the return of Mexican families from the United States. This demands attention in many respects, but one of those that has the most repercussions is the inclusion of the children of these families in the Mexican school system." And in the United States of America, she reminded, him, undocumented immigrants were not eligible for financial aid of any kind. "Mexico cannot continue deprecating its human talent," she told him. "We cannot hold ourselves back in this manner. Investment in human capital is the most effective kind. These students are an invisible population, the most unprotected, the most silenced. These young people have aspirations like any other Mexican student; many are exceptionally brilliant and with the highest promise, but they find themselves in No Man's Land. Nobody claims them; they don't exist in the eyes of the Mexican government, nor for the United States either."

Méndez then upped the ante, calling for nothing less than transnational citizen action. "These students can be one of the forces of progress for both nations," she declared. "Why do we keep denying them this possibility? We do not have the luxury of divided efforts. . . . We can't draw borderlines between nations that share the same route—this route that represents the generating of citizens with the capacities that our world demands. Activism is a privilege," she told the President. "I feel proud to exercise it. Our capabilities can elevate us in the face of adversity and transform crisis into opportunity."[19]

When President Calderón congratulated President Obama in 2012 for the executive action temporarily allowing undocumented student-age immigrants to remain in the country, the Mexican head of state must have had in mind the sentiments of people such as Rita Méndez.

Responding to US Immigration Policies

When the immigration-reform marches burst onto the national scene in 2006, some fifteen hundred Mexican immigrant "hometown associations" (HTAs, Clubes de Oriundos) were important to that effort. HTAs have come a long way since the founding of the first such groups in response to the implementation of the Western Hemisphere quota in 1968. Starting that year, suddenly no more than twenty thousand immigrants would be allowed to enter the United States annually from Mexico (other than immediate family members). This low numerical ceiling, which has scarcely risen in the ensuing years, makes it impossible for many if not most Mexican immigrants to receive official permission to enter a land a) that is contiguous with their own, b) that is formerly their own, c) that has long been a site of migration, and d) whose economy has long been tied to their own.

Fifteen percent of Mexican immigrants surveyed in 2006 claimed HTA affiliation, and participation in these groups often leads to involvement in US civic life, according to a survey of Chicago immigrants, the majority of them Mexican.[1] No wonder such major politicians as the mayor of Chicago and the governor of Illinois took part in the 2006 march organized to a large extent by a federation of HTAs, the Federación de Clubes Michoacanos de Illinois (FEDECMI). Encouraged, organizers in Chicago teamed up with their cohorts in Los Angeles to plan a nationwide demonstration in 2006 for immigration reform. The result constituted the largest marches in the histories of both cities.

The seeds for this Chicago/Los Angeles nexus were planted in the 1970s, when young people working in Southern California with Bert Corona and Chole Alataorre came to Chicago "to begin organizing the undocumented in the Pilsen barrio," according to the director of the University of Chicago's Human Rights Program, Susan Gzesch. She pointed out that in the Chicago barrio, the Californians "worked with local Mexican-American/Chicano leaders, including students who had become politically active at the University of Illinois-Chicago to protest INS [Immigration and Naturalization Service] raids. Settlement houses in traditional Mexican neighborhoods were transformed from purely service-providers to centers of community activism."[2]

Back home, the California activists "had organized against a succession of bills aiming to curb or criminalize immigration," recalled Javier Rodríguez, who explained that this came about when he and other young people

> ... decided to join forces with Bert Corona, a legendary figure in the immigrants' rights movement. He was from the binational community in El Paso/Ciudad Juárez, but had come to California in the 1930s, working as a longshoreman before becoming a labour organizer. In 1968 he and Soledad Alatorre founded CASA, the Centro de Acción Social Autónomo [sic], which aimed to organize the immigrant community and provide them with legal advice, documentation, help with housing and so on. . . .
>
> CASA was the first to organize undocumented immigrants, though it also focused more generally on working-class Mexican-Americans. . . . We held marches, started petitions and a lobbying campaign, set up mailing lists. We defended people who had been fired for being undocumented, and went to challenge Immigration and Naturalization Service raids when they took place.[3]

The young activists began by simply going up to people who were outside the office waiting for the bus, where the organizers heard such things as "they gave me a document and I don't know what it says" and "I don't speak English, and the boss gave me yet another form." So noted Chole Alatorre, who added, "The students, who knew English and Spanish, would say to them, 'Don't worry. Look: go over to that office over there, and they don't charge a cent. . . . ' And many people began to come—and thus we began."[4]

Among those early volunteers who went on to national leadership roles, Alatorre cites José Gutiérrez of Latino Movement USA and María Elena Durazo, executive secretary-treasurer of the Los Angeles County Federation of Labor. Alatorre says of Durazo, "I feel proud that . . . she has said, 'Chole is my mentor.' She was helping when she was a university student, was a volunteer." When Durazo alerted Alatorre and Corona to striking immigrant workers who were facing reprisals by local police, CASA encouraged the young woman to represent them there, says Alatorre, adding, "She had a lot of responsibility—and a lot of affection for the people."

Another such protégé was Gloria Saucedo, a prominent figure in the immigrant movement and the leader of today's main offshoot of CASA. As one activist told the Los Angeles newspaper *La Opinión* in 2005, "Luckily Gloria Saucedo, a former student of Bert Corona's and head of the immigrant advocacy Hermandad Mexicana Nacional had set up Placita Olvera Working Group that November"[5]—just one month prior to the passage of a bill reclassifying as a felony offense even minor violation of immigration regulations. Approved by the House of Representatives without fanfare at the height of the Christmas season, the Sensenbrenner Bill caught everybody by surprise, which made Saucedo's Placita Olvera Working Group of critical importance.[6]

With the Senenbrenner Bill, everyone knew someone who would be considered a felon for coming—or, even, for not turning in someone who had resided in the United States with no hope of doing so legally. The organizing of US Mexicans against such a prospect constituted the latest in a long line of barrio actions in the face of problematic US policies: complicated, often manipulative, and frequently misunderstood, even by the experts.

Immigrants from Mexico historically were relatively free to enter the United States, and sometimes the government officially sponsored recruitment of temporary Mexican workers. Nonetheless, officials periodically carried out mass expulsions. Moreover, as all of the decisions were overlain with nativism. On the one hand, Mexican immigration was not subject to any numerical limit until 1968, even as the US government created contract labor programs for recruiting Mexican workers during World War I and from 1942–64. On the other hand, these workers were not eligible for permanent residency, let alone citizenship, unless they went home and re-entered as regular immigrants. And in times of public anxiety— over the economy, national security, or both—government authorities would suddenly conduct massive immigration sweeps on often-questionable grounds, with some US citizens of Mexican ethnicity even caught in the dragnet.

The first major Mexican immigration roundup came after World War I, when an economic downturn combined with the Red Scare tactics of US attorney general A. Mitchell Palmer. *Mutualista* associations from Texas to Indiana mobilized to assist the thousands of people being pressured to return to Mexico. Some of these "repatriados" had themselves been recruited as temporary contract laborers when the United States entered the war and faced a labor shortage. Many of those forced to leave were in such desperate straits that Mexican president Alvaro Obregón promised to send financial aid to the Texas consulates. The money was slow in arriving, however, and much of it never materialized. In this crisis the women's organization Cruz Azul mobilized, truly earning its "brigade" moniker.

The San Antonio Cruz Azul brigade led the way, but the Dallas Cruz Azul assisted over one thousand desperate people, and the Laredo Cruz Azul provided so many return train tickets that it nearly depleted its treasury.

These women, as immigrants themselves, mobilized despite any deportation risks they themselves might have faced. At the same time, many of the Cruz Azul organizers were married to professionals, and the women used those connections to lobby employers, calling on them to stop singling out Mexicans for dismissal. The request was largely in vain, for as women and Mexicans, in the end they had little bargaining power with business executives.[7]

Organizing by Mexican mutual aid organizations occasionally did yield results, as in Los Angeles in 1926, when La Confederación de Sociedades Mexicanas and the Liga Protectora Latina, supported by the consulate, successfully defeated an anti-immigration bill. The proposal would have required the city council to exclude from municipal projects any contractors that hired noncitizens.[8] This success was particularly notable, for that same year a bill was introduced in Congress to establish a restrictive quota on Mexican immigration.

Pushing for the quota bill was the American Federation of Labor (AFL), which argued that US job applicants were disadvantaged by growers recruiting in Mexico. The AFL was ignoring the many immigrants who were themselves forming unions, with many in the AFL invoking stereotypical language to buttress their economic argument. Such racist talk constituted the first principle for the bill's sponsor, Congressman John Box of Texas; no friend of organized labor, Box drew mainly on the Social Darwinist theories popular among many social scientists and the "half-breed" stereotypes still held by many Anglo-Texans. "No other alien race entering America provides an easier channel for the intermixture of blood than does the mongrel Mexican," the Congressman declared, adding that "their presence and intermarriage with both white and black races . . . create the most insidious and general mixture of white, Indian and negro blood stains ever produced in America."[9]

Even those members of Congress who opposed the Box Bill nonetheless agreed with him that Mexicans should not be encouraged to become permanent, equal members of US society. Employers made the case that unlike Europeans or Asians, Mexicans crossed an adjacent border and would return home once they had accumulated some savings. When pressed by skeptics, growers said that these workers could be sent back by the authorities, if necessary. This wholesale characterization of Mexicans as temporary and solely as laborers—rather than as individuals deserving an equal place in US society—rendered people from Mexico vulnerable to both employer exploitation and official immigration sweeps. The "alien" label also connoted "subversive," with Congressman Box charging that "an effort is being made to make Mexico the basis of operations for the Bolshevist and red operations in Texas and America."

After the defeat of the Box Bill, the State Department attempted to mollify the proposal's supporters by tightening visa procedures. Congress, for its part, established the Border Patrol, along with new entrance requirements and a "head tax." Mexican *mutualista* organizations presciently recognized that these seemingly minor policy changes could provide legal pretexts for future immigration sweeps. The Alianza Hispano Americana (AHA) noted with alarm that on the one hand, someone not able to document that a job awaited them risked being rejected as "likely to become a public charge," but on the other hand, anyone producing such documentation ran the risk of being deemed in violation of the law that prohibited US companies from contracting abroad for workers.

Mexican mutual aid/self-help groups held meetings in major Mexican population centers but also in rural outposts such as the dusty little South Texas town of Cotulla. The local Comisión Honorífica invited the Mexican consul in Laredo to come and inform cotulla residents about the policies. The June 1929 meeting was held with much fanfare, according to *La Prensa* of San Antonio, which reported that a fancy motorcade of women and children escorted the Consul to the meeting site, the local "Mexican" school. There he was greeted by the local orchestra, which serenaded him with the Mexican national anthem, and he addressed an audience of one thousand five hundred.[10]

The public nature of this event was truly amazing, given local Anglo attitudes. "We don't want them to be associated with us. We want them for their labor," the resident of a nearby town told a researcher at that time, with another quoted as saying, "They increase like rats. If something is not done we will soon be shoved out of the picture."[11] Segregation was wholesale in Cotulla, with the local "Mexican" school separate and unequal from the "American" one. It seems surprising that the segregationist school board would have countenanced such a large, public, Mexican-run affair—even if it took place after the school year ended, as is likely—but perhaps the board members did not mind as long as it occurred on the Mexican side of the tracks.

The "Mexican" school's principal, meanwhile, had departed at the end of the term. This principal was none other than Lyndon Baines Johnson. But even if the Comisión Honorífica had wanted to use the building during his school term, Johnson likely would not have opposed the idea. Even though he was distantly related to the local segregationist judge and was praised by the segregationist school superintendent, the young principal was known for his dedication to the students, such that Johnson's teaching staff criticized him for "fraternizing" with the Mexicans.

At any rate, the meeting at Johnson's school was an important one, for within a few months the *San Antonio News* was reporting "a hegira of Mexican people who were thrown into a panic by deportations, arrests,

Figure 4. A photo of the segregated "Mexican" school in Cotulla, Texas, taken one month before the meeting held on the premises by the local Comisión Honorífica to address recent changes in US immigration policy. Lyndon Baines Johnson is the tall figure in the center, behind the students. (Courtesy LBJ Library photo by Unknown)

rumors."[12] With the onset of the Depression, officials from the Southwest to the Midwest rounded up people in the barrios on the flimsiest of charges.[13] *Mutualista* associations across the country demanded that municipalities at the very least provide aid for the people being repatriated under such duress. The organizations also lobbied the Mexican national government for transportation, free shipment of personal belongings, relief funds, and resettlement land grants. The Confederación de Sociedades Mutualistas and the Cruz Azul in Los Angeles were especially active, calling for an immediate end to this policy that they scored for specifically targeting immigrants from Mexico.

From its base in Mexico, meanwhile, the Unión de Repatriados Mexicanos accused the Mexican government of reneging on its promises to aid those repatriated. The Unión's lobbying made little headway with the Mexican authorities, in part due to the opposition of many people in Mexico, themselves struggling to survive and skeptical of any program to assist folks who had left the "homeland" in the first place. Also lobbying the

Mexican government were repatriated members of the AHA, but to little effect. As AHA members, however, they remained eligible for the group's considerable benefits.

It worked both ways; this expansion in Mexico may help explain why the Alianza's membership increased at a time when economic depression and repatriation pressures were decimating *mutualista* groups. This decline also was part of a general trend among mutual benefit societies of every ethnic and racial group, however, all of which faced competition from New Deal social programs and from commercial insurance companies that were lifting their exclusion of non–Anglo-Saxons. Despite such pressures, some *mutualista* associations still managed to provide critical assistance at this desperate time, with many a widow painstakingly writing heartfelt thanks in pencil on plain brown tablet paper.[14]

When the United States entered World War II, officials turned around and sponsored a recruitment program. Dwarfing the World War I version, the 1942 Bracero contract labor agreement remained in effect until 1965. Neither this fact, nor the lack of a Mexican quota, however, prevented another spasm of mass arrests at the height of McCarthyism in the 1950s.

One main target was the Alianza Nacional México-Americana (ANMA), a trailblazing advocate for immigrant rights, with many varied sponsors, but nonetheless labeled "Communist" by the federal government. ANMA functioned along the lines of a mutual aid group: by and for its members, mostly from the barrios, with Spanish used much of the time, and with several *mutualista* groups participating in its founding. The new organization broke new ground with its goals, however, as when it called on the United Nations to investigate the conditions of immigrant workers in the United States on behalf of what ANMA called "the traditional rights of the Mexican people to migrate to the borderlands without being prosecuted."[15] And ANMA affiliated with diverse groups far beyond the Mexican community. The 1949 founding convention included not only progressive *mutualista* and labor organizations but also the American Civil Liberties Union and several African American newspapers, along with the Communist Party.

The FBI simply labeling ANMA "Communist" rendered its largely immigrant leadership liable to prosecution under the 1950 McCarran Act, which gave the federal government sweeping powers to deport anyone considered a Communist, and the 1952 McCarran-Walter Act, which provided for stripping US citizenship from immigrant Americans deemed disloyal and for deporting "undesirable aliens." ANMA leaders were targeted even though none of the charges led to convictions. Then in 1954, at the same time that Senator Joseph McCarthy was on nationwide television making reckless charges of Communist infiltration in the federal government, the Eisenhower administration instituted Operation Wetback. The government reported that this unprecedented dragnet resulted in more than one million people being deported to Mexico by year's end.[16]

The role of working nationally on behalf of Mexican immigrants now fell to another Alianza: the venerable mutual aid group AHA. Like ANMA—but also like many traditional *mutualistas* before it—the AHA provided legal aid, establishing a center in the largest Mexican barrio in the nation, East Los Angeles. The AHA took the lead in a number of immigration court cases, notably when the Supreme Court ruled in its favor, restoring the citizenship of Daniel Castañeda González.[17] AHA also worked on court cases with the major Mexican American civil rights organizations of the time, but only on civil rights cases, for the League of United Latin American Citizens (LULAC), Mexican American Political Association (MAPA), and GI Forum focused on combating discriminatory laws against US citizens of Mexican descent. Here they made civil rights history. At the same time, most of the "GI Generation" of Mexican Americans did not question the reigning labor and liberal view of immigration policy, which emphasized punishing employers that hired immigrants who had entered the country without official permission, and even called for some immigration restrictions.

LULAC, MAPA, and the GI Forum, along with the AFL, lobbied for termination of the Bracero Program, arguing that someone entering as a contract laborer was legally tied to a single employer for a specifically limited period of time—forbidden to quit, let alone become a citizen or even a permanent resident. It was the only situation under which quitting a job constituted breaking the law. The leaders of the liberal wing of the Democratic Party saw immigration restriction as a progressive counter to exploitive employers. GI Forum ally Dr. Ernesto Galarza knew that those who complained about employer abuse or tried to sign up braceros as union members often found themselves targeted as "Communists." At the same time, these anti-Communist liberals kept their distance from ANMA, with the red baiting suffered by immigrant-rights advocates only serving to make the Cold War liberals even more vocal in their patriotism. Their lobbying resulted in the termination of the Bracero Program in December 1964.

The following year, Congress enacted the Hart-Celler Act, including a provision that would establish a strict limit on the number of people allowed to enter from the Western Hemisphere. GI Forum leader Dr. Héctor P. García lobbied against the Western Hemisphere quota, calling it "not only discriminatory but insulting" for suddenly forbidding the entry of most Mexicans, with their long history of crossing back and forth over the border. This position stood alongside the GI Forum's strong opposition to temporary contract labor programs and its call for sanctioning employers who hired undocumented applicants, but the latter stances would fall by the wayside in the 1970s.[18]

The open attitude toward immigrants traditionally taken by the *mutualista* organizers re-emerged and came to dominate the national discourse thanks to the work of immigrant organizers such as Chole Alatorre and Bert Corona. They recognized immediately the problems posed by the new policies. "The revisions in the immigration laws that had been made in 1965 and also in the 1970s for the first time placed a limit on immigration from Mexico and Latin America," Corona recalled. "Whereas before Mexicans could easily migrate across the border, as they had been doing since the nineteenth century, now immigration from Mexico was restricted to twenty thousand people annually. This was a ridiculous figure, given the previous levels of Mexican immigration; there was no way the quota could be enforced."[19]

To make matters worse, this stricture went into effect at a time when the number of people seeking to enter the United States from Mexico was increasing exponentially, as, for example, with all of the men who had applied for the Bracero Program that was now being terminated. And as Corona pointed out, "The Mexican economy failed to provide adequate employment. Although the Mexican government had increased investments in luxury tourist facilities, these did little to produce jobs for an expanding population."

Ironically, more than a few analysts mistakenly ascribe this rise in Mexican immigration to the 1965 immigration act itself—the very legislation that instituted the quota! This is largely a case of mistaking correlation with causation. The 1965 Hart-Celler Immigration Reform Act—spearheaded by the descendants of Jewish and Italian immigrants and signed by President Lyndon Johnson at the foot of the Statue of Liberty—famously abolished the discriminatory quotas that had severely restricted the entrance of people from southern and eastern Europe and had virtually excluded Asians. This change did open the door for Asian immigration, and both Asian and Latin American immigration increased exponentially after 1965. But as Corona and Alatorre witnessed firsthand, the law proved draconian for Mexican immigrants. Although the 1965 Act allotted the same percentage of slots to every sending region regardless of race, ethnicity, or religion, and although the discriminatory categories were scrapped in favor of non-racist criteria such as marketable skills, imposing a very limited numerical quota meant that Mexican migration—which predated the border itself—was suddenly and permanently restricted.[20]

Except for a few loopholes—notably for immediate family members—and a temporary amnesty in the 1980s, the numerical quota remains an insurmountable legal barrier for most Mexican immigrants. But where could Mexican immigrants turn in this crisis situation? In the 1970s the mighty AHA had faded away, while LULAC, the GI Forum, and MAPA were still mostly emphasizing legislation that would punish employers of undocumented immigrants.

"As part of my decision to organize the undocumented, I removed myself from MAPA," Corona recalled.[21] A MAPA founder, he had been deeply involved in its major campaigns against segregation and voting discrimination. Like many other World War II veterans, he thought that mobilizing for civil rights required tactics that transcended the old *mutualista* approach. Corona noted that in "the mutual-benefit societies/*logias* and the church groups, few leaders inspired the Mexicans to participate in formal politics or to use political action to redress grievances. Nothing was being done to build a political base in order to elect Mexican candidates to office." As a result, MAPA "had grown considerably in the 1960s, from nothing to one hundred five chapters."

On the other hand, Corona's experience in the armed forces differed from that of most MAPA members. As he saw it, "I entered the service as a buck private, and I left as one. I paid the price of having been involved in progressive causes and was one of those stigmatized and red-baited because of my involvement [in radical labor groups of the 1930s]." By the 1970s, he became increasingly alienated from MAPA because, he said, "MAPA had fulfilled some of my expectations, but not all, especially with respect to bringing in large blocs of working people—including immigrants. . . . This was especially critical because of the increasing number of Mexican and other Latino immigrants coming into the country." In the Mexican American civil rights groups, Corona saw what he considered a worrisome trend: "Increasingly middle-class lawyers were coming to be the driving force inside the chapters. Here we had a people who were ninety-five percent workers being led by five percent lawyers and other professionals. It just didn't make sense." This, even as he was hearing about "mass raids in downtown L.A." by immigration authorities, who, he said, "would seal off the entrances of a factory or a big apartment complex and force everyone to prove their citizenship or status . . . raided bus stops . . . in some case broke into homes and, without warrants, arrested people who turned out to be US citizens. . . . [O]fficers claimed, as they still do, that they could detect 'illegals' merely by looking at them . . . this was blatantly racist. But it took place all over southern California."[22]

Corona and Mexican immigrant Chole Alatorre, whom he knew from the labor movement, picked up where the AHA had left off. They set up shop in Alatorre's living room out of necessity but also as a way to organize deep in the Los Angeles immigrant community. They operated along the lines of mutual aid, soliciting both grievances and donations throughout the neighborhood. They also linked up with virtually the only California association by and for Mexican immigrants at that time, the San Diego–based Hermandad Mexicana Nacional (HMN). Founded in 1951 by veteran labor organizers Phil and Albert Usquiano, HMN had grown to four chapters but was on the brink of collapse, mainly due to investigations of Phil Usquiano by the powerful House Un-American Activities Committee. Corona and Alatorre took charge of the organization and shifted the locus to Los Angeles.

This was in 1968, the same year that the Western Hemisphere quota went into effect, and anxious immigrants by score came to HMN's local outreach centers, which the organizers dubbed CASA (Centro de Acción Social Autónoma). According to Alatorre, "We informed people that . . . they did not have to incriminate themselves"—that the only information the immigration authorities could legally demand was a person's name and address and that an immigrant "had a right to an attorney and to be released on bail." They made clear to immigrants that, as Corona put it, "Every person in the US, regardless of citizenship status, is covered and protected by the US Constitution."

Confusion on this point was exacerbated by the Immigration and Naturalization Service (INS), as the federal agency was then known. Echoing the repatriation procedures of previous eras, the INS sometimes pressured those apprehended to sign an agreement to return "voluntarily." According to Corona, "Out of some seven hundred thousand recorded voluntary departures in the late 1960s and early 1970s, only about one hundred people had been given the right to legal counsel." HMN/CASA filed suit and the policy was revised, at least on paper. The immigrant activists filed other suits as well, a number of which led the courts to overturn deportation decisions "based on the facts revealing that people had been improperly or falsely arrested with no proof that they were deportable," said Corona.[23] They were taking the AHA's approach to a new level.

The immigration activists used to their advantage the main loophole in the quota: that it did not apply to immediate family members. As Corona explained, "Many people who had been here for years, with immediate family members who were permanent residents or citizens, found they could appeal their deportations." Even so, says Alatorre, the immigration service made excuses for withholding the application forms, telling Corona that they had run out of them. Undaunted, he said, "Never mind, we'll make copies."[24] Using a hand-cranked mimeograph machine and cheap, tan-colored paper donated by a union at Alatorre's prompting, they produced hundreds of forms and helped the immigrants fill them out. The authorities, however, rejected them outright on the grounds that they were not printed on white paper. Angry, the organizers said, "We pay taxes; why can't we get the forms?"

They complained to Senator Alan Cranston and, Alatorre says, the immigration officials "sent us *boxes* of them!" Events nonetheless took an ominous turn. A worker at the local post office told the organizers that their mail was being held up, purportedly because officials wanted to know the meaning of the Aztec eagle emblazoned on the organization's return address. When HMN/CASA leaders threatened to picket the post office, the officials reacted angrily, but the mail went out.

Many a time, when immigrants were tempted to give in in the face of threats, Corona preached to them about their rights, noted Alatorre: "Bert got a hold of the Constitution of the United States in Spanish. He said, 'Look! Look what it says! This Constitution written by people who had been foreigners when they came here! It does not say, as does the constitution of Mexico, for example, "All Mexican *citizens* [sic] have a right to this, that, and the other." . . . The constitution of the United States is not made this way, as so many constitutions are made. . . . The constitution of the United States is not made that way because all of them were undocumented, were foreigners, and they made it "all PEOPLE"—it's made for the *people*, not just for *citizens*.'"

Four years after the quota went into effect, the California legislature began considering a bill to penalize employers of "illegal aliens." HMN/CASA, while equally critical of these growers, nonetheless argued that such immigrants did not embody illegality any more than did someone with a traffic ticket, and that these were productive members of society. As former labor activists, Alatorre and Corona also made the case that this type of legislation, far from helping unions, would enable businesses to discriminate against anyone who "looked illegal" and as such would be used by employers to harass Mexicans trying to organize their fellow workers. HMN/CASA led protests across California, with immigrants and their supporters personally lobbying the legislators in Sacramento. The bill became law, but the California Supreme Court ruled it unconstitutional on the grounds that immigration regulation was the purview of the federal government.

The quota remained in effect, and with the possibility of apprehension always hanging in the air, who could be trusted? Best to rely on one another, now that even going to a beach or to an amusement park meant having to keep an eye out for *la migra,* with something as simple as a CASA potluck supper serving as an emotional lifeline. Alatorre and Corona knew that even if the *mutualista* movement itself was in permanent eclipse, the *mutualista* ethos remained essential. "We needed voluntary services in maintaining our offices, gathering food and clothing, and in our public demonstrations against the INS and the Border Patrol," said Corona. "We were an extended family, which looked after the needs of all its members." He also made a historical comparison to the mutual aid aspects of ANMA, for which he had served as Northern California director. "As had been the case with ANMA, our general meetings with the Hermandad were family-based," he explained. "We talked about how the immigration laws were affecting our people."[25]

Within a few years, the HMN/CASA claimed thousands of dues-paying immigrant members, with many of the members volunteering for their organization. But the volunteering transcended mutual aid, for folks not aided by the group also played an important part, including law students, Chicano undergraduates, social workers, priests, nuns, and ministers. By combining forces they were able to serve tens of thousands of immigrants within a few years, and by 1973 they had expanded to San Diego, Oakland, San Antonio, Seattle, Chicago—even New York City. With this growth, however, came organizational challenges. Some of the younger activists, especially in more distant chapters, spent much of their time putting forth a Marxist critique of the capitalist economic system. This faction did not gain much traction at the grassroots, however, and it was on the wane by the end of the 1970s. It was the specter of just such problems that had prompted so many traditional *mutualista* associations to prohibit discussion of political ideologies.

Through all the organizational turmoil, Corona and his colleagues kept up their lobbying efforts, with their group constituting "the premier migrant rights advocacy organization in the country," in the words of historian Armando Navarro.[26] In the halls of Congress they pointed out the unrealistic, unworkable nature of current regulations, especially given the contributions immigrants were making to US society. These immigration-reform lobbyists also scored economic policies of both the US and Mexican governments that they said were driving people out of Mexico.

Corona and his cohorts did not, however, emphasize the argument that "they do the work Americans won't do," for these veterans of the labor movement knew that this was the mantra of business leaders—the same people bent on keeping unions out of their factories and fields. Plus this corporate-led argument against restriction explained why so many progressive and labor Democrats continued to hold to the view that immigration policy should emphasize punishing employers for hiring people that came from Mexico without legal approval.

Little by little the arguments espoused by HMN/CASA, so similar to those of the *mutualistas* before them, began to take hold. Corona recalled an emotional meeting with Democratic liberal lion Ted Kennedy. This meeting in the marble halls of power was a far cry from the limited effects of the *mutualista* efforts of yore, and yet it was the testimony of Mexican immigrant members of Corona's group that shook the senator most deeply, such that the famously eloquent public figure barely managed a reply. It struck Corona that it was in fact these "illegals in the shadows" who had changed the mind of a man at the center of power.

Ted Kennedy's shift was emblematic. The old labor/liberal approach emphasizing punishment of employers was now increasingly on the defensive. Although the 1986 immigration law did include employer sanctions, questions of racial profiling hobbled their implementation and were a factor in the ongoing rethinking of the immigration issue within the Democratic Party. Moreover, in order to pass the legislation, it included for the first time a provision providing temporary amnesty for some undocumented immigrants. HMN/CASA leaders had pushed for a total amnesty, and they criticized the outcome.

But something was better than nothing, so they spearheaded the law's implementation. They filed a successful lawsuit that required immigration officials to disseminate information about the program more clearly and thoroughly. The association's offices assisted some one hundred sixty thousand people in a number of states to qualify for amnesty and, if they wished, for citizenship. The activists won grants for this work from foundations interested in civic engagement, but questions arose about how the money was being administered, with suits and counter-suits, even as Corona was going into physical decline and finally passed away in 2001. The HMN eventually was legally cleared, but it never fully recovered.[27]

By this time, the Mexican immigrant HTAs were beginning to proliferate, with the members banding together in ways reminiscent of *mutualistas* in times past. HTAs have provided mutual support in the face of seemingly impossible barriers to legalization, such as quotas enforced with increasing rigor after the 9/11 attacks heightened the crisis mentality of the general public. If your members all hail from your own hometown, so much the better, given this climate of fear and mistrust. The militarization of the border rendered Mexican immigrants increasingly stranded in the United States, unable to visit family members back home, an unintended consequence of restrictive immigration policies. HTAs became increasingly attractive. Sharing a frustrated longing to visit their loved ones, immigrants from the same hometown began raising money for parks and schools and water systems, making concrete their love for the community of their birth.

HTA membership ranks also grew thanks to the temporary amnesty of the 1986 law. In addition, this legislation enabled hundreds of thousands of people to become citizens—the vanguard of those chanting, "Hoy Marchamos, Mañana Votamos" ("Today We March, Tomorrow We Vote"). Many of the HTAs and related immigrant organizations have spearheaded efforts to register immigrant voters. In Chicago, for example, they have been key players in a citizenship program sponsored jointly by the state of Illinois and the Illinois Coalition of Immigration and Refugee Rights. Called the New Americans Initiative, its first director was a leader of a federation of Michoacán HTAs: Federación de Clubes Michoacanos de Illinois (FEDECMI).

Also active in Illinois's New Americans citizen project is an umbrella group comprised of eight federations, each representing a different Mexican state. Together, this "Confederation of Federations" represents some one hundred HTAs. Founded in 2005, it is called the Confederación de Federaciones Mexicanas (CONFEMEX). CONFEMEX has been especially active in suburban Chicago counties, registering people and answering their questions about the electoral process.

With these new voters, the counties find themselves trending away from their traditional Republican voting patterns. This rising organizational prowess serves as a reminder that Latinos, mostly Mexican, constitute the fastest-growing segment of the voting population, especially in the crucial "swing" states. Illinois, for instance, voted Republican in every presidential election from 1971–80, but since then has voted Democratic in every contest. Mexican immigrants constituted 29.5 percent of the Illinois population in 1990 and 40.4 percent in 2008, making them the largest immigrant group in the state. These political ramifications have not escaped the notice of elected officials such as Barack Obama, as when, in the heat of the 2008 campaign, he eloquently invoked the Illinois citizenship campaign. Meanwhile he tapped as cochair of his 2008 national presidential campaign one of Chole Alatorre's protégés, California labor leader María Elena Durazo.

Such support cannot be taken for granted, however, with Durazo and HTA confederations among those who spearheaded the 2010 mass immigration marches emanating from Los Angeles. Explaining this resurgence of protests, an official from Alatorre's HMN said, "It is necessary to raise the volume. Officials are accustomed to us marching, and sometimes even march with us, but they approve the laws that affect us, and the President has deceived us once again" in tabling action on immigration reform and, in fact, deporting the most people in US history. They were heard at least in part, given that in the heat of the 2012 campaign, President Obama issued the executive order deferring deportation of student-age undocumented immigrants, with HMN a major implementer of that change.

Also influential on the student-immigrant issue has been the Confederación de Federaciones Mexicanas en Norteamérica, comprised of over three hundred HTAs representing some forty-five thousand California residents.[28] "These Hometown Associations are becoming extremely powerful and influential," notes the head of the California Community Foundation, Antonia Hernández: "powerful here in the United States because they are a form of mutual organizing and civic engagement, and in Mexico because of their ability to leverage money they send. . . . They're highly organized."[30] All of this is a far cry, of course, from the peripheral political position of the *mutualista* movement.

And yet the example of HTA civic activism that leapt out to Hernández was one that echoed the approach employed by *mutualista* associations. She and the Los Angeles county supervisor once met with a HTA of people from a town in Oaxaca. According to Hernández, with regard to immigration, "We said, 'You know, we need money desperately in order to keep the issue alive, and pursue litigation.'" A savvy, veteran organizer and litigator, Hernández heads one of California's most important foundations and formerly directed the Mexican American Legal Defense and Education Fund. Nonetheless, she was very impressed by the group's response. "One middle aged man said, 'Señora Hernández, Señora Molina, Do not worry, we will get the money.' We asked, 'How?' 'Do not worry. We will raise the money among our peers.'" In something of an echo of Los Angeles *mutualistas*, Hernández added, "They had a dance, they had a tamalera, and they came back and they brought money. The thing is: they said, 'We know how to do it. We make these posters and put them on lampposts and stuff and we charge $10, $15 dollars.' It's entertainment and they raise money, and they bring it to us. Did they have a formal committee? I don't know . . . but the thing is that they were able to connect with their network to accomplish a goal."[31]

And just as some *mutualista*-style groups established national networks—notably the AHA and Cruz Azul—this seemingly marginal HTA of Oaxacan immigrants belongs to a Oaxacan federation that in turn belongs to a confederation of HTA federations from ten Mexican states. "It is just a matter of finding the means on how you're going to engage, and people say, 'I get it,'" says Hernández. "That's the key to civic engagement."

PART II

Mutualismo and Civil Rights Organizing

Mutual Aid and the Legacy of Conquest

At the very time that the 2008 presidential campaign was escalating, Barack Obama and John McCain both addressed the two leading civil rights organizations founded by Mexican Americans, the League of United Latin American Citizens (LULAC) and National Council of La Raza (NCLR). As LULAC points out, Mexican-heritage voters constitute the largest cohort of a national voting bloc of Latino voters that "proved decisive in the key battleground states of Virginia, New Mexico, Colorado, Nevada, Ohio, Indiana and Florida."[1] People of Mexican ethnicity constitute two-thirds of the rapidly growing Hispanic population, and despite popular perceptions, most of this growth has come from people already residing in the United States rather than immigrants.

As the leading Latino civil rights organization, NCLR constitutes the leading minority organization in the country, period, given that Latinos constitute the nation's largest minority group. Thus, Senator McCain proudly noted that he has twice received NCLR's congressional leadership award, while Senator Obama told the convention, "You hold this election in your hands. And I'm not taking a single Latino vote for granted in this campaign."[2] The Republican nominee in 2012 skipped the NCLR meeting, and President Obama followed Mitt Romney's lead, but in the wake of his sound defeat, much of the analysis focused on the need for the GOP to reach out to the Latino community, which voted in record numbers, with NCLR instrumental in the get-out-the-vote campaigns.

"The leading voice for the Hispanic community, National Council of La Raza . . . has become a formidable force for social change, recognized for . . . unparalleled policy advocacy efforts at the national level," notes *Forces for Good*.[3] This book also points out, however, that NCLR often works through community mutual aid–style organizations, "building and serving a national network of three-hundred affiliated community-based organizations." And although in his 2008 NCLR address candidate Obama lauded the group's civil rights advocacy, this former community organizer invoked more of a grassroots, mutual aid model in the windup. "We're going to change the direction of this country from the ground up," he declared. "That's how we will make the system work for *everyone*—for *every-*

one!—by living up to the ideals of NCLR, the ideals reflected in your name: 'La Raza.' 'The people.'"[4]

Even as NCLR was born out of the civil rights struggles of the mid-twentieth century, it has long been influenced by the *mutualista* ethos as well. These two organizational strands have been explicated by the leader most associated with NCLR's phenomenal rise, Raúl Yzaguirre. He cites a major Mexican American civil rights group founded in 1948, the American GI Forum, as central to his own organizational education. Yzaguirre joined the GI Forum in his teens because, in his words, "Intimidation is nothing new to a Mexican American and old-time civil rights activist like me." He says, "I grew up in McAllen, Texas and saw how election policies were biased against minorities, [with the main elections] always held in the summer when Mexican Americans were working on farms up North and could not vote. Our polling place was positioned catty-corner to the office of 'Whispering Tom' Mayfield," the constable elected to keep law and order, and the reputed murderer of several Mexican Americans in the 1920s.[5]

Yzaguirre's debt to the GI Forum is such that he wrote the introduction to a history of the organization and interrupted attendance at the Olympic Games to attend the funeral of GI Forum founder Dr. Héctor P. García. "It was impossible for me to stay away. Dr. Héctor is most responsible for me being part of the movement."

But Yzaguirre also has long made the point that NCLR's activist legacy dates back much further: to the venerable *mutualista* movement. "It's a largely unknown, untold story," he noted. "I'm fond of saying that my organization had its roots with the *Mutualista Movement* . . . in the 1800's, the mid-1800's. This was a struggle to protect ourselves against a lot of injustices and lots of discrimination—first, all over the Southwest, and then the Midwest."

He vividly recalls that in his hometown of San Juan, Texas, on the "Mexican" side of town, people met at the *mutualista* hall to "organize independent political movements. . . . We were having a meeting there. I say 'we'— I was just watching; I was a little boy—and I remember Tom Mayfield and his goons breaking it up." Still, as Yzaguirre notes, the *mutualista* in question, Sociedad Mutualista Obrera Mexicana, "had branches all over the country, a confederation." The *mutualista* awarded Yzaguirre a small scholarship, which made it possible to go off in pursuit of education. And this vote of confidence from people organizing in the face of discrimination helped set the young man's path. "I, personally, was impacted by those kinds of organizations," he notes.

The *mutualista* movement "formed the framework for a lot of civil rights activities," Yzaguirre stated in a speech before the Equal Employment Opportunity Commission. Even these civil rights professionals had never heard of the *mutualista* members that, in the wake of the US conquest, banded together for mutual protection. One of the very few organizational studies to recognize this link is an analysis of the nonprofit sector by Charles T. Clotfelter and Thomas Erlich, which makes the point that "Today, Latino advocacy and support groups like National Council of La Raza . . . continue to push for many of the same causes championed first by the *mutualistas* of the 1870s."[6]

This ignorance comes as no surprise to Raúl Yzaguirre. "Empirically speaking," he says, "I think that I could prove to you beyond a shadow of a doubt [that] the gap between the numbers of Latinos, the length of residence in this country," on the one hand, "and the awareness of Americans of this large group of other Americans," on the other hand, "is wider than for any other group in this country. . . . We need to recapture our historicity." He decries the situation in which this major US population group is "grossly misunderstood because there are not the kinds of books . . . available to Americans that explain . . . who we are as a people, and what our civil rights struggle has been all about." He worries that "part of the reason that Hispanic civil rights history has been so neglected is the fact that Americans are loath to [recognize] a reality that, historically, Latinos first became citizens of the United States not by choice, but by conquest."[7]

Yzaguirre's own heritage bears this out. From childhood he knew that the Yzaguirres claimed a Texas land grant dating from 1721, but he also knew that their descendants faced subjugation by the Anglo victors. "I remember my grandmother talking about something called the 'race war' and I knew that there had been killings of a lot of our folks," he notes, adding, "I remember my grandmother telling me about mothers who would confront the Texas Rangers and beat their hands on the men's chests and say, 'What have you done with my son? Why did you kill him?'" She brought the message home to young Raúl, recounting that his grandfather "was almost lynched by the Texas Rangers for the crime of being on the streets after dark because he had two jobs and he didn't come home before dark on his second job. There was a curfew for Mexican-Americans in Texas. Lots of these kinds of things happened time and time again," he notes.

Or as veteran civil rights attorney Antonia Hernández puts it, Mexicans "didn't move; the border moved." This "fluidity," as Hernández calls it, was reinforced by the continuous movement of Mexicans back and forth across the greater border region. "The connection of the Italians to Italy has been broken, the connection of Germans was broken to the home country," but for people of Mexican background, "It's deep in the people who were here, and it's deep in the people who came here . . . the chain has not been broken." And memoirist John Phillip Santos quotes an uncle as saying that when he immigrated to San Antonio in the 1910s, "It didn't really feel like we were leaving Mexico, except most of the streets were paved. . . ."[8]

The growing *mutualista* movement reflected and reinforced this sense of belonging that transcended the border. Soon after it was laid down, mutual aid and Mexican cultural and patriotic societies enabled Californios "to reestablish their mutual social relations during a period when their society was being wracked by the tremendous changes wrought by Americanization and urbanization," as historian Albert Camarillo puts it. For his part, the leading Tejano historian Arnoldo De León has written that "*sociedades mutualistas* appeared among Texas Mexicans in the 1870s in part in reaction to the afflictions many Tejanos experienced at the hands of white society." Before the end of the nineteenth century, Laredo had a dozen, and Corpus Christi over thirty.[9]

Catarino Garza was able to found a number of *mutualista* organizations because, as one South Texas journalist puts it, "He secured the admiration of South Texas Mexicanos with his fiery speeches in defense of minority rights and his promotion of *mutualista*, or Mexican self-improvement societies." Yes, Garza was famed for his raids on the oppressive regime of Mexican dictator Porfirio Díaz, and while his band doubtless included some of his *mutualista* members, those organizations were located in Texas for the mutual aid and protection of Mexican Texans outnumbered and overpowered by the Anglo newcomer.

Garza's newspapers, such as *El Mutualista*, denounced unjust actions by Texas authorities, as in 1888, when he published accusations that US customs inspector Victor Sebree had murdered a Tejano supposedly trying to escape. He then killed another Texas Mexican he had taken into custody. This was in conjunction with a partner, Sheriff W. W. Sheley, who stood accused by local Mexicans of having abetted the lynching of more than one Tejano. When Sebree encountered Garza in Rio Grande City, the officer promptly shot him, although not fatally. Garza's supporters, a throng that grew to some 200 people, pursued and threatened Sebree. He reached the safety of a military installation, where the protestors dispersed upon the order of the post commander.

Anglo-Texans meanwhile besieged the governor with messages that they were being attacked by Mexicans. He responded by dispatching the state's entire force of Texas Rangers plus 250 officers from the surrounding counties. He also issued a call for the US Third Cavalry. Garza, recovering from his wounds, wrote a book-length manifesto chronicling the depredations against Mexican Texans: *La lógica de los hechos: o sean observaciones sobre las circunstancias de los mexicanos in Texas, desde el año 1877 hasta 1889 (The*

Logic of Events: Observations on the Circumstances of Mexicans in Texas from the Year 1877 until 1889).[10]

Garza's ally against Porfirio Díaz and in the *mutualista* movement, Víctor Ochoa, also pressured US authorities. At an 1891 rally of some three hundred people in El Paso, Ochoa called for "organization for self protection," where he "urged Mexican citizens of El Paso to stand shoulder to shoulder . . . in demands" that included a set wage scale for city employment and equal pay for equal work for El Pasoans of Mexican descent, according to contemporary press accounts. Unlike most *mutualistas,* this group also protested city hall's policy of recruiting workers from Mexico for lower wages, even as all of Ochoa's *mutualista* group welcomed—even recruited—Texas Mexicans regardless of citizenship or immigration status.[11]

Meanwhile, conquered Mexicans engaged in savvy—even subversive— use of holiday celebrations. "In order to reinforce group solidarity and keep Anglo cultural influences at bay, the *mutualistas* sponsored traditional dances, barbeques, and celebrations of Mexican patriotic holidays," two political scientists have noted.[12]

Between 1850 and 1900, some fifteen organizations in Los Angeles were involved in hosting Mexican holiday festivities, but even these many activities were dwarfed by the countless festivals in Texas, the center of the US Mexican population at that time. This was the case even as the Texas celebrations of Mexican Independence Day, in effect, were honoring the country defeated by Texans in 1836 and by the United States in 1848: victories central to the lore of Texas history. "Through the *mutualistas,*" in the words of one study, "the webs of race, class and culture created a tight bond of interdependence among Mexicans living in territories they believed properly belonged to Mexico."[13]

Texas-Mexican mutual aid groups were well positioned to navigate this treacherous cultural terrain. Organized among themselves at the barrio level in the Spanish language, and relying on their own shared resources, they could operate independently, below the radar screen of the Anglo authorities. These associations drew strength from an identity that predated the arrival of US forces, while the mutual aid roots ran deep, dating from colonial times.

Emulating their cohorts back in Spain, skilled workers in northern New Spain set up cooperatives: *gremios,* or guilds. They pooled their resources to facilitate production of their items, both secular and religious. Another colonial mutual aid organization, notably but not exclusively in New Mexico, was the *cofradía,* or brotherhood, a lay-run association usually affiliated with a local church. Some *cofradías* established emergency benefits for widows and orphans, much like the burial and sickness insurance so prevalent in the later *mutualista* movement. As colonists, these settlers exhibited something of the imperialist perspective that considered the native peoples inferior, even heathens, and after annexation to the United States, some of their descendants would claim Spanish or European blood so as to distance themselves from the "half-breed" epithet. Still, the picture was complicated, for *mestizos* constituted many if not most of the colonists who settled in the future US Southwest.[14]

Mutualista groups managed to reinforce the sense of their land as still somehow Mexican without drawing the attention of Anglo society. For instance, a number of Texas *mutualista* associations were named after the Texan who was the hero of Cinco de Mayo, Ignacio Zaragoza, but few non-Tejanos had any idea that Zaragoza hailed from Goliad, Texas, when it still was part of Mexico and was called La Bahía. That Zaragoza had been born in Texas was not only a source of pride but also an implicit challenge to the account of Texas history put forth by the victors.[15] According to *The Handbook of Texas*, to this day, "Each year on May 5, Zaragoza societies meet throughout Mexico and in a number of Texas towns. In the 1960s General Zaragoza State Historic Site was established near Goliad to commemorate Zaragoza's birthplace." In the late nineteenth century, however, the *mutualista* members by necessity marked their Texas-Mexican heritage more indirectly, as when they linked up with other *mutualista* associations just across the new border.[16]

The mutual aid groups were also adept at using their Mexican celebrations to navigate the fraught post-conquest power dynamics. Older Texas Mexicans could recall that the Mexican state of Texas celebrated for three days in 1825 when the Mexican president declared the first national celebration of independence from Spain. After annexation, the organizers ranged from founding families to laborers, as in 1877, when workers at San Antonio's rock quarries led the festivities. Some members of the founding families gave speeches, but "led by a brass band, about a dozen of [the] poorest class marched . . . through rain and mud" holding aloft both Mexican and US banners, according to the San Antonio *Express,* and the next few years the largely working-class Sociedad Mutualista "Benevolencia Mexicana" was in charge.

These celebrations attracted many Anglos, even in Texas, despite the state's particular brand of triumphalist history. In San Antonio, the Mexican festivities came to be known as the most impressive and entertaining of any of the city's events, with the biggest and most beautiful parades followed by festivals featuring the liveliest music, the tastiest food—even the most romantic atmosphere, the many paper lanterns casting shadows on the trees at nightfall. And although the Texas-Mexican cultural displays may have been taken by the more prejudiced Anglo-Texans as evidence of an emotional, backward—even childlike—people, nonetheless these cele-brations served as a vivid reminder that Texas had been, and to some extent remained, Mexican.[17]

While so very Mexican in identity, these parades also adhered to the routine typical of Texas processions at that time: bands, women in sym-bolic historical roles, and in the case of San Antonio, participation by local military units and fire companies. Then there was the fact that German and Italian mutual aid associations occasionally took part in Mexican holi-day events, with the *mutualistas* reciprocating, as when Antonio P. Rivas and Juan Cárdenas of Sociedad Mutualista Mexicana served as marshals of the German Volkfest in 1885. Mexican community groups sometimes took part in celebrations for US holidays as well. Thus, seven *mutualista* organizations marched in San Antonio's Fourth of July parade, along with numerous German associations, several Irish, one French, and one Italian. Interestingly, this most patriotic of days was marked by bilingual speeches. Two thousand people listened to orations in English and German at River-side Park, while over twice as many people gathered at San Pedro Springs for declamations in English and Spanish. That year, Uncle Sam himself was portrayed by a Mexican Texan, Antonio P. Rivas.[18]

This honor likely accrued not from his *mutualista* affiliation but from his ties to a founding San Antonio family; in other words, Tejanos and Tejanas were seen as having European heritage rather than mestizo. This was sig-nificant at a time when racism was rife. African American organizations were notably absent from the many parades, despite the longstanding im-portance of African American mutual aid associations in US society, dating back to the founding in 1787 of the Free African Society of Philadelphia, and with many such groups active in Texas soon after emancipation. The African American community "was almost powerless to extract essential services from white society," in the words of one historical study.[19] African Americans were not even allowed to march along the parade route used by everyone else, reflecting the pattern of isolation expressed in the rise of Jim Crow laws and lynchings.

At the same time, lynchings of Mexican ethnic people were also on the rise in the late nineteenth century. No wonder some mutual aid groups were founded with the word "protection" in their name. By the mid-1890s, these included San Antonio's Sociedad de Protección de Trabajadores Unidos and El Paso's Unión Fraternal Mutualista "La Protectora."[20] The few Mexican Texan men holding minor public offices tried to cling to their positions and act as brokers to the increasingly powerless Mexican community.

Take Juan Barrera, a Bexar County (San Antonio) clerk in the 1880s. In 1868 he had been among the founders of the political group El Club

México-Texano, which had affiliated with the Republican Party and supported racial equality. Barrera also cofounded clubs supporting the 1872 presidential candidacy of Ulysses S. Grant. Barrera's father had served as governor of San Antonio until Santa Anna forced him out, at which point the elder Barrera fought alongside Anglo-Texans against the Mexican dictator. In the new US state of Texas, he became constable and then a deputy county clerk in the 1870s. That office passed to the younger Barrera in 1883, the same year that he joined Sociedad Mutualista Mexicana.[21]

Doubtless Barrera's municipal post made him an attractive candidate for this *mutualista* society, and such strategizing was important as Tejanos' precarious hold on political office continued to diminish. Increasingly they found themselves regularly outvoted by an influx of Anglo newcomers with the railroad's arrival to the region after 1875. Intermarriage between Anglo men and mexicanas became rarer, while the Anglo tendency to see residents with Mexican backgrounds as inferior aliens was reinforced. In the words of historian Roberto Calderón, "Extensive land loss and disregard of rights contributed to this state of affairs. Similarly, language differences, limited educational and economic opportunities, lack of citizenship, racial and national prejudice, gerrymandering, poll taxes, and efforts to hamper full Tejano participation in politics combined to undermine Tejano political representation."[22]

The early, post-conquest *mutualista* movement was, if anything, more pronounced in the northern New Mexico/southern Colorado region. The new US boundary line creating Colorado partly out of northern New Mexico in effect divided into two US territories a people that for generations had turned to each other for mutual aid and companionship in this remote, harsh, but spectacularly beautiful land. As New Mexican community organizer María Varela puts it, "By its nature survival and thriving in this kind of setting requires cooperation. There is no new idea; there are always shoulders ideas stand on." She speculates that the mutual aid ethos may well live on in communities "where penitentes really modeled this way of taking care of people."[23]

The penitentes—La Hermandad Penitente—had been established in New Mexico along the lines of cofradías in the 1700s. "As a mutual aid association, they functioned as a civil and ecclesiastical association, leading the community in prayer, worship and catechism. They made sure that everyone had the basics for a decent quality of life through collective irrigation and harvesting of lands," according to one scholar.

With the conquest came the official outlawing of the Penitentes on the part of the new United States–based Catholic hierarchy. These bishops, who replaced the ones from Mexico, voiced concern over certain flagellation practices, but also—perhaps especially—looked askance at the autonomy exercised by the religious associations.[24]

Figure 5. A morada, or meeting place, of the Brothers of Light, better known as Los Penitentes, Abiquiu, New Mexico, from c. mid-1700s. (Photo by James Evangelista)

Even as Penitentes went underground, their ethos lived on, with their method of justice anticipating today's innovative "restorative justice" movement. The Penitentes instituted judicial procedures based on the common good, with punishment in the form of restitution. If a local civil court judge knew that the convicted person was a Penitente, the person often was remanded to the organization for the meting out of a sentence appropriate to the damage suffered by the victim. Today, advocates of such restorative justice cite studies showing the ineffectiveness of wholesale incarceration, and they call for sentences that require the convict to compensate the victim and/or participate in a drug rehabilitation program, for the mutual benefit of the perpetrator, the victim, and society at large.[25]

Early mutual aid in this region also presaged today's ecological concerns. The rising global issue of water rights is echoed in this remote mountain region, where to this day local landowners share communal water rights, (acequias), as they have done since before their conquest by the United States. Every year residents of northern New Mexico celebrate their communal tradition on the feast of San Isidro (Saint Isidore), the patron saint of agriculture. In the words of anthropologist and New Mexico native Rubén Martínez, "Formalization of the principle of mutual aid can be traced to the communal nature of the acequias in northern New Mexico and to the emergence of the penitente brotherhoods."[26]

Figure 6. Two Penitente leaders in northern New Mexico/southern Colorado: José Pablo Archuleta, b. 1838, and his son, Francisco Antonio Archuleta, b. 1883. (Photo by Rubén Archuleta)

As for *mutualista* activities in bordering Colorado, one of the founders of NCLR, Herman Gallegos, speaks of "the excruciating circumstances under which they lived—being born in an adobe house without a nurse or anything." Gallegos speculates that "mutual self-help" arose as a consequence, particularly with regard to respectful treatment of the deceased. "My grandfather was a member of the *mutualistas*," he said, "and he was very much celebrated when he passed away."[27] One Colorado *mutualista* group attained particular fame, the Sociedad Protección Mutua de Trabajadores Unidos (SPMDTU) (Mutual Society of United Workers), and the organization has made clear that it was founded in response to the discrimination that came with the US cession. As its own history notes, the SPMDTU arose from "the need to organize to protect themselves from the considerable discrimination that had already developed in the county of Conejos and in this part of south-central Colorado . . . since the treaty of G-H [Guadalupe-Hidalgo] in 1848."[28]

In 1900, SPMDTU founder Celedonio Mondragón convened the first meeting at his home in Antonito, Colorado, ten miles north of New Mex-

Figure 7. The Sociedad Protección Mutua de Trabajadores Unidos headquarters, listed on the National Register of Historic Places. (Photo by Rubén Archuleta)

ico. He had been born in a nearby town, and his parents hailed from a community in New Mexico's Sangre de Cristo Mountains. Mondragón set up a shop in Santa Fe where he sold the fine silver jewelry that he crafted himself.

Modeled on two New Mexico groups, SPMDTU eventually grew to some seventy chapters in Colorado, New Mexico, and Utah. The organizational benefits included not only funeral and medical insurance but also payment to workers laid off or wrongfully dismissed, with the society also serving as an informal employment information center. The SPMDTU also lobbied both the Colorado and New Mexico legislature on equal educational spending and preservation of Hispanic culture in the state curriculums. The headquarters served as centers for community meetings and celebrations, and a few do so to this day, with the Antonito headquarters and a few other chapters still active.

The SPMDTU went into decline with the waning of the *mutualista* movement, but the SPMDTU also suffered because the "Anglo has come to dominate so much of the valley," in the words of two social geographers. Even so, "vestiges are still evident in some of the acequia communities," writes anthropologist Rubén Martínez.[29] The society mainly sponsors a few college scholarships, and this echoes the modest aid, but robust vote of support, that launched civil rights leader Raúl Yzaguirre as a young man in

Figure 8. Some early leaders of the Alianza Hispano Americana. (For a photo of early female Alianza leaders, see chap. 10.) (Courtesy Ryder Ridgway Photographs, Arizona Collection, Arizona State University Libraries)

the 1950s. For his part, Yzaguirre noted that "some of these organizations still exist" when he outlined the importance of the *mutualista* legacy to the modern civil rights movement.[30]

The giant 1848 land cession to the United States was not the final ignominy, however, for in 1853 Mexico sold one additional piece of land. A strip of northern Sonora suddenly became part of Arizona, and the troubles that ensued for the local residents led to the founding of a Tucson organization that would become the first national Latino organization in the history of the United States: the Alianza Hispano Americana (AHA). From its founding in 1894, the Alianza took seriously the concept of protection in the face of an often-hostile world. One of the first leaders, attorney Carlos I. Velasco, put it this way: "As children of this country, being born here, do we not have an equal or a greater right to formulate and maintain the laws of this land that witnessed our birth than naturalized citizens of European origin? Yes. Nevertheless, the contrary occurs."[31]

At the same time, the anti-Chinese attitudes prevalent among Arizona Anglos were to be found among members of the AHA as well. "What was happening in Arizona, of course, was the brutal but effective creation of an economic pecking order organized largely along ethnic lines," notes historian Thomas Sheridan.[32] The corporate and agribusiness moguls "without exception, were Anglo. The precarious middle class of small business owners and farmers was mostly Anglo but included some Mexicans," although the latter were increasingly losing out. As for the working class, it was "Anglos pitted against Mexicans, Mexicans against Native Americans, and everyone against the Chinese," with Native Americans basically shunted aside.

Historian Linda Gordon notes this prejudice among both Anglo and Mexican miners, even as the latter were experiencing discrimination themselves. A number of AHA chapters encouraged Mexican ethnic residents to exercise their rights, as in Morenci, Arizona, where the organization accused judges of stealing the fees charged by the court. Thus the Alianza, writes Gordon, "Urged Mexicans to become citizens and . . . challenged discrimination and abuses on the basis of a solid understand of American law." With the AHA leading the way, *mutualista* organizing would reach its peak in the early decades of the new century. Existing groups would find their ranks swelling, and many more *mutualista* groups would be founded, mostly by the immigrants coming during the first mass Mexican immigration to the United States. Even so, they were coming to a land that predated the border, as did the *mutualista* idea itself.[33]

Mutual Protection against Discrimination

The new, modern century did not herald an age of racial enlightenment. The 1900s and 1910s witnessed a record number of Mexican lynchings, followed in the 1920s by a hardening of segregation policies. No wonder *mutualista* efforts to band together in the face of discrimination increased—efforts that prefigured the much more prominent Mexican American civil rights movement that came to overshadow them.

Many of the antidiscrimination actions in the early twentieth century arose as spontaneous efforts at mutual protection. In New Mexico, people banded together in protest rallies that came to be known as "juntas de indignación." Impassioned speeches denouncing racism and discrimination led to demands for justice that were published in the barrio press and were presented to local authorities. Nowhere were popular protests more evident than in Texas, however, as the state with the largest Mexican population and home to the Texas Rangers: lionized by Anglo-Americans but viewed by many Tejanos and Tejanas as "los rinches"—akin to storm troopers. "I often cite the fact that there were a lot of killings of our community that have largely been untold," civil rights leader Raúl Yzaguirre noted. "In my own state of Texas, some—perhaps as many as 5,000 of our folks—were killed . . . in the early 1900's." He stressed that the story of these incidents "goes largely unnoticed and unreported."[1]

In 1911 in Waco, Texas, for instance, Tejanas organized a mass-membership defense committee in response to the near-lynching and subsequent arrest, on questionable grounds, of a fifteen-year-old named León Cárdenas Martínez. "We, the undersigned women, met at Mrs. Dolores G. de López's home with the purpose of uniting forces to lend moral, collective and financial aid to the defense of León Cárdenas Martínez," they declared.[2] The teen had been attacked by a mob of Anglo-Texans, as described by his father in a statement to the Mexican ambassador.

> Immediately on being arrested he was taken to the place where the crime was committed (three miles out of town). And on arriving there, the officers told him to say if he was the guilty party, under the assurance that they would protect him from the wrath of ranchers who wanted to lynch him.

Under such pressure León was compelled to answer in the affirmative. At this particular time, Jim Mayfield appeared on the ground and, placing a double-barreled shot gun against his head, threatened to kill him unless he gave all the particulars in connection with the killing of Miss Emma Brown. . . . While this was going on, the sheriff in the County did all in his power to control the fury of the maddened mob . . . the jail was assaulted, the jailer overpowered . . . about twenty Americans, well-armed and on horseback, went to the Meat Market, my place of business, and . . . gave me two hours' time in which to leave town . . . the initiative, a threat on my own life . . . compelled me by force to follow the road . . . through the open desert . . . without even allowing me to provide myself with water for my family. . . .

They produced no evidence through witnesses at his trial, except the confession he was compelled to make, and it must be taken into consideration that he was forced to do this to save his life.[3]

The women who mobilized the protest, in their words, "By unanimous decision, then agreed to call the new body the DEFENSE COMMITTEE [*sic*]." They pledged a) to publicize in the newspaper *El Internacional* the fact that the members "completely support . . . the parents of the Cárdenas Martínez boy"; b) to communicate with "representatives of the Mexican government offering our moral aid in raising the funds that such a case requires"; c) "to send a petition letter to the Governor of Texas asking for suspension of the sentence"; and d) "finally, to carry out all tasks necessary in order to save our defendant from the gallows." The Defense Committee reported that it had "made extensive petitions in local neighborhoods" to drum up community support so that people "could offer their timely and efficient aid in the defense." Meanwhile the organization's statement caught the attention of the largest-circulating and most important Spanish-language newspaper in the United States at that time, *La Prensa* of San Antonio, which published the statement in full.[4]

That year, concern over such depredations led *mutualista* and fraternal organizations from across the state to convene in Laredo for El Primer Congreso Mexicanista (First Mexicanist Congress). Responding to this call issued by the Laredo newspaper *La Crónica* were such leaders as educator Simón Domínguez, who had established links among various Tejano mutual aid and fraternal organizations. He also connected these Texas organizations to their counterparts in Mexico. Indeed, as another delegate put it, those meeting "made no distinction based on country of birth or citizenship," and he added that "we who have been born in this country understand our responsibilities as citizens, but we also feel a profound love for and the most exalted interest in our mother race because we are by destiny her progeny."

A consensus emerged at the conference, as one speaker put it, "That Mexican workers who labor in a mill, on a hacienda, or on a plantation establish Ligas Mexicanistas" (Mexicanist Leagues). Then, supported by the barrio press and by mexicanos of stature, "They will be able to strike back at . . . some bad children of Uncle Sam who believe themselves better than Mexicans."[5] A resolution was adopted calling for a "Gran Liga Mexicanista" (Great Mexicanist League) to oversee the effort statewide. This "Gran Liga" evidently never materialized, but in the years immediately following the Congreso a number of mutual aid organizations began antidiscrimination initiatives. Some longstanding *mutualista* groups expanded their legal aid and protection activities, numerous new groups were established with a focus on protection, and a South Texas legal aid and protection league was established.

Among the legal defense initiatives undertaken by traditional *mutualista* groups was a protest launched in 1917 when yet another suspected murderer of a Mexican was allowed to go free, this time in Hondo, Texas. Despite the possibility of threats against its own members, a *mutualista* organization painstakingly gathering eyewitness accounts and sent the evidence to Governor James Ferguson. A number of other *mutualista* groups circulated a petition, which they then delivered to the Mexican ambassador to the United States (and future Mexican president), Ygnacio Bonillas. The ambassador then wrote to the State Department, asking the US government, in Bonillas' words, "To apply to the proper authorities with a view to the punishment of those who may be guilty of Señor Perez's death." Not that the *mutualista* groups were calling for the death penalty; as one Tejano leader had written to the previous Texas governor, most of these organizations were opposed to capital punishment. They just wanted justice.[6]

The 1910s also saw the emergence of a number of *mutualista* "protective" groups called Agrupación Protectora Mexicana. For instance, Agrupación Protectora Mexicana in San Antonio pledged to fight violence and theft of local Mexican property, while the Houston group worked in tandem with the consul to combat threats against immigrants by unscrupulous employers. This initiative anticipated the legal programs of today's immigrant worker centers, which have "a mission of creating mutual aid organizations that educate workers and provide tools for empowerment," in the words of one study.[7]

Not that history simply repeats itself; for one thing, some of the members of the 1910s associations were not immigrants. Also, sometimes the Mexican Revolution of the 1910s proved a major complication, especially along the border. One leader of Agrupación Protectora Mexicana in Laredo, Emeterio Flores, put it this way: "The influx of refugees from Mexico who, it seems, are almost generally revolutionarily inclined at all times, have great influence on their countrymen who were here prior to them." Even more, Flores decried the vigilantism aimed at Texas Mexicans, notably the escalating repression by Anglo-Texans in reaction to the 1915 rebellion by some Tejanos at San Diego, Texas. This, even as Flores, like most in the *mutualista* movement, did not subscribe to the Plan of San Diego's call for US Mexicans to counter the discrimination they faced by founding a new borderlands nation entirely.[8]

Meanwhile, a league of mutual-protective associations, La Liga Protectora Mexicana, was founded in 1917 by Manuel Gonzales. Although only eighteen years old, Gonzales was clear about his mission: "To remain Mexican but take advantage of the American life through citizenship. I was born poor, grew up poor . . . with poor people, of my *raza, mexicanos,* and I realized clearly the iniquitous exploitation of which they have always been victims." He voiced the hope that legal advice, along with "encouraging them to organize," would mean that "the authorities would be compelled to respect their rights."[9]

Born in the Lower Rio Grande Valley of Texas and raised in San Antonio, Manuel C. Gonzales may have come from a family of humble means, but he was the grandson of General José María Carbajal of San Antonio, who was one of the Tejanos that fought alongside Anglo-Texans against the dictatorship of Santa Anna. Like most Mexican Texans, Carbajal refused to support the Republic of Texas when it joined the Union in 1845, and he fought against US forces when they invaded Mexico the following year. His grandson attended Clay Commercial College in Austin, leaving prior to graduating to work as a law clerk: first for a Hidalgo County judge, then for the law firm of Love & Patterson, convincing them to sponsor the Liga Protectora Mexicana. While founded by Gonzales via the law firm, the Liga drew upon the familiar mutual aid model, with members paying dues that would enable a group of mainly laborers and farm workers to band together—in this case, for legal counsel that they otherwise could not afford.

In its inaugural year of 1917, La Liga Protectora Mexicana reported just seventy-three members, which Gonzales attributed to "bad crops and wartime conditions," but a few years later the league claimed over five hundred members and was pursuing hundreds of legal cases, often regarding land tenure laws and contracts. The Liga also addressed harassment by law enforcement officials, as when two Liga Protectora members from Mercedes, Texas, were detained by the police while traveling to Brownsville and the Liga dispatched a representative who persuaded the authorities to release the two men.[10] Despite the long odds, the Liga also lobbied the Texas State Legislature for legal reforms. In 1918 the association asked several legislators to introduce a bill "prohibiting any sheriff, deputy sheriff, or constable from aiding or accompanying any one in acquiring possession . . . of any property, except when the sheriff or other official has a written mandate from the court. . . ." This would have helped to eliminate the landholders' use of local law enforcement officials to harass tenants. Two years later the organization sought laws protecting tenants' shares of their crops, as landlords frequently claimed as their own cotton that belonged to the renters. To remedy this inequity, the Liga lobbied for a law to annul growers' sale of land when he had taken advantage of the tenant. The organization asked other Tejano groups to join in lobbying for this bill, but evidently it was not enacted.

If this mutual legal aid society could not change the state legislature, at least it could equip members to better navigate the legal system. The organization outlined for its members the nature of the political process, explaining pending legislation and publishing a handbook of Texas laws that were relevant to renters, laborers, shopkeepers, and small contractors. One hundred seventy-five pages and fully indexed, the guide was published bilingually in order to enable tenant farmers and workers to show the landlord or employer the supporting legal evidence. The handbook emphasized landlord-tenant contracts with an eye to tenants' rights, and it outlined the procedure for the new workers' compensation law. Enacted in 1913, it was overseen starting in 1917 by the Industrial Accidents Board. The Liga noted that the Board usually ruled in the plaintiff's favor and in fact had incurred the displeasure of some insurance firms. At the same time, the law excluded from the program farm workers and railroad and streetcar workers, many of whom were Mexican; moreover, the law made employer participation in the workers' compensation system voluntary. To this day, Texas is the only state that does not mandate workers' compensation on the part of private employers.[11]

Despite the Liga Protectora Mexicana's many activities and the fact that its founder would become an attorney and would help establish the mighty League of United Latin American Citizens (LULAC), in a sense the Liga was a league in name only, operating out of the law offices of Love and Patterson. In contrast, the Phoenix-based Liga Protectora was a league totally by and for US Mexicans, and within a few years of its founding in 1915 it had established chapters from the Southwest to the Midwest. Just as the latest spate of Texas lynchings had sparked the Primer Congreso Mexicanista, with its call for a great statewide league, so a grisly event in Arizona was the immediate spur for the founding in Phoenix of La Liga Protectora Latina.

When five Mexicans were condemned to hang in 1915, the Liga organized defense efforts and, along with the Mexican consul, met with the governor, George P. Hunt. Four of the men were eventually executed, even though Hunt was personally opposed to capital punishment and even though all of the others on death row—six white and one African American—received reprieves. The Liga went on to spotlight the mistreatment of workers in the Arizona mines, and the organization offered such traditional *mutualista* benefits as sickness and burial insurance, along with educational and social programs. At its peak, the Liga reported some four thousand members across the Southwest.

In California, meanwhile, protests arose in 1923 when Aurelio Pompa was convicted of murder and sentenced to death despite conflicting accounts by Anglo and Mexican witnesses, with the latter maintaining that the accused acted in self-defense—and, especially, with the capital punishment decree handed down after two mistrials. When the sentence was announced, onlookers reacted so angrily that the district attorney asked to be escorted from the courtroom with police protection. *Mutualista* organizations mounted a campaign that gathered almost thirteen thousand signatures on a clemency petition. The Supreme Council of the Alianza Hispano Americana (AHA) wrote to the governor asking for clemency, while Sociedad Mutualista Melchor Ocampo enlisted the Mexican consul in Los Angeles to do the same.

When the consulate successfully solicited a letter of support from Mexican president Alvaro Obregón himself, Pompa's mother seized this opening. "I take the liberty of writing to this letter to you because . . . you so kindly offered to help my son, Aurelio Pompa," she wrote to the Mexican president. "After having exhausted all legal resources to save my son from the terrible death penalty to which he is sentenced, the only thing left . . . is to ask for forgiveness. . . . In the immense darkness of my grief I see grace for my son as a ray of hope" that the president could influence the California governor to commute the sentence. Even the presidential effort was to no avail; Pompa was executed in 1924.[12] The outrage and fear coursing through the California barrios manifested itself in the corrido "Vida, Proceso, y Muerte de Aurelio Pompa" ("Life, Trial and Death of Aurelio Pompa"). This ballad, in the great Mexican corrido tradition, arose from the grassroots and made its way into the annals of music history.

> . . . Twenty thousand signatures
> Asked the Governor for pardon,
> All the newspapers asked for it too,
> And even Obregón sent a message.
>
> All was useless; the societies,
> All united, asked for his pardon.
> His poor mother, half-dead already,
> Also went to see the Governor.

"Farewell my friends, farewell my village.
Dear mother, cry no more.
Tell my raza not to come here.
For they will suffer here; there is no pity here.

The jailer asked him, "Are you Spanish?"
"I'm Mexican, and proud of it,
Even though they deny me the pardon". . . .

Such cases continued to surface over the decades, as when the AHA petitioned the Arizona governor for clemency on behalf of Angel Serna in 1950. The organization asked for suspension of the execution order to allow the consideration of further evidence, but to no avail. Serna was taken to the gas chamber.[13]

Mutualista groups also strove to combat Mexican stereotyping in the new motion picture industry, beginning with the first major movie filmed on location in Texas, *The Heart of the Sunset*. When local production began in 1917, a number of San Antonio *mutualista* groups protested on the grounds that that the movie was racist, taking their complaint all the way to the Mexican ambassador in Washington.

The story centered on a white damsel attacked by a Mexican "bandit." This villain, Longorio, ordered his entourage to murder the husband of "the beautiful Alaire." In rode the hero, a Texas Ranger, who rescued Alaire. Longorio and his men set fire to the couple's place of refuge, however, and the US Cavalry came to the rescue, escorting the hero and heroine back to the United States of America. In real life, the US Cavalry had just returned from Mexico, having invaded in a fruitless search for Francisco "Pancho" Villa: a revolutionary leader, but labeled a "bandit" by much of the US press. Thus did the movie recast the headlines of the day in a triumphalist fantasy.[14]

The Wilson administration that sent US forces after Villa was the same White House that three years earlier had screened the movie *The Birth of a Nation*, also known as *The Clansman*, after the novel. Both lionized the Ku Klux Klan, and this helped boost the Klan's ranks. In Texas at its high point in 1923, the Klan boasted a paid membership of one hundred fifty thousand, at which time it was estimated that the majority of the Texas House of Representatives legislators were members. This reincarnated Ku Klux Klan expanded beyond attacks on African Americans to now also target Jews, Catholics, and immigrants. Mexicans fell into two of those categories, even as many Texans also considered them "half-breed" non-whites.

Such sentiments were not limited to supporters of the Klan. Governor James Ferguson of Texas, who was known to oppose the Klan, nonetheless spoke in favor of segregating Mexicans on the grounds that they were inferior, declaring, "We have a separate coach law to separate white and black, and to keep down trouble, the Mexican must be separated too. We are not going to give more privilege to the Mexican than we do to the Negro, who is far superior to the Mexican in every attribute that goes to make a good citizen. I dare the legislature to ignore this situation. The Mexican people have not improved one bit in civilization, and they are more blood thirsty than ever."

The governor concluded that if Mexican immigration were not stopped, "the spirits of our ancestors will haunt us and the ghosts of Texas heroes will walk in the night to reprove us." Thus did he draw on the victor's version of history even as he spoke of what he considered a new, growing threat.[15]

For his part, Texas congressman John Box, who introduced legislation calling for a Mexican Quota, made reference to the long history of ethnic Mexicans residing in Texas, but he characterized this heritage as evidence of their unfitness for US citizenship, declaring, "Americans found that they could not live with them on genial terms in Texas 80 years ago. In a contest which arose then the Mexican showed both his inferiority and his savage nature. The same traits which prevailed with them in the days of the Alamo and Goliad show themselves in the dealings with each other and with America now."[16]

In California the Klan targeted Mexican farmworkers, as when members threatened laborers in Santa Barbara County by appearing in the fields in full regalia.[17] Mercedes Acasan García recalled in the San Diego area that "at first the Mexican field hands were curious at the sight of these strange men on horses shrouded with snowy gowns and huge, spotless cardboard hoods over their faces," with the white hoods at first seeming perhaps to be the garb of Penitentes of New Mexico. But as she tearfully recalls, all these years later, "Any Mexican worker who challenged authority or appeared suspicious of one thing or another would forfeit his life." García herself was no stranger to danger, having served in the Mexican Revolution as a teenager, but the harassment by the Klan prompted her to join a *mutualista* group for protection. In recent years anti-Mexican rallies organized by the Ku Klux Klan have resurfaced, as with a 2006 event in Alabama. Such demonstrations are rare in the new millennium, however, with the Ku Klux Klan having largely been relegated to the periphery of American life.[18]

To the extent that Mexican mutual aid organizations of a century ago were comprised of people banding together in the face of racist threats, these groups resembled the mutual aid associations founded by African Americans. This is not to say that *mutualista* groups recruited African American members, but almost no *mutualista* groups had racially exclusionary membership rules, nor did they exclude ethnic Mexicans who were partly of African or Asian heritage. The mutual aid associations also did not favor people of European descent over mestizos—at least not officially.[19]

Even something as seemingly frivolous as a beauty pageant served to challenge the "Nordic" standards promoted by eugenicists and the Ku Klux Klan. The magazine of the AHA described with equal enthusiasm candidates for queen ranging from a contestant "as pure white as powdered sugar" to a "tropical beauty of nutty brown," even as the AHA was one of the few *mutualista* associations that officially excluded any race—in their case, Asians and sometimes African Americans. Nonetheless, the Alianza's beauty pageants were used to advance justice issues of Mexicans regardless of racial background, with the Alianza member Jesús Franco writing that the pageant "aims to interest the local authorities so that they may recognize our souls have justice, and so that they have appreciation for our colonia." Franco, a clerk for the El Paso municipal government, reported that "already there have been cases in which the top authorities in the places in which there were these Alianza festivals have revised their judgments regarding our colonias, such that incalculable advantages have been achieved."[20]

Meanwhile many of the Mexican Americans returning from service in the Great War were galvanized to fight injustices they continued to face back home, even while in uniform. That same uniform empowered them, for nothing so clearly demonstrated one's bona fides as a loyal US citizen. They founded such organizations as Sons of America and Sons of Texas, also known as Orden Hijos de América and Orden Hijos de Texas. With their emphasis on the equal rights for US citizens of Mexican descent, these groups contrasted markedly with the transnational orientation of the *mutualista* organizations.

Indeed, when leaders of the Sons/Hijos and related groups founded LULAC in 1929, they restricted membership to US citizens. LULAC leaders aimed to engage Washington decision makers directly, not through the local Mexican consul. These budding civil rights organizers knew that although *mutualista* groups had opposed myriad injustices, few discriminatory laws had been overturned in the process. In a few cases the movement's emphasis on Mexican culture actually enabled segregation, as when the Owensmouth, California, board of education suggested that the rising number of Mexican schoolchildren be taught separately and Mutualista Sociedad Benito Juárez suggested that the school district rent its hall. The city agreed, and the new school at Mutualista Juárez boasted a number of settlement house–type services for these immigrant children, but it also constituted the first segregated "Mexican" school in the San Fernando Valley. Officially labeled as an "annex" to the Anglo elementary school, the

Mexican facility doubtless was inferior. As LULAC leader and education professor Dr. George Sánchez would write in 1951, after twenty-five years of studying districts that had "Mexican" and "American" schools, "A segregated school is an inferior school."[21]

For many ethnic Mexicans coming of age in the United States of the 1920s, the *mutualista* trans-border ethos was of little account when it came to fighting injustice. National Council of La Raza (NCLR) cofounder Herman Gallegos recalled the disenchantment felt by his father, growing up in southern Colorado and witnessing the limited power of *mutualista* organizations. "One of my grandfathers had his cattle ripped off by Texas gunslingers, and the sheriffs and the county didn't help, and there were no organizations you could go to, because you were pretty isolated—there was nothing—and that added to the bitterness." By the 1940s "'Mutualism' was now considered obsolete," notes historian Cynthia Orozco. "Self-help was re-defined to mean leadership by the male Mexican American middle class through an organization rather than cooperative effort by all members of La Raza."[22]

This is not to say that there was a clean break with *mutualismo*. The LULAC founding document, in words that could have been written by La Liga Protectora Mexicana, pledged "to create a fund for our mutual protection, for the defense of those of us who are unjustly persecuted and for the education and culture of our people." Many LULAC founders had learned the organizational ropes in the *mutualista* movement, such as Liga Protectora Mexicana leader Manuel C. Gonzales, who served as an officer at LULAC's founding convention—itself held at a *mutualista* hall.[23] Moreover, when LULAC began to focus on desegregation lawsuits, some of them were carried out in coordination with mutual-benefit associations, notably the AHA.

The AHA itself won a historic if limited anti-segregation victory when its lawsuit forced Tolleson, Arizona to end its segregation policies. The ruling applied only to that particular town, but on the strength of that decision several other districts voluntarily desegregated their schools when the AHA issued suits against them, as did Winslow, Arizona, with regard to its discriminatory swimming pool policies. On the heels of the Tolleson victory, the AHA was instrumental in helping found in 1951 a civil rights coalition that spanned the entire Southwest, the American Council of Spanish-Speaking Organizations (ACSSO). With seed money that former LULAC president Dr. George Sánchez obtained from the Marshall Trust, the ACSSO worked toward equal treatment under the law.

In 1955 the AHA established its own Civil Rights Department, headed by trailblazing community organizer and political scientist Ralph Guzmán. That year he began working with the NAACP on a major school desegregation case against El Centro, California, which segregated whites from both Mexicans and African Americans. The suit reached the Federal Court of Appeals, which ruled against the school district. Thus, the AHA had come a long way from origins that included racially exclusive membership rules—a fact made evident in 1957 when the organization offered honorary membership to Louis Armstrong.[24]

The AHA had reached the big time. John F. Kennedy's presidential campaign tapped an AHA official to head the Viva Kennedy! outreach to Latinos, and after the election the grateful candidate named several AHA members to governmental posts. These appointments were virtually all of a ceremonial nature, however, with Mexican Americans having little voice in White House decision making. And while the AHA name "Alianza" inspired the title of the Kennedy administration's signature Latin American program, Alianza para el Progreso (Alliance for Progress), this inspiration was something of a fluke. The Kennedy aide who suggested the name "Alianza," Richard Goodwin, did so without any knowledge of the AHA per se. During a campaign swing through the Southwest, Goodwin was tasked with writing a speech about the presidential candidate's Latin American proposals. And as the aide recalled, "To dramatize the policy we needed a name—at least I thought we did—something that would establish Kennedy's proposals as a successor to the Good Neighbor policy of Franklin Roosevelt. It should be in Spanish, I thought, to demonstrate that . . . we envisioned a partnership. . . . Unfortunately my search for a ringing slogan was handicapped by almost complete ignorance of Spanish. Looking down at the empty seat beside me, I saw a magazine published by a Mexican-American society in New Mexico [sic], serendipitously discarded by an earlier passenger, and entitled *Alianza*. Perfect."[25]

After 1960 the AHA went into steady decline, however, plagued by internal dissension, financial mismanagement, and an inability to compete with LULAC and the GI Forum, which were winning major civil rights victories for Mexican Americans, as with 1965 Voting Rights Act provisions covering the Southwest. That same year, when these civil rights groups opposed a proposal by Senator Sam Ervin to institute a Western Hemisphere immigration quota, they likely were motivated at least in part by Ervin's segregationist history, even if their stance did mark the beginning of a turn toward immigration reform as a civil rights issue. But it was the AHA that pioneered this stance, with its immigration cases operating out of the group's Civil Rights Department. The first national organization to link immigrant rights with civil rights, the AHA made history—history that is as significant as it is overlooked.

Today the LULAC civil rights webpage is devoted almost entirely to immigration issues, and the organization to some extent recognizes the long tradition of this perspective. LULAC leader Jaime Martínez, for one, wrote that when he lobbies "for a just, comprehensive immigration reform, and for a temporary moratorium to protect hardworking immigrants," he draws upon the organizational legacy of his grandparents, who "taught me by example to serve our people, by involving me at an early age with the organization La Sociedad Mutualista Mexicana.'"[26] The NCLR, for its part, has brought forward the historic term "la raza" that was so often invoked in the *mutualista* era. As NCLR notes, while "La Raza" can mean "race," the term "has its origins in early 20th century Latin American literature and translates into English most closely as 'the people.' . . ."

But while NCLR's use of "La Raza" echoes the *mutualista* movement, NCLR far outpaces those earlier groups in many respects. The organization posits gender equality, with several women having served as NCLR presidents and with former NCLR vice president Cecilia Muñoz tapped by the Obama administration for a high-ranking post. Such clout is also reflected in the appointment of NCLR's longtime leader Raúl Yzaguirre as ambassador to the Dominican Republic. On the local level, the organization is impressive as well, with some three hundred affiliated barrio organizations offering assistance to people all across the land. In this sense NCLR's accomplishments dwarf those of the *mutualista* associations, even the AHA in its prime.[27]

It can seem ridiculous to even mention those faded barrio-based groups in the same breath as NCLR—the most important, largest, most powerful, sophisticated Latino organization of a growing, increasingly influential electorate—but in fact the *mutualista* associations, and the networks they fashioned, were much more self-sufficient. NCLR's vast network of barrio organizations includes many service providers dependent on government and/or foundations for their funding, with the organization's actual dues-paying membership relatively small. This conforms with sociologist Theda Skocpol's observation that major civil rights groups such as the NAACP have relatively small numbers of grassroots dues-paying members. Thus, while the AHA had a policy of providing travel money to local officers so that working class leaders could attend its national conference, recent NCLR conventions have charged high registration fees.

Not happy with this aspect of NCLR's evolution, Herman Gallegos noted that he and the other founders of the group that led to NCLR, Ernesto Galarza and Julian Samora, all envisioned an association "to negotiate with institutions instead of being handmaidens to power." Not surprisingly, the person most responsible for NCLR's rise to prominence, Raúl Yzaguirre, sees things differently. "Initially the objectives were to build an infrastructure of urban-based, community-based organizations that could deal with poverty and discrimination. The purpose of the organi-

Herman Gallegos speaking in 2008 at the conference marking the fiftieth anniversary of community organizing in California. (Courtesy CSO Project UC San Diego)

zation has expanded to other things," he noted, but added that barrio-based organizing "still remains very much in accord with what we do."[28]

Gallegos, however, says that he told a recent NCLR convention, "I know that all of you are running service-based organizations. That's not going to affect fundamental change in institutions. We have to get back to the training, development of indigenous leadership of self-help." He cited trailblazing farm labor organizer Dr. Ernesto Galarza, who "warned against taking money and depending on the compassion of others to survive. He said, 'What happens, you know, is that a liberal group will support you, and then the wellsprings of compassion will soon run dry. They'll go on to another cause, and if you have not learned how to develop a self-sustaining mode of operation, you'll collapse, or you'll become very dependent'—like the politicians that depend on the lobbyists for survival."[29]

Gallegos himself started out as a community organizer alongside César Chávez in the East San Jose barrio infamously known as "Sal Si Puedes," or "Get Out If You Can," becoming their group's president in 1960. He went on to distinguish himself in civil rights and philanthropy—and sits on several corporate boards—but he finds himself remaining impressed by the efficacy of that first calling. "After 50-some years of this kind of work," he mused, "I come out very concerned that investments in the creation of organizations that provide services to the community—badly needed as they are—may not be the answer that we need for social progress." At the same time, Gallegos takes great pride in the historic victories of NCLR, among other groups, as when he entitled his final public address "'From Sal Si Puedes' to 'Sí Se Puede'"—that is, "From 'Get Out if You Can' to 'Yes We Can,'" noting that "it's even in the national lexicon, 'Yes We Can.' One of the things we need to do is to look at these historical roots, these antecedents that made it successful . . . how the Mexican community has gotten from 'Sal Si Puedes' to 'Sí Se Puede.'"[30]

PART III

Mutualista-Style Labor Organizing

Community-based Labor Organizing

What lessons can the labor movement possibly offer for the renewal of American democracy? By any measure, unions are a diminishing presence on the national scene—even as the number of vulnerable undocumented workers has risen sharply in the past four decades. Nonetheless, some labor organizations are employing innovative, community-centered recruitment strategies that promise nothing less than a revitalization of the US labor movement. And it would likely surprise most people to learn that some of the main the leaders in this effort are those seemingly "unorganizable" Mexican workers—let alone that their work echoes *mutualista* labor organizing of a century ago.

"Reinventing American civic democracy," sociologist Theda Skocpol calls the new social unionism, citing formerly hidebound institutions such as the American Federation of Labor (AFL) as "turning some cities, like Los Angeles, into hotbeds of 'new unionism,' with Latino immigrants in the vanguard." Political scientist Immanuel Ness, for his part, suggests that "perhaps a new social movement could emerge from a common struggle uniting unions, immigrant workers and community activists."[1] For all their insights, it is not scholars but rather an organizer at the grassroots, Miriam Ching Yoon Louie, who has spotlighted the *mutualista* antecedents of this social unionism.

She explains that "by linking the *mutualistas* and other ethnically-based independent labor organizations of yesteryear with those of today, the 'big picture' expands from a single frame shot of a current struggle to a rolling documentary film that also encompasses the ethnic- and gender-based organizing of that preceded today's movement. Reclaiming and elaborating this organizing is important for all groups, but especially for immigrants."[2] For his part, Mexican immigrant farmworker Lucas Benítez, a leader of the Coalition of Immokalee Workers (CIW), says that his trailblazing labor organization echoes the ethos of traditional *mutualista* group, of members being "united to help."

Just as traditional *mutualista* groups arose out of concern for the families of the bereaved, so Benítez cites as the initial CIW project their having taken up collections to pay for the funerals and flights home of deceased loved ones. In the service of another mutual aid goal, responding to barrio needs, the CIW employs a mutual aid economic model: the cooperative. Responding to price gouging on the part of neighborhood grocers, the group established a food coop. It began informally, with members selling essential food staples in front of the CIW headquarters. CIW folks had bought the rice, beans, and oil wholesale in Miami; "Instead of $5, say, it was $1.70," he noted. Soon the local stores were lowering their prices.

CIW members also mobilize when a community back home faces a crisis, said Benítez, citing the earthquake that devastated Haiti. The Coalition transformed itself into a community clearinghouse that put local donors in contact with Catholic charities and the Red Cross. And even though many of these farmworkers were out of work due to unprecedented freezes that had ruined much of the crop, "people who had nothing more to give brought a bottle of water." An old man hobbled into the union headquarters, but instead of asking for assistance, he said, "I heard on the radio that you are collecting for Haiti. In my truck I have shoes, clothing, food. . . ."

Another community concern, the lack of local entertainment, led to Saturday night movies at the CIW hall, which also gave the association the opportunity to publicize its weekly meetings. "They are on Wednesday nights, and last week we had 90–100 people," said Benítez, adding, "We are not professional organizers; we are animators—'comunidades de base'—based on what appeals to and is familiar to the people." Comunidades de base (base-level communities) were made famous in the 1980s by Catholic grassroots organizers in Latin America who, influenced by the Church's social teaching, along with Marxist analysis, mobilized local groups for spiritual support, economic self-help, and political empowerment in the face of right-wing dictatorships. Indeed, the CIW calls itself "a community-based organization." It does not use the term "union" and does not belong to any traditional labor organization. Benítez explains that initially they sent out a survey asking people their concerns and that had the respondents called for, say, a campaign for safety in the neighborhoods, the CIW would have focused on that issue. However, at the top of the list were, he said, "Better wages and more respect from employers." Still, those are traditional trade union goals, and the CIW sometimes works with mainstream labor organizations such as the AFL-CIO, as when Coalition leaders recently spoke at an AFL-CIO training session in Florida. For its part, the AFL-CIO regularly posts CIW accomplishments on its website—and no wonder, for these farmworkers have won concessions from such corporate behemoths as McDonald's and Taco Bell.

Benítez cites as an influence the historic *mutualista* labor organizing of a century ago, particularly by mine workers along the border, and the mutuality he witnessed growing up in Mexico. On their small farm his parents

Figure 10. Lucas Benítez of the Coalition of Immokalee Workers. (Photo by Nancy Pierce)

instilled in him the principle that, although poor, "We have something important, which is our dignity as a human being and we also have our work ethos . . . I'm not going to respect the rich man if he doesn't respect me as well. It has to be mutual: respect is gained . . . and without us their enterprise is not worth a thing." His parents also would round up the children, he said, with the cry, "Let's go march alongside your striking teachers and support them!" Young Lucas was impressed as well by his grandmother, a highly respected midwife who offered her services to all, regardless of their ability to pay—what he called "this pledge to help others."[3]

Community-based mutual aid also animated the childhood of union leader Baldemar Velásquez, founder of the Farm Labor Organizing Committee (FLOC), which has won concessions from Campbell's Soup, among others. When the Velásquezes' funds ran out and they could not return to Texas from migrant work in Ohio, they became among the first families to settle out in the greater Toledo area. "There was a lot of racism in those days," he recalls, "so we tried to survive—get by—however we could." Other than the local Catholic parish, the only place they could congregate was "in people's living rooms. . . . My dad's farmhouse was kind of like the Grand Central for all the migrant workers," he said. "Since we lived there year round, all the migrants would come there to find out where they could get, like, used tires, a cheap price on a battery, things like that. So there

were people coming and going all the time, looking for my dad, because we
worked for all the farmers in that area. We knew all the labor contractors.
. . . We didn't have much power to do anything, but my dad would tell them
where to go for help—kind of like a referral center."

FLOC's first meetings were held at the Velásquez house, which had the
advantage of being "out of the way, rural, inconspicuous. We'd have 70–80
people . . . and the kids came . . . children, babies." The farmworker organizers "were all friends of my dad's, comadres of my mom's." The women
chatted in the kitchen and the men outside, where they would discuss labor issues. Young Baldemar reminded them that "this was something that
was important to the entire family—the conditions in the migrant camps,
and what we got paid—because the women were workers too." So the men
traipsed into the house, but they continued to huddle together. "Finally I
put a rule down," said Velásquez. "I said, 'Look, if we're going to found an
organization, the women have to be involved.'" He said that he made the argument that with both genders, their numbers would automatically double.
"Look, we're going to have a thirty-minute meeting, and all the women have
to come," he told them, adding that he "got everybody out there." It also
helped that "my mom was a leader of the women and I was her son, and
she'd be there supporting, adding to, what I had said." With regard to gender, "That's always a dynamic there, and if you're wise you take advantage of
it," he said, and he made reference to "a lot of organizations that failed because they weren't able to navigate that dynamic in the Latino community."

FLOC often sponsored social events, such as baseball games at which every person would have at least one turn at bat, regardless of age or gender.
"Those games ended up being a highlight," he recalls. "You could do things
nobody expected you to do . . . and there was a lot of joking . . . fun" when a
little kid or a serious, stolid older person took a swing. People bonded and
organizational information was shared, as when one of the participants
"would remind people of the dance the next Saturday at his house, and a lot
of them would go, and we'd see each other in a different setting." By this
time all of the band members were also members of FLOC. All of this, he
recalls, "Laid the roots to the organization."[4]

These activities mirrored events sponsored by *mutualista* labor groups a
century ago. *Mutualista* labor unions held celebrations deep in the barrio,
away from the prying eyes of Anglo society and convenient for neighborhood families. These labor groups often borrowed or rented the halls of
other *mutualista* groups and sometimes participated in their celebrations.
For instance, in 1917 the San Antonio–based organization of bakers called
Sociedad Morelos Mutua de Panaderos participated in the thirty-second anniversary celebration of Sociedad Mutualista Ignacio Allende. The "Panaderos," some two thousand strong, held their meetings at the headquarters of

another *mutualista* association, the venerable Sociedad Mutualista Benevolencia Mexicana, founded in 1875.[5]

At one of those meetings, Morelos Mútua de Panaderos decided to bring "the advantages of mutualism and unity to Mexican workers" by voting "to take this opportunity to escape the exploitation" by the firm of Stone and Webster, for whom they worked at San Antonio's Camp Wilson. The workers pledged to obtain "an equitable salary, hours, and working condition ... not trying to obstruct the projects but, rather, to facilitate the contracting of laborers by means of a [hiring] center that defends their interests." After several meetings, some seven hundred people voted to inform the mayor of their plans. Less than a week later, however, the leaders were arrested on undisclosed charges. Camp Wilson opened its own hiring halls run by the employers.[6]

This *mutualista* call for union hiring halls prefigured César Chávez and his United Farm Workers (UFW), who demanded such union hiring halls from growers—as does Chávez protégé Baldemar Velásquez, who in his words, "poured over" historical labor organizing precedents. Nonetheless, Velásquez did not come across the *mutualista* factor in his own research, even as he did find himself profoundly influenced by the African American civil rights movement. As a college student, Velásquez volunteered for Student Nonviolent Coordinating Committee's historic 1964 Freedom Summer voter registration campaign. Upon returning home to Ohio from Mississippi, still fired up, he organized for the Congress of Racial Equality (CORE). His CORE host in Cleveland, learning young Baldemar's own story, asked him why he did not focus on fighting the injustices faced by his own people.

He took the words to heart, with the name of his organization, Farm Labor Organizing Committee, derived in part from Student Nonviolent Coordinating Committee. While a student at Bluffton College, he was "organizing in the fields in the summers and working with my parents after school, helping them with finishing the crop. After I got done with my classes I'd drive home real quick, help them finish that last row of potatoes or cucumbers." One day, lo and behold, "I get a telegram from Dr. Martin Luther King, Jr., at the college, asking if I would go down to Atlanta and help plan the Poor People's Campaign!" Dr. King was shifting his focus to economic justice, calling on all those on the economic margins to join in a march to lobby Washington for a more equitable economy, from increased aid to poor people to decreased military spending.

At the headquarters of King's Southern Christian Leadership Conference in Atlanta, the young organizer was joined by the principal Chicano leaders of the time—all of them invited to meet with the legendary leader and his top lieutenants and discuss strategy for the planned Poor People's

March. "History before my eyes," Velásquez recalled in an address at a 2008 meeting called "Rebuilding Labor's Power." This trip back in time was also a call to action.

> The idea came up: how do we as poor people face this monolithic institutions called international corporations and financial empires. We said, "How can we compel them to talk to us? How do we *get them* to talk to us? And Dr. King made a comment that I will never forget. It's been my cornerstone. It's why I revere Ray Rodgers over at Corporate Campaign, because he showed us how to do this, and that is: Dr. King says, "When you impede the rich man's ability to make money, anything is negotiable."
>
> So remember that! Find their money line. Find their money supply, and find their Achilles heel, and anything is negotiable. That's why we can negotiate multi-party collective bargaining agreements. That's why we can get the corporations, the growers, the suppliers together, all at one table, and carve out one agreement. But we have to impact their financial ability to make money to get them to talk to us, because that talks bigger than anything. Forget the law—because then they'll supersede the law. . . . Well, this is kind of like the martial law of farm workers and the working people. So ¡P'alante!⁷ And never give up!

César Chávez was also a formidable influence on the young leader, with the name of his group, Farm Labor Organizing Committee, bearing a striking resemblance to United Farm Workers Organizing Committee, the early name of the UFW. Chávez would be the keynote speaker at the first three FLOC conventions, and from him, says Velásquez, "I learned: don't ask from somebody something you wouldn't do yourself first." He marvels that "I met both men in the matter of months—within three months, and both men had one affect on you—*both* of them. When you looked at them, when you met them—squared your eyes with theirs—you realized that you were meeting a person that laid everything on the line—their lives—for a cause, that they were going to do it no matter what. They made you feel like, 'If they can do it, I can do it too.'" Baldemar Velásquez was in it for the long haul.

There was a spiritual dimension to this call on the part of both Chávez and King—a faith that sustained them through trials and against seemingly ridiculous odds—and Velásquez made his own spiritual reference in remarks to the 2009 AFL-CIO convention.

To this group—long the nation's leading labor federation and, until a decade ago, a famed promoter of immigration restriction—Velásquez spoke of immigration reform as "a moral imperative." "Brothers and sisters," he began. "With all due respect to the religions of the world, my

Judeo-Christian heritage tells me . . . not to oppress or mistreat the alien . . . . So let's get right with God, because if you don't, Ezekiel 22:29–30 warns that He's going to be really ticked off if we do these things to these aliens. Finally, in the New Testament, those of us who call ourselves Christians, we're recipients of the greatest amnesty in the world! Didn't Jesus come, take all our sins—everything we've ever done, all the laws we broke—took them, to say, 'You're forgiven'? And who are we to deny it to anybody else?"

Like any potent tool—like fire—a perceived spiritual call can have its negative aspects, from sanctimony to messianism. Velásquez's own mentor, Chávez, became increasingly insular and authoritarian as he turned to cult-like behavior, in the process alienating nearly all of his dedicated lieutenants, who found themselves forced out of the UFW. And yet the inspiring aspects of Chávez's spiritual charism live on in those same organizers, who mostly went on to work in other labor organizations or in immigrant rights, political reform, or environmental justice.[8]

For his part, Baldemar Velásquez is careful to situate any religious reference within the broadest of humanistic frames, which is actually how most *mutualista* groups treated the topic: allowing free reference to religious feelings but seldom holding religious events. (The one exception was in the case of those *mutualista* groups founded in conjunction with parishes.) Meanwhile, it is clear in this testimony by Baldemar Velásquez that he was presenting options, not commands. And this statement climaxed not with his religious references but, rather, with a very inclusive appeal (even if he doubtless sees "inclusion" as an approach he is required to take as a Christian). "My brothers and sisters," he began in his windup, "let us be like the founders of the great unions in this hall. They were all immigrants; many of them came here without papers. So they started organizing the people— and now immigrants are joining unions at the greatest rate of any segment of the population!"

Then the FLOC leader evoked the Ellis Island immigrants that organized garment workers, mine workers—all sorts of workers—in the face of threats and in the wake of preventable tragedies such as the Triangle Shirtwaist Factory fire. Yet he skipped over the anti-immigrant policies trumpeted through most of the twentieth century by one union: the AFL itself. He also elided the fact that it was much easier to immigrate legally a century ago (with the stark exception of Asians). He appealed to the better angels of the union movement and that bedrock union tenet, solidarity, and the hall erupted in cheers when he declared, "So let's be like the founders of your unions! . . . They started organizing immigrants, and now immigrants are joining unions at the greatest rate of any segment of the population! I say: let's be like the founders of your unions, who came to this country, and organized unions; they didn't say, 'What country are you from?' They only asked, 'Which side are you on?' I'm gonna be on *your side!*"[9]

Such organizing, without regard to immigration or citizenship status, was second nature to *mutualista* labor groups of a century ago. They were typical of *mutualista* groups in general, who of course had no citizenship test for membership. Not that the *mutualista* movement was synonymous with labor organizing. After all, the typical Mexican mutual aid association provided insurance benefits, and many of these groups included some small business owners among their members. Moreover, a few "worker" *mutualista* societies in fact were headed by business owners. Then there is the case of the two *mutualista* groups founded by workers of the El Paso Smelter Company: company unions, evidently, for they were headed by plant supervisors. Smelter workers who themselves held *mutualista* leadership posts did so offsite, not surprisingly, as when an El Paso Smelter oiler served as an officer of Sociedad Mutualista "La Fraternal," which met in a neighborhood that was near but outside of the company site.

Some of the early leaders of the *mutualista* movement were active in the nation's first national union, the Knights of Labor, which peaked in the 1880s. Among the more notable was José María Flores of San Antonio, a founder of Sociedad de la Unión in 1885.[10] The role of influential organizers such as Flores no doubt helps explain why Sociedad Mutualista de La Unión emerged as the largest and most prominent Mexican association in San Antonio (not that the term *unión* carried any organized-labor connotations, with the Spanish word for trade union being *sindicato*). Flores's leadership in this high-profile *mutualista* also no doubt helped bring Mexican recruits to the Knights of Labor. The Knights' courageous recruiting of workers regardless of background (even African Americans—at least officially—but with the glaring exception of Asians) doubtless contributed to its demise, even if many other factors proved lethal, notably the combined hostility of the media, the corporate elite, and most governmental authorities.

The new AFL more than took to the heart the cautionary lessons of the Knights. As it rose to become the largest, most prominent national union, the AFL limited membership to the skilled trades and pushed for immigration restriction, all of which ended up reinforcing a strong anti-Mexican tendency among its largely Anglo rank and file. Despite it all, a few Mexican AFL locals sprang up, including one at an El Paso smelter in 1900.[11]

These pioneering union members, with their links to both the AFL and the *mutualista* movement, anticipated the UFW, which is affiliated with the AFL-CIO but originally developed along *mutualista* lines. Early on César Chávez and his fellow organizers employed "a *mutualista* approach to provide a multiplicity of services to farm workers," in the words of historian

Armando Navarro. "These included life insurance, a gas station, a grocery store, a drug store cooperative, and a medical clinic." The few traditional *mutualista* groups still surviving in the UFW era, meanwhile, tended to support the union, as in 1972 when Sociedad Mutualista in Granger, Washington unanimously voted to endorse a UFW-led consumer boycott, or in 1975 when Sociedad Progresista Mexicana Lodge #56 in the San Fernando Valley was among the sponsors of a benefit event for the UFW. Sociedad Progresista's slogan, which translates as "Works, not rationales, are love," echoed Chávez's famous slogan "deeds are love/hechos son amor." The *mutualista* ethos also provided the elegiac closing passage for an article in *The Nation* recounting the funeral of César Chávez: "Cesar, who was always good at symbols, saved his best for last: a simple pine box, fashioned by his brother's hands, carried unceremoniously through the Central Valley town he made famous. With some 35,000 people looking on . . . no one . . . could fail to hear that plain box speak. Cesar Chavez's commitment to voluntary poverty extended even unto death. And perhaps a few among the crowd would get the deeper reference. Burial insurance had been Cesar's first organizing tool. . . ."[12]

For his part, Chávez's own mentor, Ernesto Galarza, structured much of his California farm labor organizing in the 1950s around the remaining active *mutualista* groups.[13] Doubtless Galarza knew that the first major farm labor organizing in California, in the 1920s, included *mutualista* labor groups. They were instrumental in the founding of Confederación de Uniones de Obreros Mexicanos (CUOM), or the Confederation of Unions of Mexican Workers.

CUOM, reflecting its *mutualista* influences, did not focus exclusively on jobsite issues such as wages, hours, and working conditions but also set up libraries, a clinic, and legal aid. Some CUOM statements reflected radical views, such as the declaration that "the exploited class, the greater part of which is manual labor, is right in establishing a class struggle in order to effect an economic and moral betterment of its condition, and at last its freedom from capitalist tyranny," which led the Mexican consul to try to influence the internal workings of CUOM. Mainly, however, it operated "as an organization that included a wide range of tendencies," according to historian Douglas Monroy, serving as "a confederation of Mexican worker organizations—mutualistas, cooperatives, and the existing, incipient unions." CUOM was renamed the Asociación Mutualista del Valle Imperial, evidently in response to the growers' refusal to recognize any organization called a "union," and the Mexican Consul may have played a role in the group agreeing to the name change—and even promising to refrain from strikes.

But whatever the consul may have thought, "mutualista" did not mean anti-union. The wildcat walkouts that continued "were very much community affairs, rooted as they were in the mutualistas," Monroy notes. With the coming of the Great Depression and also the mass arrests of immigrants, *mutualista* groups found themselves mostly on the decline. The mighty Alianza Hispano Americana (AHA) did support the labor efforts, such as when a California AHA lodge held a fundraiser in support of striking citrus workers in 1935. The Alianza also supported farmworker strikes in Colorado, Wyoming, and elsewhere.[14]

But it was in the AHA's home state of Arizona, in the first years of the twentieth century, that the organization had the most active presence in labor actions, when the head of the AHA chapter in the mining town of Morenci, Abrán Salcido, was among the strike leaders. Although the AHA itself took no stance on labor organizing and included some business owners in its ranks, AHA venues and membership links were used by organizers such as Salcido. He had emigrated from Chihuahua, while another *mutualista* labor leader, known as Juan de la O., had been born and raised in New Mexico. Both Morenci miners were instrumental in "developing a labor organization within the womb of the mutualistas," as historian Linda Gordon puts it.

By 1901, most of the Morenci miners were Mexican, both born in the United States and from Mexico, and on June 1, 1903, some two thousand to three thousand five hundred strikers began demonstrated on the mining property: "a pretty big crowd," according to one report, "mostly Mexicans, but a lot of Dagoes, Bohunks, and foreigners of every kind. . . ."[15] The walkout was not sponsored by any official union, with the Western Federation of Miners (WFM) known to discriminate in favor of its largely Anglo/Irish membership. But to the extent that planning took place in any established organizations, it was via the mutual aid associations of the various ethnic groups, with the Mexican ones predominating. And just as the *mutualistas* united ethnic Mexicans from the United States with Mexican immigrants, the Italian and Mexican mutual aid groups also likely helped foster cooperation across nationalities.

The miners were protesting a cut in hours and wages, and less than a week into the strike they upped the demand to wage parity with Anglo and Irish miners. The workers also called for union recognition, lower prices at the company-owned store, an end to arbitrary dismissals and mandatory paycheck deductions for company medical and insurance programs, and facilities for changing into street clothes at the end of a shift. Management responded by shutting down production and refusing to negotiate. "Mexicans gathered 'two or three times a day in Morenci . . . [to] listen to leaders who are very industrious [and] have used harsh language concerning the 'gringos,'" according to historian Philip Mellinger, who notes that many if not most of these leaders were officers in Morenci *mutualista* groups.

What happened next has been recounted through the generations. Here is how it was remembered in one Morenci family: "My dad always told me he heard about the strike of 1903 from his uncles, who were miners then. He would hear them recall Abrán Salcido, a Mexican organizer from Chihuahua, who convinced the miners that they should go out on strike for higher wages. The striking miners took over the Company offices which caused the Company to ask the Governor for help. He sent a group of Arizona Rangers. When it looked like there was going to be an armed confrontation, a storm gathered and a deluge descended on Morenci, scattering Rangers and strikers alike. A torrent of water rushed through the Mexican part of town drowning many people. Federal troops arrived, proclaimed martial law and put an end to the strike. Abrán Salcido was sent to prison."[16]

Salcido was one of ten leaders, a number of them from *mutualista* groups, who were summarily convicted of rioting (and with AHA and another *mutualista* under suspicion by federal authorities). In the future, the miners of the Morenci region would stage other major labor protests, including in the 1980s, but they mostly failed in the face of obdurate, powerful, politically connected mining interests. Today the original section of Morenci itself no longer exists, "Reduced to rubble, scooped out and then filled back in with copper landfill waste," in the words of a former resident, memoirist Joaquín B. Oviedo.

These *mutualista* mine worker activists also live on through the people they inspired, notably Lucas Benítez of the CIW, who says that this saga of community-based organizing informs his own efforts as a farmworker organizer taking on some of the world's most powerful corporations. He may well see it as a case of David versus Goliath, at least in the long run— the very long run. Just such a vision was put forth eloquently by FLOC's Baldemar Velásquez. "Now I'm going to speak to you as organizers," he said in a 2008 talk. "Listen carefully. The object is not to win. That's not the objective. The object is to do the *right* and *good thing*. If you decide not to do anything, because it's too *hard* or too *impossible,* then nothing will be done, but if you go and do the right thing now, and you do it long enough, good things will happen—something's going to happen!"[17]

At least one of the principal demands from 1903 was eventually won, although it took fifty years: wage parity. This victory over discrimination serves as the coda for the prize-winning documentary *Los Mineros*. "A quietly powerful story," *TV Guide* called this chronicle of a struggle waged more than a century ago.[18]

The activism of Abrán Salcido and his comrades was also instrumental in furthering the idea that the labor movement should welcome immigrants. The labor solidarity at Morenci convinced the WFM to permanently reject the idea of excluding immigrants from membership. At the union convention later that year, several delegates spoke in favor of welcoming Mexican miners, and a former WFM president summed up much of the testimony by saying, "Discourage talk about scabs and foreigners. Foreigners are leaders in labor movements." Carrying this expansive notion one step further, the WFM would soon be instrumental in the founding of the Industrial Workers of the World, famed for recruiting members from everywhere in "one big union."[19]

Meanwhile, an Italian miner, a man very much like the ones who organized alongside *los mineros*, exercised a powerful early influence on the nation's most important labor official today: the president of the AFL-CIO, Richard Trumka. "Twelve-year-old Richard Louis Trumka was sitting on the porch of his grandfather Attilio Bertugli's house in Rices Landing, Pa., complaining bitterly to his grandpap about how badly Mine Workers were being treated," according to Trumka's biography on the AFL-CIO website.

> "What do you plan to do about it?" his grandfather asked.
>
> "When I grow up, I could be a politician," Rich replied. His grandpap feigned anger, smacking him across the back of his head. Chastened, young Trumka offered a second opinion: "I could become a lawyer and stand up for workers' rights."
>
> His grandfather, a long-time miner, allowed how that was a better idea, but added something that has stuck with Trumka ever since. "If you want to help workers," his grandfather said, "you first need to help people."
>
> Rich Trumka not only grasped the wisdom of his grandfather's counsel, it has been the encompassing vision of his leadership in the labor movement ever since: Unions must strive to uplift everybody in their pursuit of fair treatment for workers.[20]

Does the AFL-CIO president realize that Mexican miners were engaged in just such community-based labor organizing a century ago—sometimes alongside miners with the same background as his grandfather? That is an open question, but doubtless the labor leader would be heartened to learn of this link to his own story. Solidarity, indeed.

Trans-Border Organizing

Labor organizers increasingly recognize that if their movement hopes to survive in an era of global corporations, unions need to operate transnationally. For instance, in 2005, the United Steelworkers, in one of their strikes, sought the support of a Mexican union and then supported that Mexican labor group in its own job action five years later. This strike in Cananea, Sonora also was endorsed by the AFL-CIO, which "condemned" the Mexican courts for permitting the mining company, in the union's words, "To fire 1,200 striking workers," with the AFL charging that "the court effectively eliminated the right to strike in Mexico." A Mexican labor leader summed up the confrontation in the starkest terms: "If what they want are martyrs in Cananea, then they will find them here."[1]

These words carried the weight of history, for Cananea mine workers helped spark the Mexican Revolution of 1910. Some of those who helped plan the 1906 Cananea miner's strike, moreover, had been among the organizers of the 1903 miners' strike in Morenci, Arizona. As historian Rodolfo Acuña notes, the US strike "was a defining moment in the history of Mexicans not just in Arizona but in Mexico itself. It was linked to the Cananea strike of 1906, a precursor to the Mexican Revolution."[2]

One of these early transnational organizers was Abrán Salcido. Convicted of "being one of the leaders in the Morenci riots," he served his full two-year sentence in the scorching, rattlesnake-infested Yuma prison. There he served alongside several *mutualista* labor cohorts, notably Weneslado Laustaunau. The most voluble of the strike leaders, Laustaunau continued his diatribes within the prison walls. The authorities accused him of "assault with a weapon" and slapped him with a ten-year extension of his sentence, along with periodic banishment to solitary confinement in an iron cage bolted to granite rock face during the blistering Arizona summers. Laustaunau died of heat prostration on a sweltering August day in 1906.[3]

After his release, Salcido renewed his activism with a vengeance and joined up with the main worker action at that time, which was now centered in Mexico. He gave speeches decrying US mining interests that dominated Cananea. They operated with the blessing of Mexican dictator Porfirio Díaz,

Figure 11. "Mug photo" of labor/ *mutualista* organizer Abrán Salcido at the Yuma, Arizona, Territorial Prison, 1903. (Courtesy Mike Guertin, Yuma Territorial Prison)

even as they paid local Mexicans a pittance, especially in comparison with workers brought in from the United States. "Down with Díaz! Cursed be Díaz! Traitor! Tyrant of the republic! Imposter! Thief!" cried Salcido in the middle of Arizona Cinco de Mayo festivities to the delight of many in the crowd, while the "shocked" authorities, both US and Mexican, threatened him with reprisals.

Undeterred, Salcido joined the revolutionary Partido Liberal Mexicano (PLM), which had been active in the Morenci region for several years. Hounded by the authorities, Salcido left to join the revolutionary labor movement in Mexico, with upwards of one hundred other armed Mexicans following him out of the Morenci area.

In the Arizona border town of Douglas, Salcido teamed up with cohorts such as PLM leader Práxedis Guerrero, who also had recently arrived from Morenci, where he had headed Mutualista Obreros Libres. Salcido was arrested in Douglas on charges of fomenting revolution. Turned over to Mexican officials, he was fined one thousand pesos and sentenced to eight years, eighty days in San Juan de Ullúa prison. Thus, within the space of twelve months, Abrán Salcido had the dubious distinction of being incarcerated in infamously horrible detention facilities on both sides of the border.[4]

Public security forces from both nations together ultimately crushed the Cananea miners' strike, with the Arizona Rangers called in by the US owner. The Morenci and Cananea labor actions together constituted the first great strikes in the modern copper industry, an industry that had already become transnational in this early era, with the giant Phelps-Dodge mining company having built a railroad between its Sonora and Arizona mines in 1903: "the Arizona/Sonora copper barons," in the words of one historian.[5]

Mexican workers operated even more transnationally, however, notably with their *mutualista* groups, which embraced both immigrants from Mexico and people whose families had long lived in Arizona and other Southwestern states. And as historian Michael Wasserman puts it, "Miners and railroad workers in particular had experienced a wider world of labor relations across the border in the United States, which led them to protest their plight [with] newer tactics, such as migration and the organization of mutualist societies . . . and labor unions."[6]

Thus, the less-revolutionary *mutualista* labor activists operated transnationally as well. Historian David Gutiérrez cites the case of the Gran Círculo de Obreros Mexicanos (Great Circle of Mexican Workers) as part of what he calls "the transnational edge of *mutualismo*." Founded in Mexico City in 1870, the Gran Círculo not only had a number of chapters in Mexico by the early 1880s but also had established affiliates in the US Southwest by the 1890s. As Díaz loyalists took over some chapters and repressed others, Gran Círculo activists hopped the train north. In 1890, just a few years after the railroad line reached Lampassas, Texas, a Gran Círculo chapter was founded in that rural outpost, and it doubtless was linked to the larger branch in San Antonio, about one hundred miles away. Meanwhile in California, the Gran Círculo would prove instrumental in some of the farm labor organizing drives of the 1930s — organizing that in turn would influence Ernesto Galarza, the mentor of César Chávez.[7]

Mutualista labor organizations also sometimes sponsored talks by PLM radicals, as when a prominent *mutualista* labor group in Laredo hosted PLM orator Sara Estela Ramírez. The feminist revolutionary lauded *mutualista* labor groups for their solidarity and their strike committees.[8] One of the leaders of this particular Laredo labor *mutualista*, for his part, spoke movingly of worker rights and transnationalism. "It is necessary to banish from the worker the idea of always being enslaved," J. M. Mora declared, and he laid out a trans-border vision of *mutualismo*: "When all the sociedades mexicanas in the State of Texas have established relations of alliance,

it will be a league of such force and power . . . as to have great a social representation here [and] in Mexico, such that it might attract the attention of
the world."[9]

This speech took place at the historic Primer Congreso Mexicanista of
1911. The Mexicanist Congress founder, Nicasio Idar, was himself a great
champion of trans-border labor activism. Born in Port Isabel, Texas, and
educated in Corpus Christi, Idar was involved in various *mutualista* and
labor groups in Texas and then helped found an important union in Monterrey, Mexico, the Supreme Order of Mexican Railroad Workers. In 1891,
"after three years, the Order was destroyed by the repression of the Díaz
government," in the words of a Mexican historian, so the young Idar returned to Texas, settling in Laredo, where he founded the newspaper *La
Crónica*, which encouraged trans-border cooperation by *mutualista*, labor,
and Masonic groups.[10]

For their part, two of Nicacio Idar's sons together embodied transnational organizing: Federico Idar, a leading labor organizer and national
political figure in Mexico, and Clemente Idar, an important labor official
in the leading US union then and now, the American Federation of Labor
(AFL).[11] Both efforts ended tragically, and this points to the long odds of
such organizing.

Like his father before him, Federico Idar became a major figure in Mexican railroad organizing, rising to become a director of the Unión General
de Conductores, Maquinistas, Garroteros y Fogoneros. He won a seat in
the Mexican Senate and in 1937 was elected president of the Senate itself. In that capacity, Federico Idar challenged the growing hegemony of
the reigning political party, the Partido Nacional Revolucionario (PNR).
He was prescient, for the Partido Revolucionario Institucional (PRI), as
it would later be known, would control Mexican national politics for more
than half a century, but Idar paid dearly for his political integrity. While
serving his second year as president of the Senate, Federico Idar was assas-
sinated, with the principal suspect someone associated with former president Emilio Portes Gil. At that point, the Idar's left Mexico City for San
Antonio.

For his part, Clemente Idar made history as the first national Mexican
organizer for the AFL, signing up everyone from boilermakers to clerks
and tailors to beet workers in Colorado to, yes, railroad workers. During the
national railroad strike of 1922, Idar headed an organization of nearly two
thousand railroad workers in El Paso. "Organizing Mexican workers usually involved the recruitment of entire mutual aid societies," one historian
has noted about his efforts. "The workers would either retain the society as
a dual organization or supplant it with the union, which negotiated fringe
benefits in lieu of mutualism." He engaged in cross-border organizing,

Figure 12. Clemente Idar, front row, second from the right, sitting next to legendary AFL leader and co-founder Samuel Gompers (third from right). (Courtesy Nettie Benson Latin American Collection, University of Texas Libraries, the University of Texas at Austin)

as when he tried to establish links between the carpenter unions in the United States and Mexico: a visionary move, when one considers that, until relatively recently, carpenters and other skilled trades were still among the staunchest opponents of Mexican immigration.[12]

Even as Clemente Idar bravely swam against the anti-Mexican tide, he did not challenge the AFL's longstanding position in favor of immigration restriction. Doubtless that was a prerequisite for working with this most powerful of unions, which, as such, must have seemed to be the only viable labor organization in the powerfully anti-labor state of Texas. Moreover, the sole voices lobbying against immigration restrictions at the time were those of the corporate bosses, in stark contrast to today, when immigrants and their supporters lead the way in this regard. Until the 1970s, however, the Mexican immigrant voice was virtually excluded from the immigration policy debate.

Figure 13. Emma Tenayuca leading a rally in front of City Hall, San Antonio, c. 1937. (Note the word *mutualista* on the banner to her immediate right) (UTSA Special Collections, S. A. Light Collection, L-1541-D)

It was in this fraught political landscape that Clemente Idar navigated, and he managed to gain unprecedented entry into the very center of power of this largest and oldest union, working directly with the legendary founder, President Samuel Gompers. In fact, according to a nephew of Idar's, the civil rights attorney Ed Idar Jr., Gompers died in Clemente Idar's arms, at the Saint Anthony Hotel, during the Pan American Labor Conference being held in San Antonio in 1924.

Thus did Idar subscribe to the AFL's restrictive immigration stance, even as he was organizing newly arrived immigrants, and even as his brother was a leading Mexican labor official. It is likely that Clemente saw Federico's work not as contradictory but as complimentary, holding the prospect of improving the Mexican wages so that these workers would not feel the economic pressure to emigrate. Clemente and another brother, Eduardo, were among the founders in 1929 of the League of United Latin American Citizens, which required members to be US citizens, and which paid little heed to the problems of immigrants—or laborers, for that matter—focusing instead on civil rights for Mexican Americans.[13]

At this time, the union on the march was not the AFL but rather the Congress of Industrial Organizations (CIO), which was busy mobilizing workers across the land, from autoworkers in Michigan to mine workers in Appalachia to dockworkers, farmworkers, and pecan shellers in the Southwest, with the latter organized by Emma Tenayuca of San Antonio. Many of the CIO unions had been founded by European immigrants, and the CIO recruited members regardless of ethnicity or gender.

Many of Tenayuca's planning meetings took place at the headquarters of Sociedad Mutualista Benevolencia Mexicana. Founded in 1875, "La Benevolencia" had long served as a safe community spot for labor groups, as when a bakery workers *mutualista* met there in 1917 and voted to go out on strike.

Representing the pecan shellers at the national level was another Latina, Luisa Moreno. In her native Guatemala, labor unions typically had arisen from *mutualista* organizing, and now she tapped *mutualista* associations all across the United States for the CIO and for the organization she headed, the left-wing Congress of Spanish-Speaking Peoples (Congreso de Los Pueblos de Habla Española). Moreno also worked for a time as a research analyst at the Pan American Union (PAU), the forerunner of the Organization of American States.

She was hired by the director of PAU's Department of Labor and Social Education, Ernesto Galarza.[14] In 1942 he made waves by accusing the US ambassador to Bolivia of pressuring the Bolivian president not to implement the new labor code in the crucial tin industry, even as union leaders charged the dictator with having ordered the massacre of striking miners. The press widely reported Galarza's statements, prompting the State Department to issue a denial. That in turn prompted him to quit PAU in protest, which triggered even more publicity. As the *TIME* magazine profile "Man against Tin" put it, "In his cluttered office on the ground floor of the Pan American Union's exotic building in Washington, shock-haired Ernesto Galarza gazed thoughtfully through a dirt-dimmed window at the sunken gardens below. What he would do next, now that he had quit his job as Chief of the Union's Division of Labor & Social Information, he did not know. Nor did he care. He had made his point."[15]

The Roosevelt administration responded with a fact-finding commission that included US labor leaders. "It is believed that the designation of the commission is at least in part a sequel to the charges of Ernesto Galarza," reported *The New York Times*. Meanwhile, *The Nation* called for Roosevelt to "ask the Pan American Union to reinstate Ernesto Galarza as chief of its Labor and Social Information Division."[16]

Figure 14.
Ernesto Galarza,
n.d. (Courtesy
Occidental College
Special Collections
& College
Archives)

Galarza did return to his job, but three years later he quit for good, scoring "the ineffectiveness of the Division of Social and Labor Information . . . culminated in its practical absorption by the more aggressive elements of the [Pan American] Union representing business, industry and finance." He charged that "Latin American liberals, democrats and workers are also coming to the conclusion . . . that the declarations of the United States with respect to the principles of honest and democratic dealing do not apply to Latin America." Galarza had concluded that "the door to reform has been slammed shut."[17]

Galarza would now apply his transnational labor perspective to grassroots organizing by working for the National Farm Labor Union (NFLU).

Figure 15. Members of the National Farm Labor Union, 1950s. (Courtesy Occidental College Special Collections & College Archives)

This career move on the part of someone who had earned a PhD. at Columbia University and had headed an international department in Washington must have come as a surprise to Galarza's professional colleagues. But he admired the labor activism of people such as Luisa Moreno and H. L. Mitchell of the Southern Tenant Farmers Union, and Galarza himself had come from humble origins, having immigrated as a boy with his family from their mountain village in the Mexican state of Nyarit.

In an echo of the historic *mutualista* labor organizations, Galarza set up "Mexican Organizing Committees" that welcomed members regardless of their immigration status. "Galarza's union allowed Mexican people to be very Mexican. It gave everybody the sense that we could be Mexicanos and demand our rights as residents of California," one NFLU member recalled.[18]

The people Galarza recruited included contract temporary laborers, or *braceros,* as they were known. Under a wartime agreement, Mexico had agreed to allow US corporations to sign up workers for temporary employment. As the program became permanent, the Mexican government withdrew, charging that employers too often exploited the workers. Every laborer was bound by a work contract signed in Mexico, their US working conditions sight-unseen, with their legal right to stay in the United States totally tied to their temporary work contract with that one employer—to quit meant that one was subject to deportation. This power imbalance made it exceedingly difficult for labor organizers to recruit braceros, even as their vulnerable status meant that they had many grievances.

In response to this seemingly desperate situation, Galarza lobbied for an end to the Bracero Program. As such he was in line with the views of the main progressive groups in the 1950s, from labor to civil rights leaders, plus the NFLU was a constituent member of the AFL. Like Clemente Idar before him, Galarza went along with the AFL's restrictionist policies. Idar, however, did not have to contend with a contract labor program. One had been implemented during World War I—indeed braceros had replaced striking *mutualista* bakery workers in San Antonio in 1917—but the policy was terminated in 1919, shortly after Idar joined the AFL, in large part because of its lobbying.[19]

But just as AFL leaders of the 1920s had no interest in the trans-border labor expertise of the Idar brothers, so the AFL in the 1950s and 1960s ignored Ernesto Galarza's explicit transnational analysis. The Federation's leaders failed to acknowledge the fact that the Mexican immigrant, in Galarza's words, "Is forced to seek better conditions north of the border by the slow but relentless pressure of the United States' agricultural, financial and oil corporate interests on the entire economic and social evolution of the Mexican nation." Galarza himself had been offering such analysis for years, including in testimony before Congress in 1947. By the 1950s, however, red-baiting had brought such criticism of US business practices under suspicion as "anti-free enterprise." Even more, the anti-Communist juggernaut targeted anyone who had known Communists, and Galarza had made many such friends in the 1930s.

If Galarza was in a precarious spot, those old colleagues, such as Luisa Moreno, bore the full weight of the opprobrium. Moreno was deported, while Emma Tenayuca was imprisoned. She could hardly be deported, as her family had been in Texas for many generations. Thus was silenced the one segment of society speaking on behalf of immigrant workers, as in this 1940 speech by Luisa Moreno to the American Committee for the Protection of the Foreign Born: "Long before *The Grapes of Wrath* had ripened under California's vineyards, a people lived on highways, under trees or tents, in shacks or railroad sections, picking crops . . . cultivating sugar beets, building railroads and dams, making barren land fertile for new crops and greater riches. These people are not aliens. They have contributed their endurance, sacrifice, youth and labor to the Southwest. Indirectly, they have paid more taxes than all the stockholders of California's industrialized agriculture, the sugar companies, and the large cotton interests, that operated or have operated with the labor of Mexican workers."

A defiant Moreno declared, "They can talk about deporting me . . . but they can never deport the people I've worked with and with whom things were accomplished for the benefit of hundreds of thousands of workers—things that can never be destroyed."[20] Indeed, one of her colleagues from the 1940s, Bert Corona, would go on to play a major role in making mainstream the organizing of immigrant workers regardless of their legal status.

Meanwhile, a future cohort of Corona's in that campaign, Soledad "Chole" Alatorre, was signing up union members in her workplace regardless of their immigration status. Her father had been the leader of a Mexican railway union (much like Nicasio and Federico Idar), and young Chole took those lessons with her when she immigrated to California and landed a job at a Rose Marie Reid factory. It turned out that she was the perfect size to model their famed swimwear—the typical size of the average American woman—so she was asked to show off the latest styles around the plant, and Alatorre took this opportunity to speak to workers about the union. Then she was promoted to supervisor, but instead of aligning with management she used her increased autonomy to spread the word about unionizing, and she went on to work for several major unions—often the only female Mexican immigrant organizer.

Alatorre and Corona brought to their unions the *mutualista* ethos of welcoming members regardless of their immigration or citizenship status. Both activists also worked in the other direction, bringing a labor-organizing perspective to the pioneering immigrant rights group they founded in the 1970s, known variously as Hermandad Mexicana Nacional (HMN) and Centro de Acción Social Autónoma (CASA). For them, as for *mutualista* labor organizers of yore, the issue was joined: rights for *immigrant workers*. "What most distinguished CASA," writes historian David Gutiérrez, "was that . . . basing their political perspective on more than four decades of labor organizing and activism in Mexican communities in the Southwest, CASA founders, particularly Corona and Alatorre, argued that Mexican immigrant laborers represented an integral component of the American working class and that, as such, they had legitimate claims to the same rights as other workers in the United States."[21]

HMN/CASA activists would make this argument to their soul-mates in the United Farm Workers (UFW). The UFW, in turn, would advocate for immigration reform with its parent organization, the AFL-CIO.[22] Traditionally the UFW, like its parent group the AFL, emphasized elimination of the contract labor program and punishment of growers who recruited as strike breakers people who had not entered the country officially. At the same time, unlike so many in the AFL, with their discriminatory attitudes, César Chávez, like Galarza before him, always organized from the heart of the barrio community, tapping into the old *mutualista* networks.

Now HMN and CASA called on the UFW to build on that approach by widening its view of immigration. Corona kept reminding Chávez of their shared view that US transnational policies favored corporations over workers on *both* sides of the border, a critique Chávez already knew from Galarza. Meanwhile, many of the students marching with the UFW for farmworker rights also were CASA activists and were fired up by a rising Chicano movement that rediscovered *mutualismo* and emphasized pride in a Mexican heritage that predated the border itself.

Chávez could understand that perspective, for his own family's residence in the Southwest predated the US presence there. For people of his generation, however, this fact had long been seen as a US civil rights issue: that their families predated the Anglos in the region, that they themselves had fought in World War II—as was the case with Chávez—but that they faced discrimination at home. All of this prompted them to demand the rights owed to them as US citizens: a far cry from the perspective of the *mutualista*. Thus, Chávez and Corona mostly worked together on civil rights and labor rights as domestic political issues, with this connection reaching its high-water mark in the presidential campaign of 1968. The two activists had major roles in the California primary campaign of Senator Robert Kennedy. So did Chole Alatorre, and years later she recalled how she stood next to the senator at a mammoth rally in downtown Los Angeles and then shepherded him through the massive throng of excited admirers. Years later she recalled the Senator asking, "Where is that woman, 'Challie,' who saved my life?"[23]

During the 1970s, Chole Alatorre and Bert Corona spearheaded a sea change in Democratic Party and labor attitudes toward immigration policy. By now Chávez was shifting his stance. This contributed to the UFW's parent organization, the AFL, rethinking its position. So did the Federation's merger in 1955 with the CIO, which had been so animated by pro-immigrant organizers such as Luisa Moreno, Bert Corona, and Chole Alatorre. Moreover, some of the AFL's main players, notably its president at that time, George Meany, were not wedded to the traditional restrictionist stance, while Chávez himself sat on the AFL-CIO board. He would eventually be succeeded in that seat by one of his protégés, Baldemar Velásquez, who champions immigration reform and signs up contract laborers for his Farm Labor Organizing Committee (FLOC).[24]

This has resulted in a "cross-fertilization of the union movement, the concurrent reemergence of ethnic-based *mutualistas* . . . and . . . large trade unions in the process of massive rethinking and retooling," as reported in the study *Sweatshop Warrior*.[25] Thus, organized labor has played a crucial role in supporting the massive, historic immigration marches of recent years. The Social Science Research Council noted that "Los Angeles organized labor has been a potent vehicle of Latino immigrant mobilization,

Figure 16. Leaving a White House meeting on immigration reform legislation, February 5, 2013, from left to right: Eliseo Medina, Service Employees International Union; Richard Trumka, American Federation of Labor-Congress of Industrial Organizations; and Janet Murguía, National Council of La Raza. (Courtesy Getty Images)

both in the workplace and at the voting booth. That is why L.A. was at the epicenter of the immigrant rights movement that emerged this past spring, with a reported 500,000 marchers in the city's streets on March 25, 2006, and even more on May 1, when cities across the nation were engulfed in mass protest."

Labor unions were crucial in Chicago as well, with those Midwest marches critical to the national scope of the demonstrations: beyond the Southwest and into every corner of the country. As a study by the Woodrow Wilson Center notes, "Impressed by the skill of the march organizers and the spontaneous participation by dozens of individuals and informal groups (parishes, work-places, high school students, families, et al.), the Chicago and Illinois labor federations pledged critical, major financial and logistical support for the upcoming May march, overcoming their initial hesitation to march on May Day. Union funds paid for Chicago immigrant leaders to travel to California to coordinate with local organizers there."[26]

Latino and Latina leaders in the AFL-CIO have been central to the Federation as it has come into line with the unions that have a long history of labor organizing among non-WASP immigrants, such as UNITE-HERE and the Service Employees International Union (SEIU). One of SEIU's top officials, Eliseo Medina, is arguably the leading labor proponent of immigration reform. The son of a bracero, and an immigrant himself, Medina left the fields as a teen and joined the UFW, inspired by César Chávez's community-based organizing. As the farmworker founder veered increasingly toward cult-like behavior, Medina left the UFW for SEIU, carrying with him the tips he had learned from his mentor. The young organizer reached out to neighborhood leaders and clergy, doubling and tripling membership at one SEIU local after another.

Medina has never stated that the *mutualista* heritage influenced his own organizing approach, but his community-based ethos echoes that of the historic *mutualista* unions. So does his trail-blazing recruitment of members regardless of their immigration status, as with SEIU's landmark Justice for Janitor's campaign. This national victory in April 2000 may well have been the final factor tipping the AFL-CIO toward its historic pivot on the question of immigration reform later that same year.[27]

The AFL-CIO's policy shift means that, for instance, the construction trades have been organizing in tandem with the National Day Labor Organizing Network. "It may be hard to see just what immigrant day laborers, those wiry guys scrambling for landscaping jobs amid clouds of picketing Minutemen, have in common with union workers, the folks with American flags on their hard hats, but the two groups are a lot closer than you might have thought," editorialized *The New York Times,* which explained that "The bold idea behind labor's embrace of immigrants is that third-world outsourcing should stop at our borders—that the best way to help all workers is to start with those at the bottom. The less our street corners resemble a chaotic job bazaar, the better off all workers will be."[28]

Meanwhile, UNITE-HERE joined forces with the Mexican American Worker Organization (Asociación Mexicana Americana de Trabajadores) (AMAT), which has the "mission of creating mutual aid organizations that educate workers and provide tools for empowerment," as one study noted. Indeed, AMAT echoes the community-based nature of *mutualista* labor organizing, such as when AMAT, in its effort to win a labor contract for one thousand five hundred laundry and dry cleaner workers, collaborated with the local community center Casa Mexico, or when AMAT serves the immigrant community at large, as when it aided Mexican workers who suffered in the wake of the 9/11 attack.

In a sense, then, cutting-edge organizing by AMAT, day labor associations, and others carries forward a kind of mutual aid organizing evident in previous eras—including among New York City Mexicans. The small New York City Mexican community of the 1920s and 1930s included at least two *mutualista* groups, one of which, Mutualista Obrera Mexicana, was affiliated with the International Workers Order and conducted such labor-related community activities as a 1937 dance in support of striking restaurant workers.[29]

Today every national union sees transnational factors as part of their portfolio and none of them lobby for immigration restriction. The one remaining sticking point has been contract foreign labor, at least for the AFL-CIO. But while the AFL's response to exploitation of contract laborers has always been to lobby for outlawing the program, AFL-CIO board member Baldemar Velásquez emphasizes pushing for these laborers to have a path to legalization. "I tell my colleagues in AFL-CIO, 'You're right, those programs are exploitive, but we're supposed to be union organizers, we're supposed to organize workers regardless of what impediments there are and find a strategy to make it happen," says Velásquez. "And if there's a slave labor program, well, let's organize the slaves for their liberation.' Which is exactly what we did."[30] This argument evidently is taking root among the Federation leadership. In 2013, instead of rejecting a "guest worker" bill outright, they obtained from the White House a proposal that, for the first time, would guarantee these contract laborers the right to change jobs and thus not be tied to only one employer (although as of this writing, it remains to be seen whether Congress will endorse this plan).

Regardless of the twists and turns of immigration policy, however, Velásquez keeps his focus on signing up workers transnationally. As soon as "guest workers" join FLOC in Mexico, they have the right to file grievances regarding the procedures used to bring them to US workplaces. But in an echo of Monterrey labor leader Federico Idar's murder in 1938, the director of FLOC's Monterrey office, Santiago Rafael Cruz, was murdered in 2007, probably at the behest of corrupt labor contractors in his case. After being tied hand and foot, he was pummeled to death. The case remains unsolved.[31]

The murder "symbolizes the threat of what we're facing, I think, in all trade union movements today," warns Velásquez. "We're a threat to that diabolic elixir of demagogues, oligarchies, unfair trade, and financial services industry. And their moving apparatus is multinational corporations with their global structures. You see," he argued, "with Santiago, one of his responsibilities was to educate workers who are part of this 'guest worker' agreement: to teach them about the laws and the rights that they have, particularly under the collective bargaining agreement. . . ."[32]

Undaunted, the union is persevering in its attempt to further a reshaping of the global labor landscape. According to FLOC, "International structures and policies directly affect the lives of migrant workers not only in the US but other regions of the world where the same crops are grown for the same corporations in the global economy. Thus, FLOC initiated dialogs with labor unions in Mexico and other countries in response to multinational companies moving some operations across borders. One such effort has led to the establishment of a US-Mexico Commission of labor groups to oversee joint organizing and negotiation efforts among farm workers producing for the same corporations. FLOC is continuing these efforts with agricultural workers in other regions."[33]

The union calls for a "Freedom Visa": a system whereby "workers have the same rights as corporations to cross the borders between countries that have trade agreements in the search for economic well-being."

Velásquez's initiatives have earned him the highest award Mexico bestows on noncitizens, La Aguila Azteca (the Mexican Eagle), and Michigan State University (MSU) awarded him an honorary degree. In an interview with MSU media, the FLOC leader was asked what message he would give to students, and he answered, "Be knowledgeable about globalization . . . that has increasingly contradictory ramifications. . . . We have to almost be global citizens: be Americans, but try to bring our values to the rest of the world and try to create the wonderful safety nets we've created. . . ."

He also received the MacArthur Fellowship, popularly known as the "genius award." Another "genius award" recipient, Fordham law professor Jennifer Gordon, laid out the concept of transnational labor citizenship developed by FLOC, explaining in a *New York Times* Op Ed that the proposal is "based on the theory that the only way to create a genuine floor on working conditions in a context of heavy competition is to link worker self-organization with the enforcement power of the state in a way that crosses borders just as workers do." Salon.com characterizes her argument as "addressing head-on 'the dilemmas of decent work in a globalizing world" via the concept of "transnational labor citizenship."[34]

At first glance the notion of transnational citizenship for "guest workers" seems almost ludicrous. How can a union based in, say, hard-pressed Toledo, Ohio (FLOC's home base) hope to organize Mexicans in Mexico, a country with its own, dangerous challenges? Velásquez replied, "Well, I think there is some merit to trying to create a model that other people can copy," and to a meeting of labor activists he declared, "We need to internationalize our agreements: internationalize the trade union movement . . . internationalize the struggle. If they're going to globalize us to death, we need to organize to globalize them to death."[35]

He even outlines a plan for negotiating with these global behemoths: the "supply-chain" strategy. "This whole supply-chain issue: it's a very elusive concept to understand. The first thing people throw in our face is that, well, 'The company is not the employer of the people. You've got to go to the employers. You've got to blame the employer.'" Velásquez counters that if organized labor pressures family farmers, "Either the farmer pays through the nose, or the burden is put on the worker with low wages." FLOC pioneered targeting not the local farmers per se but rather their corporate customers, starting in the 1980s with a successful campaign on behalf of Ohio tomato harvesters that focused on a consumer boycott of the Campbell Soup Company.

Now the union, in organizing tobacco farmworkers across the South, is targeting one of the giants of global capitalism: JPMorgan Chase. "They're leaders in this huge group of banks that float huge loans to the R.J. Reynolds Company," says Velásquez. "Here you've got the R.J. Reynolds Company: they made record profits last year—giving themselves $60 million bonuses, they're laughing all the way to the bank—while we sit here and argue between the little players at the bottom of the supply chain." He noted that this tobacco giant has holdings in Mexico "and they mix the two tobacco sources" with impunity, even as some of the workers may well have been employed in both locales. Thus FLOC has launched a campaign to have Chase's depositors withdraw their funds.

Meanwhile with regard to US labor unions, Velásquez says, "If they don't pay attention to following the supply chain and forming joint unionizing efforts with the counterpart unions in other countries—and maybe merging into a real international union—we're going to be lost. I'm sure there are some unions that can still have a service industry and so on," he adds, "but for the most part . . . with production that make goods that people *use*, it's got to be internationalized."

Employing just such a strategy is the Coalition of Immokalee Workers (CIW): in its case, with regard to the French company Sodexo. Evidently this multinational corporation has a reputation with European consumers as an enterprise that tries to be socially responsible, but Sodexo's negotiations with the CIW stalled, so the Coalition alerted the European media to this seeming disconnect between Sodexo's reputation and its actions. CIW also mobilized its community partners in the United States, including college students whose campus food services were operated by Sodexo.

In August 2010, Sodexo and the CIW reached an accord. According to their joint news release, "The agreement puts in place a strict Florida tomato supplier code of conduct—developed and implemented with input from farm workers—that supplements Sodexo's existing supplier code of conduct. Sodexo will also pay a 1.5-cent premium for every pound of Florida tomatoes purchased, with the premium going directly to improving wages for tomato harvesters who are part of Sodexo's supply chain."[36]

Regarding transnational trade policies, notably the North American Free Trade Agreement (NAFTA), Benítez looks to the history of his own family. "My grandfather, my great-grandfather, my father—they worked on the land for decades. They planted maiz, frijol, calabaza in Guerrero. We didn't live like millionaires, we didn't live in luxury, but we had enough to eat. Then what happens? . . . NAFTA impoverishes the small farmer."[37]

NAFTA prompted Mexico to eliminate its tariff on imported crops, prompting a flood of government-subsidized agribusiness products from the United States. Speaking of his family, Benítez says, "They lost their land, then found themselves dealing with that very same agribusiness sector as farm workers in Florida! Meantime Mexico began importing a number of food staples for the first time." He notes with irony, "At this point Mexico is an exporter, but an exporter of cheap labor." One of those displaced Mexican corn farmers was Santiago Rafael Cruz, who had come north to work in the fields and became a FLOC organizer, first in the United States and then in Mexico, where he met his tragic end.[38]

Such NAFTA critiques were anticipated by Dr. Ernesto Galarza. In 1965, when business leaders lobbied successfully for a border industrialization program, they promised that factories would go up along the US side of the border in tandem with Mexican border development: the "twin plant" concept. Galarza was skeptical. He requested in vain that the Border Commission include labor representatives from *both* sides of the border, to work toward raising "Mexican levels of income to American standards," not "lowering American to present Mexican ones." Otherwise, he predicted, "goods will be manufactured at Mexican wages and re-imported for sale at American prices."[39]

Today's transnational labor organizing in the face of great odds carries forward the trans-border organizing of *mutualista* leaders of a century ago, as with Abrán Salcido, whose activities from Arizona to Chihuahua prompted retaliation by both President Theodore Roosevelt and President Porfirio Díaz. This, even if today's high-speed, cyberspace world—with FLOC and CIW on YouTube—would stun Salcido. In another sense, however, the odds against global labor organizing still seem long, given the risks, and given that millions of workers around the world—divided by race, ethnicity, geography, education, culture, religion, and politics—face multinational corporations that are famously organized, flexible, mobile, wealthy, and politically connected. And yet the high-profile nature of global corporations makes them clear targets, as with CIW spotlighting Sodexo and FLOC targeting JPMorgan Chase.[40]

Today, like a century ago, when it comes to labor organizing, the challenge is daunting. It remains to be seen whether the lessons gleaned from more than a century of trans-border labor organizing will be tapped by the leaders of today's labor movement. If, as it seems, those heading the big, national unions increasingly have transnational labor organizing experience, then the prospects for such a perspective are good, even if the odds for gaining a seat at the global negotiating table remain long.

PART IV

Barrio Community Organizing

OneLA Snapshot

"**D**id you go to the march?" asked veteran organizer Soledad "Chole" Alatorre. "I did; it was beautiful—great," she said a few hours after the mammoth Los Angeles immigration event of May 1, 2010. Despite her years, this pioneering figure was energized by having participated. In fact, that same evening she held a follow-up event in her Los Angeles area of Pacoima, long home to many Mexican-heritage people and still a destination for new immigrants. The evening's program, a May Day presentation in honor of Mexican workers, culminated with a call to community organizing—in this case banding together to fight the wave of foreclosures that were making neighborhoods such as Pacoima among the hardest hit in the nation.

Chole Alatorre says that her community organizing dates from her childhood in northern Mexico. "There was a train that passed near the house, and there were many tracks that the children had to cross to get to school," she says, noting that although adults tried to keep watch, almost daily a youngster was injured, sometimes even killed. "And so, at the dinner hour we discussed things like that. . . . And one day, we kids were talking about what could be done to stop this." Her father told them, "If you kids unite, you will be able to do something . . . make it possible for a bridge or an underpass." "And how do we do this, Papá?" the children asked. "Well, I think the first thing is to look up the city engineer. Who has a pencil?" Her sister ran to get one; meanwhile the other children asked, "How do we find him?" "Go to the general railroad offices," he told them, "and then you need to get permission from the city, so go to the city headquarters with your group." Alatorre and the other youngsters, accompanied by their parents, went to see the officials, who agreed to build the bridge, but only if the neighbors were supportive of the idea. At the suggestion of Alatorre's father, the children took a petition door to door and then presented it to the head of the municipality. They built the bridge, she recalls, adding, "It still exists."[1]

In recent decades, meanwhile, barrio communities like Pacoima all across the Southwest have given rise to some of the nation's most important community organizing. "There is that ownership—collaborative agency, mutual agency, this sense of obligation," says Ernesto Cortés Jr. of OneLA, who in the 1970s gained fame for his community organizing in San Antonio. Many of these neighborhoods had been the epicenter of the *mutualista* movement, and they now served as the epicenter of the community organizing he helped bring to life via San Antonio's Communities Organized for Public Service (COPS). COPS in turn spawned a statewide network that began holding "accountability sessions" at which major Texas political and business leaders responded to concerns raised by representatives of the constituent groups. By the 1980s, this ongoing exercise in civic engagement caught the attention of the MacArthur Foundation, which awarded Cortés its "genius" fellowship. Meanwhile Cortés headed to California, where he was instrumental in the creation of the community organization today known as OneLA, along with kindred groups across the state.[2]

These Texas and California associations belong to the Southwest Industrial Areas Foundation (IAF). With Cortés as its lead organizer, Southwest IAF constitutes a regional network of more than twenty community organizations and more than half a million families as members. As such, it represents the largest subset of the IAF, the oldest and most prominent community organization network in the United States. The IAF was founded in 1940 by Saul Alinsky of Chicago, in his words, "To restore the democratic way of life to modern industrial society." Young Ernie Cortés, for his part, journeyed to Chicago in the early 1970s for the IAF training sessions, much as a young Barack Obama would do a decade later, even if Cortés was the one who stayed rooted in community.[3]

Southwest IAF affiliates such as OneLA have been built neighborhood by neighborhood, as when OneLA-IAF community organizer Tom Holler addressed the 2010 May Day event organized by Chole Alatorre in her neighborhood. It was largely due to her acumen that Holler was speaking to a full house. She had arranged for the event, at Mary Immaculate parish in Pacoima, to immediately follow a Saturday evening Mass that was always well attended. The liturgy itself that May Day was a celebratory Worker Mass, and during the closing announcements she stepped up to the lectern. With warm enthusiasm, she invited the entire congregation to the festivities in the adjacent hall. As people drifted in they found a tempting array of goodies, from pizza to snacks, both salty and sweet.

Alatorre had made sure to involve a number of folks in the planning, including young people. A hipster type filmed the event, while the main presentations were given by two college students, including the president of the parish Social Justice Committee, Areceli Alvarez. The students informed the audience that May Day, which Mexico and many other countries mark as their Labor Day, was in fact inspired by a US event: Chicago labor organizers arrested at Haymarket Square and then unjustly convicted and

Figure 17. Soledad "Chole" Alatorre speaking on a panel at California State University, Los Angeles just five days after the May 1, 2010 immigration march and her event that same evening. (Photo by Marie Gregorio-Oviedo)

executed in May 1886. Moreover, Areceli told them, a US Mexican named González—Lucy González Parsons—was one of the most famous defenders of the "Haymarket Martyrs." Thus the audience members witnessed one of their bright, attractive young people sharing a part of their adopted land's history—a history, it turned out, that they themselves owned.

Now Soledad Alatorre took the floor. With her trademark warmth and confidence, she announced a major event: a citywide meeting with top officials to be held the very next day, which they were very much encouraged to attend. She introduced, with a flourish, OneLA-IAF community organizer Tom Holler.

Holler conveyed a genuine if quiet dedication as he explained that the next day's event would address the issue on everybody's minds: foreclosures. The OneLA meeting would take place in South Los Angeles, he said, adding that the people of South Los Angeles were looking for the support of people from the Pacoima and San Fernando Valley areas—that the event would be a great opportunity for folks from all across LA to unite in fighting this plague that was devastating many neighborhoods. The parish had rented a bus, and all were welcome to come. Many in the audience already knew Tom Holler. He had been working with the parish and with Neighborhood Legal Services "to organize hundreds of homeowners in the Pacoima area and track down their loan modification applications with lenders," according to the Los Angeles *Daily News*, which quoted Holler as saying, "We were able to unmask the fact that (the banks') foreclosure strategy (and) modification strategy weren't working, and once we were able to do that, then we had them in a position to say" to the banks, "Now let's talk about something that will work."[4] For his part, the parish's pastor, Father John Lasseigne, "teamed up with the OneLA community group," according to a CNN report, "and together they started to teach foreclosure 101 to his flock." CNN noted that Lasseigne, an attorney prior to ordination, "met with more than 300 residents in recent months and brought them together with banks to modify their loans."[5]

With Holler and Lasseigne's encouragement, people held meetings in their living rooms. They shared their concerns, for OneLA would tackle whatever issue its members chose as the top priority. They also elected leaders from among their ranks to represent them in negotiations with policy makers. Holler, meanwhile, was working for them, with his salary paid mostly out of the dues from OneLA member groups such as the parish. As Ernie Cortés explains, "So the organizers, they don't work for me, in the sense that I don't write their paychecks. I supervise them. In fact ... my salary is paid for ... from the money that comes from the organizations. They're my boss." When asked if his advice to the leaders chosen by the house meetings resembled a president reporting to a board of trustees, he replied, "Exactly."[6]

On May 2, 2010, the sun shone brightly in Pacoima as people boarded the yellow school bus for the OneLA meeting: a father and his ten-year-old daughter; two women friends chatting animatedly; a silent, dignified man with a cowboy hat and the leathery look of the borderlands; Araceli checking her cell phone. Standing next to the bus and saying hello to people as they climbed aboard was Fr. Lasseigne, who then took a seat in the front. So did Alatorre and a OneLA leader from the parish, Cecelia Barragán, who also was greeting many of the folks. On the forty-minute trip, passengers chatted in Spanish and English, with some occasionally breaking into song: favorite old Spanish hymns and rancheras, mostly.

The "accountability session," as IAF calls these gatherings, was held at Harmony Elementary School in South Los Angeles. People mingled naturally—effortlessly, it seemed. In fact, however, virtually every logistical consideration had been anticipated. Each person was greeted warmly and received a OneLA-IAF sticker, along with two pieces of paper: a green sheet with the day's agenda and a yellow sheet entitled "OneLA Foreclosure Prevention Plan," both of which had the information in Spanish on the reverse side. A table held water bottles, there for the taking, along with literature about OneLA-IAF. Another table had a hand-lettered "Press" sign; among those who had signed in was someone from the *Los Angeles Times*. In the gymnasium, various leaders circulated, offering assistance and answering questions. They had been elected in the house meetings in their various neighborhoods and were identifiable by the red ribbons attached to the blue and white OneLA-IAF buttons, which made for a bit of an all-American effect. When one of them was asked if it would be all right to make an audio recording of the proceedings, she replied, "Sure." The gymnasium was filling up quickly as the Pacoima folks filed into several rows of seats. Soon people were helping each other adjust headphones, for it turned out that there would be simultaneous translation.

From the stage, meanwhile, a very different sound was emanating than Spanish: Gospel music, movingly sung by an African American choir. People were starting to sway to the beat as waves of sound were carrying waves of words:

> I need you to survive.
> I pray for you, you pray for me, I need you to survive.
> We're all a part of God's body, I need you to survive.
> I love you, I need you to survive.

The key signature kept rising—higher and higher—creating escalating waves of sound:

> I love you, I need you to survive.
> I won't harm you with words from my mouth
> I love you, I need you to survive.

By now members of the audience were joining in:

> I love you. I need you to survive.
> You are im-por-tant to me: I need you to sur-vive

The music might remind many of church, but it also could resonate with nonbelievers—this sound that echoed the blues and Motown and traditional folk spirituals, this sound that brought forth something deep from America's cultural groundwater.[7]

"Today we will be calling on the banks to come together with OneLA to revitalize our homes," began Maxine McNeal of the OneLA delegation from St. Brigid parish. Then OneLA leader Robert Cordova of the (hosting) Harmony Elementary School asked for approval of the agenda, saying, "Here today are public officials and representatives from the banks. We will be asking them to support our agenda. Everyone should have a copy of today's agenda. If you have one, raise it in the air." After the assembly approved the agenda by acclamation, Cordova suggested a few ground rules: "While we want to be respectful to our guests, the most important people on the stage will be our leaders. It is OK to prod our guests for our agenda, but we do not boo our guests; instead there is a more powerful way to show our disapproval"—through resolutions and organized actions.

The presence of IAF leaders from across California was noted by speaker Zita Davis, also from South Los Angeles. This grassroots African American woman then introduced the amazing assemblage of important officials seated on the stage behind her: a Los Angeles County supervisor; two Los Angeles city councilmen; the local state assemblyman; JPMorgan Chase's director of community relations; an executive vice president from One West Bank, and the man of the hour—the government official in charge of administering the federal mortgage relief funds allocated to California— the executive director of the California Debt Limit Allocation Committee.

Saying "we are here to do the people's business," Davis concluded by presenting Father Tom Frank to deliver the focus statement. "How are we are doin'?" he began. "We of St. Brigid's are proud to be here today . . . and it isn't about profits and stockholders, is it?" The audience shouted back, "No!" This obviously was not going to be your typical focus statement— and he was just getting started.

> Profits are really important to businesses: that's their bottom line. . . . OneLA sees the value of profits. But the profit motive is only as good as long as it values the human person and recognizes the right of everyone here to participate in our economic system. . . . Yes, corporations are considered legally corporate persons, and so it is important that they recognize that they are part of this community, too. And so it's about more than just profit, Amen?
> "Amen."

Just when it seemed as if the priest was heading into a stem-winder, however, he began to employ business terminology.

> We have come not to beg, but rather as stakeholders. And let's face it: as citizens of these United States, it seems like we are stockholders too, aren't we? We are stockholders not only in those federal funds that were distributed to our corporations, but we are stockholders in the life of the community. . . .
> We have come to this table with *money* and a *plan*. . . .
> We have seen the government avoid foreclosure on Wall Street. We are here to collaborate with the financial system and our communities and the people's government to avoid foreclosure on *Main Street*. . . . We are here to take

our seat at the table. We are here to participate: to hold ourselves and our financial institutions and our government accountable.

Thus did he take the language of the financial sector and bend it toward justice (as Reverend Martin Luther King Jr. might have put it when he said, "The arc of the moral universe is long, but it bends toward justice"). The Catholic pastor summed things up by addressing the long-term situation: that this approach, by benefitting the local community, would benefit business and government as well. Then he asked everyone to stand and said, "Let us pray. God of Creation, God of all humanity, God who makes all things new, a God who gives us true freedom under God's heaven, a God who never forecloses on us. . . . Lord God we ask you to let your blessings flow down upon us. Let your wisdom flow in us and through us as we seek to do the people's business today and choose not foreclosure but to be revitalized. That includes all here present on both sides of the table here today, on both sides of the podium today: let God's love flow forth from Harmony Elementary School with the Good News—the good news of revitalization."

Continuing in an even-tempered voice, this Catholic cleric nonetheless ended with the call-and-response format so closely associated with Baptist preachers like Dr. King:

Let the church say "Amen."
Amen.
Let the church say "Amen."
Amen.
Let the church say "*A-men.*"
Amen![8]

Applause and cheers erupted, and the cheers started up again as each IAF contingent stood to be recognized: South Los Angeles, the San Fernando Valley, the (downtown) Metro Cluster. On and on it went, including groups from more affluent areas such as greater San Francisco. All this time, the dignitaries sat onstage watching and waiting, and now it became apparent that they would have to listen to a parade of individuals stepping up to the floor microphone, each with a tale of foreclosure problems. These busy officials could have been forgiven for thinking, "Oh, no: an afternoon of rambling complaints!" But only three homeowners spoke, and they limited their remarks to three minutes each—another indication of good planning. Besides, time was precious to the community people as well.

The first testimony came from a man who said that "it is very difficult to service a loan for $330,000 when your house is only worth $100,000." Next came a strong, dignified voice: "Good afternoon. My name is José

Gómez from Mary Immaculate in the San Fernando Valley, and my family and I are one of thousands who are in danger of losing our home." He reported "getting the run-around each time we call, but we are here today to demonstrate that we are not giving up." Gómez ticked off the names of several banks and said that he was one of many who wanted these institutions "to fork out money for the OneLA plan for principal reduction." That constituted his entire statement.

He was followed by an African American woman from South Los Angeles. As she spoke, it became clear that her testimony would be different: that she was something of a power player. "I work in the housing office at USC," she began, "and I work with the banks to provide mortgages for the employees, but . . . because of Bank of America's poor service we removed them from our USC website." This got the bank's attention, she said, and she concluded that with regard to homeowners, "It's time for . . . the banks to respond with the respect and attention."

Next came a man with a bland, middle-management look about him. "My name is Ron Mulvihill," he began. "I'm here for the Society of Saint Vincent de Paul, the Los Angeles County Committee Board." That identifier would make any Catholic sit up and take notice—including any Catholics among the bankers onstage. The Catholic answer to Volunteers of America or the Salvation Army, St. Vincent de Paul is active in many if not most parishes across the United States. Indeed, the scope of this organization is tremendous, with the gigantic Los Angeles archdiocese having more Catholics, more parishes—and thus more St. Vincent de Paul chapters—than any other diocese in the country, even as Catholicism itself is the largest denomination in the nation.

"The Los Angeles Council of St. Vincent de Paul has been working with the poor of our city since 1908, and our motto is: 'No act of charity is foreign to the Society,'" Mulvihill began. Then he explained that "over the last several years our parishes and our Society have been overwhelmed with calls by people struggling with foreclosures and mortgage repayments. That, coupled with the vast numbers of working families facing foreclosures just, uh, put us in a bind. And we were seeing that the options being offered . . . are modifications that aren't truly modifications. We've seen that these really aren't solutions." Now he came to the main point: "So we were happy to learn about the OneLA plan of principle reduction and the importance of showing that that plan works. That's why we have joined OneLA as a dues-paying member institution, and we've taken a pro-active approach to prevent future homelessness in the city of Los Angeles by committing up to one million dollars for a pilot program of the principle reduction of the OneLA plan right here in South Los Angeles."

Cheers and stomping from the crowd ensued, but Mulvihill continued

Figure 18. Southwest Industrial Areas ⁻ Foundation lead organizer Ernesto Cortés Jr. (Courtesy David Weisman, Conservation History Association of Texas 2002)

in an even tone, one that belied the significance of his message: "We are here today to challenge the banks to come on/get on board, in implementing this principle-reduction plan. We also want to challenge other non-profits, city and county officials, and government, to join us in our efforts to allocate money to the OneLA principle-reduction plan. Thank you."

Taking in the proceedings unobtrusively from the sidelines, quietly exchanging the occasional word, were Tom Holler and Ernie Cortés. They were among the few audience members wearing business clothes, in their cases likely out of respect for the IAF organizations that collectively employed them. At the same time, their attire was nondescript, Cortés' in particular: jacket, shirt, tie all of the same muddy color, one that did little for this somewhat short, balding man with a rumpled air about him. But, then, his job was not to stand out—not to lead—but rather to facilitate: to support, to serve the Southwest IAF. Both of them operate under the iron rule of community organizing laid down by Saul Alinsky: "Never do for others what they can do for themselves."[9]

Then came the event centerpiece: the OneLA-IAF Foreclosure Prevention Plan. It was presented by a OneLA community leader and frequent spokesperson, attorney Yvette Mariajimenez, deputy director of Neighborhood Legal Services in Pacoima. The plan proposed that in the case of houses now valued at far less than their mortgage amount, federal funds pay banks the difference if the banks would charge the customers mortgages pegged to the houses' current market value. She did not explain these provisions very systematically or define the concepts involved, nor did the handout. On the other hand, both made clear that a pilot project based on the plan was operating in the San Fernando Valley. This demonstration case was made possible by the money from St. Vincent de Paul, along with one million dollars obtained by the local city council member Richard Alarcón. It was being administered by Bank of America, with JPMorgan Chase poised to join in as well. Mariajimenez asked those assembled if they wanted such a program to be implemented in South Los Angeles, and of course the answer was "Yes!"[10]

The crux of the matter, however, was whether the OneLA formula would be applied to the seven hundred million dollars allocated by the Obama administration for the entire state. The executive director of the California Housing Authority, Sean Spears, was asked to share with the audience a letter he received from the treasurer of the state of California. Sporting a OneLA-IAF sticker, no less, Spears stepped forward and read aloud State Treasurer Bill Lockyer's statement that "it is very important to include this plan" in the Housing Authority's proposal to the White House. At the same time, Lockyer did not specify what percentage of the money should be allocated for the OneLA formula, while Spears merely spoke of the need for "extraordinary effort on the part of borrowers and lenders."

In contrast, Los Angeles County Supervisor Mark Ridley-Thomas exhorted OneLA to keep up the fight. "I believe the OneLA strategy to call on the banks to be held accountable in this agenda for principle reduction is important," he said, adding that he and his cohorts on the Board of Supervisors needed to strategize ways to move this agenda "across the length and breadth of the county of Los Angeles." He then stated that "the reason we got in this shape in the first place was because of unmitigated, unbridled greed." He seemed to mean greed on the part of the bankers and real estate people but not on the part of buyers. Indeed, none of the OneLA presenters raised the issue of irresponsible financial overreaching on the part of any mortgage purchasers. At the same time, the supervisor implicitly answered that charge by citing misleading, hard-sell practices that targeted the customers least able to fend them off. "I fought this issue . . . on the City Council. It was the most extensive predatory lending ordinance in the whole country," he noted, adding ruefully, "The financial industry with its lobbyists overturned that. . . . And the California Supreme Court said the ordinance was too strong in protecting the people that were negatively affected by it, and that the banks needed to be cut some slack. So they mean business. The only thing we ultimately get is what we *fight* for. . . . It's time for us to organize, and OneLA has my support, my respect, for its effort to cause people to be protected and respected for the dignity and worth that was given us by God our Creator."

When asked if he would put forth a resolution to the County Board of Supervisors for the Board to endorse the OneLA plan as the best use of the seven hundred million dollars, the supervisor said that the Board was in talks with the Department of Housing and Urban Development (HUD) about this. While less than specific, at least he promised to pursue this issue he was on record as supporting so strongly.

When state assemblyman Mark Davis was asked if he would present a resolution to the California State Assembly to endorse the plan, however, he answered unequivocally "Yes." Then came city councilman Alarcón—he of the pilot project—who stated that "the OneLA plan saves six homes for every one by the banks." This was of utmost importance, he said, given "estimates of three million foreclosures in US this year, and most of them in California." In his own district of Pacoima, "It has been averaging a thousand a month for over three years—and it's going to continue!" he cried. "So if we want to take the $700 million, we must use it to maximize the number of homes that are saved; otherwise we are throwing the government's money *away*." Meanwhile, Chole Alatorre remarked to a member of the audience, "He says I mentored him." This son of Pacoima wound up his statement—and wound up the crowd—with a powerful litany.

> It was my pleasure to work with OneLA to sit down and map out this program.
> It was my pleasure to work with OneLA to go to Washington and demand from HUD a better understanding of why a principle of justice is necessary, for loan modification is not working.
> It is my pleasure to work with OneLA to go to Congress and meet with the various Congress members that could make the difference here.
> It *must* be a wiser investment. We can do it—and it starts with *you*.
> I am *for* OneLA.
> I am *for* wise investment in foreclosure assistance.
> I am *for* saving homes and the positive effect that this can have.
> Working together we *can* make this happen.
> A lot of education is needed; this is not easy stuff to understand.
> Spread the word, and we'll save more homes.

As the cheers died down, and with less than ten minutes left in the ninety-minute program, the bankers were finally called on to speak. Rather, they were called on to answer a few specific questions, culminating with: "Are you willing to work with OneLA to bring this program forward?" Both men replied with pleasant but vague formulations, as when one said, "We will continue to work with them. I can't come back and say we'll participate in the program because we don't have the authority to do that. We expressed support to the extent that we could." The audience members applauded politely.

The assembly concluded with a call to action by Father Paul Spellman. His long, flowing blond and white mane drew everybody's attention back to the stage one last time. "Brothers and sisters," he began, "we are just beginning, and we cannot sit around and just wait for something to happen." He explained that business is cyclical, and provided evidence, saying, "Prior to being a priest I spent eighteen years as a certified public accountant, and I began my career with a company called Price Waterhouse. That's gone," he said. Then he ticked off banks that got gobbled up, including by one of the financial institutions represented on the stage. Warning that real estate is very changeable, very cyclical, Spellman said that even as they were meeting, speculators were scooping up foreclosed houses in order to sell them expensively when the market rebounded. "And what area is very close to the water and very close to Los Angeles? South Los Angeles—exactly." He concluded, "We cannot wait for the market to turn around. We don't want houses being flipped; we want stabilization in our communities. We don't want foreclosure; we want revitalization. Let the church say 'Amen.'"

The event adjourned five minutes ahead of schedule, ending with an invitation to attend an evaluation session immediately afterwards. This meeting took place in a much smaller room, the school library, with the organizers having estimated correctly that only a small fraction of the assembly would show up. This meant, however, that the session likely drew the most motivated members, those best able to take advantage of the professional strategy tips from Holler and Cortés. Robert Cordova of Harmony Elementary introduced the session by noting that "there was a partnership between the [San Fernando] Valley and South LA." Yvette Mariajimenez chimed in, "All of us noticed how many people from the Valley were here." Applause and cheers followed. "We also want to thank people who were new and had a speaking role," she said, asking them to stand up. "We want to recognize turnout," she added; "you all filled the house like you fill this evaluation room."

At this point Tom Holler was given the floor to cheers, which he ignored. "I want to talk with you a little bit about the politics of today, some of the things that happened," he began. The organizer cited IAF representation from around the state and called on Mark Linder, from the Monterey-area affiliate, for his assessment. Holler was, in effect, demonstrating inclusion and diversity by soliciting comments from a middle-class/suburban constituency from outside Los Angeles. Next he spotlighted the questions posed by Yvette Mariajimenez to government officials, which made them sharpen their comments. He remarked that she and Linder "made clear the difference between the city's plan and the OneLA plan," although in fact one could argue that the explanations could have been clearer. Holler pointed out that "the banks are trying to equivocate, trying to drag their feet a little bit, trying to make it sound like they're doing something," and then added, "Father Paul Spellman picked up on that, didn't he?" Holler characterized Spellman's closing remarks and Fr. Franks' opening ones as "a kind of a bookend effect," that this was "important because it represents your institutional power." He did not elaborate, perhaps not wanting to use a sectarian term such as "parishes," let alone "the Church." And while praising Fr. Frank's presentation, Holler nonetheless cautioned, "We've got to remember we've got people here from other religions"—again with an eye to inclusion and diversity.

Above all, the organizer drove home the point that "the whole thing is about power: real power, the power of people organized together with a plan." He explained this by referencing the many house meetings so integral to the process. "You can articulate that plan to each other: get eight, ten people together, tell your stories, just like the stories were told in here. Did they interest people in here when they told their stories? Well, there are lots of people out there; they don't have anybody to tell their stories to. . . . When they tell the story they get energized, there's some hope; they hear other people, and maybe they can do something about it. And if you have teams organized in each of those districts, with a plan, and get lots of those people . . . hundreds of house meetings, you're getting thousands of people. . . . Then the perceptions of power by other centers of power is going to be increased."

At this critical moment, right when people were mentally processing this call to empowerment, someone interrupted to ask if the session could be translated. Just the tiniest flicker of annoyance flitted across Holler's face. He said that the entire assembly had been translated, but then quickly added, "Someone want to summarize, just briefly?" and used both languages in his own closing sentences. At any rate, the woman interrupting evidently thought his point should not be missed by anyone, plus a summary in Spanish meant that many in the room got the message twice.

Now it was time to hear from the head of the Southwest IAF, and Ernie Cortés ambled up to the front of the room. He only spoke for a moment, but he made that moment count. The master teacher, he was personable and clear, utilizing concrete examples culminating with a challenge that also constituted a positive vision. "Congratulations. I'd like the rabbis to come forward," he said, to long applause. "We need to multiply their numbers, because institutional power has much more capacity for staying, much more capacity for sticking with it." And indeed, the highly influential Wilshire Boulevard Temple is an enthusiastic OneLA participant. "For those of you who are interested in making L.A. a better place to live—we need you!" declares the Temple's bulletin. For its part, the *Jewish Weekly* of Los Angeles, in a laudatory profile of OneLA entitled "Pursuit of Justice," added for good measure, "The most famous IAF veteran is ex-Chicago organizer Barack Obama."[11]

But even as Cortés was highlighting support coming out of the Jewish community, he was making a larger point—a sophisticated structural point. "Institutional power *perdures*, it *lasts*," he said, choosing a verb whose Spanish cognate, "perdurar," is much more commonly used than its English equivalent. "Like Mr. Cordova, we need other people here who are leaders: from trade unions; from synagogues; from mosques, or other institutions—with their people, and their money, and their leadership." He cited another institutional example, "St. Vincent de Paul: money, energy, hope, OK?" Cortés noted that with regard to the banks, the St. Vincent de Paul representative "can put money in; he can take money out." Thus did he explain the sophisticated concept of structural power—a concept typically underplayed in a media landscape that tends to privilege individualism.

In so doing, moreover, the veteran organizer squared the circle with regard to the tricky subject of religious affiliation, showcasing the rabbis but then giving a nod to the St. Vincent de Paul Society. After this lesson in coalition building, Cortés reiterated Holler's—IAF's—point that power emanates from the neighborhood house meetings. OneLA was doing a great job, he said, adding, "Hey—give yourselves a hand." Thus did people leave the event laughing and applauding, but with a charge to go back to the neighborhood and redouble their house meetings.[12]

Four months after this "accountability session," the California Housing Finance Agency (CalHFA) announced its plan. The Authority allocated twenty million dollars to the OneLA model, but the bulk, seven hundred million dollars, was assigned to the plan as originally formulated by the federal government. Yvonne Mariajimenez of OneLA called the decision a bank bailout, and she was seconded by the chief financial officer of the city of Los Angeles, the city controller, and even the mayor himself. Mayor Antonio Villaraigosa sent a letter to CalHFA objecting to the formula and declaring that "limited resources should be used efficiently to impact the highest number of homeowners."[13] Thus, OneLA lost that round overall despite having the mayor on its side.

At any rate, the folks at OneLA indicated that they would continue working on the issues of concern to them, come what may. At an "accountability session" a few months later, some four hundred OneLA-IAF members met with public officials, this time calling on them "to make the new health care law more affordable and accessible to all the community." This venue, in contrast to the previous one, was a Jewish temple in Beverly Hills.

OneLA-IAF's broad coalition, along with its impressive pipeline to top decision-makers, together serve as stark reminders of the ways in which the Southwest IAF contrasts with the *mutualista* networks of yore. Nonetheless, in characterizing the IAF's bedrock ethos as "collaborative agency, mutual agency," Ernie Cortés echoes the approach expounded long ago by the *sociedades mutualistas*. "We organize people not just around issues, but around their values," he says. "The issues fade, and people lose interest in them. But what they really care about remains: family, dignity, justice, and hope."[14]

The Power to Protect What We Value

In the barrios that provide so much of the support for the Southwest Industrial Areas Foundation (IAF), the emphasis on organizing among community members has a long history. While unloading freight at the rail yard, over a beer at the pool hall, picking endless rows of cotton, while hanging clothes out to dry, people touted the benefits of mutual support. "I still remember it so clearly," Texas community activist Viviana Cavada recalled from her childhood: hearing the adults saying, "We need to get health going, to take care of these people from the moment they are born to the day that they die. And have a *mutualista* club where they can even have the burial." She adds for emphasis, "People didn't even have any place to be buried in or any money even to bury them." Or as a leader of Sociedad Mutualista Ignacio Allende in San Antonio noted back in the 1920s, "For that reason the *sociedades mutualistas* say 'One for all and all for one.' The avaricious, to the contrary, say, 'All for us and the people can drown.'"[1]

As with IAF groups such as Communities Organized for Public Service (COPS) and OneLA, most of the *mutualista* activists came from the working class. Not unusual was the El Paso officer of Sociedad Mutualista "La Constructora" who lived in the wagon yard where he worked.[2] The leaders of *mutualista* groups in 1920s San Antonio included a teamster (Sociedad Mutualista Mexicana), a shoemaker (Sociedad Mutualista "Amigos del Pueblo"), a blacksmith ("Union Católica Mutualista"), and a printing press operator (Sociedad Mutualista Miguel Hidalgo). Then there was the case of Guadalupe M. Báez, a cowboy in the stockyards and a longtime president of Sociedad de La Unión. This cowboy headed the largest, most prominent *mutualista* organization in the city that itself served as the unofficial capital of US Mexicans at the time. A prominent speaker for "La Unión" by 1890, President Báez was exhorting his members to foster "a culture of good harmony" as late as the 1930s.[3]

A smaller but significant percentage of the leaders held minor municipal jobs. For instance, a clerk at the El Paso courthouse, Pedro Calendaria, served as secretary and president of Sociedad Mutualista "La Fraternal Number 30" in 1913 and two years later was elected president of the El Paso chapter of the mighty Alianza Hispano Americana (AHA). Calendaria was "a faithful servant of the community," another community leader recalled years later. And just as the Southwest IAF includes more than a few professionals among its members, so did the *mutualista* associations. Typically neighborhood professionals or owners of barrio businesses, they had a stake in the local community even as the *mutualista* network and attendant press coverage provided them with customers or clients and publicity. For example, the founding director of a school in Laredo, Simón Domínguez, belonged to some ten organizations and served as president of Sociedad Mutualista Hijos de Juárez in 1907.[4] A few *mutualista* associations were founded by professionals, and not surprisingly these groups had a larger percentage of leaders from that class. The most notable case was the AHA, but even in the AHA many of the officers were laborers. Thus, while the top officers of the Alianza chapter in El Paso in 1913 were a physician and a civil engineer, the very next year one of the officers was a laundry worker.[5]

Like the Southwest IAF meetings, those of the *mutualistas* typically were conducted by the largely working-class officers in a professional manner, complete with parliamentary procedure.[6] Most of the mutual aid groups that survived longer than a year or two also kept careful records, a practice that was reinforced by state insurance regulations instituted by the 1920s. At any rate, members were keenly aware that solvency was essential to the survival of the insurance benefits that they cherished and that they supported with their dues.

People active in *mutualista* operations strove to protect what they valued. Regarding mutual benefit societies in general, historian David Beito has noted that "Unlike private companies, they drew on extensive reserves of membership solidarity. It might be one thing to bilk a commercial insurance company with a phony claim, but the mutual benefit nature of fraternal coverage, not to mention the fact that it was fairly easy for lodge members to check up on each other, served as effective deterrents to malingerers."[7]

By efficiently pooling their resources, groups with larger memberships such as San Antonio's Sociedad Mutualista "Amigos del Pueblo" were able to count on more than one thousand dollars in monthly income—at a time when many Mexicans were making a dollar a day—and word of such success in turn attracted more members. San Antonio principal Charles Arnold noted in the 1920s that "even the poorer men, women and children pay their weekly installments of five and ten cents on a life insurance policy of one or two hundred dollars . . . laborers, clerks, salesmen, fruit vendors, small shopkeepers."[8]

Smaller *mutualistas* also made their mark, particularly in isolated rural communities. A resident of Creedmore, Texas, asked the San Antonio newspaper *La Epoca* to convey his gratitude to Sociedad Funeraria de Agri-

Figure 19. A cemetery founded in 1924 by Sociedad de Agricultores "Mariano Escobedo," Pflugerville, Texas. (Photo by Pamela A. Stephenson)

cultores Mariano Escobedo, which provided him with $48.25 during his ill-ness. Word of such aid doubtless helps explain the Creedmore *mutualista's* ability to establish branches in other rural Texas towns as well.[9]

At the same time, the *mutualista* movement was plagued by internal problems that dwarf any in the Southwest IAF, from financial misman-agement to factionalism, both between groups and within them. In San Antonio, countless *mutualista* organizations disappeared after a few years. Or take the case of two *mutualistas* in East Chicago, Indiana: one folded two years after its 1922 founding, the other, founded in 1924, suffered from a split in 1926 (with the controversy centering on dissatisfaction over the small size of the benefits being paid out). Meanwhile, the strong Mexican ethnic identity of the *mutualista* movement could lead to cultural parochial-ism. This is a view rejected by Alinsky and Cortés, as with the inclusive IAF name "one LA." As Ernesto Cortés told a television interviewer, "There is a plurality to our selves that goes beyond being Mexican or gay or male or female or whatever it is. We are multiple persons."[10]

When it comes to policy issues, however, in a sense, COPS and OneLA are only one step removed from the *mutualista* heritage. COPS's success in wresting educational reform legislation from the Texas state legislature, while unprecedented in scope, nonetheless echoed trailblazing lobbying of the 1930s that was driven to a large extent by *mutualista* associations. In 1934, the Pro-Schools Defense League (Liga Pro-Defensa Escolar), later known as the School Improvement League, fired off hundreds of telegrams to state legislators, calling for a decrease in school board members' terms from six years to two in order to make them more responsible to parents on the West Side of San Antonio. Sociedad Mutualista de la Unión's telegram read, "Our organization composed of more than 500 members request you support bill . . . shortening term members school board."[11] The *mutualista* association followed up with a fundraiser featuring one of the great celebrities of the age, famed songwriter Agustín Lara, along with historian Dr. Carlos E. Castañeda of the group League of United Latin American Citizens—an organization also central to the effort. This event grossed seven hundred dollars at a time when local pecan shellers were making pennies a pound. The pressure and publicity from the West Side groups led the school district to promise improved facilities, additional teachers, and two new schools.[12]

OneLA-IAF recognizes its organizational heritage. Its publication "A Legacy of Organizing in Los Angeles County Over the Past Eight Decades" notes that the very first California IAF organization, the Community Service Organization (CSO), emerged after World War II "through a mutualista, or mutual-aid structure, in which members pooled their money to start purchasing cooperatives and revolving loan funds," as one social scientist puts it.[13] CSO pioneer Herman Gallegos recalls that the organization looked to the *mutualista* example, recruiting people at "three dollars a year . . . by offering a funeral benefit program." The organizers wagered that that these benefits would remind older residents of the *mutualistas* and would attract younger folks, including immigrants. Gallegos points out that they "fought for a dozen years to get old age security for non-citizens, and we succeeded." The CSO also successfully assisted tens of thousands of people with the naturalization process. In fact, the CSO constituted a rare organization that was looking out for the rights of immigrants in the 1950s. The group also successfully campaigned against police brutality, with some members of the Los Angeles Police Department actually going to jail. "That story impressed more people than almost anything else," Gallegos recalls of this historic breakthrough, and it stands in stark contrast to the limited success of the protests carried out by the *mutualista* generation.[14]

Like the *mutualista* groups that preceded it and the Southwest IAF that followed in its wake, the CSO focused its organizing on the neighborhood level. Describing this method, Gallegos explained that "leadership emerges from the ranks of people who have learned the discipline of one-on-one, of building individual trust, which is the core of organizing." The approach, says Gallegos, is not to tout the organization at the outset but rather to tap into a person's own priorities and links to the community. "You meet someone for the first time, and you say, 'Tell me about yourself. Where do you live? Oh, you have kids?' You're basically getting to know each other— 'Oh, yeah, I used to live there'—then at some point saying, 'By the way, I'm having a meeting at Mrs. Borges's house . . . and she's inviting some people from the barrio to go; it's going to be at 7 o'clock. Do you think you could go, and bring a couple of people there—bring your wife, some compadres to go there? I want to talk about some of the things that we can do together.'"

The CSO's demise by the mid-1960s was due to a number of factors. By this time there was no longer a *mutualista* movement to reinforce its neighborhood-centered approach to organizing. The more politically oriented civil rights groups were on the rise, especially the Mexican American Political Association (MAPA). Gallegos notes that the CSO "was originally called 'Community Political Organization [CPO]'" and as such had successfully championed a voter registration drive in 1947 that helped elect the first Mexican-heritage person to the Los Angeles City Council, Ed Roybal. The CPO became the CSO because its parent organization, the IAF, eschewed party politics, much like the *mutualista* groups before it. "A lot of people left to join MAPA, and I thought it was fine," said Gallegos.

Just as *mutualista* associations could not compete with the New Deal social programs, so the CSO could not compete with the Community Action Programs (CAP) of Lyndon Johnson's Great Society. Begun in 1964, and taking a leaf from community organizing, CAP called for "maximum feasible participation of the poor" in social service programs. "Everything that CSO was doing on a volunteer basis—classes in citizenship, basic English, immigration and so on: all of these would be done by CAP agencies," says Gallegos. Meanwhile, he viewed with concern CAP's attempts at social change being thwarted by local city officials enraged at the notion of taxpayer dollars going to organizations mobilizing protests against municipal policies. "Mayors would not allow some community organization to 'Mau-Mau' city hall," he recalled. At the same time Gallegos had his own, very different, misgivings about CAP. "I remember going to some of those meetings, and I became very concerned . . . 99% of the people were on the [federal] payroll! You can't organize change on this. . . . As soon as the money ran out, they ran out. . . ." Saul Alinksy, the creator of community

Figure 20. Leaders of the Community Service Organization, 1950s. César Chávez is in the first row, second from the right. Herman Gallegos is in the first row, fifth from right. Next to him in the plaid shirt is Industrial Areas Foundation (IAF) lead California organizer Fred Ross. Next to Ross is Ed Roybal, who in 1949 became the first Mexican American elected to the Los Angeles City Council and in 1962 was elected to Congress. IAF founder Saul Alinsky is the figure with glasses standing to the far left. (Courtesy Walter P. Reuther Library, Wayne State University)

organizing as a profession, was blunter, calling the CAP approach "political pornography."[15]

The CAP tale strengthened the IAF argument that community organizing should be based on mutual support, on funds raised by the members themselves. Or as Ernesto Cortés says with regard to some of the prominent groups in the Southwest IAF, "If you look at COPS or OneLA or Valley Interfaith or Pima County PCIC in Tucson or EPISO . . . you'll find Mexican American leadership/mexicano leadership/latino leadership organizing their congregations to raise money for dues, and they also do fundraising events of all kinds."[16]

Cortés also, however, witnessed the limits of traditional *mutualismso*. Growing up, he saw people paying mutual aid dues even as the economic and educational conditions in their neighborhood remained abysmal. No wonder Southwest IAF groups have long sought alliances with powerful nonpartisan institutions in the community, such as parent teacher associations (PTAs) and labor unions. In the case of OneLA, these entities range from Harmony Elementary School to the Society of St. Vincent de Paul to Wilshire Boulevard Temple. "Mediating institutions," Cortés calls them.

They have been tapped by the Southwest IAF to great effect, according to Herman Gallegos: more so, he says, than the alliances he and a young César Chávez attempted when they were spearheading the CSO. "The kind of work Ernie Cortés does they call 'relational organizing.' They work with religious and community groups that pay dues to support the organizer," says Gallegos, adding, "It's these relationships—across racial, ethnic, income lines—that I think gives the new model vibrancy." Associating with permanent, national institutions provides ongoing structural support, from announcements in the weekly Temple bulletin to a school bus for a meeting across town, courtesy of Mary Immaculate parish. Moreover, established institutions such as major religious denominations can fend off attacks from powerful foes. The forces that destroyed the community-organizing network Association of Community Organizations for Reform Now (ACORN) have been largely unsuccessful in similar attacks on one of IAF's principal longtime supporters, the Catholic Campaign for Human Development (CCHD). To take on CCHD is to take on its creator and patron, the US Conference of Catholic Bishops.[17]

But what would IAF founder Saul Alinksy—this Jewish, self-proclaimed radical—think of the IAF today sometimes being supported by the Catholic bishops?! Actually, Alinsky was in a sense joined at the hip to a Catholic bishop, Bishop (later Archbishop) James Sheil of Chicago. "Alinsky brought his ideas first to Bishop Sheil," according to a seminal study of the IAF, which notes that "by 1940 Alinsky and Bishop Sheil had formally organized the Industrial Areas Foundation."[18]

For his part, Ernie Cortés links Catholic social teaching to Saul Alinsky's iron rule of community organizing: "Never do for others what they can do for themselves." Writing in the progressive magazine *The American Prospect*, Cortés explains, "The Iron Rule is actually a more prosaic way of talking about subsidiarity. The documents of Vatican II consistently remind us of the importance of subsidiarity—the notion that decisions should be made at the most local level of capability in a society," with this common sensibility "close to the Tocquevillian understanding of the importance of intermediary institutions for effective democratic participation."[19]

Typically, *mutualista* organizations eschewed or even prohibited sectarian religious discussions, even as they often made reference to God in their founding documents, while on ceremonial occasions groups often employed religious symbols such as Our Lady of Guadalupe. They also sometimes made tactical alliances with religious organizations, as when the Liga Mutualista Mexicana in Los Angeles asked for the assistance of a Catholic settlement house. A number of Catholic *mutualista* groups also arose, and while their explicit denominational affiliation contrasts with the IAF, these groups bear out Ernie Cortés's theory about the utility of mediating institutions, for the Catholic associations constitute a disproportionate percentage of the historic *mutualista* organizations that have survived to this day.

A parish in Premont, Texas, for example, is home to Sociedad Católica Mutualista (Catholic Mutual Society), with twelve chapters in six other South Texas towns. The story began in San Diego, Texas, on Holy Thursday of 1934, when a group of men organized to keep vigil before the tabernacle of the Blessed Sacrament. They prayed together, all wearing identical homemade uniforms. "Noting their strong conviction, Fr. Zavala urged them to form a Society for mutual material aid and spiritual encouragement," according to one local account, and Sociedad Católica Mutualista (Catholic Mutual Society) was born. "Fr. Zavala and the governing board wrote the first Constitution which has since served as the basic rule of this Society. Besides paying their annual dues, members would contribute to a death fund. This fund was used to help out a member's family when that person passed away."[20]

By the end of the month, forty men had joined, and within a few years chapters had been established in twenty South Texas towns. In fact there is a link between Father Juan Zavala and Father John Lasseigne, the great champion of OneLA as pastor of Mary Immaculate in Pacoima. Originally from Texas, Lasseigne is a member of the same religious order that encouraged the work of Sociedad Católica Mutualista (Catholic Mutual Society), the Oblates of Mary Immaculate.[21]

On the other hand, Lasseinge is involved not with *mutualistas* but rather with the IAF—yet another indication that the barrio mutual aid associations have virtually disappeared. Even at its peak, the *mutualista* movement paled in comparison to the influence of today's Southwest IAF. It has prodded public officials to initiate billions of dollars in projects for underserved neighborhoods across the region, beginning in the 1970s with the well-known drive by COPS in San Antonio for sewers on the West Side. From San Antonio, the IAF spread to the Lower Rio Grande Valley, where it successfully agitated for decent housing in a number of unincorporated barrios along the Mexican border. IAF affiliates in other southwestern cities have gained such public improvements as sidewalks and parks. Meanwhile, major governmental initiatives jump-started by the IAF, notably in the Southwest, have included public works projects, living-wage ordinances, and educational reforms.[22]

In one respect, however, the Southwest IAF would seem to fall short in comparison to the *mutualista* movement of yore, and that is transnationally. The IAF has only three international affiliates, all in English-speaking countries, and the organization's website makes no mention of any transnational initiatives. Contrast this with the cross-border organizing of so many *mutualista* organizations, led by the Alianza Hispano Americana, with chapters from New York City to Mexico City.

There is, however, a sense in which the Southwest IAF lives out a bedrock value that transcends borders, for its member groups have always welcomed people regardless of immigration or citizenship status. And just as *mutualista* membership included both Mexican immigrants and Mexican-heritage people whose families had long resided in the United States, Cortés himself embodies both heritages. His father's parents came as immigrants fleeing the upheaval of the Mexican Revolution, while his mother's family has called Texas home for countless generations. Or, as a leader of Sociedad Mutualista Ignacio Allende of San Antonio put it, while friction sometimes arose "between Mexican-Texans and immigrants from Mexico," they were "all united as one sole family."[23]

The cutting-edge civic engagement of the Southwest IAF is radical organizing in both senses of the word—trailblazing and deeply rooted—for its ethnic Mexican members include people crossing the border today but also a people whose history in the region predates the border itself. Most studies of the Southwest IAF overlook this major breakthrough: redefining civic engagement by ignoring distinctions created by borders. As we have seen with OneLA, people from suburb and barrio alike unite in support of common civic goals, without regard to citizenship status. They manage to do this, moreover, without shying away from the immigrant issue itself. The official immigration statement by the Southwest IAF says it best.

> Fully committed to comprehensive immigration reform, the Southwest IAF organizations have been actively working at federal, state and local levels for more humane conditions for immigrants. Affiliates organize native-born as well as foreign-born supporters for national reform, educate recent immigrants with financial and know-your-rights toolkits in predominantly-immigrant institutions, and work to support policies which protect immigrants while defeating those which would unfairly penalize them for their status. . . . All immigration initiatives are deeply rooted in the faith and democratic teachings of member institutions and seek to connect leaders across race, ethnic and language lines.

Southwest IAF transcends citizenship distinctions and advocates for undocumented residents but manages to do so in a manner that does not alienate the average Anglo-American. Thus, the group website notes that the Iowa affiliates "have led voter education initiatives on the fiscal and economic impacts of immigration," while it is the California affiliates that have engaged in direct advocacy that "successfully changed vehicle impoundment laws in urban municipalities and equipped thousands of individuals with government accepted photo-ID cards [and] the Arizona network successfully blocked scores of anti-immigrant legislation."[24]

Southwest IAF immigrant activities mirror some of those carried out by Mexican immigrant hometown associations (HTAs), such as organizing through barrio-based soccer leagues, and both the Southwest IAF and the HTAs are involved in immigrant reform efforts. HTA activities, for their part, increasingly mirror Ernie Cortés's concept of tapping "mediating institutions." According to one Washington, DC think tank, "Mexican migrants have become more engaged with their US communities, working with the PTA, faith-based initiatives, neighborhood organizations, trade unions, canvassing and other efforts in support of candidates for election for school boards and city councils." In the process, "many Mexican migrants are becoming full members of *both* US and Mexican societies at the same time, constructing practices of what we could call 'civic binationality' [*sic*]." Thus does immigrant-based organizing meet Alinsky-style organizing in visionary trans-border civic engagement. Even if HTA and IAF links are yet to be made explicit, doubtless these Mexican hometown groups would embrace the idea of "power to protect what we value."[25]

This slogan may be most closely associated with Ernie Cortés and the Southwest IAF, but "the power to protect what we value" is, in a sense, even more deeply rooted in the Chama Valley of northern New Mexico. For hundreds of years people here have banded together to preserve the very land that gives them life, with this heritage having spawned its own brand of cutting-edge civic engagement. While lacking the great breadth of the Southwest IAF, the Chama Valley organizing, with its generations of agrarian *mutualismo*, is radical—radical in the literal sense of going to the root.

The area's community organization Ganados del Valle (Livestock of the Valley) "turned around the economy of the Chama Valley region by linking economic, cultural, and environmental sustainability and survival." This is according to the committee that nominated Ganados organizer María Varela among the "1,000 Women for Peace" that the committee collectively put forward for the Nobel Peace Prize. As the nomination statement put it, "In support of these businesses and projects, Ganados established a loan fund, a scholarship fund, a land fund, a work-based college program, and many workshops and opportunities for training and teaching."[26] Varela also won the MacArthur Foundation "genius" fellowship and was named one of the heroes of the magazine *Mother Jones.*

As Varela explained to the magazine reporter, "I saw pastures empty of sheep and villages full of old men and women," and state government officials had only one answer: "Put in a ski resort or write it off." She wondered, "Why can't we use the resources and the talents of the people here? Our ancestors came to this valley nearly 200 years ago seeking pasture for their sheep. They lived off the land . . . through cooperation and self reliance. The land took care of the people and the people took care of each other. But when the occupation came, it was all pretty much one way out to large feed lots in the Midwest. . . . Other people build their wealth on our resources."

Varela says that this tendency was reinforced by "federal policy around agriculture [that] destroyed the agricultural base of these communities to the point where these small-scale livestock growers were called 'hobby farmers,' which infuriated people." Agricultural Extension programs, for their part, labeled the traditional Churro sheep a "primitive breed," even though, as Varela points out, the traditional breeds were "really adaptable to these high mountain areas" because the wool could be washed at home, while the breed the market liked for its more tender meat has greasy wool that requires expensive, industrial-size processing facilities. "I think the people immersed in the regular markets were behind the times," concludes Varela. "When we in 1988 were taking organic lamb to the Santa Fe Farmers Market . . . we were niche marketing . . . and we had a softer footprint on the environment, because these sheep, as one Navaho woman told me, 'Aren't as greedy.'"[27]

The revitalized herds led to Tierra Wools, a cooperative of fine woven fabrics that resuscitated the local weaving skills and textile designs. As these enterprises evolved, they joined together in a mutual aid network, but one that faced challenges. "Our staff had no health insurance; we're not making very much money. . . ." says Varela. "We would have long talks. And finally, I thought, 'Well, what if we developed an organizational collaboration,' because we didn't want to create a second organization; we just wanted to create a collaboration around things as fundamental as finding insurance for a larger pool of people than just our little staff group, and . . . to supply technical assistance to each other instead of hiring these outside 'guns for hire' that you had to educate in order for them to share with you their tools. Not all were bad, but there were many that were not great. And so we thought, 'We can do this.'"

The textile cooperatives in the Chama Valley were adept at bookkeeping and marketing, while a nonprofit in Taos was successful at landing government grants, said Varela, "So there were ways we thought we could

Figure 21. María Varela, n.d. (Photo by Valerie Santagto, www.photosantagto.com)

be of mutual assistance to each other." She notes that they were "trying to bring that concept into a different environment that still had its fundamental roots in the sort of mutual help and self-sufficiency model of early *mutualistas*." Interestingly, Varela attributes the decline of the *mutualista* groups in no small part to unscrupulous commercial insurance companies. They lured members away with promises of cheaper policies, "but the payout was peanuts," she explains. Varela was told by clinic clients that they had commercial burial insurance for a loved one who had just died, "and it would be $200 after they paid out weekly for years."

Meanwhile, she says, the local folks involved in trying to establish the cooperative initiatives "absolutely recognized" the historical continuity with the *mutualista* tradition, while "the funders didn't have a clue," she said, "and even though I probably tried to explain it pretty well in the proposals . . . it just didn't resonate with them. And to me, this was such an exciting idea! Here we were, taking on kind of an old cultural form!" For one thing, the venerable Sociedad Protección Mutualista de Trabajadores Unidos still operated in the region. As for Varela, a northern transplant, "I can't tell you where I came across—or who told me about—*mutualistas,* but I started searching them out," she recalls, "and I was struck by how similar they were to what we were trying to do. It was in that northern New Mexican cultural ecology that there was this concept, and things don't go away: somehow you hear, or it's part of an ethos, or it's there in the social fabric of the culture."[28]

María Varela, as a community organizer, recognizes that the mutual aid ethos also is reflected in the iron rule of community organizing, "Never do for others what they can do for themselves." Thus, she turned down an offer to run VISTA (Volunteers in Service to America, "the nation's domestic Peace Corps") because she considered government-run community organizing ineffective. And while Varela did not train in Chicago with IAF, she came out of the world of Chicago social justice organizing that spawned it.

In a South Chicago Catholic high school, Varela became involved with the association that would first teach her to organize: Young Christian Students (YCS). "We were trained in the social inquiry method ('Observe, Judge, Act') to remove barriers to Christian love in our communities," she has written, adding, "Now that I reflect on the process, YCS trained us to the fundamentals of community organizing and research methodology . . . . It starts with local knowledge and through reflective action the structural roots of community dysfunction are revealed."[29]

The YCS and Young Christian Workers (YCW) organizations were brought from Europe to Chicago not long after Saul Alinsky founded the IAF there, and one of the important YCS/YCW figures, Reverend John (Jack) Egan, also was an early, strong supporter of the IAF. He even asked Alinsky, the Jewish radical, to teach a course on community organizing to local priests. According to Egan's biographer, who quotes Alinsky's biographer, Alinsky saw in the priest "a young man who had the potential to become what Alinsky had found to be so elusive: a crack organizer with whom he could work as a brother, or perhaps as a father, sharing and rejoicing in the adventure, the jousting, the fun, the power, and the nobility of a just cause." The Alinsky biography, in turn, quotes Egan as saying that his friendship with Alinsky was one "'that perdures' [he likes that word and concept] 'to this very day even though Saul died in 1972. We were very, very close.'"[30]

Referencing the activism of YCS and kindred groups, historian Jay Dolan notes, "Not so tradition bound as East Coast Catholicism, the church in the Midwest has been more open to change. The center where much of this renewal first developed was the Archdiocese of Chicago." Thus, while María Varela was learning from YCS that young people were the bedrock of the Church, her parents were participating in the kindred Christian Family Movement, which brought families together and led them to question the blockbusting of their South Chicago neighborhood by real estate interests.[31]

Questioning was nothing new in their family, according to María Varela. Her grandfather questioned the anti-Mexican sentiment in San Antonio, where the Varelas had come in flight from the Mexican Revolution. In fact, he questioned the Texas prejudice to such an extent that the family had picked up and moved to New Jersey. While in high school there, Varela's Mexican-born father met her mother, who was of Irish-German descent and who, at age eleven, had lost her own mother, a textile worker, to tuberculosis. In this marriage, "ethnic identity primarily came from the stories told when our tribe gathered and the uncles recounted the adventures and pranks of Los Rodríguez-Varelas' childhood in Mexico," wrote Varela. Even though her Mexican grandfather emphasized speaking English in his home, "the Mexican stories loomed large."

María Varela, like Ernie Cortés, has been known to cite the social encyclicals of the Church, and they both see the encyclicals' connection to the *mutualista* ethos, notably Pope Leo XIII's *Rerum Novarum* (1891), which famously stated the right of workers to organize and praised "various benevolent foundations established by private persons to provide for the workman, for his widow or orphans, in the case of sudden calamity, in sickness, and in the event of death."[32]

A worldwide phenomenon, the YCS had leaders "involved in independence movements and resistance efforts in the Third World," Varela noted, adding, "several were disappeared or killed." This, she said, reinforced the notion "that as Christians we were to be actively engaged in dismantling racism, economic injustice, anti-democratic forces and unjust wars. We were part of a movement to be a 'servant' church engaged in the world." This sensibility was underscored by the reforms of the Second Vatican Council (1962–65) and by the theology of liberation and base communities that emerged in its wake in Latin America and also in the Hispanic areas of the United States, as Ernie Cortés has noted, citing their influence on his own organizing ethos.[33]

Varela was a YCS officer while attending Milwaukee's Alverno College in the early 1960s, where she served as student body president, and upon graduation she was tapped by the national YCS in Chicago. "I was the circuit rider: first in the Midwest, and then in the Boston area," she recalls. She spoke to YCSers about the Christian call to social justice, citing the example of the students who were putting their lives on the line for racial equality. "Did you hear about the Freedom Rides?" she asked, adding, "They burned the buses; there were students on them. If you don't want to go, will you raise money for these organizations that are trying to break apartheid?" On her visits to Catholic campuses, some of what she heard was a suspicious anti-Communism, which in turn crystallized her sense "that we lived in a ghetto; Catholics lived in a ghetto . . . and so the thought was: 'Why not join the National Student Association [NSA] . . . which addressed the major issues of the day: racism; international relations; war and peace; poverty?' . . . because our job was to be yeast in the world, not a lump of rock."

Varela represented the YCS at the NSA conventions, where she came to the attention of Students for a Democratic Society (SDS) founders Tom Hayden and Al Haber. They asked her to participate in the drafting of the official documents stating the SDS principles, including the famous 1962 Port Huron Statement. "Perhaps the most important legacy of the Port Huron Statement," writes Hayden, "is the fact that it introduced the concept of participatory democracy to popular discourse and practice. It made sense of the fact that ordinary people were making history, and not waiting for parties or traditional organizations. . . . It proved to be a contagious idea."[34]

The students had to overcome an ideological split, and among those SDSers who credit Varela with having resolved it is Tom Hayden, who has written that, "On the one hand, there were followers of the theologian Reinhold Niebuhr, influenced by the atrocities of the Holocaust and Stalinism, who had asserted that 'the children of darkness,' the political realists, were in their generation wiser than 'the foolish children of light,' the pacifists and idealists. On the other side were the Enlightenment humanists who believed in infinite perfectibility through education and nonviolence as adopted by Gandhi and Martin Luther King Jr. Agreement was reached when Mary Varela, a Catholic Worker activist [sic], inspired by Pope John XXIII, suggested that we follow the doctrine that humans have 'unfulfilled' rather than 'unlimited' capacities for good, and are 'infinitely precious' rather than 'infinitely perfectible.'"

At this time the civil rights confrontations were escalating in the Deep South, and an SDS founder, Sandra (Casey) Carson Hayden, asked Varela to leave YCS and join the Student Nonviolent Coordinating Committee (SNCC) in Mississippi. Despite her fears of the murderous violence, Varela answered the call. "From Harvard, from Howard—me from Alverno—we were taught that we were under the leadership of the local people, people that this society considered as ignorant," she has recalled. SNCC practiced what SDS preached, and Varela maintains that "the support of SNCC for men *and* women to translate ideas into action resulted in the piloting of innovative programs that would influence the fields of policy, education, and community development all over the country."[35]

Varela's organizing expertise derives from many sources, from YCS to SDS to SNCC, but when it comes to her famed organizing in New Mexico, the lessons derived from the local organizing heritage have been crucial. "Within these homelands are the taproots of our cultures," she writes by way of explaining how in 1968 she came to join the New Mexico movement that was demanding the land rights first promised to the local residents by the 1848 Treaty of Guadalupe Hidalgo. She photographed—documented— the movement's activities for the Chicano newspaper *El Grito del Norte*. She also recorded local community organizing, such as the establishment of an agricultural cooperative and La Clínica del Pueblo. One morning in 1969, as Varela recounts, she was awakened by an urgent call: La Clínica "had been torched. Some local Anglo ranchers and businessmen, threatened by the land grant movement's success, had hired two young men to set the fire. It was a flashback to the South. I decided to . . . work full time for La Cooperativa Agrícola and La Clínica del Pueblo."

She came to see that La Clínica del Pueblo, like the *mutualista* organizations of yore, was formed by people who banded together for mutual protection and assistance in a threatening world. Not that Varela and her cohorts held discussions about this organizational history. "We were not doing this out of a philosophical kind of perch," she says, "we were doing it out of our experience . . . a method developed out of experience." Varela also had the genius to see that the sophisticated funding concept of "hard money" in fact had played out for generations in *mutualista* financial operations, which relied not on the goodwill of donors but rather on membership dues.

"Whether at La Clínica or with Ganados, we were looking for hard sources of money," she explained. "And with Tierra Wools—while it's limping along because this economy had been very hard on it, plus other internal issues with them . . . it's *there* because it has a source of hard money. Otra Vuelta, the other business that we started, is there . . . because, again, it's all sales." Calling La Clínica "our *mutualista*," Varela noted that this institution has survived for more than four decades because "at La Clínica it was what you charged the patients—and even though it was on a sliding fee scale—it was revenue that came in."

Thus does La Clínica echo La Clínica Beneficencia, which operated during the 1920s in San Antonio and which also relied mainly on funds from the community itself, notably from the women's organization Cruz Azul and local *mutualista* groups. The clinic also obtained a grant from the federal government—the Mexican government. These efforts evidently paid off; the treasury grew from $1,163.14 in 1924 to about $4,000 just one year later, at which point the organization established a public clinic for "poor mexicanos." Inaugurated May 30, 1925, the facility included an operating room as well as a reception area that could accommodate sixty patients. Five Mexican-heritage doctors lent their services, one of them a woman, Delfina R. del Castillo. On the other hand, the medical treatment in the 1920s at La Beneficencia was free of charge, and this lack of "hard" money may help explain the clinic's demise, even if the decisive factors likely were the onset of the Depression and wholesale immigrant roundups of the early 1930s. In the meantime, against the odds, some two hundred people visited the clinic every month for medical attention, prescriptions, and adult education classes.

From clinics to agricultural cooperatives, over the generations and against the odds, community-based mutual aid efforts have provided life-sustaining support to their members. In the process they have developed an expansive notion of civic engagement, with this community-organizing ethos—this "power to protect what we value"—revitalizing and expanding the very notion of democratic engagement itself.[36]

The Bones of Community Organizing

While often overlooked, women's initiatives have been crucial to barrio mutual aid, both historically and in contemporary times. Take the clinic "La Beneficencia," which offered trailblazing medical services to the San Antonio Mexican community in the 1920s: it was sponsored by the women's group Cruz Azul Mexicana. Drawing support from both barrio *mutualista* groups and the Mexican consulate, Cruz Azul linked the back streets of the Mexican West Side to the marble halls of Mexico City. As award-winning community organizer María Varela puts it, "Men are the flesh and women are the bones of community organizing."

Mutualista associations famously arose out of concern that the beloved dead be treated with respect, and women traditionally were in charge of a crucial component: the formal viewings of the deceased. Women made sure that the table was draped in a white cloth; that candles were placed at the four surrounding points in the form of a cross; that blocks of ice were set underneath the table to help preserve the body of the dear departed, with a heavy iron object placed on the deceased's stomach to prevent bloating.

Women typically hosted the people who came to mourn and pay their respects, and if a layperson were to lead the group in the recitation of the Rosary, often it was expected that this would be done by a senior female relative. After the funeral, the mourners would return to the house, where women led the prayers and the mourning rituals. Then, for nine days, older female parishioners particularly respected for their piety conducted a Novena for the spiritual intention that the soul of the deceased might find peace in heaven. Women also typically were in charge of the gravesites.[1]

Women founded some of the earliest *mutualista* associations, such as in 1875, when "We signatories, Hispanic-American women of San Francisco, California" established the Sociedad Hispano-Americana de Benevolencia Mutua "under the patronage of Santa Mónica" with the goal of "promoting the moral union and cooperation of nuestra raza in California." To this end, they vowed "to protect ourselves in cases of need; to assist each other with spiritual and corporal aid in case of illness; to provide our deceased sister with a decent burial and in conformance with our holy faith; to aid the families of the departed; to stimulate ourselves in the observation of our holy religion."

The founders carefully spelled out the vigils held for ill members. "There will be six assigned persons for each infirm woman. . . . [T]hey will carry out their vigil taking turns, two each night" so that family members could get some rest. The visitors were to take turns through the night and "console the ill person with all amiability and patience and according to all the prescriptions of the physician." Benevolencia Mutua cautioned members to "not judge anything regarding the house or family nor propose any new medicines nor censure the doctor nor talk coarsely in such a way as to bother the ill person or the family. Nor will they accept payment, food, or drink, nor will they bring any liquor with them."[2]

This emphasis on proper deportment was likely not coincidental at a time when women of every ethnic background were expected to be the guardians of propriety. However, these rules were presented not as etiquette but rather as important tools for implementing Christian love. Other rules made clear the leadership duties of their president, from preserving order to assuring fair elections. "In case of a tie, her vote will be decisive."[3]

Across the Southwest, women founded a number of such groups from the 1870s onward, including many named for Josefa Ortiz de Domínguez, a hero of Mexican Independence. The president of San Antonio's Sociedad Mutualista Josefa Ortiz de Domínguez gave a speech at the twenty-sixth anniversary celebration of the male-led Sociedad Mutualista Benito Juárez—at a time when society at large still frowned on women speaking in public, particularly to men. Meanwhile, in the rural outpost of Alpine, Texas, Sociedad Mutualista Josefa Ortiz de Domínguez was founded in the centenary year of Mexican independence, 1910. The leaders, while noting the importance of women as the leading educators of their children, made clear that "in this present century of emancipation and progress, the female, that medium of humanity, has taken a very active part in reclaiming her rights. Little by little she is . . . understanding that she must oblige herself to more be more noble and have higher goals than that which, in other times, made her a slave to man."[4]

Women also have long taken the lead in Sociedades Guadalupanas, which have been active in barrios nationwide for a century. Predictably associated with the events marking the feast of Our Lady of Guadalupe on December 12, Las Guadalupanas also sometimes have operated as *mutualista* groups, complete with illness and death benefits. Las Guadalupanas, like Cruz Azul and *mutualista* groups, have contributed to an ethos of grassroots activism: a "social ecology" of community organizing, to borrow a term from María Varela. Several leaders of a chapter in San José, California, including Ramona Ortiz and her daughter, were also active in the Community Service Organization (CSO), that important, early Industrial Areas Foundation (IAF) community-organizing effort in the 1950s and 1960s. The famed IAF San Antonio organization of the 1970s, Communities Organized for Public Service (COPS), also had a number of leaders from the ranks of the Guadalupanas, while a Sociedad Guadalupana member in an Oakland, California parish linked up with the IAF-affiliated Oakland Community Organizations (OCO). OCO called for increased responsiveness from the educational system, in the process obtaining homework centers and smaller, more community-friendly schools. This Guadalupana member happened to be a man, and Las Guadalupanas are notable on that score: they are mainly led by women but have active male participation as well. It should be noted that the typical Sociedad Guadalupana was based in a parish; the pastor served as the chaplain and wielded various degrees of influence, but in many cases these organizations serve as an example of the "third space" that US Mexicans carved out for themselves within dominant society institutions.[5]

Not that women played equal public roles in the traditional *mutualista* movement. As with most formal organizations—whatever their type, whether in Mexico or the United States—officers in mixed-gender *mutualista* groups were mostly men. Women almost never served as presidents, even though they occasionally held other posts, such as when dressmakers Juanita and Elvira Castro were officers of the mixed-gender Sociedad Mutualista Ignacio Allende of San Antonio in the 1920s.

Some *mutualista* societies established "auxiliaries." The very name conjures up the helpmate, subordinate model that posited the man as the head of the family, but women ran these groups autonomously and sometimes resisted male attempts at subordination. Angie Morales, the head of the auxiliary of Houston's Sociedad Mutualista Obrera Mexicana in the 1930s, recalled years later that "the men did not trust the ladies too well. They wanted to have a man at all of our meetings. It used to irk me," she noted, "because sometimes we wanted to discuss things and we did not want men there, but they were always there as sort of watchdogs, to see that we performed right, I guess." When she protested, the man said he kept an eye on them because they were such a small group, but she recalled retorting that, actually, the women needed to send a representative to watch the men, as "we had ninety members present, and their group hadn't have but thirty or forty present!"[6]

On the other hand, the largest mutual aid–style organization, the mighty Alianza Hispano Americana, officially made women equal members in 1913, evidently in response to the state having given women the

Figure 22. Alianza Hispano Americana officers María Delgado, María Lopes, and Lupe Castillo, n.d. (Courtesy Ocampo Family Photographs, Chicano/a Research Collection, Arizona State University Libraries)

right to vote the previous year.[7] Welcoming women also was the easiest way to swell the membership rolls, and within a decade the Alianza became the first national Latino organization in US history.

"During the first half of the twentieth century, the Alianza was the best-funded, best-established, and most aggressive of all mutualista organizations," historian Juan Gómez Quiñones notes. And the Alianza chapter in the unofficial capital of US Mexicans, San Antonio, at one point in the 1920s had a woman as its president: Luisa M. González, a midwife by profession. Her presidency remained the rare exception amid a masculine hegemony, as reflected in such unequal terms as "auxiliary" and, in the case of the Alianza, such male terms as "fraternity" and "lodge."[8]

But their actual role was a powerful one, for women controlled much of the money and information. Typically they provided the funds essential to the organizational projects because they were in charge of the fundraisers, such as bazaars. And rooted as they were in the neighborhood, they often had the most accurate, up-to-date news of barrio issues and members, both actual and potential, and served as the best eyes and ears of *mutualismo,* touting its virtues and telegraphing its events throughout the neighborhood. Also rarely acknowledged, then or now, is the extent to which the men serving as the presidents stood on the shoulders of the women who were keeping family life afloat—and, indeed, keeping much of barrio life afloat.[9] Whether in mixed-gender or women-only groups, "Women, through *mutualistas,* sought to help their neighbors," notes historian Vicki Ruiz, who makes the point that these women were often well known in their neighborhoods: "They worked within their communities in a public way, although their labor generally remained invisible outside the barrio."[10]

In contrast, the Mexican American groups that would eclipse the *mutualista* associations in the 1930s were founded mainly by men, many of them veterans of World War I. They mobilized to fight injustices they faced back home, even while in uniform, and even after having risked their lives for their nation. That same uniform empowered them, in the sense that nothing so clearly demonstrated one's bona fides as a US citizen, but it was a uniform that no women had worn. The veterans founded such organizations as Sons of America and Sons of Texas, also known as Orden Hijos de América and Orden Hijos de Texas. Virtually no women joined, and none held office. For instance, Santiago Tafolla headed the Sons/Hijos, but neither Delfina Tafolla nor Micaela Tafolla were Sons/Hijos leaders, even though Delfina was an officer in the Cruz Azul and Micaela was a prominent social worker.

The Sons/Hijos, in turn, would lead to the founding in 1929 of the League of United Latin American Citizens (LULAC), which by the 1940s would eclipse the Alianza Hispano Americana as the most prominent organization of Mexican-heritage people. As historian Cynthia Orozco has noted, "'Mutualism' was now considered obsolete; self-help was re-defined to mean leadership by the male Mexican American middle class through an organization rather than cooperative effort by all members of La Raza."[11]

She cites the mutual aid vision laid out in 1911 by the delegates from Texas and nearby Mexico at the Primer Congreso Mexicanista in Laredo—a convention that very much included women. They set up the Liga Femenil Mexicanista (League of Mexican Women), which issued a call for women's mobilization on such issues as bilingual education for needy children. President Jovita Idar knew the problems firsthand, for she had turned to journalism after having taught under deplorable conditions at a segregated South Texas "Mexican" public school (as she would have not been hired by the local "American" school despite her teaching certification). With the

Mexican Revolution erupting within walking distance of her Laredo home, Idar helped found the Cruz Blanca, which aided wounded revolutionaries, and the Liga Femenil Mexicana soon faded from the scene.

Another Liga at this time, La Liga Protectora Latina, illustrates some of the problems Mexican women faced within their own community. Liga Protectora Latina initially arose in vigorous defense of two Mexican men who were convicted of killing their wives. Liga founders could well argue that such an accusation was unprovable and that racists commonly hurled such charges about supposed attacks on women, but having these particular cases be the galvanizing cause for the League's formation would seem to have belittled the issue of domestic violence. There also is some evidence that US law gave women more legal redress in such cases than they had in Mexico. Besides, even as women "were increasingly becoming members of mutualistas," at that very time the new "civil rights organizations, considered a male domain, defined women as incidental to organizing," as historian Cynthia Orozco perceptively notes.[12]

On occasion Mexican American civil rights groups did work with women's organizations, as when the men allied with the female-led Mexican parent teacher association (PTA) in anti-school segregation suits. Then there is the case of María Hernández, who cofounded a *mutualista* group and went on to be an important supporter of LULAC. She also was one of the founders of the Liga Pro-Defensa Escolar (School Improvement League) that protested the grossly-unequal school facilities on San Antonio's largely Mexican West Side. Hernández publicized all these activities on her popular Spanish-language radio show.

María Hernández was the only woman to give a speech at the School Improvement League's historic 1934 meeting, even though women constituted the majority of the hundreds of participants. Forty years later, however, when women from those same neighborhoods participated in meetings for COPS-IAF, they constituted a majority of the official leaders as well. And while the School Improvement League made history with the improvements they obtained in school facilities, the Alliance Schools Project spearheaded by COPS and other Texas IAF groups yielded truly amazing results: higher student scores on standardized achievement tests and, at the same time, better satisfaction ratings on the part of *both* parents and teachers—this according to a 2008 report by the Annenberg Institute for School Reform, Brown University. Still, the goals and meeting locations were much the same, with the house meetings so central to IAF organizing echoing those held by people such as María Hernández.[13]

Straddling the *mutualista* generation of the early 1900s and the community-organizing generation of today is Chole Alatorre. She is active in the IAF, while in 1968 she cofounded the immigrant rights group that stood on the shoulders of barrio mutual aid efforts going back to the 1910s. She explained that when she and Bert Corona set up the La Hermandad Nacional/Centro de Acción Social Autónoma (HMN/CASA), "We'd have a dinner: two or three people would host it, and everybody else would come and help prepare the meal. I'd get together with two women from my neighborhood, you know? So we'd make the meal, and in the evening the people would come for the meal. That's how we got the funds to be able to set up the office, and that's how we opened the first office," which was in her house. "We had the desk right here," she said, pointing to a spot in her living room. There HMN/CASA cofounder Bert Corona, as the college graduate, would check people's immigration paperwork. "He would sit and try to help, in whatever way possible, the workers that would come in." And in order to raise funds for the association, she says, "We had meetings—like we do now in the parish's house meetings for OneLA."[14]

The HMN/CASA house meetings of the 1970s resembled the ones so integral to the IAF, as with the house meeting held by its budding CSO in the 1950s. Almost half of the CSO-IAF founders were women, including María Durán, who hosted organizational meetings in her home. And Lucy Ríos, referring to Saul Alinsky's main operative in California, recalls, "We decided to have Fred Ross in the house. Fred Ross came to the house to talk about the Industrial Areas Foundation; even Alinsky came a couple of times. My house was the office, and we took messages and everything." As CSO spread north from its Los Angeles origins to the San Jose area, Helen Delgadillo recalled that "Fr. Ralph Dugan brought César Chávez and Fred Ross to my house, to try to get . . . a few other people to start registering voters, and that's how it started."[15]

Women were important on all fronts for the CSO. "In order to have some money to help out, we would work like the dickens, making tamales, to have dances," said Cecilia Sánchez. When the CSO turned to a mutual financial aid model, the credit union, Flavia Vásquez headed the first credit union in 1964, while Margot Benavides was the president of another one four years later.

For her part, Dolores Huerta of the CSO went on to be the chief legislative liaison and a legendary leader of the United Farm Workers. Or, as Bert Corona put it, "Many women were active in the CSO, as officers, organizers, and door-to-door voter registrars." At least one of the presidents of the entire CSO operation was a woman, Ursula Gutiérrez.

But even though the CSO led the way with regard to women leaders, the names commonly associated with the CSO nonetheless all belong to men: Fred Ross, Ed Roybal, César Chávez. In the words of historian Margaret Rose, women have constituted the "invisible backbone of barrio organizational activity." And women often learned to organize from other women.

Rita Medina credited the CSO with getting her "very, very involved—really helping the community," but she noted that in fact she first learned of community involvement from her mother, who always inculcated the idea of mutual aid. "When we were young, my mother was a very 'service person': made us go help neighbors, friends, whoever needed help." Young Rita didn't mind doing so—not even when it meant helping wash diapers—but she was embarrassed to visit someone in jail. Unfazed, her mother would simply say, "Go help. Mrs. So-and-so's husband is in jail" or "Her son is in Juvenile; they don't speak English." Medina notes, "So I was used to it: helping in the community."[16]

As in California, women's community activism long went unheralded in New Mexico. It was not until 1989 that a book by historian Sarah Deutsch documented the many ways Mexican-heritage women of the northern New Mexico and southern Colorado region systematically navigated their fraught post-conquest world. While these women dealt with the US authorities when necessary and adopted newcomer innovations that could be useful, such as the sewing machine, they preserved what they could of their lives, from an emphasis on the Spanish language to maintenance of handicraft skills. As both Varela and Deutsch explain, women had an additional reason to view US authorities with suspicion, for the conquest brought with it a loss of property rights for women. English Common Law did not recognize the property protections upheld by the Spanish and then Mexican legal systems; meanwhile, traditionally in rural New Mexico, the wife inherited the bulk of the property and daughters inherited equally with sons.

As men left for jobs in the agribusinesses and mines of the industrializing West in the face of costly legal land suits and rising real estate taxes, women worked to hold the homes and communities together. Increasingly women fashioned networks of mutual economic and social support, even as they found it difficult to maintain these networks in an expanding corporate economy. No wonder many folks turned for mutual protection to rising *mutualista* groups such as the Sociedad Protección Mutua de Trabajadores Unidos. This put women at a disadvantage, however, to the extent that so many of these groups were run by men—at least officially.[17]

In the 1980s in the Chama valley of New Mexico, women began a new chapter of mutual aid by forming weaving cooperatives, often utilizing textile designs handed down from one generation of women to another over the centuries. "Women grow organisms, and these need the time to take to grow," says Varela. "There's nothing we can do about that. You have to grow the organism in relationship to the ingredients that you have, that the community has—that the people you are working with have." Meanwhile, "men often build . . . a structure, and that's what they're trying to do . . . and construction's based on a square, usually." And you cannot pay much

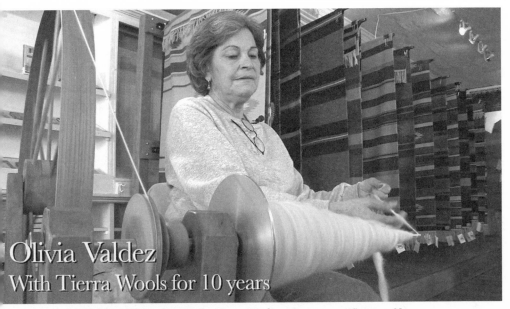

Olivia Valdez
With Tierra Wools for 10 years

Figure 23. From the PBS program on the Tierra Wools project, 2009. (Courtesy New Mexico Public Broadcasting Service)

attention to the community because you are concentrating on the blueprint and mechanics of building. "You find the incipient leadership there—often among women, but not always—and you create a space where that leadership can grow and develop, and people can begin to feel strong enough to articulate what they want or need." And if it works, you are "mutually supporting each other financially, emotionally and then through the organization."

At the same time, Varela cautions against rigidly applying any model. "I'm not saying this is foolproof at all. . . . It can buy you 20–25 years that makes some kind of difference in people's lives. . . ." Organizing for social change is especially challenging in rural areas, she points out, given the small pool of people from which to draw the leadership, and that it takes generations to "reverse the patterns of colonialism; you can't reverse colonialism in, like, three-year 'funding cycles.'" Thus, the cooperative enterprises in Chama Valley have fallen on hard times in recent years, even as they have established models that provide important templates for organizing efforts far and wide. Ganados del Valle, the vibrant economic cooperative on the *mutualista* model that was operated by shepherds in the region, "is right now dormant, but I find so often . . . that it inspires," says Varela. People come and seek them out, wanting to apply the Ganados principles in other projects. "So your hope," says Varela, "is that while it may light the fire in one community for maybe a generation and a half, it has the potential to light the fire in other communities for longer than that." Meanwhile, the women's weaving cooperative, Tierra Wools, lives on. Moreover, the organizational half-life of the women in the valley is akin to the legacy left by the women organizing a century ago for mutual aid and protection.

María Varela also reminds us that many crucial historical events were never written down and can only be recovered—if at all—through oral traditions.[18] To the extent that women have been the bones and men the flesh of community organizing, it would seem that women have constituted the "bones" that undergird much of the historical record itself.

PART V

Big Media, Big Money, and *Mutualista* Organizing

The Media Angle

Coverage of mutual aid organizing by US Mexicans has been largely limited to the Spanish-language media. Even the hometown associations (HTAs) (asociaciones oriundos), despite their role in the huge immigrant marches, remain largely unreported by the mainstream media. No wonder the coverage of these nationwide demonstrations gave the impression that they had emerged out of nowhere. Moreover, given the anti-Mexican sentiment in some quarters, "Had a *single* car been burned by immigrant protesters in the US, one can be sure that the televised image would have been repeated so many times on Fox News that viewers would have gotten the impression that hundreds of cars were burned," noted a report by the Woodrow Wilson Center.[1] Orderly behavior on the part of so many marchers all across the country did not, however, prevent prominent talk radio host Rush Limbaugh from referring to Mexican immigrants as "a renegade, potential criminal element . . . poor and unwilling to work."

This kind of talk on the airwaves is nothing new, says Chole Alatorre. She and Bert Corona had faced such vitriol back in the 1970s. As Corona put it, "The level of hysteria and hype this issue generated . . . got out of hand and became almost comical and ridiculous. On some radio talk shows, the host and the people who called in blamed every problem imaginable on 'illegal aliens.' I remember a group called the American Association to Protect Taxpayers, who complained that the long gas lines during the Middle East crisis in 1973 were really being caused by 'illegal aliens' using up all the gas. . . ."[2]

Not that the leading, respected newspapers employ this kind of rhetoric. Today *The New York Times* would never editorialize, as it did in the 1930s, that "it is folly to pretend that the more recently arrived Mexicans, who are largely of Indian blood, can be absorbed into the American race." But if the most prestigious publications do not engage in such sentiments, they seldom treat recently arrived Mexican immigrants as civic actors.[3]

Antonia Hernández, head of the Los Angeles Community Foundation, contrasts this neglect with the extensive reporting on grassroots immigrant organizing by *La Opinión* of Los Angeles, which, in her words, "plays a critical role in getting the word out." The publisher, Mónica Lozano, has a background that includes community organizing, so when her publisher father asked her to take over the family business, she approached the venture with an organizer's perspective: "If I was interested in making a difference, there was nothing more important, or at least more accessible, than *La Opinión*."[4]

The widest-circulating Spanish-language newspaper in the United States, *La Opinión* has been the lead player in a nationwide effort to promote naturalization and voter registration, Ya Es Ahora (Now Is the Time), which one study had called "an innovative Spanish-language media campaign" that in one year "managed to enroll 300 organizations, operating more than 400 citizenship centers and organizing 200 citizenship workshops." The results of such efforts have been seismic. As CNN reported, in 2012 Latinos for the first time comprised ten percent of the electorate, and with the "Latino vote key to Obama's reelection." With this the fastest growing demographic in the nation, notably in crucial "swing" states, the Republican Party has been scrambling to lessen its anti-immigrant reputation.[5]

Despite all of this, however, the immigrant mutual aid groups themselves still remain under the radar screen of the mainstream media. It is *La Opinión* that provides information on some of the oldest and largest HTA networks, such as the Southern California federation of immigrants from the state of Zacatecas, Federación de Clubes Zacatecanos del Sur de California. The federation's president, Manuel Salazar, explained that his organization was involved in the Zacatecan government's 3x1 construction program, under which the state contributed three state dollars for every dollar sent to Zacatecas by the Zacatecan clubs. Thus, "It is painful," he told the reporter, to find the ex-governor of Zacatecas charged with links to a drug cartel. But Salazar also stressed that "if the government of the state and some of the municipalities are in discord, this doesn't impede us." The head of community outreach for this federation of Zacatecan HTAs, María Jiménez, made the same point even more emphatically. "These accusations ought to be kept in perspective," she told *La Opinión*. "One needs to take into consideration all the good that is being done, people working so that Zacatecas can keep moving forward," and despite threats of violence in their home state, "Our seventeen federations will continue here in pursuit of a more just society."[6]

Today *La Opinión*'s "beat" very much includes news by and for immigrants from across Latin America, but the periodical also maintains its strong, historic connection to the Mexican community. Mónica Lozano explained to National Public Radio that her newspaper continues the mission begun by her grandfather, Ignacio Lozano Sr., who founded *La Opinión* as an independent daily newspaper for Mexican immigrants. Publication began on September 16, 1926: Mexican Independence Day. This date was no coincidence, for the newspaper championed "El México de Afuera" (Mexico Abroad), promising "to provide news of the native homeland as well as of the new country for the growing Mexican population in southern California."[7]

Ignacio Lozano Sr. was born near Monterrey, Mexico, in 1886, less than forty years after the new US border was laid down just one hundred miles to the north. In 1908, as events in northern Mexico were hurdling toward revolution, Lozano headed to San Antonio, where he founded *La Prensa*. In the 1920s, presciently recognizing that Los Angeles would overtake San Antonio as the population center, he founded *La Opinión* there, even as *La Prensa* had become the widest-circulating Spanish language newspaper in the United States.

Its extensive coverage of mutual aid endeavors included detailed accounts of women's groups, notably those founded by exiles, such as Cruz Azul Mexicana, from reports on its clinic project to accounts of a few internal squabbles. Sometimes *La Prensa* featured Cruz Azul on page one, as in 1926, when a large photo of the group served as the centerpiece for the main story, on Mexican Independence Day events. *La Prensa*'s competitors also reported on Cruz Azul, as in 1928, when the more radical *El Heraldo de México* scored the group for holding a benefit dinner at the swank Gunther Hotel rather than "in the heart of the barrio." In contrast, *La Epoca* gave the event highly favorable coverage, and no wonder, for the founding president of Cruz Azul, María Luisa Garza, was the newspaper's editor. As such, she was that rare woman: supervising the work of male professionals.[8]

Garza was a trailblazing woman journalist in other respects as well, from publishing a regular column to founding her own newspaper. Her column appeared in *El Imparcial de Texas* under the penname Loreley, and although her writing did not directly challenge the notion of a woman's "sphere," she reported on such women's activism as the Pan American Women's Conference of 1922, in which she participated. Garza also founded the newspaper *Alma Femenina*—first in San Antonio and then in Los Angeles. Meanwhile, her organization Cruz Azul published the magazine *Revista Azul*, which could be found in barrios from the Southwest to the Midwest and beyond. That *Revista Azul* constituted one of the first nationally distributed Latina periodicals in the United States likely was facilitated by Garza having herself been a prominent media figure.[9]

María Luisa Garza's five press outlets also point to the profusion of periodicals founded by US Mexicans. Some thirty such newspapers were circulating at this time in San Antonio alone, while others sprang up in Mexican communities large and small all across the United States. As in San Antonio, many of these publications were the work of émigré professionals who disseminated news of local *mutualista* activities. Newspapers in Chicago and Iowa even went so far as to call for the formation of statewide *mutualista* alliances.[10] Conversely, *mutualista* organizations sometimes were instrumental in sponsoring local newspapers, as with *El Amigo del Hogar* in northwest Indiana and Detroit's *El Eco de la Patria,* with mostly working-class *mutualista* members joining forces with the more elite publishers to put out a periodical for the community.

Many of the émigré publishers had fled the Mexican Revolution and called for Mexicans in the United States to remain loyal to the Madre Patria, its traditional culture, and its Catholic religion. *El Heraldo de México* of Los Angeles, for example, dismissed the 1917 Mexican constitution—still in effect today—as "Bolsheviki." Predictably, their overall positive reports on the *mutualista* movement mostly ignored mutual aid labor unions.[11]

Some of the émigré publishers reflected the opposite end of the political spectrum, however, and these exiled revolutionaries had a complicated relationship with *mutualista* organizations. The most prominent, the revolutionary Partido Liberal Mexicano (PLM), was on record criticizing *mutualista* groups as "bourgeois" even as some PLM editors were founding their own *mutualistas* in the United States. In the party's radical organ *Regeneración,* PLM cofounder Ricardo Flores-Magón scored a California *mutualista* that reneged on its promises to its members, and he warned, "Don't spend your money on *mutualista* societies, Mexican workers, as these societies only serve to make good salaries for . . . the board of directors, while for the members there is nothing. Everyone unite in the Partido Liberal Mexicano, which doesn't ask, or take." He found these leaders wanting in radical fervor. "*Mutualismo* distracts the worker from the straight path that he ought to follow to conquer: Bread, Land, and Liberty for all," Flores-Magón declared, adding for good measure, "*Mutualismo* doesn't depart from capitalism because it isn't instituted to attack Capital. True, it does make it possible for proletariats to associate with each other to mutually help one another, but this is not salvation. War on Capital and on the Authorities, Mexicans!"[12]

Regeneración was published between 1900 and 1918 from ever-shifting US locales—Texas, Missouri, California—as Ricardo Flores-Magón and his brother Enrique endeavored to stay one step ahead of the Mexican and US federal agents pursuing them on charges of weapons smuggling and sedition. In an effort to avoid detection by the authorities, at least one PLM chapter posed as a traditional *mutualista* organization. In Cost, Texas, the PLM club—one of more than 160 PLM chapters in the state—proposed this ploy to Ricardo Flores-Magón. He replied, "The idea that you have of a *mutualista* society is magnificent, don't forget it, and do implement it for the cause." For good measure, he added, "It is hoped that you can

Figure 24. Revolutionary journalist Práxedis Guerrero, who founded several *mutualista* societies in the United States.

send us funds . . . write me in care of the editors of *Progreso* in San Antonio, Texas." Eight days later the leader of the Cost PLM chapter reported to Flores-Magón that the *mutualista* cover was in place. The group sent Flores-Magón $6.00 toward the PLM's expenses, plus $2.25 for the Cost club's subscription to *Regeneración*.[13]

On the other hand, a number of PLM leaders founded *mutualista* associations, including several by prominent *Regeneración* contributor Práxedis Guerrero, who went on to fame as one of the first casualties of the Mexican Revolution, with a Mexican town renamed in his honor. Doubtless this enemy of imperial power would have been happy to know that his eponymous municipality had been founded in 1849 by "Mexicans from Texas and New Mexico who did not want to lose their nationality with the implementation of the Treaty of Guadalupe-Hidalgo"—this according to the official municipal history of Práxedis Guerrero, Mexico.[14]

Another PLM activist, writer and publisher Sara Estela Ramírez, called herself "a fervent admirer of the *mutualista* movements." Her newspaper,

like so many women's *mutualista* groups, took as its inspiration Josefa Ortiz de Domínguez, the Mexican independence figure. She is known as "La
Corregidora," and Ramírez used that name for her radical periodical. In an
address to the Sociedad de Obreros, Igualdad y Progreso (the Equality and
Progress Society of Workers) in Laredo, the publisher of *La Corregidora,*
noted that "we celebrate the twenty-fourth anniversary of the well-known,
as it is respected, Sociedad de Obreros." Ramírez went on to laud

> Twenty four years of noble struggle . . . twenty four years of joining souls
> through the principle of humanity . . . an altruism that permits us to fulfill
> our obligation to our beloved comrade, to visit him in sickness, to console
> him in sorrows and to give him our hand in every bitter hour and in every
> test, even to bid him farewell when his turn comes to return to eternity. That
> is mutualism. . . . Mutualism needs the vigor of struggle and the firmness of
> conviction to advance in its unionizing efforts; it needs to shake the apathy
> from the masses . . . it needs hearts that say, "I am for you, I want you to be
> for me"; mutualism has need of us workers. . . . May you, beloved workers,
> integral part of human progress, yet celebrate uncounted anniversaries, and
> with your example may you show sociedades how to love each other so that
> they may be *mutualistas* and to unite so that they may be strong.[15]

Even some newspapers founded by counter-revolutionaries joined with
mutualista organizations in defending the rights of US Mexicans. While *El
Heraldo de México* of Los Angeles did rail against Bolshevism, the newspaper also published the first novel narrated from the point of view of a
working class Mexican immigrant, and in 1919, in association with local *mutualista* groups, *El Heraldo* founded a league pledged to defend the
rights of US Mexicans, La Liga Protectiva Mexicana de California.

This initiative echoed the call for such leagues issued a few years earlier
by *La Crónica* of Laredo when it famously convened the Primer Congreso
Mexicanista. *La Crónica* mobilized *mutualista* and other barrio organizations in part by documenting injustices in grisly detail, notably in an article
by Jovita Idar about the lynching of Antonio Rodríguez in 1910. He had
been arrested in Rock Springs, Texas, on the charge of murdering a local
Anglo woman and then had been dragged from his cell by a mob and tied
to a tree, where he was set afire. "The crowd cheered when the flames engulfed his contorted body," she reported. "They did not even turn away at
the smell of his burning flesh and I wondered if they even knew his name."
She then addressed the general scandalous state of affairs, writing, "There
are so many dead that sometimes I can't remember all their names."[16]

The numerous Ligas Protectivas/Ligas Protectoras that emerged in the
wake of that congress were chronicled by many Mexican periodicals in

Texas. *El Imparcial de Texas* of San Antonio reported that the Liga Protectora Mexicana was providing legal aid in much of South Texas and was lobbying the state legislature for legal reforms. The group's founder M. C. Gonzales published his own newspaper, *El Luchador* (*The Fighter*). That this periodical was issued bilingually was unusual—and telling, given that a decade later Gonzales would be among the Mexican ethnic leaders establishing a civil rights league with an English-language name and that was restricted to US citizens: the League of United Latin American Citizens. Meanwhile in Arizona, the Liga Protectora Latina's founder published the newspaper *Justicia*, writing in 1910 that he had nearly been lynched in 1898 when he expressed opposition to the US involvement in the war with Spain. Such publishers helped the Liga Protectora Latina spread to various other parts of the Southwest.[17]

Even decades earlier, however, journalists had avidly chronicled *mutualista* activism. In 1879, *El Horizonte* of Corpus Christi had urged its readers to become members of the Sociedad Mutualista Benito Juárez, writing, "We Mexicans in Corpus have always been considered unworthy of even the title of foreigner. They have stepped over our rights; they have denied us even the few guarantees owed to a citizen and we have been, in short, miserable pariahs, without a future. . . ." The editors vowed that "from today . . . they will respect our rights and we shall not be the object of their jokes and insult."[18]

Indeed, journalism that supported community activism dates from the time of the US acquisition of the Southwest. Writers in the 1850s for such periodicals as *El Regidor* in San Antonio and *El Clamor Público* in Los Angeles decried the discrimination experienced by longtime residents of territories newly added to the United States. Nowhere was this sentiment more evident than in New Mexico. Proclaiming "la defensa de nuestro pueblo" ("the defense of our people"), these newspaper folks crafted a counter-narrative to Manifest Destiny, in their case championing a supposedly superior culture of graciousness and commonality rooted in a Hispanic heritage. It should be recalled that this was taking place at the same time that New Mexican villagers—many of them women—for their part were striving to preserve their Spanish language, their agronomy, and their crafts.[19]

A century later, this ethos was embraced by the Chicano/Chicana movement, even as these activists, in stark contrast to their predecessors, took pains to note the importance of the indigenous/Native American presence that predated the Spanish conquest, and with some of the Chicanos/Chicanas also employing a Marxist analysis. Leading the call for a renewal of cultural and political self-determination was *El Grito del Norte* (The Shout/ Cry of the North). Published from 1968 to 1973 and covering northern New Mexico and southern Colorado, it pledged "to advance the cause of

Figure 25.
Elizabeth
"Betita"
Sutherland
Martínez, c. late
1980s. (Photo
by Margaret
Randall)

justice for poor people and preserve the rich cultural heritage of la Raza in this area."[20] The principal editor, Elizabeth "Betita" Martínez, arrived in New Mexico fresh from *The Nation* by way of civil rights organizing in Mississippi with the Student Nonviolent Coordinating Committee (SNCC). For her lifetime of contributions, Martínez would be among the "1,000 Women for Peace" collectively nominated for the Nobel Prize in 2005.

Fellow honoree María Varela also was active in SNCC, where she took some of the group's most important photographs. Varela then joined *El Grito del Norte,* where she documented Chicano activism, from the land grant organizers making headlines in northern New Mexico to the political and cultural creativity radiating out of the Denver barrios. In 1969, Varela conveyed the electricity of a Denver conference by Rodolfo "Corky" Gonzales's Crusade for Justice when she wrote in *El Grito del Norte,* "'Conference' is a poor word to describe those five days. It was in reality a fiesta: days of celebrating what sings in the blood of a people, who, taught to believe that they are ugly, discover the true beauty in their souls during years of occupation and intimidation. Coca-Cola, Doris Day, Breck Shampoo, the Playboy Bunny, the Arrow shirt man, the Marlboro heroes, are lies. 'We are beautiful.' This affirmation grew into a grito, a roar, among the people gathered in the auditorium of the Crusade's Center."[21]

This incandescent activism flared briefly and then faded. María Varela went on to her award-winning organizing in the region, while Betita Martínez transferred her journalistic locus to California and wrote the monumental *500 Years of Chicana Women's History*. An entire chapter is devoted to "Las Mutualistas: Surviving with Mutual Aid," which notes that "women often initiated the creation of *mutualistas* in the years 1920–30, at a time when they constituted the most important social organizations for Chicanos." As for her years publishing *El Grito del Norte*, she recalled years later, "If ever there has been a chapter of the US Left with deep cultural roots in every sense, it is the movimiento of New Mexico."[22]

Increasingly, however, radio had come to overshadow the press as the communication partner with grassroots organizers. Making this point, civic leader Antonia Hernández cited hugely popular radio host Eddie "Piolín" Sotelo, saying, "El Piolín was the one that incited hundreds of thousands to go out and demonstrate" in the mass immigration marches. Echoing this point is the Executive Director of the Coalition for Humane Immigrant Rights, Angelica Salas. Noting that many of the DJs, such as "El Piolín," are themselves immigrants, she says, "Radio, unlike TV, focuses on how to effectively speak to the common man and woman and thus has been able to generate a great deal of enthusiasm."[23]

Media ratings indicate that Hispanics lead all population groups in the number of hours spent listening to the radio, likely due to the strong bonds forged with the hosts—who listen affectionately to immigrant callers and give advice on navigating US society—along with the comforting sound of one's favorite music from home. Moreover, radio can be accessed while doing manual labor or childcare and requires no reading. Summing this up, a social science study characterizes the radio personalities as "mouthpieces" for immigrant concerns and, as such, "an overlooked intermediate mobilizer."[24]

In January 2006, when immigration-rights activists held a news conference to announce plans for mass demonstrations protesting the Sensenbrenner Bill (which would have made being undocumented a felony), the immediate effect was limited. No representatives from any major civil rights or labor groups were on board—not even from the Coalition for Humane Immigrant Rights. It was at this point that some members of the original planning committee were invited to appear on *Piolín por la Mañana*, the top morning show in Los Angeles. The result was historic.

These leaders included Javier Rodríguez, whose immigrant-rights mentors in the 1970s had been the two leaders who had been organizing immigrants along the lines of the old *mutualistas,* Chole Alatorre and Bert Corona. "El Piolín" ended up featuring Rodríguez and the other guests for the entire morning. "That was it, man!" Rodríguez told *The Los Angeles Times*. "They gave us four hours and we went at it. We talked about the need for people to come out." The next morning, while appearing on the competing radio show of Ricardo "El Mandril" Sánchez, Rodríguez suggested on air that the rival radio personalities, just this once, unite to support the effort to defeat this bill that they all thought was engendering such fear and anger in community.[25]

With this idea, Javier Rodríguez was drawing on his many years of having operated at the intersection of journalism and immigrant advocacy. Back in the 1970s he had worked for the seminal periodical *Sin Fronteras* (Without Borders). Published by Corona and Alatorre, it laid out the arguments that would form the dominant frame for advocates of comprehensive immigration reform. Rodríguez proudly recalls those years, including the fact that his brother José was the top vendor of *Sin Fronteras* (due to his own community activism and his many connections as co-owner of a popular Mexican restaurant).

When Javier Rodíguez issued his challenge to "El Mandril," the radio personality responded in a dramatic fashion. Then and there—on the air—the host called up his rival, El Piolín. "It was fascinating, to say the least," Rodríguez recalled. "Here were the two top DJs, competitors, coming forth and saying, 'We're going to march with you, we're going to get everybody together.'" Soon all the major Spanish-language radio personalities were on board. Within days the radio personalities staged a dramatic joint appearance on the steps of the Los Angeles City Hall, where they urged the public to join them at the upcoming march. "From there it just blew up," said one organizer.[26]

For all their influence, these media celebrities are mouthpieces, not organizers. The drive-time shows are entertainment, after all—music interspersed with contests and banter—sometimes silly, sometimes raunchy, sometimes a combination of the two. As a Chicago radio personality, Javier Salas, told a leading Mexico City newspaper, "The responsibility of the media is basic, but we can't be the protagonists." He cited the immigrant clubs and federations as central to organizing the marches, adding, "We can't relegate the leadership to jokesters—that harms the community."[27]

The head of the major immigrant-rights group Latino Movement USA, Juan José Gutiérrez, put it this way to journalist Roberto Lovato: "The DJs played a role, an important role, but they let us put our message in their medium. . . ." As an organizer, he noted, "Since January I've been to about thirty-five different cities and seen old and new leadership coming together to create something that has never been seen before." His own involvement, like that of Javier Rodríguez, dates from Gutiérrez's days with Chole Alatorre and Bert Corona. As journalist Lovato explains, "Juan José

Gutiérrez started as a young organizer distributing mimeographed copies of the radical newspaper *Sin Fronteras* to immigrant workers in the face of hostility from the anti-Communist right."[28]

While unprecedented in its scope, the role of radio personality as mobilizer is not brand new. Popular DJs had promoted earlier immigration demonstrations, notably the 1994 protest against California Proposition 187, limiting undocumented immigrants' access to public services, and since the 1960s, Radio Campesina has served as the mouthpiece for the United Farm Workers Union. Even back in the 1930s, some of the very first Mexican disc jockeys in the United States, mostly immigrants, gave airtime to barrio groups defending the rights of Mexicans.

The first major Mexican radio personality in Los Angeles, Pedro González, provided immigrants with an important media mouthpiece. Relegated to the graveyard schedule (4 to 6 a.m.), his show caught on nonetheless. "Los Madrugadores" ("those up at dawn") featured not only music but also reports on local activities. That news proved crucial in the depths of the Depression, as Los Angeles authorities began pressuring thousands of people to return to Mexico.

When González noted, on air, that these roundups were forcing some US citizens to leave the country, local authorities attempted to revoke his broadcast license. Arrested on a rape charge, he served six years of a fifty-year sentence at San Quentin. The radio personality was released early after he conducted a hunger strike and due to a concerted campaign mounted by his wife. It was supported by *mutualista* and related organizations, along with the Mexican Consulate and two Mexican presidents. The plaintiff later recanted, saying that she had been promised she would be spared punishment for a crime if she would press charges, but neither this revelation nor the presidential appeals resulted in a retrial. In 1940 González was deported to Tijuana, where he become an important radio personality, with his programs reaching north across the border. Eventually González was able to return to California, and in his later years he was the subject of a PBS documentary.

Or take the pioneering radio professional and Mexican immigrant María L. de Hernández of San Antonio, who began broadcasting in 1932. Hernández promoted barrio activities, notably the 1934 meeting of the organization she cofounded, the School Defense League (Liga Pro-Defensa Escolar). The event, demanding educational equality, drew ten thousand people, "Perhaps the largest rally ever held by Mexican Americans in San Antonio," according to *The Handbook of Texas*. The group was short-lived, however, and even as radio programs spread word of organizational activities, these same media outlets contributed to the demise of traditional *mutualista* activity by offering a free, modern source of entertainment and virtual companionship. Not until the new millennium would Mexican immigrant radio hosts and Mexican immigrant organizations systematically combine—with resulting demonstrations that, for the first time, gained the attention of the major national media.[29]

Today's Spanish-language radio hosts, mostly from Mexico, not only serve as effective local mouthpieces but also as powerful national megaphones. Take Piolín's program, the number one morning show in Los Angeles and the number one morning drive-time show of any kind in the entire United States. *Piolín por la Mañana*, moreover, belongs to the Univisión network, which sometimes beats the major networks in the national ratings. But while in the same league as ABC, NBC, and CNN, Univisión also has strong links to immigrant organizations still virtually unknown to the mainstream media, as when four Univisión radio stations served as official sponsors of festivities organized by an HTA alliance, the Federación Jalisco del Norte de California.

And just as her grandfather pioneered Spanish-language press coverage at the national level, so Mónica Lozano has pioneered such coverage at the global level. *La Opinión* is an important player on the World Wide Web via the consortium ImpreMedia, which calls itself "the No. 1 Hispanic News and Information Company in the US in Online and Print." ImpreMedia and Univisión also have been powerful instruments for the voter-registration project that *La Opinión* had helped launched: Ya Es Ahora (Now Is the Time). This voter initiative has also been promoted by Eddie "Piolín" Sotelo, working with *La Opinión*, the National Association of Latino Elected Officials, and National Council of La Raza (NCLR). Again demonstrating his flair for the dramatic, the media star chose the giant NCLR convention as the venue for announcing, "My community has inspired me to take action and become a US citizen. My hope is to inspire others to do the same."[30]

Meanwhile, as Chief Executive Officer of ImpreMedia, Mónica Lozano is a major national player, named by President Barack Obama to his Outside Economic Advisory Board. All of this far outstrips the dreams of any Mexican woman a century ago, or even the most ambitious and successful male Mexican ethnic journalists and organizers of yore, notably her grandfather.[31] And obviously no organization of the *mutualista* era, not even the Alianza Hispano Americana—with its nationwide magazine *Alianza* and with members that included important media figures such as Ignacio Lozano—could have envisioned anything like the media reach of today's organizations.

Even the networks of humble immigrant HTAs have a surprisingly extensive media presence. The articles about HTAs published in *La Opinión* automatically are lodged in its major website, impremedia.com, while the HTA networks maintain their own sophisticated websites. This would doubtless surprise most media observers; after all, many if not most of the members toil in the shadows at low-wage jobs and speak limited English. Moreover, typically each federation limits itself to people hailing from one specific region, such as Zacatecas. Nonetheless, the Zacatecan association's website includes a number of sophisticated features, all of them in Spanish. For instance, the page called "Get Ahead! Zacatecas Community Plaza" has information on adult education programs; government forms in PDF files; an evaluation of the Mexican leadership in the California American Federation of Labor-Congress of Industrial Organizations (AFL-CIO), and trans-border press coverage, such as from Mexico City's *La Jornada*. Events publicized on the site range from the agreement signed by the Federation with Western Union to promote projects in Zacatecas to the celebration marking the thirtieth anniversary of the Federation's founding. This is but one of many Zacatecan immigrant websites featured on the website of the Federation of Zacatecan organizations, Consejo de Federaciones Mexicanas en Norteamérica (COFEM). And COFEM is part of an even bigger website, a "network of Mexican migrant leaders and organizations," the Red Mexicana de Líderes y Organizaciones Migrantes, with HTAs from every region of Mexico, from Baja, California to the Yucatan, and now located across the United States.[32]

Websites are also of critical importance to the farm labor organizations founded by Mexican-heritage leaders. This online presence can answer that of corporate agribusiness, especially given that both the United Farm Workers and Farm Labor Organizing Committee (FLOC) are linked to the website of the mighty AFL-CIO. For its part, the Southwest Industrial Areas Foundation, with its many barrio community organizations, also has numerous, informative webpages and links. However, the lead organizer Ernie Cortés, still prefers the telephone, perhaps in recognition of most barrio residents' relatively limited access to the Internet. It is also the case that websites can disappear as quickly as they appear, as happened with the site launched by the Villa Guerrero HTA.[33]

Permanent and sophisticated beyond belief, however, is the website of NCLR, reflecting its status as the leading Hispanic organization and civil rights organization in the United States—lesser-known than the National Association for the Advancement of Colored People, but representing the nation's largest, fastest-growing minority group and largest immigrant group. At a recent NCLR convention, President Emeritus Raúl Yzaguirre outlined the overall media situation with regard to Latinos.

Yzaguirre began with a gloomy assessment of the present landscape, saying, "We just don't have any other population of that significance that is so unknown, so invisible . . . in our media, in our decision-making process. We are truly an invisible minority in this country." He cited a poll showing that "Latinos are perceived more negatively than any other group in this country and . . . for reasons that are totally opposite to reality. . . ." At the same time, he cited as a hopeful sign the campaign bastadobbs.com, which demanded that CNN fire anti-immigration host Lou Dobbs, with the website claiming a large role in Dobbs leaving the network. "We're on our way," Yzaguirre concluded, "and as an old community organizer by trade I'm used to starting with small groups and building and building and building to larger and larger audiences, so this is where we are today, but we're going to be in a much better place in the future."[34]

Indeed, it would seem that ethnic Mexicans, and Latinos in general, are poised to take their place on the main media stage. But even as barrio-based organizations experience media exposure beyond the wildest dreams of *mutualista* leaders, a new, problematic factor has arisen: increasing control of the Spanish-language media by powerful financial interests. Take *La Opinión:* although the Lozanos still run the newspaper, fifty percent of the publication is now owned by the Tribune Corporation. As for *La Opinión*'s parent company, Impremedia, its website reports that "ImpreMedia is backed by a private investment group led by Clarity Partners, Halyard Capital, ACON Investments, and the Lozano family. . . . Clarity Partners is a private equity firm based in Los Angeles, managing over US$1 billion . . . . Halyard is a private equity firm based in New York, with over $600 million of capital. . . . ACON Investments is a diversified private equity firm based in Washington, DC, with more than $400 million of capital. . . ." Meanwhile, in June 2006 the Board of Directors of Univisión announced that the company had been acquired by "a consortium of investors, headed by Texas Pacific Group, Inc. and Thomas H. Lee Partners."[35]

Almost no journalists have looked at the ways the priorities of such investors square with those of grassroots barrio organizations. In the case of FLOC, at least, there would seem to be a clear conflict between its activities and the interests of the media outlets covering those same activities, given that FLOC is currently protesting policies of the major investment firm JPMorgan Chase. One of the few organizations addressing this issue as it affects the Latino community is the National Hispanic Media Coalition (NHMC). NHMC has lobbied the Federal Communications Commission for policies to encourage, in the Coalition's words, "More diversity, competition and localism in broadcast media." In so doing, the NHMC has partnered with religious, civil rights, and media reform groups, and in July 2010 the NHMC was "pleased [to announce that] the FCC has begun a comprehensive review of its media ownership rules."[36]

Of course the Internet offers a powerful alternative media outlet for such entities as FLOC, but the Web, for its part, may be headed in a direction that favors privileged access for corporations. A few Latinos have joined those countering with a call for "net neutrality." Such liaisons are embryonic. On the other hand, just as barrio organizers a century ago publicized their activities in a variety of ways, so today some leaders also think creatively. Citing the example of FLOC organizing director Leticia Zavala, journalist Roberto Lovato noted, "Grassroots leaders like Zavala mix, scratch and dub different media (think [social media] and text messaging, radio and TV, butcher paper and bullhorns) while navigating the cultural, political and historical currents that yoke and inspire the diverse elements making up this young, decentralized, digital-age *movimiento*."[37]

"That Reciprocity that Makes Us Human"

Mutual aid organizing by US Mexicans can seem so peripheral as to be invisible: day laborers wiring money to their hometowns, or a faded *mutualista* sign on a dilapidated building. Yet, as we have seen, barrio mutual aid activity has a long if overlooked history that continues to reverberate in cutting-edge ways. Moreover, this influence even extends to the elite world of corporate philanthropy. Some of the biggest players, such as the Global Business Network's Monitor Institute, argue that the *mutualista* model is essential for the future of philanthropy itself.

The Global Business Network/Monitor Institute publication *Looking Out for the Future: An Orientation for Twenty-first Century Philanthropists* features the article "Mutualismo Not Filantropía." Employing the "futures scenario" tool currently all the rage among policy professionals, the report argues that community philanthropy, in particular, should consider the *mutualista* approach. This particular "futures scenario" posits the historic *mutualista* model as applied to the community foundation of Cedar Rapids, Iowa. "After becoming the first community foundation in a predominantly white area to adopt the Mexican *mutualista* (mutual aid) model," they write, "the Greater Cedar Rapids Community Foundation (GCRCF) announced in 2024 that it had more than doubled its endowment, and that its education and neighborhood safety programs had helped lower high-school dropout rates and decrease juvenile crime by more than 50 percent."[1]

According to this scenario from the Monitor Institute, the so-called Greater Cedar Rapids Community Foundation decided to implement the *mutualista* after having seen the success in El Paso of philanthropies that had tapped their own local *mutualista* tradition. "Renaming itself the El Paso Mutual Aid Society in the '00s, it joined with others across the US in experimenting with endowed community hubs that solicit money from residents of all income levels and play an active broker role for their constituencies." The futures scenario included an initiative "to coordinate remittance giving back to home communities in Mexico," recognizing what immigration scholars call "philanthropy from below." In general, the Cedar Rapids plan looked to the way that "El Paso began using its assets"—that is, longstanding mutual aid that could be harnessed "to operate credit services, to provide sickness and death benefits, to represent and advocate for local residents . . . and to offer social and educational programs to community members."

For the benefit of its audience of philanthropy professionals, the Monitor Institute explains that "The El Paso *mutualista* itself was adapted from earlier Mexican traditions of *sociedades mutualistas* and the mutual aid societies that helped Mexican-American immigrants adjust to the US in the late nineteenth century." The scenario builds to an impressive conclusion, citing the 2024 executive director of the Greater Cedar Rapids Community Foundation, one Simone Johnson, on the effectiveness of the *mutualista* model, having her report that "In Texas, contributions from everyone, even very poor residents, helped create new bonds and an unbelievable spirit of fraternity in the community. But it isn't just Latinos that want stronger connections between donors and the recipients of their giving. It took us awhile to work through the growing pains, but just like in El Paso and Corpus Christi, folks here in Cedar Rapids didn't want some cold institution that just collected money from rich people and gave it at a distance to poor ones. They wanted a place that would bring people together to share and help each other—to build a real community that looks out for its own."

The scenario also cites a supposed 2024 philanthropy expert at Indiana University to the effect that "some people didn't think that a model that emerged in Latino communities would translate so well to a predominantly white area like Cedar Rapids, but there is no denying the results. *Mutualistas* are simply more fluid and dynamic than previous models for community philanthropy, and they are much more connected to all parts of the community."[2]

When presented with this scenario, a pioneer with regard to US Mexicans and philanthropy, Herman Gallegos, responded that in fact the actual community fund operating in El Paso works quite well—"does important work." Gallegos explained that the El Paso community foundation began with about ten families donating about ten thousand dollars each, and now, "for a miniscule amount of money," the foundation provides professional accounting expertise for local donors, issuing checks on their behalf to whatever community group the grantee has designated. He said that in general, however, philanthropic support is lacking for this type of community chest, particularly when compared to the major, sustained help given to the United Way and other such prominent community foundations.[3]

Gallegos cites the problem of boards run by members of the founding elite in a community. He has worked for decades to change that, as when he was invited onto the board of the San Francisco Community Foundation, recalling that he convinced the directors to add an Asian member. Today the board has a majority of women and minority trustees. His actions are hardly surprising, given his long experience in civil rights and community organizing and, in particular, as a cofounder of Hispanics in Philanthropy (HIP) in 1983. HIP was established, in its words, "To promote stronger partnerships between organized philanthropies and the latino community."[4]

A few years later, the Foundation Center—the main clearinghouse for the field—published a HIP study coauthored by Gallegos. In tracing the history of donations among Hispanics in the United States, the study notes that "the goal of self-help continues today in ways similar to the first mutual aid associations founded by Mexican-Americans."[5] And, indeed, *mutualista* groups reached out to the community from the outset, as in the 1870s with Sociedad Beneficiencia of San Antonio, which established such community services as a lending library. And from the mighty Alianza Hispano Americana to the little *mutualista* group in Creedmore, Texas, these associations engaged in philanthropic endeavors. As for HIP, "From its inception, HIP has been an organization rooted in the Latino tradition of giving," as their website puts it, noting that the organization "aimed at addressing the needs of Latino communities by creating a network of philanthropists representative of and sensitive to those needs."[6]

HIP's sensitivity to community needs echoes Gallegos's own experiences as a community organizer for the Community Service Organization (CSO) in the 1950s. "What made the CSO important was the link to the poorest of the poor," says Gallegos. And as a study on philanthropy "in a changing America" notes, the CSO was "serving as more of a *mutualista* to southern California Latinos." Gallegos likened this to today's immigrant organizing in a depressed area of Colorado. Members of a Mexican hometown association in a Colorado barrio banded together to raise money for HIP matching funds, and he remarked with reference to this *mutualista* heritage that the founder of community organizing, "[Saul] Alinsky said there are some groups that will never die, that if they still even just have a name, they will not disappear."[7]

HIP is also a player among foundations, as when it was listed in 2011 as an advisor to the Monitor Institute, the publisher of that 2024 *mutualista* scenario. This reflects the fact that the Hispanic community is crucial, given the demographics. Forward-thinking people in the world of philanthropy recognize that the nation's largest minority group and largest immigrant group is also the youngest population group by far. Mainly for that reason, it is growing at a much faster rate than the US population at large (with immigration a secondary factor). This insight was reported by a foundation, the Pew Charitable Trust. Crunching the 2010 census numbers, the Pew Hispanic Center found that Texas experienced the nation's largest rise in population, with almost two-thirds of this due to Hispanics, and with most of this population, both native-born and immigrant, of Mexican background.[8]

Figure 26.
Antonia
Hernández,
executive director
of the California
Community
Foundation.
(Photo by Juan
Alaniz)

In philanthropy strategy, one reality that has received comparatively little attention, however, is Mexican women's philanthropic leadership. After all, historically, women ran much of the fundraising that undergirded the *mutualista* projects, from disaster relief to cultural and educational programs to legal aid and defense funds to the very concept of caring for the deceased that sparked *mutualismo* in the first place. Today, meanwhile, women are major players in philanthropy, as with Elisa Arévalo and Luz Vega-Marquis, the cofounders of HIP along with Herman Gallegos.

Then there is Antonia Hernández, executive director of the California Community Foundation. She was born in Mexico to parents who had been, in her words, "pushed" into Mexico during the Depression-era immigration sweeps, even though they themselves had been born and raised in the United States. According to Hernández, identifying the main potential donors in Los Angeles means recognizing that the largest cohort is Latino and that "vast numbers" of Angelenos are immigrants from Latin America, Asia, and elsewhere.

They already donate, she points out: "They get together and pool their money to help one another. . . . That's philanthropy—sharing beyond family for a common good, the sense of affinity—whether they give to a church or a mutual." She says she speaks from the heart as she tells them, "You're very giving. You send to your relatives in the home country; you help relatives here who are having a hard time. You know, you're very giving. All I'm asking you is to extend that affinity you know to an affinity for L.A." Building on their familiarity with mutual aid, she applies that concept to more formal civic involvement. "I tell them, 'In America there are two R's: there's your rights and there's your responsibilities, and that the more that you take your responsibilities seriously, the more your rights will materialize. And the more you engage in community the more vibrant a community will be.'" And, she says, "Once you explain it to them, they get it. So for me, civic engagement is: how do you talk to an individual to connect the dots to make them see their connection to the city they live in?"[9]

This giving has a built-in transnational aspect, of course. No wonder the Monitor Institute *mutualista* "futures" scenario factored in the role of immigrant remittances to Mexico. "Trans-local civic engagement," some scholars call it. This recognition dates back to the 1920s, when a US foundation, the Social Science Research Council, commissioned Mexican anthropologist Manuel Gamio to head a study of Mexican immigration in which Gamio used remittance statistics, which he found more reliable than US Census figures. The report resulted in his landmark book *Mexican Immigration to the United States,* which included a list of "Some Mexican Societies in the United States." They ranged from forty-four in California to "more than twenty societies in Michigan," in a Mexican population of little more than six thousand individuals.[10]

The Gamio study doubtless is well-known to the HIP cofounders; in fact, one of them, Elisa Arévalo, has been the longtime vice-president and Latino remittance acquisition marketing manager at Wells Fargo Bank. "HIP works with international partners to address issues of immigration, remittance, and the role of philanthropy," according to a Monitor Institute report that concludes that HIP "is on the right track."[11] Herman Gallegos also has important business links, sitting on several corporate boards, where he tries to bring the voice of the barrio to corporate decisions; he cites the example of having influenced Verizon to improve its service to barrio customers.

Another member of that Verizon board was someone from Mexico, which on the face of it would seem to be a move in the direction of diversity and responsiveness. This man, however, is in fact the wealthiest person in the world, Carlos Slim Helú. His vast holdings include over eighty percent of the Mexican telephone system. This makes him a symbol of the concentration of wealth that has accompanied much of the transnational economic development. And while supporters of this trend claim that the middle class has grown, in fact there is little evidence that the gap between the rich and the poor in Mexico has diminished appreciably in recent decades, while under the Slim telephone monopoly, Mexicans have been trailing other Latin Americans in cellphone use.

Moreover, the economic change experienced by Mexico has contributed to dislocations, particularly in the rural sector, and thus to the rise in the number of people leaving Mexico out of economic necessity. If Carlos Slim is the symbol of transnational wealth born of wealth concentration, the Zapatista revolt against the 1994 North American Free Trade Agreement has been recognized as "The first announcement to the world that grassroots people are creating new self-healing civic groups in response to corporate globalization," as veteran activist Grace Lee Boggs put it. She noted that now "there may be as many as half a million of these groups, most of them small and barely visible in every country around the world. These self-healing civic groups and communities connect mainly through networks. So Solidarity is beginning to mean the linking or networking of these communities in North and South America and around the world."[12]

Community organizer María Varela outlined these global factors as she has seen them play out in northern New Mexico, writing in 2000 that "in this process of organizing to survive, my vecinos and I are joining together with other communities, other cultures in other ecosystems" in a sustainable environmentalism that "values and takes great stock in the observations and experiences of rural people who live on and watch the land," in the process wedding this ethos to "the best of modern technology."

She contrasted this effort at grassroots mutual aid with "ecosystems taken care of by weekend or summer stewards—ivory tower researchers, corporate conservation warriors, and urban-based policy makers" where "gated and fenced 'public' wilderness areas and baronial land holdings will benefit the few. Ancient sciences will become extinct. Human, plant and animal health will decline because their ability to regenerate each other will have been destroyed." Varela laid out the stakes: "Rural communities are more than pretty backdrops to sell jeeps, butter or laundry soap. Rural communities contain important cultural wellsprings, which recharge the cultural diversity of this nation. Rural communities are critical buffers to watersheds, wildlife and human habitats, sacred places and scenic treasures. Many rural human habitats contain generations of people with longterm experience in living on and watching the land."

But if the stakes are high, "The result is awesome to envision: the regeneration of rural America, which will draw forward the future of this nation from ancient well springs of our cultural heritages."[13]

To this high-stakes debate, Ernesto Cortés brings a more positive—what he might call a more pragmatic—approach: that there are no permanent enemies, only permanent issues. In this vein, Herman Gallegos, who sits on corporate boards, is of course a former community organizer. He also helped found the precursor to National Council of La Raza (NCLR) in part with seed money from organized labor. NCLR, for its part, has a corporate advisory board and many business sponsors (more than two hundred thousand dollars apiece from twenty-two separate corporations in one recent year), but NCLR's silence on labor issues was broken in February 2013 when the civil rights group supported a boycott of the Hyatt corporation organized by the union UNITE HERE on behalf of its striking hotel workers.

Meanwhile, although the Southwest Industrial Areas Foundation (IAF) member organizations occasionally partner with businesses, they work more closely with labor, and Ernie Cortés has long cited trade unions as Southwest IAF's among the crucial "community-based institutions," as he wrote decades ago. He explained that "if we are interested in restoring broadly shared prosperity to the United States, we must take action to reverse the deterioration . . . of those community-based institutions (i.e., labor unions, schools, churches, and other voluntary associations) that were the foundation of civic culture and historically have buffered working families from the worst effects of a changing economy."

When presented with the *mutualista* futures scenario posited for Cedar Rapids by the Monitor Institute, Cortés responded somewhat mordantly that the authors might want to look at the community organizing actually taking place in Cedar Rapids. The IAF has established A Mid-Iowa Organizing Strategy (AMOS)—"Creating a Community Where All Can Succeed!"—whose organizing meetings draw such top officials as Senator Charles Grassley. As for the Monitor Institute, it would seem that its corporate affiliation sometimes affects its analysis, as when one of its reports noted the great funding opportunities offered by the exponential increase in the number of billionaires in recent years, with the whole issue of growing income inequality left unaddressed. This, even as the increased concentration of wealth has been linked to the exponential growth of corporate influence on the political process, according to a number of analysts who, in turn, spotlight community organizing as one of the few civic counterweights to this trend.[14]

Or, as Ernie Cortés has long said, "There are only two ways to build power . . . organized money or organized people." In the wake of the 2010 Supreme Court decision *Citizens United,* allowing virtually unlimited corporate political contributions, the question of organized people versus organized money would seem more urgent than ever. Just a few months after the decision, in the congressional off-year elections, spending reached four times the previous levels. It would seem that organized money is winning out, regardless of political party, with corporations able to obtain ever-more favorable policies, from tax breaks to outsourcing, in the process becoming even more profitable and, thus, more politically powerful.

On the other hand, organized people have more numbers. They also have more time, as César Chávez explained to a young Baldemar Velásquez. He recalled the famed farmworker organizer saying, "Look, Baldemar: we've got nothing, and the opposition's got power and money. . . . So the competition is between time and money—our time and their money—and there's a lot more time than there is money, and money's going to run out before time, so as long as we are not going to give up, we're going to win."[15] Plus, two can play the transnational game, from the labor organizing in Mexico by Baldemar Velásquez's Farm Labor Organizing Committee (FLOC) to the hundreds of US-based immigrant groups linked to their Mexican hometowns, and with grassroots transnational activism dating from the earliest days of the *mutualistas*.[16]

But what of the fact that Ernie Cortés, Baldemar Velásquez, and María Varela all received "genius" grants from an entity funded with corporate profits, the MacArthur Foundation? Some foundations even directly support community organizing, and there is a debate among grassroots activists as to whether these initiatives work to curb corporate power or tend to co-opt grassroots activism. In any event, community organizers continue to emphasize "hard money" via member financial contributions, with foundation grants being at most a supplemental funding source.

Could Southwest IAF, FLOC, NCLR, and other such organizations forge a campaign finance-reform coalition? If so, this coalition would represent a giant, young, fast-growing demographic, one of political importance, in that it is located mostly in crucial "swing" states. Could such a coalition in turn coalesce with established, well-known, highly professional campaign finance reform organizations such as Common Cause and Public Citizen?

The odds are against such a broad, heterogeneous coalition. The same corporations that are working mightily to preserve their advantage in campaign spending also are able to curry Latinos by loudly trumpeting their sympathetic immigration stance in the corporate-dominated media, including the Spanish-language media. Besides, overturning *Citizens United* would require a constitutional amendment, and most such efforts have failed over the course of US history. On the other hand, the vast majority of Americans seem to be arriving at a consensus, however fragile, in favor of comprehensive immigration reform, even as a whopping eighty percent of those polled indicated opposition to the *Citizens United* decision.

In his organizing efforts, Ernesto Cortés has learned not to demonize corporate players but, rather, to treat them as equals. This approach reflects hardheaded realism, but even more, it stems from Cortés's deeply rooted

Figure 27. Fred Ross Jr., second from right, taking notes at the 2008 Community Service Organization reunion. (Courtesy CSO Project UC San Diego)

belief that we all are called to love one another. "The enduring principle that often gets overlooked—that power of love," as labor organizer Fred Ross Jr. called it at a CSO-IAF reunion. He noted that his father "was operating—as were you—out of love for one another."[17]

Ernie Cortés put it this way in a PBS television interview: "Love implies relationship. It requires reciprocity. If you're not reciprocal, if you're not mutual, then you're nothing, which means you lose a dimension of your humanity." Evoking the venerable principle of mutual aid, he asks: "How do we begin to reconnect with other human beings and create that solidarity, that mutuality, that reciprocity that makes us human?" At a time when the very notion of *E Pluribus Unum* is under threat from powerful economic interests, the question of reciprocity, of mutuality, constitutes a challenge but also a hope—the hope of democratic renewal.[18]

Notes

Acknowledgements

1. Bill Moyers, *Moyers on America: A Journalist and His Times*, ed. Julie Leininger Pycior (New York: The New Press, 2004).

Introduction

1. Jonathan Fox, "Reframing Mexican Migration as a Multi-ethnic Process," *Latino Studies* 4, no. 1–2 (2006), 39–61.

2. Juan Carlos Romero Hicks, "Comisión Estatal de Apoyo Integral a Los Migrantes y Sus Familias," http://www.guanajuato.gob.mx/gestiones/romerohicks/cuarto/social/sdsh2.pdf, 23–26; Tereso Ortiz Alvarado, "Historia," http://www.redesmexico.mx/index.php?option=com_con tent&view=article&id=991:Dallas%20/%20Dallas%20-%20M%C3%A9xico%20Casa%20Guanajuato.%20&catid=97:estados-unidos&Itemid=125 (accessed 8/19/13); Gustavo Cano and Alexandra Délano, "The Institute of Mexicans Abroad: The Day After . . . After 156 Years," American Political Science Association, September 2–5, 2004, 31; "Mexico: Migrants, Remittances, 3XI," *Migration News*, October 2009, http://migration.ucdavis.edu/mn/more.php?id=3548_0_2_0; Geo-Mexico, "Mexican Home Town Associations (HTAs) and Their Considerable Effectiveness," http://geo-mexico.com/?p=5589 (accessed 1/7/13); Federación Jaliscence, "Patrocinador," http://fedjalisco.org/category/patrocinadores/ (accessed 8/19/13); Jonathan Fox and Xóchitl Bada, "Migrant Civic Engagement"; Mexico Institute, Woodrow Wilson International Center for Scholars, "2006 Presidential Election Votes by State and Party," http://www.wilsoncenter.org/news/docs/MexicoGovernmentStats1.pdf; Kay Briegal, "Alianza Hispano-Americana," PhD diss., University of Southern California, 1974, 94–99; *Alianza*, October 1932, 20.

3. The uneven pattern of this segregation serves as a reminder that the practice was not ubiquitous throughout the entire Southwest, in contrast to the situation for African Americans in the Deep South. Thus, David Montejano found that Mexicans in Texas counties with cash-crop economies experienced wholesale segregation, while those in ranching counties largely did not. David Montejano, *Anglos and Mexicans in the Making of Texas, 1836–1986* (Austin: University of Texas Press, 1987); Briegal, "Alianza Hispano Americana," chapter 1; Julie Leininger Pycior, "Sociedades Mutualistas," *Handbook of Texas Online*, http://www.tshaonline.org/handbook/online/articles/ves01 (accessed 2/18/2013).

4. Raúl Yzaguirre, "Comments of Raúl Yzaguirre," *EEOC History: 35th Anniversary*, http://www.eeoc.gov/eeoc/history/35th/voices/yzaguirre-text.html (accessed 1/25/11).

5. For an eloquent immigrant rights statement given to an AFL-CIO convention, see FLOC President Baldemar Velásquez at http://www.youtube.com/watch?v=z_IbmChlmdw (accessed 2/24/13). Steven Greenhouse, "North Carolina Growers' Group Signs Union Contract for Mexican Workers," *The New York Times*, September 17, 2004; Baldemar Velásquez, speech to Labor Notes conference, August 15, 2008; http://www.youtube.com/watch?v=ZRm1HFPgBto&feature =related (accessed 2/21/11); Farm Labor Organizing Committee, "Justice for Santiago Rafael Cruz," http://www.aflcio.org/content/download/6872/74284/file/2009res_64.pdf (accessed 8/24/13); Pycior, "Sociedades Mutualistas."

6. Chuck Collins and Felice Yeskel, *Economic Apartheid in America: A Primer on Economic Inequality and Insecurity* (New York: The New Press, 2011), 84.

7. Author interview with Soledad "Chole" Alatorre, May 3, 2010, Pacoima, CA; Soledad Alatorre to author, telephone conversation, May 1, 2010; Industrial Areas Foundation, "Locate IAF Facilities," http://www.industrialareasfoundation.org/affiliate-members (accessed 8/24/13); author notes on Worker Mass and May Day commemoration, May 1, 2010, Pacoima, CA; author interview with Ernesto Cortés Jr., May 19, 2010, New York City; Harry C. Boyte, "Seeds of a Different Politics," *The Good Society* 19, no. 1 (2010), 70–73; Hezekiah Walker, "I Need You to Survive," http://www.youtube.com/watch?v=LUUHPDUsLJo (accessed 3/2/11); OneLA-IAF, "Agenda: OneLA Assembly" and "OneLA-IAF Foreclosure Prevention Plan," n.d., Los Angeles; author audio recording, OneLA-IAF assembly, May 2, 2010, Los Angeles.

8. "NCLR President and CEO," http://www.nclr.org/index.php/about_us/leadership/ (accessed 2/24/13).

9. The classic account of the GI generation of Mexican Americans is Mario García, *Mexican Americans: Leadership, Ideology, and Identity, 1930–1960* (New Haven: Yale University Press, 1989). Yzaguirre interview.

10. María Varela received the MacArthur "genius" award and was one of one thousand women collectively nominated for the Nobel Peace Prize. She also is a veteran of Student Nonviolent Coordinating Committee organizing in Mississippi, and before that, she was a national leader of the Catholic social justice group Young Christian Students and a founder, in 1962, of Students for a Democratic Society. Alatorre interview; García, *Mexican Americans*, Part Two, "Labor and the Left"; María Varela, interview with author, April 22, 2010, Providence, RI; María Varela, telephone interview with author, May 2, 2010; Jim Christensen, "Heroes and Heroines: María Varela, an Authentic 'Milagro,'" *Mother Jones*, January 1989, 27–28; María Ochoa, "Cooperative Re/weavings: Artistic Expression and Economic Development in a Northern New Mexican Village," *Mexican American Women: Changing Images/Perspectives in Mexican American Studies*, 5, (1995), 122, 144, n. 1; Sociedad Protección Mútua de Trabajadores Unidos, http://www.spmdtu.org/ (accessed 8/19/13); "María Varela," *Peace Women around the Globe*, http://www.1000peacewomen.org/eng/friedensfrauen_biographien_gefunden.php?WomenID=883 (accessed 2/18/13); Leslie G. Kelen, *This Little Light of Ours: Activist Photographers of the Civil Rights Movement* (Oxford, MS: University of Mississippi Press, 2012), 10; Julie Leininger Pycior, "Important but Neglected: Midwest Latino/a Biography and Memoir," Julian Samora Research Institute, Michigan State University, http://jsri.msu.edu/upload/events/20thAnniversary/Pycior.pdf (accessed 8/24/13).

11. One of the few national radio programs about Latino activities, *Latino USA*—evidently the only such national program on public broadcasting—is relegated to the off hours in New York City, for instance, despite the metropolitan area's importance as both a media center and a Latino population center. WNYC, "Latino USA," http://www.wnyc.org/shows/latino-usa/about/ (accessed 2/25/13); "Hispanics in the News: An Event-driven Narrative," Pew Research Hispanic Center, http://www.pewhispanic.org/2009/12/07/hispanics-in-the-news-an-event-driven-narrative/ (accessed 2/25/13).

12. Antonia Hernández, telephone interview with author, March 10, 2010; Federico A. Subervi-Vélez, Marc Brindel, Juandalynn Taylor, and Renée Espinoza, "Spanish-language Daily Newspapers and Presidential Elections," in *The Mass Media and Latino Politics*, ed. Federico Subervi-Velez (New York: Routledge, 2008), 86; Xóchitl Bada, Jonathan Fox, Robert Donnelly, and Andrew Selee, *Context Matters: Latino Immigrant Civic Engagement in Nine U.S. Cities* (Washington: Reports on Latino Immigrant Civic Engagement, Woodrow Wilson International Center for Scholars, 2010); Marisela Chávez, "Mónica Lozano," in *Latinas in the United States: A Historical Encyclopedia*, eds. Vicki Ruiz and Virginia Sánchez Korrol (Bloomington: Indiana University Press, 2006), 412–413; Juan García, *Mexicans in the Midwest, 1900–1932* (Tucson: University of Arizona, 1996), 131–149, 156, 163, 174, 185.

13. Hernández interview; James E. García, "Spanish-language Radio," in *Encyclopedia of Latino Popular Culture*, eds. Cordelia Candelaria, Peter J. García, and Arturo J. Aldama (Westport, CT: Greenwood Publishing, 2004), 788–791; Ed Morales, "The Media is the *Mensaje*." *The Nation*, May 15, 2006, http://www.edmorales.net/articles/mediaismessage.html (accessed 1/7/11); Adrian Félix, Carmen González, and Ricardo Ramírez, "Political Protest, Ethnic Media and Latino Naturalization." *American Behavioral Scientist* 52, no. 618 (2008), http://www.

rebelion.org/noticias/2006/4/30005.pdf (accessed 1/7/11); Jesús Rangel, "Story of a Mexican Immigrant 'Hero,'" *The New York Times*, January 7, 1985, http://query.nytimes.com/gst/fullpage. html?res=9A0DE1D81F38F934A35752C0A963948260 (accessed 1/9/11); "Univision Beats All the English-language Broadcast Nets in Monday Ratings," *TV Week*, http://www.tvweek.com/ blogs/tvbizwire/2010/12/univision-beats-all-the-englis.php (accessed 1/10/11); Brian Seltzer, "TV Viewing Continues to Edge Up," *The New York Times*, January 2, 2010, http://www.nytimes. com/2011/01/03/business/media/03ratings.html?_r=1&scp=1&sq=univision+ratings+monday+ night&st=nyt (accessed 1/10/11); Federación de Clubes Zacatecanos del Sur de California, http:// www.federacionzacatecana.org/index.php?sectionName=home&subSection=news (accessed 1/10/11); Federación Jalisco del Norte de California, http://fedjalisco.org/category/patrocina- dores/ (accessed 8/19/13); COFEM: Consejo de Federaciones Mexicanas de Norteamérica, http:// www.cofem.org/home.html (accessed 1/10/11); Club Barrio del Gpe. Mezquitillo, San Francisco del Rincón, Gto., http://francorrinconenses.blogspot.com/ (accessed 1/11/11); "Impremedia Part- ners with LAT Careers," http://www.reuters.com/article/2010/08/17/idUS137441+17- Aug-2010+BW20100817 (accessed 8/24/13); "Univisión Ya Encontró Comprador," http://www .univision.com/content/content.jhtml?cid=900813 (accessed 1/12/11).

14. National Hispanic Media Coalition, "NHMC Advocates for More Diversity, Competition and Localism in Broadcast Media," http://www.nhmc.org/content/media-ownership (accessed 1/12/11); Roberto Lovato, "Voices of a New Movimiento," http://www.thenation.com/article/ voices-new-movimiento (accessed 2/24/13); Centro de los Derechos del Migrante, Inc., http:// www.cdmigrante.org/ (accessed 8/19/13).

15. The company representing corporations in negotiations with unions is Deloitte, http:// www.deloittelegalce.com/en/content/comprehensive-legal-advisory-services-acquisition- manufacturing-company (accessed 2/24/13). Author interview with Herman Gallegos, February 2010, San Francisco; San Francisco Foundation, "Board of Trustees," http://www.sff.org/about/ who-we-are/board-of-trustees/?searchterm=gallegos (accessed 1/20/11); Hispanics in Philan- thropy, "Our Story," http://www.hiponline.org/about/our-story (accessed 8/19/13); Katherine Fulton and Andrew Blau, "Mutualismo Not Filantropolía" (Global Business Network/Monitor Institute, 2005), http://www.futureofphilanthropy.org/files/finalreport.pdf, 41–42 (accessed 1/16/11).

16. National Council of La Raza, *NCLR Annual Report, 2009*, May 18, 2010, http://www. nclr.org/index.php/publications/nclr_2009_annual_report/ (accessed 2/24/13); David Moberg, "Labor's Turnaround: The AFL-CIO Has a Plan to Turn around the Movement," *In These Times*, March 3, 2013, http://inthesetimes.com/article/14678/labors_creaky_turnaround/ (accessed 3/9/13).

17. *Religion and Ethics Newsweekly*, "An Interview with Ernesto Cortes," March 1, 2001, http:// www.pbs.org/wnet/religionandethics/episodes/march-2-2001/an-interview-with-ernesto-cor- tes/3456/ (accessed 1/3/13).

18. Julie Leininger Pycior, *LBJ and Mexican Americans: The Paradox of Power* (Austin: Univer- sity of Texas Press, 1997), introduction.

19. One early study on the *mutualista* topic is *Mutual Aid for Survival: The Case of the Mexican American* by José Amaro Hernández (Malabar, FL: Krieger, 1983). Stephen J. Pitti, *The Devil in the Silicon Valley: Northern California, Race, and Mexican Americans* (Princeton: Princeton University Press, 2003), especially 62, 97, 105–118, 125, 132–133, 155, 159–161.

20. Roberto R. Calderón, *Mexican Coal Mining Labor in Texas and Coahuila, 1880–1930* (Col- lege Station: Texas A&M University Press, 2000); Rodolfo Acuña, *Corridors of Migration* (Tucson: University of Arizona Press, 2007); Elliot Young, *Catarino Garza's Revolution on the Texas-Mexi- can Border* (Durham: Duke University Press, 2004).

21. Julie Leininger Pycior, "Important but Neglected: Midwest Latino Biography and Mem- oir," http://jsri.msu.edu/upload/events/20thAnniversary/Pycior.pdf (accessed 7/30/13); Bada, et al., *Context Matters: Latino Immigrant Civic Engagement in Nine U.S. Cities*; Immanuel Ness, *Immigrants, Unions, and the New U.S. Labor Market* (Pittsburgh: Temple University Press, 2005).

22. A useful source for mutual aid (including by *mutualistas*) as it operated on the ground in a particular city is *San Antonio on Parade*, by Judith Berg Sobré (College Station: Texas A&M Uni- versity Press, 2003). David T. Beito, *From Mutual Aid to the Welfare State* (Chapel Hill: University

of North Carolina Press, 2000); Theda Skocpol, *Diminished Democracy: From Membership to Management in American Civic Life* (Norman: University of Oklahoma Press, 2004).

23. Report, 2012, of anonymous scholarly reviewer commissioned by Texas A&M Press for this book manuscript.

Chapter 1

1. Author interview with Soledad "Chole" Alatorre, May 3, 2010, Pacoima, CA.

2. For his efforts, Benítez was honored with the Robert F. Kennedy Memorial Human Rights Award in 2003. Alan Zagier, "Laborers-Turned-Activists Win RFK Human Rights Award," *Boston Globe*, November 19, 2003; Katrina vanden Heuvel, "Modern Slavery," http://www.thenation.com/blog/modern-slavery (accessed 3/29/13); Alatorre interview.

3. Adrian D. Pantoja, Cecilia Menjívar, and Lisa Magaña, "The Spring Marches of 2006: Latinos, Immigration, and Political Mobilization in the 21st Century," *American Behavioral Scientist* 52, no. 499 (2008), http://abs.sagepub.com/cgi/reprint/52/4/499.

4. Alatorre interview.

5. Xóchitl Bada, Jonathan Fox, Robert Donnelly, and Andrew Selee, *Context Matters: Latnio Immigrant Civic Engagement in Nine US Cities* (Washington: Reports on Latino Immigrant Civic Engagement, Woodrow Wilson International Center, 2010), 58.

6. Alatorre interview.

7. Bada, et.al., *Context Matters: Latino Immigrant Civic Engagement in Nine US Cities*, 58; "Director of Immigrant Rights Organization Latino Movement USA," Democratic Underground, http://www.democraticunderground.com/discuss/duboard.php?az=show_mesg&forum=364&topic_id=1130201&mesg_id=1132461 (accessed 1/27/11); Alatorre interview; Mario T. García, *Memories of Chicano History: The Life and Narrative of Bert Corona* (Berkeley: University of California Press, 1994), 294; Hermandad Nacional Mexicana poster featuring Bert Corona, 2010, author's collection.

8. Instituto de los Mexicanos en el Exterior, *Directorio de Organizaciones y Clubes de Oriundos,* keyword "mutualista," http://www.ime.gob.mx/DirectorioOrganizaciones/busqueda.aspx; Briant Lindsey Lowell and Rodolfo O. de la Garza, "A New Phase in the Story of Remittances," in *Sending Money Home: Hispanic Remittances and Community Development* (Lanham, MD: Rowan and Littlefield, 2002), 15; Carol Zabin and Luis Escala, "From Civic Association to Political Participation: Mexican Hometown Associations and Mexican Immigrant Political Empowerment in Los Angeles," *Frontera Norte* 14, no. 27 (2002), 7–42, http://www.redalyc.org/pdf/136/13602701.pdf (accessed 8/19/13); Cecilia B. Imaz, "Las Organizaciones Sociales de Migrantes en Los Estados Unidos: El Caso del Club Social De Jala, Nayarit, en California y Su Gestión para La Co-existencia de Tradiciones Populares," in *Nuevas tendencias y desafíos de la migración internacional México-Estados Unidos*, ed. Raúl Delgado Wise (Mexico City: UNAM, 2004), 10–14; Gaspar Rivera-Salgado and Luis Escala Rabadán, "Collective Identity and Organizational Strategies of Indigenous and Mestizo Mexican Migrants," in *Indigenous Mexican Migrants in the United States*, eds. Jonathan Fox and Gaspar Rivera-Salgado (La Jolla: Center for US-Mexican Studies, University of California, San Diego, 2004), 163; Federación de Clubes Zacatecanos, "Historia de la Federación, http://www.federacionzacatecana.org/ (accessed 1/6/13); Jonathan Fox and Xóchitl Bada, "Migrant Civic Engagement," Research Paper Series on Latino Civic and Political Participation, no. 3, June 2009, Woodrow Wilson Center Mexico Insititute, www.wilsoncenter/migrant participation (accessed 5/30/10).

9. *La Prensa*, January 12, 1926, 5; Sociedad de la Unión, Libro de Actas, 1919–20, condolence cards sent to member relatives as a result of virtually every meeting. See, for example, "Asuntos Generales," Libro de Actas, 1922–27, 158, 199, Sociedad de la Unión Papers, Our Lady of the Lake University, San Antonio (hereafter OLLU); "Potosinos de Houston," "Negocios en México" blog, January 3, 2008, http://www.chron.com/spanish/la-voz/article/Potosinos-de-Houston-interesados-en-crear-1992784.php (accessed 8/24/13).

10. Sociedad de la Unión, "Constitución y reglamento interior," OLLU, 4; Sociedad de la Unión, "85avo. aniversario," OLLU, 3; Sociedad Benevolencia Mexicana, "Reglamento," 8–9, 24, 28–29; David T. Beito, "Thy Brother's Keeper," *Policy Review* (Fall 1994), http://www.unz.org/Pub/PolicyRev-1994q4-00055?View=PDF (accessed 8/19/13).

11. Alianza Hispano Americana, 5, 7, 8, 36, 42; *La Prensa*, November 25, 1925, 12; Benevolencia Mexicana, "Reglamento," Dolph Briscoe Center for American History, University of Texas (hereafter CAH), 9–15, 22–24, 27, 30; Sociedad de la Unión, constitution, OLLU, 1, 3–6, 8, 10, 12–14.

12. Author interviews with Lucas Garza, November 15, 23, and 25, 1976, San Antonio; *La Prensa*, August 20, 1924, 8; February 13, 1925; Section Two, 8; June 14, 1925, 8; Jules A. Appler, *General Directory and Householder Directory of Greater San Antonio, 1921–1922* (San Antonio: Tower Publications, 1923), 365, 517, 605, 669, 723; Sociedad de la Unión, "85avo aniversario," 5, OLLU; Briegal, 67–68; interview with John Solís, November 17, 1976, San Antonio; Manuel G. Gonzales, "Carlos I. Velasco and the Defense of Mexican Rights in Territorial Arizona," in *En Aquel Entonces*, eds. Manuel G. Gonzales and Cynthia M. Gonzales (Bloomington: Indiana University Press, 2000, 102; Judith Berg Sobré, *San Antonio on Parade*, (College Station: Texas A&M University Press, 2003), 96; José Amaro Hernández, *Mutual Aid for Survival: The Case of the Mexican American* (Malabar, FL: Robert Krieger Publishing Company, 1983), 65; Kay Briegal, "Alianza Hispano Americana," PhD diss., University of Southern California, 1979, 77.

13. Alatorre interview; Hernández, *Mutual Aid for Survival;* Luin Goldring, "The Mexican State and Transmigrant Organizations: Negotiating the Boundaries of Membership and Participation," *Latin American Research Review* 37, no. 3 (2002), 62, 71; COFEM, "Clubs/Organizations," http://www.cofem.org/clubs.html; Mario T. García, *Memories of Chicano History: The Life and Narrative of Bert Corona* (Berkeley: University of California Press, 1994), 294; Cecilia B. Imaz, "Las Organizaciones Sociales de Migrantes en Los Estados Unidos: El Caso del Club Social De Jala, Nayarit, en California y Su Gestión para La Co-existencia de Tradiciones Populares," in *Nuevas tendencias y desafíos de la migración internacional México-Estados Unidos*, ed. Raúl Delgado Wise (Mexico City: UNAM, 2004), 56–59; Louise LaMothe, "Oral History of Antonia Herández," January 20, 2006 (ABA Commission on Women in the Profession), http://www.c-spanvideo.org/program/294199-1 (accessed 8/24/13); KCET, "Local Hero: Antonia Hernández," http://www.kcet.org/socal/local_heroes/hhm/local-hero-antonia-hernandez.html (accessed 1/29/11); Esmeralda Bermudez, "A Muralist's Masterpiece Tells the Story of the Mexican People," *Los Angeles Times*, July 3, 2010, http://articles.latimes.com/2010/jul/03/local/la-me-muralist-20100703.

14. Bada et al., *Context Matters: Latino Immigrant Civic Engagement in Nine U.S. Cities*, 58; "Mexicans to Meet: New 'Liga Mutualista Mexicana' Plans Activities," La Prensa, January 8, 1917; Albert Camarillo, *Chicanos in a Changing Society: From Mexican Pueblos to American Barrios in Santa Barbara and Southern California, 1848–1930* (Cambridge: Harvard University Press, 1979), 147–155; Stephen J. Pitti, *The Devil in the Silicon Valley: Northern California, Race, and Mexican Americans* (Princeton: Princeton University Press, 2003), 106–111.

15. Susan D. Greenbaum, "A Comparison of African American and European-American Mutual Aid Societies in 19th Century America," *Journal of Ethnic Studies* 19, no. 3 (1991), 95–119; Lowell and de la Garza, "A New Phase in the Story of Remittances," 15; Carol Zabin and Louis Escala, "From Civic Association to Political Participation," *Frontera Norte*, no. 27, 2002, 7–42.

16. Armando Labra, interview by Sherry Linkon, Center for Working Class Studies, Youngstown State University, June 24, 2009, Youngstown, OH, http://www.google.com/url?sa=t&rct=j&q=&esrc=s&source=web&cd=1&ved=0CCoQFjAA&url=http%3A%2F%2Fsteelvalleyvoices.ysu.edu%2FMexican%2FLabra%2FInterview.doc&ei=Ns7dUdOvE5St4APa7oGYDg&usg=AFQjCNFpLW13WV9eI4pdomycyY2Am_5s4w&sig2=yoxzeCHofi1YhyERZf5POg&bvm=bv.48705608,d.dmg.

17. Ernie Brown, "Mexican Society Preserves Culture," *The Vindicator*, May 6, 2001; Garcia, *Memories of Chicano History*, 294–295.

18. José Amaro Hernández, *Mutual Aid for Survival: The Case of the Mexican American* (Malabar, FL: Robert Krieger Publishing Company, 1983), conclusion; Joe Franco, *Pueblo Chieftain*, October 12, 2009; "José G. Carrales," *Corpus Christi Caller-Times*, February 22, 2006; "María Galván," *Corpus Christi Caller-Times*, March 8, 2007; Zabin and Escala, "From Civic Association to Political Participation: Mexican Hometown Associations and Mexican Immigrant Political Empowerment in Los Angeles," 7–42; Dennis Valdés, *Al Norte* (Austin: University of Texas Press, 1991), 162.

19. Robert Courtney Smith, *Mexicans in New York City: Transnational Lives of New Immigrants* (Berkeley: University of California Press, 2006), 12.

20. *Mutualista* groups also sprang up in more far-flung Mexican communities, such as Saginaw, Michigan. Juan Ramón García, *Mexicans in the Midwest, 1900–1932* (Tucson: University of Arizona Press, 1996), 77, 149, 158–162, 167, 170–172, 183–189; Dionicio Nodín Valdés, *Barrios Norteños: St. Paul and Midwestern Mexican Communities in the Twentieth Century* (Austin: University of Texas Press, 2000), 41, 46, 75, 77, 80; Bada, Fox, Donnelly, and Selee, *Context Matters*, 18–22; De Paul University and FEDECMI-Casa Michoacán, "Presencia Michoacana en el Medio Oeste," De Paul University, June 4–5, 2010, jmorelia@hotmail.com posting on the "Historia Chicana" list-serv [historia-1 @mail.cas.unt.edu]; Betsy Guzmán, "The Hispanic Population: Census 2000 Brief" (US Census Bureau, 2001), Table 2, "Hispanic Population by Type for Regions, States and Puerto Rico," http://www.census.gov/prod/2001pubs/c2kbr01-3.pdf; "Hispanics and the 2008 Election: A Swing Vote?"

21. For the number and duration of El Paso *mutualista* groups, see the organizational listings, 1890–1930, in John F. Worley and Company, *El Paso City Directory*, El Paso: Press of John F. Worley; F. B. Payne, *City Directory of Laredo, Texas* (Laredo, TX: F. B. Payne and Company, 1912), 162–164; Ernest H. Miller, *Corpus Christi, Texas City Directory* (Asheville, North Carolina: The Miller Press, 1929), 539–540; Thomas H. Kreneck, *Pueblo: History of Houston's Mexican American Community* (Houston: Houston International University, 1989), 30, 45, 92; Arnoldo De León, *Ethnicity in the Sunbelt: Mexican Americans in Houston* (Houston: University of Houston Series in Mexican American Studies), no. 4, 38; Teresa Paloma Acosta and Ruthe Winegarten, *Las Tejanas: 300 Years of History* (Austin: University of Texas Press, 2003), 210; *Houston Press*, February 20, 2003; "La Sociedad Cuauhtemoc," *San Marcos Daily Record*, July 6, 2007; *Waco Tribune-Herald*, May 27, 2005 and August 30, 2008; Roberto Gutiérrez Turrubiartes, "Urgen más oportunidades para frenar la migración," *El Sol de San Luis*, August 5, 2007; David Gutiérrez, *Walls and Mirrors*, Berkeley: University of California Press, (1995), 27–29; anonymous, "Ignacio Seguin Zaragosa," *The Handbook of Texas*, http://www.tsha.utexas.edu/handbook/online/articles/ZZ/fza4.html; Sobré, *San Antonio on Parade*, 48; Josef Barton, "Czech and Mexican Immigration," in *European Immigrants in the West*, ed. Frederick Luebke (Albuquerque: University of New Mexico Press, 1998); Caja 37/exp.14/f.3, 1914, Fondo Departamento del Trabajo, Serie Conflictos, 1911–14, Archivo General de la Nación, Mexico City; Roberto R. Calderón, "Unión, Paz, y Trabajo: Laredo's Mexican Mutual Aid Societies, 1890s," in *Mexican Americans in Texas History*, eds. Emilio Zamora et al. (Austin: Texas State Historical Association, 2000), 68.

22. Sociedad de la Unión even had its own anthem, "Gran Marcha de La Sociedad de La Unión." Secretaría de Relationes a la Comisión de Bibliotecas, June 11, 1928, 1–3, Sociedad de la Unión Collection; journal of "La Unión" library, Sociedad de la Unión Collection, OLLU; Secretaría de Relaciones to Secretaría de Educación Pública de México, April 29, 1929, Jesús Gamboa papers, San Antonio; *La Prensa*, February 13, 1925, sec. 2, 8; Sociedad de La Unión, "Reseña Histórica," in the anniversary program, 1927, folder 1, box 27, Escobar Collection, Benson Latin American Collection, University of Texas.

Chapter 2

1. Rodolfo García Zamora, "Collective Remittances and the 3x1 Program as a Transnational Social Learning Process," http://www.docstoc.com/docs/39986452/Collective-Remittances-and-the-3x1-Program-as-a-Transnational (accessed 7/15/13).

2. Juan Carlos Romero Hicks, "Comisión Estatal de Apoyo Integral a Los Migrantes y Sus Familias," http://www.guanajuato.gob.mx/gestiones/romerohicks/cuarto/social/sdsh2.pdf (accessed 8/24/13), 23–26; Gustavo Cano and Alexandra Délano, "The Institute of Mexicans Abroad: The Day After . . . After 156 Years," American Political Science Association, September 2–5, 2004, 31; "Mexico: Migrants, Remittances, 3x1," Migration News, October 2009, http://migration.ucdavis .edu/mn/more.php?id=3548_0_2_0; Geo–Mexico, "Mexican Home Town Associations (HTAs) and Their Considerable Effectiveness," http://geo-mexico.com/?p=5589 (accessed 1/7/13); Federación Jaliscence, "Patrocinador," http://fedjalisco.org/patrocindores/ (accessed 8/19/13).

3. Xóchitl Bada, "The Binational Civic and Political Engagement of Mexican Migrant Hometown Associations and Federations in the United States," http://www.iai.spk-berlin.de/fileadmin/ dokumentenbibliothek/Iberoamericana/2007/Nr_25/25_Bada.pdf (accessed 8/24/13).

4. As one historian put it, although Díaz's "centralization and capitalism appeared to have triumphed, Mexico's common people had waged steady resistance . . . they adopted newer tactics, such as migration and the organization of mutualist societies." Mark Wasserman, *Everyday Life and Politics in Nineteenth Century Mexico: Men, Women, and War* (Albuquerque: University of New Mexico Press, 2000), 10; Génaro Padilla, *My History, Not Yours: The Formation of Mexican American Autobiography* (Madison: University of Wisconsin Press, 1993), 16–17; Gilbert M. Cuthbertson, "Catarino Erasmo Garza," *The Handbook of Texas*, http://www.tsha.utexas.edu/handbook/online/articles/GG/fga38.html; Elliot Young, *Catarino Garza's Revolution on the Texas-Mexican Border* (Durham, NC: Duke University Press, 2004), 40; Benjamin Heber Johnson, *Revolution in Texas: How a Forgotten Rebellion and Its Bloody Suppression Turned Mexicans into Americans* (New Haven: Yale University Press, 2003), 25–26, 39.

5. Young, *Catarino Garza's Revolution on the Texas-Mexican Border*, 295–300.

6. Garza's battle with combined Colombian and US forces took place in the Colombian state of Panama, and a few years later the United States would change sides, helping Panamanian rebels break away from Colombia after that government rejected the US proposal to build and own a Panamanian canal: the very kind of imperialism that Garza deplored. Américo Paredes, *A Texas-Mexican Cancionero: Folksongs of the Lower Border* (Austin: University of Texas Press, 1995), 229; Young, *Catarino Garza's Revolution on the Texas-Mexican Border*, 24, 27, 41, 52, 295–300; Padilla, *My History, Not Yours;* Joe Baulch, "Garza War," *The Handbook of Texas*, http://www.tsha.utexas.edu/handbook/online/articles/GG/jcgwk.html; Cuthbertson, "Catarino Erasmo Garza"; "The Men Shot in Mexico," *The New York Times*, October 25, 1891, 2; "The Garza Revolution," *The New York Times*, January 10, 1892, 5; Félix D. Almaráz Jr., "Francisco I. Madero and the Texas Prelude to the Mexican Revolution," Bexar County Precinct 4 Newsletter.

7. Armando Navarro, *Mexicano Political Experience in Occupied Aztlán: Struggles and Changes* (Lanham, MD: Rowman Altimira Press, 2005), 149; Teresa Paloma Acosta, "Víctor Ochoa," *The Handbook of Texas*, http://www.tshaonline.org/handbook/online/articles/foc05; Smithsonian Institution, "Overview of the Collection, Victor L. Ochoa Papers," http://americanhistory.si.edu/archives/AC0590.pdf and "Víctor Ochoa," http://www.smithsonianeducation.org/scitech/impacto/graphic/victor/index.html (both accessed 1/31/11); Thomas Cole National Historic Site, "This Is Where American Art Was Born," http://www.thomascole.org/ (accessed 1/31/11).

8. The Santos memoir was a finalist for the National Book Award. John Phillip Santos, *Places Left Unfinished at the Time of Creation* (New York: Viking, 1999), front cover, 13, 51, 91–94.

9. Julie Leininger, *Chicanos in South Bend: Some Historical Narratives* (Notre Dame: Centro de Estudios Chicanos e Investigaciones Sociales, 1976), 5.

10. For more on Cruz Blanca, see chapter 1. Sociedad Mutualista Mexicana, *Pro-Mexico;* Gilbert G. González, *Mexican Consuls and Labor Organizing: Imperial Politics in the American Southwest* (Austin: University of Texas Press, 1999); Consul at El Paso to the Subsecretary, Secretaría de Relaciones Exteriores, November 26, 1929, ASRE, IV-100-43, 11/26/29, Archives of the Secretaría de Relaciones Exteriores, Mexico City hereafter SRE; Julie Leininger Pycior, "The Mexican Community in New York City: Precursors," New York State Historical Association, 2005; Nancy Baker Jones, "Villegas de Magnón, Leonor," *Handbook of Texas Online*, http://www.tshaonline.org/handbook/online/articles/fvi19 (accessed 1/7/13).

11. *La Prensa*, November 21, 1921, 5; February 11, 1922, 8; February 12, 1922, 8; March 4, 1922, 8; March 23, 1923, 1; November 30, 1924, 2; April 1, 1925, 1; March 11, 1925, 12; April 11, 1925, 1; May 5, 1925, 1; April 15, 1925, 1; July 24, 1925, 1; July 29, 1925, 1; July 18, 1925, 7, 12; May 20, 1925, 2; May 25, 1925, 8; June 1, 1925, 1; September 20, 1925, 16; September 22, 1925, 10; August 31, 1925, 1; January 29, 1925, 1; May 5, 1925, 1; May 20, 1925, 12; October 4, 1925, 8; June 19, 1927, 5; April 22, 1928, 1; January 18, 1920, 15; *La Epoca*, September 4, 1921, 6; March 5, 1922, 1, 8; April 23, 1922, 1; May 9, 1926, 4; March 13, 1927, 6; September 11, 1927, 5; *El Heraldo Mexicano*, May 5, 1928, 1; November 4, 1928, 2; January 20, 1929, 2; March 13, 1927, 5; January 29, 1928, 1; April 22, 1928, 5; April 22, 1928, 5; June 10, 1929, 1; David Gutiérrez, *Walls and Mirrors: Mexican Americans, Mexican Immigration, and the Politics of Ethnicity* (Berkeley: University of California Press, 1995), 32–34, 102–104, 228; Manuel Gamio, *Life Story of the Mexican Immigrant* (New York: Dover Press [reprint], 1971), 10; Sociedad de la Unión, Libro de Actas, 1922–26, 411, 414, 506, OLLU.

12. Alatorre interview.

13. *La Prensa*, November 21, 1921, 5.

14. Antonia Castañeda, remarks presented at "Las Tejanas: 300 Years of History, a Symposium," University of Texas at Austin, October 17, 2003; *La Prensa*, April 15, 1925, July 24, 1925, 1; July 29, 1925, 1; July 18, 1925, 7, 12; May 20, 1925, 1; May 25, 1925, 8; June 1, 1925, 1; September 20, 1925, 16; September 22, 1925, 10; August 31, 1925, 1; January 29, 1925, 1; May 5, 1925, 1; May 20, 1925, 12; October 4, 1925, 8; June 19, 1927, 5; April 22, 1928, 1; January 18, 1920, 15; *El Heraldo Mexicano*, May 5, 1928, 1; November 4, 1928, 2; January 20, 1929, 2; March 13, 1927, 5; January 29, 1928, 1; April 22, 1928, 5; April 22, 1928, 5; June 10, 1929, 1; Adriana Ayala, "Negotiating Race Relations through Activism: Women Activists and Women's Organizations in San Antonio, Texas, during the 1920s," PhD diss., University of Texas, 2005, chapter 4: "Cruz Azul: Soldaderas de la Colonia"; Emma Pérez, *The Decolonial Imaginary: Writing Chicanas into History* (Bloomington: Indiana University Press, 1999), 97–98; Alatorre interview; brochure, Comisión Honorífica of Pueblo, CO, "Loor Eterno a Los Héroes de la Independencia Mexicana," 1925, pf F784 P9L58, Bancroft Library, University of California, Berkeley; Edwin B. Adams, vice-consul of N. Laredo, to Sec. of State, May 9, 1922, 702.1200/15, box 6366, RG 59, Department of State National Archives; ASRE, IV-100−26, Institucion filantropicas mex.'s to consular general of San Antonio, SRE Archives.

15. Rosales, *Pobre Raza*, 195; Gilbert González, *Mexican Consuls and Labor Organizing* (Austin: University of Texas Press, 1999), 62–73.

16. Kay Briegal, "Alianza Hispano-Americana," PhD diss., University of Southern California, 1974, 94–99; *Alianza*, October 1932, 20.

17. Cecilia B. Imaz, "Las Organizaciones Sociales de Migrantes en Los Estados Unidos: El Caso del Club Social De Jala, Nayarit, en California y Su Gestión para La Co-existencia de Tradiciones Populares," in *Nuevas tendencias y desafíos de la migración internacional México-Estados Unidos*, ed. Raúl Delgado Wise (Mexico City: UNAM, 2004), 26–28.

18. Imaz, "Las Organizaciones Sociales de Migrantes en Los Estados Unidos," 26–28.

19. Jonathan Fox and Xóchitl Bada, "Migrant Civic Engagement," Research Paper Series no. 3, June 2009, Wilson Center Mexico Insitute, www.wilsoncenter.org/migrantparticpation (accessed 5/30/10); Mexico Institute, Woodrow Wilson International Center for Scholars, "2006 Presidential Election Votes by State and Party," http://www.wilsoncenter.org/migrantparticipation (accessed 8/24/13); Susan Gzesh, "Mexico's Presidential Election: Implications for US Immigration Policy," Migration Information Source (September 2006), http://www.migrationinformation.org/Feature/display.cfm?id=420; Cecilia Imaz, http://meme.phpwebhosting.com/~migracion/modules/libro_nuevas_tendencias_de_la_migracion/5.pdf (accessed 1/25/11), 26–28; H. Nelson Goodson, "Sale of Worthless ID's and Advertising Continues," El Conquistador, December 10, 2008; Rita Méndez, speech to the 12th meeting of the CCIME, November 10–11, 2009, http://www.ime .gob.mx/images/stories/ime/CCIME/reuniones_ordinarias/xii/12_dis_rm.pdf (accessed 1/7/13); "Mexico's President Praises Obama's Immigration Shift," http://www.cnn.com/2012/06/18/politics/immigration/index.html (accessed 1/7/13).

Chapter 3

1. Michael Jones-Correa, "Mexican Migrants and Their Relation to U.S. Civil Society," http://www.wilsoncenter.org/sites/default/files/Jones-Correa%20-%20Mex%20Migrant%20US%20 Civ%20Soc.pdf (accessed 8/24/13).

2. Susan Gzesh, "Paper for the Wilson Center/Enlaces America Roundtable," http://www .wilsoncenter.org/sites/default/files/Chicago%20Eng.pdf (accessed 8/24/13); Jonathan Fox, "Binational Citizens," *The Boston Review*, http://www.bostonreview.net/jonathan-fox-civic-binationality-mexican-migrants (accessed 7/16/13); Magda Banda and Martha Zurita, "Latino Immigrant Engagement in the Chicago Region," Institute for Latino Studies, University of Notre Dame, http://latinostudies.nd.edu/assets/95265/original/ (accessed 7/16/13); Illinois Coalition for Migrant and Refugee Rights, "Latino Vote Pivotal in Close Mid-term Election," http://icirr .org/es/content/latino-vote-pivotal-close-mid-term-elections (accessed 8/24/13).

3. "Jesse Díaz and Javier Rodríguez: Undocumented in America," *New Left Review,* 47 (September–October 2007), http://www.newleftreview.org/?view=2689 (accessed 2/6/11).

4. "Díaz and Rodríguez: Undocumented in America"; author interview with Soledad "Chole" Alatorre, May 3, 2010, Pacoima, CA; author telephone interview with Soledad Alatorre, May 18, 2010.

5. "Díaz and Rodríguez: Undocumented in America."

6. "Díaz and Rodríguez: Undocumented in America."

7. Julie Leininger Pycior, "Ahead of Their Time to No Avail: The American GI Forum and the Immigration Reform Act of 1965," American GI Forum/Texas A&M Corpus Christi History Conference, Corpus Christi, March 27, 2008; Adriana Ayala, "Negotiating Race Relations through Activism: Women Activists and Women's Organizations in San Antonio, Texas, during the 1920s" PhD diss., University of Texas, 2005, 111–113; Juan Ramón García, *Mexicans in the Midwest, 1900–1932,* (Tucson: University of Arizona Press, 1996), 44–45.

8. Rodolfo Acuña, Corridors of Migration (Tucson: University of Arizona Press, 2007), 223–224; F. Arturo Rosales, *Testimonio: A Documentary History of the Mexican American Struggle for Civil Rights* (Houston: Arte Público Press, 2000), 122–125; F. Arturo Rosales, *Pobre Raza: Violence, Justice, and Mobilization among México Lindo Immigrants, 1900–1936* (Austin: University of Texas Press, 1999), 27–30, 133–134, 138–139, 151; Albert Camarillo, *Chicanos in a Changing Society: From Mexican Pueblos to American Barrios in Santa Barbara and Southern California, 1848–1930* (Cambridge: Harvard University Press, 1979), 152.

9. Ian Haney-López, *Racism on Trial: The Chicano Fight for Justice* (Cambridge: Harvard University Press, 2004), 59.

10. Julie Leininger Pycior, *LBJ and Mexican Americans: The Paradox of Power* (Austin: University of Texas Press, 1997), 12, 249, n. 15.

11. Pycior, *LBJ and Mexican Americans,* 10.

12. Kay Briegal, "The Alianza Hispano-Americana," PhD diss., University of Southern California, 1974, 111–114; Pycior, *LBJ and Mexican Americans: The Paradox of Power,* 10–14; LBJ Library, "Lyndon B. Johnson with students and fellow teachers [sic] . . . ," serial number 29-5-2, http://www.lbjlibrary.net/collections/photo-archive.html (accessed 1/9/13).

13. Francisco Balderrama and Raymond Rodríguez, *Decade of Betrayal: Mexican Repatriation in the 1930s* (Albuquerque: University of New Mexico Press [revised], 2006), 41, 99, 147, 161, 205–206, 252; Aristide Zolberg, "A Century of Informality Along the U.S.-Mexican Border," *Border Battles: The U.S. Immigration Debates,* Social Science Research Council, August 17, 2006, http://borderbattles.ssrc.org/Zolberg/; Matt S. Meier and Feliciano Rivera, *Dictionary of Mexican American History* (Westport, CT: Greenwood Press, 1981), 264, 300–302; Kelly Lytle Hernández, "The Crimes and Consequences of Illegal Immigration: A Cross-border Examination of Operation Wetback, 1943–1954," *Western Historical Quarterly* (Winter 2006); Mark Reisler, *By the Sweat of Their Brow: Mexican Immigrant Labor in the United States, 1900–1940* (Westport, CT: Greenwood Press, 1976), 59–61; Jeffrey Garcilazo, "McCarthyism, Mexican Americans, and the Los Angeles Committee for Protection of the Foreign-Born," *Western Historical Quarterly* 32, no. 3 (2001), 276.

14. Balderrama and Rodríguez, *Decade of Betryal,* 41, 99, 147, 161, 205–206, 252; Briegal, "The Alianza Hispano-Americana," 113–120; Stephen J. Pitti, *The Devil in Silicon Valley: Northern California, Race, and Mexican Americans* (Princeton: Princeton University Press, 2003), 106–111; García, *Mexicans in the Midwest,* 189; Adriana Ayala, "Negotiating Race Relations through Activism: Women Activists and Women's Organizations in San Antonio, Texas in the 1920s." PhD. diss., University of Texas, 2005, 124–125; David Beito, "Thy Brother's Keeper," *Policy Review* (Fall 1994), 6–8; correspondence, Sociedad Mutualista Melchor Ocampo, 1926–41, Benson Latin American Collection, University of Texas (hereafter BLAC).

15. Jeffery Garcilazo, "McCarthyism, Mexican Americans, and the Los Angeles Committee for Protection of the Foreign-Born," *Western Historical Quarterly,* 32, no. 3 (2001), 276.

16. For the story of Operation Wetback, see Juan Ramón García, *Operation Wetback* (Westport, CT: Greenwood Press, 1979). Mario T. García, *Mexican Americans: Leadership, Ideology and Identity, 1930–1960* (New Haven: Yale University Press, 1989), 202; Pycior, *LBJ and Mexican Americans: The Paradox of Power,* 63–64, 77–79.

17. The immigration service had revoked Daniel Castañeda González's citizenship on the grounds that he had left the United States in order to avoid military service during World War II. The defense argued that he lived in Mexico purely for personal reasons and without knowledge of any US military obligations. The highest court agreed with the AHA attorneys that the immigration agency had not proven willful intent as prescribed by the McCarran-Walter Act. Pycior, "Ahead of Their Time to No Avail: The American GI Forum and the Immigration Reform Act of 1965"; Zolberg, "A Century of Informality along the US-Mexican Border"; Briegal, "The Alianza Hispano Americana," 181–183, 199; Cynthia Orozco, "American Council of Spanish-speaking People," The Handbook of Texas, http://www.tshaonline.org/handbook/online/articles/AA/pqa1. html (accessed 5/7/10); Teresa Paloma Acosta, "Alianza Hispano Americana," http://www.tsha-online.org/handbook/online/articles/AA/vna2.html (accessed 5/17/10); Garcilazo, "McCarthyism, Mexican Americans, and the Los Angeles Committee for Protection of the Foreign-Born," 273–295.

18. Pycior, "Ahead of Their Time to No Avail."

19. Mario T. García, Memories of Chicano History: The Life and Narrative of Bert Corona (Berkeley: University of California Press, 1995), 317.

20. Presciently but futilely, the Johnson administration, led by Secretary of State Dean Rusk and Senate sponsor Philip Hart, had lobbied in vain against the Western Hemisphere quota, warning that sudden imposition of a strict numerical quota in this adjoining region would prove unworkable. For most of the bill's supporters, however, such as Representative Peter Rodino of New Jersey, equal numerical percentages applied worldwide seemed eminently fair at face value. Meanwhile, conservative restrictionists such as powerful Senator Sam Ervin of North Carolina dismissed out of hand any call for a flexible Western Hemisphere policy. Pycior, "Ahead of Their Time to No Avail"; author telephone interview with Antonio Hernández, March 1, 2010; García, Memories of Chicano History, 287–290; Jennifer Ludden, "1965 Immigration Law Changed Face of America," National Public Radio, May 9, 2006, http://www.npr.org/templates/story/story. php?storyId=5391395 (accessed 1/16/12).

21. García, Memories of Chicano History, 287.

22. García, Memories of Chicano History, 287–295.

23. García, Memories of Chicano History, 290–295, 307–309.

24. García, Memories of Chicano History, 309; Alatorre interview.

25. García, Memories of Chicano History, 63, 287–295; University of San Diego, San Diego History Center, "Luisa Moreno and the Beginnings of the Mexican American Civil Rights Movement," http://www.sandiegohistory.org/journal/97summer/morenoimages.htm; Alatorre interview; House of Representatives, Committee on Un-American Activities, "Investigation of Communist Activities in the State of California" (Washington: Government Printing Office, 1954); Mario Compeán, "Mexican Americans in the Columbia Basin: A Historical Overview," Columbia River Basin Ethnic History Archive, http://www.vancouver.wsu.edu/crbeha/ma/ma.htm; John Flores, "Bert Corona," Encyclopedia of U.S. Labor and Working-Class History, ed. Eric Arnesen (New York: Routledge, 2007), 324–327.

26. Armando Navarro, The Immigration Crisis (Lanham, MD: Rowman and Littlefield, 2009), 108.

27. During this period, the Hermandad Mexicana Nacional underwent a temporary and somewhat confusing rechristening as CASA-HGT. CASA/Centro de Acción Social Autónoma already was the name of the service centers run by the Hermandad Mexicana Nacional. Meanwhile the "HGT" part of "CASA-HGT" stood for "Hermandad General de Trabajadores (workers)" and thus constituted a modification of the Hermandad's original name. García, Memories of Chicano History, 296, 300–302; Navarro, The Immigration Crisis, 99, 108–109, 383–385, 500–526.

28. "Continúa la movilización para la reforma migratoria con una marcha en los angeles," La Prensa (San Antonio), March 26, 2010, http://www.laprensasa.com/25_hispanos/633102_con-tinua-la-movilizacion-por-la-reforma-migratoria-con-una-marcha-en-los-angeles.html (accessed 8/24/13); Douglas Massey et al. Beyond Smoke and Mirrors: Immigration in an Era of Economic Integration (New York: Russell Sage Foundation, 2003), chapter 1; Migration Policy Institute, "Illinois: Social and Demographic Characteristics," http://www.migrationinformation.org/datahub/state.cfm?ID=IL; Fox and Bada, "Migrant Civic Engagement"; CONFEMEX, "Quienes Somos,"

http://www.confemexusa.com/quienes_somos.html and "Celebran Miembros de CONFEMEX Su 6to Aniversario," http://www.confemexusa.com/archive/sexto_aniveresario_confemex .html (accessed 2/13/11); "Governor Quinn Joins ICIRR to Celebrate 50,000 New Citizens," New Americans Initiative, 2011, http://icirr.org/content/governor-quinn-joins-icirr-celebrate-50000-new-citizens-1 (accessed 8/24/13); "Illinois Voting History," http://www.270towin.com/states/Illinois (accessed 1/9/13); Barack Obama, speech to the League of United Latin American Citizens, July 8, 2008 (transcript), http://www.realclearpolitics.com/articles/2008/07/obamas_speech_to_lulac.html (accessed 2/13/11); "Maria Elena Durazo," http://www.launionaflcio.org/section/leadership/# (accessed 2/13/11); cofem.org (accessed 2/13/11); "Continúa la mobilización para la reforma migratoria con una marcha en los angeles," *La Prensa* (San Antonio), March 26, 2010; "Start of Deferred Action Gives Immigrants a Reason to Celebrate," *Las Vegas Sun*, January 9, 2013 (accessed 1/9/13), http://www.lasvegassun.com/news/2012/aug/16/legal-residency-sight-deferred-action-program-gets/; "2012 COFEM Annual Conference and Expo," http://www.hispaniclifestyle.com/blog/articles/community/2012-cofem-annual-conference-expo/; "Rita Mendez signed the petition: Stand with President Obama: Pass the DREAM Act," http://www.change.org/users/556249 (accessed 1/7/13); author telephone interview with Antonia Hernández, March 1, 2010.

29. Hernández interview.

30. Hernández interview.

Chapter 4

1. League of United Latin American Citizens, "Historic Latino Voter Turnout Helps Elect Barack Obama," http://lulac.org/news/pr/historic_turnout/ (accessed 5/10/10).

2. John McCain, address to National Council of La Raza, July 14, 2008, http://www.mccain.senate.gov/public/index.cfm?FuseAction=PressOffice.Speeches&ContentRecord_id=0378B4AD-377F-4064-B50D-B6394B966DCD (accessed 8/19/13).

3. Leslie R. Crutchfield and Heather McLeod Grant, *Forces for Good: The Six Practices of Six High-Impact Nonprofits* (New York: Jossey-Bass, 2007), 44–45.

4. Gar Alperovitz, *America beyond Capitalism: Reclaiming Our Wealth, Our Liberty, and Our Democracy* (New York: Wiley, 2005), 159; Rogelio Saenz, "Latinos in America 2010," *Population Bulletin Update* (December 2010), http://www.prb.org/pdf10/latinos-update2010.pdf (accessed 1/6/10); Martin Kettle, "The Hispanic Vote Shaped the Contours of This Election," *The Guardian*, November 7, 2008, http://www.guardian.co.uk/commentisfree/2008/nov/07/barack-obama-south-west-hispanic (accessed 5/10/10); Barack Obama, address to National Council of La Raza, July 13, 2008, http://www.whitehouse.gov/photos-and-video/video/2011/07/25/president-obama-addresses-council-la-raza (accessed 8/19/13); Julia Preston and Fernanda Santos, "A Record Latino Turnout, Solidly Backing Obama," *The New York Times*, November 7, 2012, http://www.nytimes.com/2012/11/08/us/politics/with-record-turnout-latinos-solidly-back-obama-and-wield-influence.html?_r=0 (accessed 1/10/12).

5. Editors of *Black Issues in Higher Education, The Unfinished Agenda of the Selma-Montgomery Voting Rights March* (Hoboken, NJ: John Wiley and Son, 2005), 110; Raúl Yzaguirre, "Comments of Raúl Yzaguirre," EEOC History: 35th Anniversary, http://www.eeoc.gov/eeoc/history/35th/voices/yzaguirre-text.html (accessed 4/14/10).

6. Yzaguirre, "Comments of Raúl Yzaguirre"; Charles T. Clotfelter and Thomas Ehrlich, *Philanthropy and the Non-Profit Sector in a Changing America* (Bloomington: Indiana University Press, 2001), 260–261.

7. Editors of *Black Issues in Higher Education, The Unfinished Agenda of the Selma-Montgomery Voting Rights March*; Raúl Yzaguirre, "Civil Rights and the Hispanic Voter: The Legacy of Willie Velásquez," June 19, 2008, http://www.youtube.com/watch?v=dTqIq2qb1Vo (accessed 4/14/10); Raúl Yzaguirre, "Liberty and Justice for All," in *Latinos and the Nation's Future*, eds. Henry Cisneros and John Rosales (Houston: Arte Público Press, 2009), 33; Raúl Yzaguirre, telephone interview with author, August 24, 1992.

8. For the "legacy of conquest" as it played out in the American West, the trailblazing work is Patricia Nelson Limerick, *The Legacy of Conquest: The Unbroken Past of the American West* (New

York: Norton, 1987). "Ready to Rumble: Civil Rights Heavyweight Raul Yzaguirre on Life, the Evolution of the NCLR, and giving Latinos a Fighting Chance," *Latino Leaders* (December 2001), http://www.highbeam.com/doc/1G1-113053334.html (accessed 8/24/13); author telephone interview with Antonia Hernández, March 1, 2010; Richard Griswold del Castillo, *La Familia: Chicano Families in the Urban Southwest, 1848–Present* (Notre Dame: University of Notre Dame Press, 1974), 96; David Gutiérrez, *Walls and Mirrors: Mexican Americans, Mexican Immigrants, and the Politics of Ethnicity* (Berkeley: University of California Press, 1995), 36; William A. Das, "For Whom and for What? The Contributions of the Non-Profit Sector," the Aspen Institute, http://www.aspeninstitute.org/policy-work/nonprofit-philanthropy/archives/whom-what-contributions-t (accessed 8/19/13); Emilio Zamora, "Labor Formation, Community, and Politics: The Mexican Working Class in Texas, 1900–1945," in *Border Crossings: Mexican and Mexican-American Workers*, ed. John Mason Hart (Wilmington, DE: Scholarly Resources, 1998), 155; Kenneth Mason, *African Americans and Race Relations in San Antonio, 1867–1937* (New York: Garland Publishing Co., 1998), 61; "The Garza Revolution," *The New York Times*, January 10, 1892; John Phillip Santos, *Places Left Unfinished at the Time of Creation* (New York: Viking, 1999), 91.

9. Albert Camarillo, *Chicanos in a Changing Society: From Mexican Pueblos to American Barrios in Santa Barbara and Southern California, 1848–1930* (Cambridge: Harvard University Press, 1979), 120; Arnoldo De León, *The Tejano Community, 1836–1900* (Albuquerque: University of New Mexico Press, 1982), 194–196; Armando Navarro, *Mexicano Political Experience in Occupied Aztlán* (Lanham, MD: Rowman Altimira Press, 2005), 147; Roberto Calderón, "'Unión, Paz y Trabajo': Laredo's Mutual Aid Societies, 1890s," in *Mexican Americans in Texas History*, eds. Emilio Zamora, Cynthia Orozco, and Rodolfo Rocha (Austin: Texas State Historical Commission, 2000), 72–73.

10. Gilbert M. Cuthbertson, "Catarino Erasmo Garza," *The Handbook of Texas*, http://www.tsha.utexas.edu/handbook/online/articles/GG/fga38.html (accessed 1/16/12); Elliott Young, *Catarino Garza's Revolution on the Texas-Mexican Border* (Durham: Duke University Press, 2004), 292; Camarillo, *Chicanos in a Changing Society*, 119–120; Arnoldo De León, *Mexican Americans in Texas* (College Station: Texas A&M University Press, 1999), 75–76; David Romo, "Ringside Seat to a Revolution," *The Texas Observer*, January 13, 2006, 26–27, http://www.texasobserver.org/article.php?aid=2114; Alicia A. Garza, "Rio Grande City Riots of 1888," *Handbook of Texas Online*, http://www.tshaonline.org/handbook/online/articles/RR/jcr3.html (accessed April 20, 2010).

11. For the history of relations among US Mexicans, see David Gutiérrez, *Walls and Mirrors: Mexican Americans, Mexican Immigrants, and the Politics of Ethnicity* (Berkeley: University of California Press, 1995). "Inventor and Revolutionary: Víctor Ochoa," http://www.smithsonianeducation.org/scitech/impacto/graphic/victor/index.html; Teresa Paloma Acosta, "Victor Ochoa," *The Handbook of Texas*, http://www.tsha.utexas.edu/handbook/online/articles/OO/foc5.html; Archdiocese of Los Angeles, "Historical Order of Bishops," http://www.archdiocese.la/about/heritage/bishops.html#amat (accessed 4/19/10).

12. Benjamin Márquez and James Jennings, "Representation by Other Means: Mexican American and Puerto Rican Social Movement Organizations," *PS: Political Science and Politics* 33, no. 3 (2000), 541.

13. Márquez and Jennings, "Representation by Other Means," 641; Richard Griswold del Castillo, *The Los Angeles Barrio, 1850–1890: A Social History* (Berkeley: University of California Press, 1979), 134–135.

14. Hubert Herring, review of Manual Carrera Estampa, *Los Gremios Mexicanos: La Organización Gremial en Nueva España*, *American Historical Review* 62, no. 1. (1956), 169–170; Armando Navarro, *Mexicano Political Experience in Occupied Aztlán*, 146; Gloria Fraser Giffords, *Sanctuaries of Earth, Stone and Light: The Churches of Northern New Spain* (Tucson, University of Arizona Press, 2007), 410, n. 10; Instituto de Antropología e Historia, "Los Gremios y Cofradías en Nueva España," http://www.gobiernodigital.inah.gob.mx/Exposiciones/gremios_cofradias/index.html (accessed 1/10/13); David A. Badillo, *Latinos and the New Immigrant Church* (Baltimore: Johns Hopkins University Press, 2006), 7.

15. *La Prensa*, January 24, 1924, 9 and February 13, 1925, 8; author interview with Lucas Garza, November 17, 1976, San Antonio.

16. Griswold del Castillo, *The Los Angeles Barrio*, 134–135; 541; Cuthbertson, "Catarino Erasmo

Garza"; Young, *Catarino Garza's Revolution on the Texas-Mexican Border*, 292; Arnoldo De León, *The Tejano Community, 1836–1900*, (Alburquerque: University of New Mexico Press, 1982), 194–196; Navarro, *Mexicano Political Experience in Occupied Aztlán*, 147; "Zaragoza, Ignacio Seguín," http://www.tshaonline.org/handbook/online/articles/fza04 (accessed 1/11/13); *La Prensa*, January 24, 1924, 9, and February 13, 1925, 8; author interview with Lucas Garza, November 17, 1976, San Antonio; Calderón, "'Unión, Paz y Trabajo': Laredo's Mutual Aid Societies, 1890s," 72–73.

17. Judith Berg Sobré, *San Antonio on Parade* (College Station: Texas A&M University Press, 2003), 86–89, 95–97; De León, *The Tejano Community*, 177–181; Cuthbertson, "Garza, Catarino Erasmo"; Young, *Catarino Garza's Revolution on the Texas-Mexican Border*, 292; De León, *The Tejano Community, 1836–1900*, 177–181, 194–196; Navarro, *Mexicano Political Experience in Occupied Aztlán*, 147; Calderón, "'Unión, Paz y Trabajo': Laredo's Mutual Aid Societies, 1890s," 72–73.

18. De León, *The Tejano Community*, 177; Sobré, *San Antonio on Parade*, 40, 48–49, 87, 90.

19. Robert A. Calvert and Arnoldo De León, *The History of Texas* (Arlington Heights, IL: Harlan Davidson, 1990), 72.

20. Arturo Rosales, *Pobre Raza: Violence, Justice, and Mobilization among México Lindo Immigrants, 1900–1936* (Austin: University of Texas Press, 1999), 26; Calvert and De León, *The History of Texas*, 144, 172; National Humanities Center, "Toolbox Library: Primary Resources in U.S. History and Literature: The Making of African American Identity, Volume I," http://nationalhumanitiescenter.org/pds/maai/community/text5/text5read.htm (accessed 2/14/11); Theda Skocpol, "What a Mighty Power We Can Be: African American Fraternal Groups and the Struggle for Equal Rights," http://www.slideshare.net/jsucus/african-american-fraternal-groups-talk-presentation (accessed 4/22/10); Laura Gómez, *Manifest Destinies: The Making of the Mexican American Race* (New York: NYU Press, 2007), 3–6.

21. Sobré, *San Antonio on Parade*, 11, 40, 77, 80–90.

22. Mark Reisler, *By the Sweat of Their Brow: Mexican Immigrant Labor in the United States, 1900–1940* (Westport, CT: Greenwood Press, 1976), 156, 161, 170–174, and chapter 8, "The Politics of Restriction"; Robert R. Calderón, "Tejano Politics," *The Handbook of Texas*, http://www.tshaonline.org/handbook/online/articles/TT/wmtkn.html.

23. María Varela, interview by author, April 22, 2010, Providence, RI.

24. Conquest by the United States brought the Church in this region under the authority of the diocese of St. Louis, Missouri, which sent to this former Mexican land, now part of the United States, prelates from—France! Bishop (later archbishop) Jean-Baptiste Lamy prohibited most activities of the Hermanos Penitentes, and even some popular priests of Mexican background were shunted aside—most notably the chaplain for the penitentes, Reverend Antonio José Martínez. Ordained one year after Mexico won its independence from Spain, Martínez was trained in canon law and founded a seminary that had graduated sixteen priests by 1834. The next year he established the first printing press and publishing house west of the Mississippi as well as schools for settler and tribal children alike. Nonetheless, Archbishop Lamy ordered that Martínez and six other native New Mexican priests be excommunicated. The conquest mentality even entered the annals of American literature, with Jean Lamy the hero versus an uncultured Father Martínez in the major work *Death Comes to the Archbishop*, by Willa Cather. Thus was established the dominance of nonnative clergy. Indeed, the bishop for Texas, Jean Marie Odin, first suggested to Lamy that he replace the Mexican priests with Frenchmen. Mexican bishops were also succeeded by Europeans in the US state of California. That some of the priests hailed from Spain, and thus spoke the same language as their parishioners, hardly resolved the problem of a foreign clergy unfamiliar with both US and Mexican culture. Colorado State Archives, "History FAQs," http://www.colorado.gov/dpa/doit/archives/history/histfaqs.htm (accessed 4/19/10); Alberto L. Pulido, "Mexican American Catholicism in the Southwest: The Transformation of a Popular Religion," in *En Aquel Entonces: Readings in Mexican-American History*, eds. Manuel G. Gonzales and Cynthia M. Gonzales (Bloomington: Indiana University Press, 2000), 88–93; Ray John de Aragón, *Padre Martínez and Bishop Lamy* (Santa Fe, NM: Sunstone Press, 2006), back cover; Willam H. Wrothe, "Lamy, Jean-Baptiste," *New Mexico Office of the State Historian*, http://www.newmexicohistory.org/filedetails.php?fileID=501 (accessed 4/19/10).

25. After the subjugation of the Hermandad Penitente, the gorras blancas (white caps) arose. This group stealthily but systematically attempted to cut down fences and derail trains of the

"land-grabbers." But in contrast to Texas, where *mutualista* leaders such as Catarino Garza echoed those rebellious sentiments, in New Mexico *mutualista* groups typically distanced themselves from the *gorras blancas*. F. Arturo Rosales, *Testimonio: A Documentary History of the Mexican American Struggle for Civil Rights* (Houston: Arte Público Press, 2000), 29–30; New Mexico Office of the State Historian, "Ortero, Miguel A.," http://www.newmexicohistory.org/filedetails. php?fileID=4783 (accessed 4/21/10); Pulido, "Mexican American Catholicism in the Southwest.

26. San Isidro was a Spanish saint, hence the connection to colonial New Spain. At the same time, he is the official patron of farming for the universal Catholic Church, with the US Catholic Rural Life Conference, for example, having Saint Isidore as its patron saint. Rubén Martínez, "Chicano/a Land Ethics and a Sense of Place," *Culture & Agriculture* 29, no. 2, (2007), 113–120, http://www.americancatholic.org/features/saints/saint.aspx?id=1384; *St. Anthony Messenger Press/* Franciscan Communications, "Saint Isidore the Farmer," http://www.americancatholic.org/ features/saints/saint.aspx?id=1384 (accessed 4/19/10); Colorado State Archives, "History FAQs," http://www.colorado.gov/dpa/doit/archives/history/histfaqs.htm (accessed 4/19/10); Pulido, "Mexican American Catholicism in the Southwest"; Varela interview; Larry J. Siegal, *Criminology* (Florency, KY: Cengage, 2008), 480; "Los Penitentes," http://www.eljeferuben.com/lospenitentes.html (accessed 1/10/13).

27. Herman Gallegos, interview by author, February 10, 2010, San Francisco.

28. José Timoteo López, *La Historia de la Sociedad Protección Mutua de Trabajadores Unidos* (New York: Comet Press Books, 1958), 5–15, 26, 48–61.

29. Kate A. Berry and Martha L. Henderson, *Geographic Identities of Ethnic America* (Reno: University of Nevada Press, 2002), 195–197; Martínez, "Chicano/a Land Ethics and a Sense of Place," 115–117.

30. Another Trinidad, Colorado *mutualista* association still in existence is the Confederación Mutualista Mexicana e Hispano Americana, which reported assets of $127,075 as of 2008. IMPLU Corporation, "Confederación Mutualista Mexicana e Hispano Americana," http://www. implu.com/nonprofit/840260776 (accessed 5/14/10); "SPMDTU," www.spmdtu.org (accessed 8/19/13); Ernest Gurulé, "An Organization is Born," *La Voz Nueva*, November 25, 2009, http:// www.lavozcolorado.com/news.php?nid=4282&pag=0&st=0 (accessed 4/20/10); "La Cultura," http://hispanonewmexico.com/?page_id=6 (accessed 4/3/13); "2012–2013 SPMDTU Grant Application Now Available!" http://spmdtucouncir7.org/?p=47 (accessed 4/3/13).

31. Teresa Paloma Acosta, "Alianza Hispano Americana," *The Handbook of Texas*, http://www .tsha.utexas.edu/handbook/online/articles/view/AA/vna2.html; Thomas E. Sheridan, "Race and Class in a Southwestern City: The Mexican Community of Tucson, 1848–1941," in *Beyond 1848*, ed. Michael R. Ornelas (Dubuque, IA: Kendall-Hunt Publishing Co., 1993), 69; Gutiérrez, *Walls and Mirrors*, 96; Manuel G. Gonzales, "Carlos I. Velasco and the Defense of Mexican Rights in Territorial Arizona," in *En Aquel Entonces: Readings in Mexican-American History*, eds. Manuel G. Gonzalez and Cynthia M. Gonzales (Bloomington: Indiana University Press, 2000), 97–99, 102; *Alianza*, March 1954, 2.

32. Sheridan, "Race and Class in a Southwestern City: The Mexican Community of Tucson, 1854–1941," 73.

33. Linda Gordon, *The Great Arizona Orphan Abduction* (Cambridge: Harvard University Press, 1999), 101, 185.

Chapter 5

1. Heroic popular depictions of the Texas Rangers include the television shows *The Lone Ranger* (1949–57), http://www.imdb.com/title/tt0041038/ and *Walker, Texas Ranger* (1993– 2001), http://www.imdb.com/title/tt0106168/ (both accessed 2/16/17), while the counterview of "los rinches" lives on in the ballad/corrido "Gregorio Cortez," as performed by such popular groups from the border region as Los Alegres de Terán on their 2007 release *15 Corridos Famosos*, http://www.cduniverse.com/mp3search.asp?HT_SEARCH_Info=17285364&HT_ SEARCH=mp3album&style=mp3 (accessed 2/16/11). Cortez was also the subject of the 1982 feature film starring Edward James Olmos, *The Ballad of Gregorio Cortez*, which aired later that

year on the PBS series *American Playhouse*. Pat Aufderheide, "An Actor Turns Activist," *Mother Jones Magazine* VIII, no. IX (1983), 60; Raúl Yzaguirre, "Comments of Raúl Yzaguirre," EEOC History: 35th Anniversary, http://www.eeoc.gov/eeoc/history/35th/voices/yzaguirre-text.html (accessed 4/14/10).

2. F. Arturo Rosales, *Testimonio: A Documentary History of the Mexican American Struggle for Civil Rights*, 111–113, 120–121.

3. The version of the Defense Committee declaration as published a few years ago lists the president's signature as a male name—Wenceslao de Méndez—but the declaration's text referred to the president of the protestors as a woman, Mrs. Wenceslao de Méndez. Rosales, *Testimonio: A Documentary History of the Mexican American Struggle for Civil Rights* (Houston: Arte Público Press, 2000), 111–113, 120–121; José María Fernández, *The Biography of Casimiro Barela* (Albuquerque: University of New Mexico Press, 2003), 64–64.

4. Rosales, *Testimonio: A Documentary History of the Mexican American Struggle for Civil Rights*, 111–113, 120–121; José María Fernández, *The Biography of Casimiro Barela* (Albuquerque: University of New Mexico Press, 2003), 64–64.

5. Arturo Rosales, *Pobre Raza: Violence, Justice, and Mobilization among México Lindo Immigrants, 1900–1936* (Austin: University of Texas Press, 1999), 11; Arnoldo De León, *They Called Them Greasers: Anglo Attitudes Toward Mexicans in Texas, 1821–1900* (University of Texas Press, 1983), 104; Richard R. Flores, *Remembering the Alamo: Memory, Modernity and the Master Symbol* (Austin: University of Texas Press, 2002), 6; Rebecca Anne Todd Koenig, "Antonio Rodríguez," *The Handbook of Texas*, http://www.tshaonline.org/handbook/online/articles/RR/fr099.html; William D. Carrigan and Clive Webb, "The Lynching of Persons of Mexican Origin or Descent in the United States, 1848 to 1928," *Journal of Social History* 37, no. 2 (2003), 411–438; Julie Leininger Pycior, "Tejana Activism, 1910–1930," De León Lecture, University of Houston-Victoria/Victoria College, April 30, 2005.

6. The translation of Ambassador Bonillas' message is that of the State Department. Ygnacio Bonillas to Travis Polk, 7/17/17, 311.12, box 3572, RG 59, National Archives; Simón Domínguez to Oscar Colquitt, n.d. (1911?), box 2DG5, Dolph Briscoe Center for American History; Ralph W. Steen, "Ferguson, James Edward," *The Handbook of Texas*, http://www.tshaonline.org/handbook/online/articles/FF/ffe5.html.

7. Emilio Zamora, *The World of the Mexican Worker in Texas* (College Station: Texas A&M University Press, 1995), 106, 205; Roberto Calderón, "Unión, Trabajo, y Progreso: Laredo's Mexican Mutual Aid Societies, 1890s," in *Mexican Americans in Texas History*, eds. Emilio Zamora, Cynthia Orozco, and Rodolfo Rocha (Austin: Texas State Historical Commission), 72–77; José Limón, "El Primer Congreso Mexicanista: A Precursor to Contemporary Chicanismo," in *Latino/a Thought: Culture Politics and Society*, eds. Francisco H. Vásquez and Fernando D. Torres (New York: Rowan and Littlefield, 2002), 108; Teresa Palomo Acosta, "Primer Congreso Mexicanista" *The Handbook of Texas*, http://www.tshaonline.org/handbook/online/articles/CC/vecyk.html; Pycior, "Tejana Activism"; Nancy Jones, "Jovita Idar," *The Handbook of Texas*, http://www.tshaonline.org/handbook/online/articles/fido3 (accessed 2/28/11); Cynthia Orozco, "League of United Latin American Citizens," *The Handbook of Texas*, http://www.tshaonline.org/handbook/online/articles/LL/we11.html; Saumathi Jayaraman and Immanuel Ness, *The New Urban Immigrant Workforce* (Armonk, NY: M. E. Sharpe, 2005), 78; National Day Labor Organizing Committee, "Program Areas," http://www.ndlon.org/en/program-areas (accessed 8/24/13).

8. Emeterio Flores' own rising revolutionary fervor can be seen as early as 1913, when he called on Tejanos to support the revolutionary forces of Venustiano Carranza. Benjamin Heber Johnson, *Revolution in Texas: How a Forgotten Rebellion and Its Bloody Suppression Turned Mexicans into Americans* (New Haven: Yale University Press, 2003), 59–60, 70,145–148.

9. Cynthia Orozco, "Manuel C. Gonzales" *The Handbook of Texas*, http://www.tshaonline.org/handbook/online/articles/GG/fg057.html (accessed 8/25/13).

10. Orozco, "Manuel C. Gonzales"; "Carbajal, José María Jesús," *The Handbook of Texas*, http://www.tshaonline.org/handbook/online/articles/CC/fca45.html (accessed 8/25/13).

11. The Liga handbook was written in 1919 but publication was delayed until 1920 due to a paper shortage. Also, in 1917 the Liga reported that members paid $337 in dues, which was spent as follows:

Publications, publicity $36.00
Organizing committee 27.00
Travel fare for members 24.00
Stamps 6.00
Forms 18.00
Attorney fees 106.00
Salary for secretary 87.50
Desk 5.00
Typewriter ribbon .75

El Imparcial de Texas, August 4, 1919, 5; October 9, 1919, 5; November 6, 1919, 4; November 20, 1919, 5; March 18, 1920, 13; June 10, 1920, 6; Rosales, *Pobre Raza,* 26–27; Texas Department of Insurance, "About Workers' Compensation," http://www.tdi.state.tx.us/wc/dwc/index.html; Sanford N. Greenberg, "White Primary," *The Handbook of Texas,* http://www.tshaonline.org/handbook/online/articles/WW/wdw1.html; Orozco, "League of United Latin American Citizens"; Orozco, "Manuel C. Gonzales."

12. Rodolf Acuña, *Corridors of Migration* (Tucson: University of Arizona Press, 2007), 223–224; Rosales, *Testimonio,* 122–125; Rosales, *Pobre Raza,* 27–30, 133–134, 138–139, 151; Albert Camarillo, *Chicanos in a Changing Society: From Mexican Pueblos to American Barrios in Santa Barbara and Southern California, 1848–1930* (Cambridge: Harvard University Press, 1979), 152; Scott Christianson, *The Last Gasp: The Rise and Fall of the American Gas Chamber* (Berkeley: University of California, 2010), 238; Manuel Servín, *An Awakened Minority: The Mexican-Americans* (Beverly Hills: Glencoe Press, 1974), 178; Kay Breigal, "The Alianza Hispano-Americana," PhD diss., University of Arizona, 1974, 168–170.

13. Rosales, *Pobre Raza,* 27–30, 133–134, 138–139, 151; Christianson, *The Last Gasp,* 238; Manuel Servín, *Mexican Americans: An Awakened Minority* (Berkeley: Glencoe Press, 1974), 178.

14. President Woodrow Wilson had ordered the invasion in response to Villa having raided the town of Columbus, New Mexico, after the White House favored his revolutionary rival, Venustiano Carranza, with arms deals. *La Epoca,* July 28, 1918, 5; *El Imparcial de Texas,* January 17, 1918, 11; IMBD, "Heart of the Sunset (1918)," http://www.imdb.com/title/tto184556/; "Heart of the Sunset (1918), Review Summary," *The New York Times,* http://movies.nytimes.com/movie/94588/Heart-of-the-Sunset/overview (accessed 1/12/13); Nancy De Los Santos, *The Bronze Screen,* http://www.thebronzescreen.com/chapters.php (accessed 4/30/10); Friedrich Katz, *The Life and Times of Pancho Villa* (Palo Alto: Stanford University Press, 1998), 500; John H. Slate, "Film Industry," *Handbook of Texas Online,* http://www.tshaonline.org/handbook/online/articles/ecfo1 (accessed 1/17/12); *Birth of a Nation,* AMC Filmsite, http://www.filmsite.org/birt.html; Thomas Cripps, "'Art [and History] by Lightning Flash': *The Birth of a Nation* and Black Protest," Center for History and New Media, http://chnm.gmu.edu/episodes/the-birth-of-a-nation-and-black-protest/ (accessed 8/24/13).

15. F. Arturo Rosales, *Testimonio,* 116.

16. Judith Berg Sobré, *San Antonio on Parade* (College Station: Texas A&M University Press, 2003), 82–89; David Montejano, *Anglos and Mexicans in the Making of Texas, 1836–1986* (Austin: University of Texas Press, 1987), 92, 95; Richard Griswold del Castillo, *La Familia: Chicano Families in the Urban Southwest, 1848 to the Present* (Notre Dame, IN: University of Notre Dame Press, 1984), 43.

17. Roberto R. Calderón, "*Unión, Paz, y Trabajo:* Laredo's Mexican Mutual Aid Societies, 1890s," in *Mexican Americans in Texas History,* eds. Emilio Zamora et al. (Austin: Texas State Historical Association, 2000), 68; David E. Lorey, *The U.S.-Mexico Border in the Twentieth Century* (Wilmington, DE: Scholarly Resources, 1999), 30; Manuel Gamio, *Mexican Immigration to the United States* (New York: Dover Press, 1971), 11; Carlos Salas, "The Impact of NAFTA on Wages and Incomes in Mexico," in "NAFTA at Seven: Its Impact on Workers in All Three Nations, Briefing Paper 106," eds. Robert Scott, Carlos Salas, and Bruce Campbell (Washington: Economic Policy Institute, 2001), http://www.epi.org/publication/briefingpapers_nafta01_index/ (accessed 9/24/13); Louis Gerard Mendoza, *Historia: The Literary Making of Chicana and Chicano History* (College Station: Texas A&M University Press, 2001), 64–65; Gustavo Cano and Alejan-

dra Délano, "The Institute of Mexicans Abroad: The Day After . . . After 156 Years," *American Political Science Association*, September 2–5, 2004, http://ccis.ucsd.edu/2006/04/the-mexican-government-and-organised-mexican-immigrants-in-the-united-states-a-historical-analysis-of-political-transnationalism-1848–2005-working-paper-148/ (accessed 8/24/13); Martha Menchaca, *The Mexican Outsiders: A Community History of Marginalization and Discrimination in California* (Austin: University of Texas Press, 1995), 51–58; Stephen J. Pitti, *The Devil in the Silicon Valley: Northern California, Race, and Mexican Americans* (Princeton: Princeton University Press, 2003), 110.

18. Rosales, *Testimonio*, 116; Cynthia Orozco, *No Mexicans, Women or Dogs Allowed: The Rise of the Mexican American Civil Rights Movement* (Austin: University of Texas Press, 2009), 28; Camarillo, *Chicanos in a Changing Society*, 148–152; Carlos Larralde and Richard Griswold del Castillo, "San Diego's Ku Klux Klan, 1920–1980," *San Diego History* 46, nos. 2 and 3 (2000), http://www.sandiegohistory.org/journal/2000-2/klan.htm (accessed 2/21/11); Menchaca, *The Mexican Outsiders*, 51–55; Anti-Defamation League, "Ku Klux Klan: Recent Developments," http://www.adl.org/learn/ext_us/kkk/changes.asp?LEARN_Cat=Extremism&LEARN_SubCat=Extremism_in_America&xpicked=4&item=kkk (accessed 2/21/11).

19. Charles B. Williams Jr. and Hilda H. B. Williams, "Mutual Aid Societies and Economic Development: Survival Efforts," in *African Americans in the South: Issues of Race, Class and Gender*, eds. Hans A. Baer and Yvonne Jones (Athens: University of Georgia Press, 1992), 27; Theda Skocpol, "What a Mighty Power We Can Be: African American Fraternal Groups and the Struggle for Equal Rights," http://www.slideshare.net/jsucus/african-american-fraternal-groups-talk-presentation (accessed 5/5/10); Teresa Paloma Acosta, "Alianza Hispano Americana," *The Handbook of Texas*, http://www.tshaonline.org/handbook/online/articles/AA/vna2.html (accessed 5/6/10); Sociedad de la Unión, Libro de Actas, 1914–31 (six volumes), "Solicitudes," Our Lady of the Lake University Archives (hereafter "OLLU"); Teresa Paloma Acosta and Ruthe Winegarten, *Las Tejanas: 300 Years of History,* (Austin: University of Texas Press, 2003), 210.

20. File 32, "Organo de la Alianza," box 3, AHA Collection, Arizona Collection, Arizona State University Archives, Tempe, AZ.

21. For an example of mutual aid in opposition to segregated facilities, see Arnoldo De León, *San Angelenos: Mexican Americans in San Angelo, Texas* (San Angelo: Fort Concho Museum Press, 1985), 29–33. Judith Rosenberg Raftery, *Land of Fair Promise: Politics and Reform in Los Angeles Schools, 1885–1941* (Stanford: Stanford University Press, 1992), 112–113; Julie Leininger Pycior, *LBJ and Mexican Americans: The Paradox of Power* (Austin: University of Texas Press, 1997), 15.

22. Author interview with Herman Gallegos, February 10, 2010, San Francisco. Armando Navarro, *Mexicano Political Experience in Occupied Aztlán* (Lanham, MD: Rowman and Littlefield, 2005), 204–207; *La Epoca*, September 28, 1926, 6; *La Prensa*, September 12, 1926, 3; Cynthia E. Orozco, "The Origins of the League of United Latin American Citizens (LULAC) and the Mexican American Civil Rights Movement in Texas with an Analysis of Women's Political Participation in a Gendered Context, 1910–1929," PhD diss., University of California, Los Angeles, 1992, 228, 265, 302–303, 322; Julie Leininger Pycior, "Tejanas Navigating the 1920s," in *Tejano Epic: Essays in Honor of Félix Almaráz, Jr.,* ed. Arnoldo De León (Austin: Texas State Historical Association, 2005), 71–81; Jovita González, *Life along the Border,* ed. María Eugenia Cotera (College Station: Texas A&M Press, 2006), 111–116.

23. Gallegos interview; Cynthia Orozco, "Manuel C. Gonzales," *The Handbook of Texas*, http://www.tshaonline.org/handbook/online/articles/GG/fgo57.html; Rosales, *Pobre Raza*, 135–136.

24. Briegal, "The Alianza Hispano Americana," 170–185, 199; Cynthia Orozco, "American Council of Spanish-speaking People," *The Handbook of Texas*, http://www.tshaonline.org/handbook/online/articles/AA/pqa1.html (accessed 5/7/10); Acosta, "Alianza Hispano Americana," http://www.tshaonline.org/handbook/online/articles/AA/vna2.html (accessed 5/17/10); Matt S. Meier and Margo Gutiérrez, "Ralph Guzmán," in *Encyclopedia of the Mexican American Civil Rights Movement* (Westport, CT: Greenwood Press, 2000), 101; Jeffrey M. Garcilazo, "McCarthyism, Mexican Americans, and the Los Angeles Committee for Protection of the Foreign-Born," *Western Historical Quarterly* 32, no. 3 (2001), 273–295.

25. For Mexican American complaints about being ignored by the Kennedy administration, see Ralph Estrada, "Equity and Political Progress," *Alianza* LVII, no. 3 (1961), 6. Briegal, "Alianza Hispano Americana," 204–205; Richard Goodwin, *Remembering America: A Voice from the Sixties* (New York: Harper and Row, 1988), 108–109.

26. Julie Leininger Pycior, "Ahead of Their Time to No Avail: The American GI Forum and the Immigration Reform Act of 1965." American GI Forum/Texas A&M Corpus Christi History Conference, Corpus Christi, TX, March 27, 2008; Lizette Janess Olmos, "Profile: Jaime Martínez," *LULAC News* (May/June 2007), 18, http://www.lulac.net/publications/lulacnews/2007mayjun.pdf (accessed 2/21/11).

27. National Council of La Raza, "NCLR Affiliate Network," http://www.nclr.org/index.php/nclr_affiliates/affiliate_network/ (accessed 8/24/13); Embassy of the United States—Dominican Republic, "President Obama Announces Nomination of Raul H. Yzaguirre, Sr., to Become U.S. Ambassador to the Dominican Republic," http://santodomingo.usembassy.gov/pr-091130.html (accessed 5/12/10); Michael A. Fletcher, "Obama Appoints White House Speechwriting and Intergovernmental Affairs Heads," http://voices.washingtonpost.com/44/2008/11/26/obama_appoints_white_house_spe.html (accessed 5/12/10).

28. In terms of global economic issues, NCLR has been circumspect, with its website making virtually no mention of the North American Free Trade Agreement, for example; http://www.nclr.org/index.php/site/search_results/?cx=000638822871137547098%3Awrwrlgwzing&cof=FORID%3A10&ie=UTF-8&q=nafta&sa=Search (accessed 8/24/13); Theda Skocpol, *Diminished Democracy*, Norman: University of Oklahoma Press, 2004, 116–119, 135, 136, 146, 173, 190, 195–196, 201, 202; "Ready to Rumble: Civil Rights Heavyweight Raul Yzaguirre on Life, the Evolution of the NCLR, and Giving Latinos a Fighting Chance," *Latino Leaders* (December 2001), http://law-journals-books.vlex.com/vid/rumble-heavyweight-raul-yzaguirre-nclr-56471996 (accessed 8/19/13).

29. Gallegos interview.

30. Gallegos, who was born in 1930, chose to give his final public address in 2009 not to Washington, DC decision-makers or at some big convention, but back in the East San Jose barrio where he began his organizing. Navarrette interview; Gallegos interview.

Chapter 6

1. Theda Skocpol, *Diminished Democracy: From Membership to Management in American Civic Life* (Norman: University of Oklahoma Press, 2004), 266–267; Immanuel Ness, *Immigrant Unions and the New U.S. Labor Market* (Pittsburgh: Temple University Press, 2010), 191.

2. Miriam Ching Yoon Louie, *Sweatshop Warriors: Immigrant Workers Take on Local Factories* (Cambridge: South End Press Collective, 2001), ii, 195–197, 220; William Greider, *Who Will Tell the People: The Betrayal of American Democracy* (New York: Simon and Schuster, 1992), 193–194; Anya Kamenetz, "The Shape of Unions to Come," tompaine.com, January 30, 2007 (accessed 3/24/10); Skocpol, *Diminished Democracy*, 215, 221–222, 266–267; Gar Alperovitz, *America beyond Capitalism: Reclaiming Our Wealth, Our Liberty, and Our Democracy* (New York: Wiley, 2005), 159.

3. Author interview with Lucas Benítez, February 22, 2010, Immokalee, FL; Julie Leininger Pycior, "Transnational Labor Organizing: Lessons from the Mexican-heritage Community," lecture at the Julian Samora Research Institute, Michigan State University, March 17, 2010; Penny Lernoux, *Cry of the People* (New York: Doubleday, 1980), 40, 389, 514; Mike Hall, "Florida Activist Training Draws 200 Union Members," *AFL-CIO Now Blog*, November 6, 2009, http://blog.aflcio.org/2009/11/06/florida-activist-training-draws-200-union-members/ (accessed 3/31/10); Coalition of Immokalee Workers, "About CIW," http://ciw-online.org/about.html (accessed 4/1/10).

4. Author interview with Baldemar Velásquez, March 21, 2010, Toledo, OH; Arturo Cano, "Baldemar Velásquez," *La Jornada*, January 1, 2009, http://www.jornada.unam.mx/2009/01/12/index.php?section=sociedad&article=034n1soc (accessed 4/7/10).

5. *La Prensa*, February 28, 1919, 6; November 21, 1922, 8; May 3, 1923, 7; June 10, 1926, 6; Thomas P. Rogers, "The Housing Situation of Mexicans in San Antonio" (master's thesis, Uni-

versity of Texas, 1927), 8–10; Sociedad de la Unión, Libro de Actas, 1914–15, Our Lady of the Lake University Archives (hereafter "*Ollu*"), San Antonio; 293, 294, 304, 312–313, 318–319, 329, 343, 356, 396, 400–401, 409, 412–413, 443, 471; Libro de Actas, 1916–19, 58–59, 64–65, 134, 172, 178, 210, 269, 353–354, 368, 382, 386, 397, 399; Libro de Actas, 1922–26, 139, 159–160, 162–163, 304, 425, 437, 516; Libro de Actas, 1926–29, 47, 52, 259, 430; Libro de Actas, 1929–30, 253, 258.

6. *La Prensa*, July 5, 1917, 7; July 9, 1917, 5; July 11, 1917, 1, 5; July 24, 1917, 5; July 13, 1917, 5; July 3, 1919, 8; July 4, 1919, 8.

7. "¡P'alante!" or "¡Para adelante!" ("Ever onward!" or "Onward and upward!") is a colloquial, emphatic version of "adelante"/"onward."

8. Labor Notes, "Rebuilding Labor's Power," August 15, 2008, http://www.youtube.com/ watch?v=ZRmiHFPgBto (accessed 4/2/10); Clem Richardson, "Corporate Campaign, Inc.'s Ray Rogers," *Daily News*, August 21, 2008; Miriam Pawel, *A Union of Their Dreams: Power, Hope, and Struggle in Cesar Chavez's Farm Worker Movement* (New York: Bloomsbury Press, 2009), chapter 19, "The Purges" and "Epilogue"; Randy Shaw, *Beyond the Fields: Cesar Chavez, the UFW, and the Struggle for Justice in the Twenty-first Century* (Berkeley: University of California Press, 2008), chapter 10, "Decline of the UFW," and chapter 11, "Harvesting Justice beyond the Fields: The Ongoing Legacy of UFW Alumni"; Frank Bardack, "Cesar's Ghost: Decline and Fall of the UFW," in *César Chávez: A Brief Biography with Documents*, ed. Richard W. Etulian, 170.

9. Velásquez interview; Baldemar Velásquez, remarks at the AFL-CIO convention, Pittsburgh, 2009, http://www.youtube.com/watch?v=z_IbmChlmdw (accessed 7/22/13); W. K. Barger and Ernesto Reza, *The Farm Labor Movement in the Midwest* (Austin: University of Texas Press, 1994), 66–80; Farm Labor Organizing Committee, FLOC, AFL-CIO, http://www.supportfloc.org/ Pages/default.aspx (accessed 8/24/13).

10. Judith Berg Sobré, *San Antonio on Parade* (College Station: Texas A&M Press, 2003), 92; David Beito, "Thy Brother's Keeper," *Policy Review*, 1994, www.unz.org/PUb/PolicyRev-199494–000055?View=PDF (accessed 8/19/13); Worley, *El Paso City Directory*, 1900: 92–93; 1911: 33, 740; 1916: 83 (Dallas: John F. Worley Directory Co.); *La Prensa*, February 13, 1925, section two, 8; Texas Department of State, *Official List of Notaries Public of the State of Texas* (Austin: Department of State, 1922), 21; Phyllis McKenzie, *The Mexican-Texans* (College Station: Texas A&M University Press, 2004), 91; *El Paso City Directory*, 1901: 92; 1907: 40–41; 1903: 92; 1906: 40–41; Cleofas Calleros, in collaboration with Marjorie F. Graham, *El Paso Then and Now* (El Paso: American Printing Co., 1954).

11. Texas Department of State, *Official List of Notaries Public* (Austin: Department of State, 1922), 21; Phyllis McKenzie, *The Mexican-Texans* (College Station: Texas A&MM University Press, 2004), 91; *El Paso City Directory*: 1901, 92; 1904, 40–41; 1903, 92; 1906, 40–41; Calleros, *El Paso, Then and Now*, 176.

12. Ted Escobar, "Mutualista Delegates Vote to Back UFW," *Tri-City Herald*, June 20, 1972; Armando Navarro, *Mexicano Political Experience in Occupied Aztlán: Struggles and Change* (Walnut Creek, CA: Alta Mira Press, 2005), 283, 375; "United Farm Workers of America, AFL-CIO Premiere," April 16, 1975, http://www.farmworkermovement.us/ufwarchives/elmalcriado/Scott/ Brochure_001.pdf (accessed 2/23/11); José Pitti, Antonia Castañeda, and Carlos Cortés, "A History of Mexican Americans in California," http://www.lasculturas.com/lib/sd/blsd092200a.php (accessed 2/24/11); Bardack, "Cesar's Ghost."

13. Julie Leininger Pycior, "Vale Mas La Revolución Que Viene: Ernesto Galarza and Transnational Scholar Activism," in *Leaders of the Mexican American Generation* [working title], ed. Anthony Quiroz (Urbana: University of Illinois Press, forthcoming); Stephen J. Pitti, *The Devil in Silicon Valley: Northern California, Race, and Mexican Americans* (Princeton: Princeton University Press, 2003), 139–141.

14. Pitti, *The Devil in the Silicon Valley*, 111–119, 139; José Amaro Hernández, *Mutual Aid for Survival: The Case of the Mexican American* (Malabar, FL: Robert E. Krieger Publishing Company, 1983), 78–79; Gilbert González, "Company Unions, the Mexican Consulate, and the Imperial Valley Agricultural Strikes, 1928–1934," *The Western Historical Quarterly* 27, no. 1 (1996), 53–73; Kevin Starr, *Endangered Dreams: The Great Depression in California* (New York: Oxford University Press, 1996), 65; Douglas Monroy, *Rebirth: Mexican Los Angeles from the Great Migration to the Great Depression* (Berkeley: University of California Press, 1999), 61–66, 223–232; Lizabeth

Haas, *Conquests and Historical Identities in California, 1769–1936* (Berkeley: University of California Press, 1995), 159, 206–207; Barbara Driscoll, *The Tracks North: The Railroad Bracero Program of World War II* (Austin: University of Texas Press, 1999), 30.

15. Linda Gordon, *The Great Arizona Orphan Abduction* (Cambridge: Harvard University Press, 2001), 226.

16. Joaquín B. Oviedo, *Morenci Memories: True Tales of Copper Town* (N.P.: iUniverse, 2004), 9.

17. Benítez interview; Theodore Roosevelt, *The Winning of the West* (New York: G. P. Putnam's Sons, six volumes, 1889–96); Phil Mellinger, "The Men Have Become Organizers: Labor Conflict and Unionization in the Mexican Mining Camps of Arizona, 1900–1915," *Western Historical Quarterly* 23, no. 3 (1992), 323–331; Thomas G. Dyer, *Theodore Roosevelt and the Idea of Race* (Baton Rouge: LSU Press, 1980), 52–53, 61, and chapter 6, "Race, Immigration and Imperialism"; Rodolfo Acuña, *Corridors of Migration: The Odyssey of Mexican Laborers, 1600–1933* (Tucson: University of Arizona Press, 2008), 189, 193–194.

18. "Los Mineros," http://www.espinosaproductions.com/productions/mineros.html (accessed 7/22/2013).

19. Andrew Leonard, "I Dreamed I Saw José Hill Last Night: Borders Can't Stop Immigration, So Why Should They Stop Unions?" http://www.salon.com/technology/how_the_world_works/2007/01/22/jennifer_gordon/index.html (accessed 4/1/10); Jennifer Gordon, "Transnational Labor Citizenship," *Southern California Law Review* 80 (2007), http://papers.ssrn.com/s013/papers.cfm?abstract_id=943061&download=yes (accessed 4/1/10); Velásquez interview; Arizona State University Archives, "The Chicana/Chicano Experience—Mining/Minería," http://www.asu.edu/lib/archives/website/mining.htm (accessed 3/2/10); Mark Wassermann, *Everyday Life and Politics in Nineteenth Century Mexico* (Albuquerque: University of New Mexico Press, 2000), 206–207; Kent Patterson, "Cananea Mine Battle Reveals Anti-labor Offensive in Mexico, United States," *Americas Program, Center for International Policy,* http://www.unions.org/home/union-blog/2010/02/12/afl-cio-mexican-court-ruling-eliminates-right-to-strike/ (accessed 8/25/13); AFL-CIONOWBLOG, "Mexican Court Ruling Eliminates Right to Strike," http://www.unions.org/home/union-blog/2010/02/12/afl-cio-mexican-court-ruling-eliminates-right-to-strike/ (accessed 8/25/13), and AFL-CIO, "Top National Officers," http://www.axisoflogic.com/artman/publish/Article_58834.shtml (accessed 8/19/13).

20. AFL-CIO, "Top National Officers," http://www.aflcio.org/About/Leadership/Executive-Council-Members (accessed 8/24/13).

Chapter 7

1. Kent Patterson, "Cananea Mine Battle Reveals Anti-labor Offensive in Mexico, United States," Americas Program www.unions.org/home/union-blog/2010/02/12/aflcio-mexican-court-ruling-elimination-right-to-strike (accessed 8/25/10).

2. Rodolfo Acuña, *Corridors of Migration: The Odyssey of Mexican Laborers, 1600–1933* (Tucson: University of Arizona Press, 2008), 112.

3. Arizona State University Archives, "The Chicana/Chicano Experience—Mining/Minería," http://www.asu.edu/lib/archives/website/mining.htm (accessed 3/2/10); Mark Wassermann, *Everyday Life and Politics in Nineteenth Century Mexico* (Albuquerque: University of New Mexico Press, 2000), 206–207.

4. Philip J. Mellinger, *Race and Class in Western Copper: The Fight for Equality, 1896–1918* (Tucson: University of Arizona, 1995), 47–72; Acuña, *Corridors of Migration,* 125–137, 172, chapter 7; David Walker, "Porfirian Labor Politics: Working Class Organizations in Mexico City and Porfirio Díaz, 1876–1902," *The Americas* (January 1981), 247–298; John Mason Hart, "The Evolution of the Mexican and Mexican-American Working Class," in *Border Crossings,* Wilmington, DE: Scholarly Resources, 1988, 5–6; Leticia Barragán, Rina Ortiz, and Amanda Rosales, "El mutualismo en México: Siglo XIX," *Historia Obrera* 10 (1977), http://www.antorcha.net/biblioteca_virtual/historia/mutualismo/mutualismo.html (accessed 8/19/13).

5. Joshua McConnell Heyman, *Working People on the Border: Life and Labor in Sonora, 1886–1986* (Tucson: University of Arizona, 1991), 30, 64; Acuña, *Corridors of Migration.*

6. Wassermann, *Everyday Life and Politics in Nineteenth Century Mexico*, 206–207.

7. Caja 37/exp.14/f.3, 1914, Fondo Departamento del Trabajo, Serie Conflictos, 1911–1914, Archivo General de la Nación (Mexico); Roberto R. Calderón, "*Unión, Paz, y Trabajo*: Laredo's Mexican Mutual Aid Societies, 1890s," in *Mexican Americans in Texas History*, eds. Emilio Zamora et al. (Austin: Texas State Historical Association, 2000), 68; Adolfo Gilly, *La Revolución Interrumpida* (Mexico City: Ediciones ERA, 2007), 56–58; Rodney D. Anderson, *Outcasts in Their Own Land* (DeKalb: Northern Illinois University Press, 1976), 80–81; *La Prensa*, April 29, 1914, 5; July 11, 1923, 7; Sociedad de la Unión, Correspondence Records, Our Lady of the Lake University Archives, San Antonio, 170, 172; Judith Berg Sobré, *San Antonio on Parade* (College Station: Texas A&M University Press, 2003), 48; Walker, "Porfirian Labor Politics: Working Class Organizations in Mexico City and Porfirio Díaz, 1876–1902," 247–290; Alice J. Rhodes, "Lampasas, Texas," *The Handbook of Texas*, http://www.tshaonline.org/handbook/online/articles/hf101 (accessed 2/28/11).

8. Rodney D. Anderson, *Outcasts in Their Own Land* (DeKalb: University of Northern Illinois Press, 1976), 228, 313; *La Prensa*, January 29, 1917, 5; February 26, 1917, 5; March 17, 1917, 6; February 18, 1919, 7; July 10, 1925, 8; February 5, 1917, 6; March 4, 1917, 6; June 3, 1917, 5; March 18, 1919, 6; January 11, 1921, 1; Moisés González Navarro, *El Porfiriato: La Vida Social* [vol. 4 of *Historia Moderna de México*, ed. Daniel Cosío Villegas (México, 1957)], 345, 349; *El Imparcial de Texas*, November 21, 1918, 12; Roberto Calderón, *Mexican Coal Mining Labor in Texas and Coahuila, 1880–1930* (College Station: Texas A&M University Press, 2000), 149.

9. Emilio Zamora, *The World of the Mexican Worker in Texas* (College Station: Texas A&M Press, 1995), 106, 205; Calderón, "Unión, Trabajo, y Progreso: Laredo's Mexican Mutual Aid Societies, 1890s," 72–77; José Limón, "El Primer Congreso Mexicanista: A Precursor to Contemporary Chicanismo," in *Latino/a Thought: Culture Politics and Society*, eds. Francisco H. Vásquez and Fernando D. Torres (New York: Rowan and Littlefield, 2002), 108; Teresa Palomo Acosta, "Primer Congreso Mexicanista," *The Handbook of Texas*, http://www.tshaonline.org/handbook/online/articles/CC/vecyk.html (accessed 2/28/11); Julie Leininger Pycior, "Tejana Activism, 1910–1930: An Overview," De León Symposium Lecture, Victoria, TX, April 30, 2005; Nancy Baker Jones, "Jovita Idar," *The Handbook of Texas*, http://www.tshaonline.org/handbook/online/articles/fido3 (accessed 2/28/11); Cynthia Orozco, "League of United Latin American Citizens," http://www.tshaonline.org/handbook/online/articles/LL/we11.html; Cynthia Orozco, "Manuel C. Gonzales," *The Handbook of Texas*, http://www.tshaonline.org/handbook/online/articles/GG/fg057.html.

10. Adolfo Gilly, *La Revolución Interrumpida* (Mexico City: Ediciones ERA, 2007), 59.

11. The story of El Primer Congreso Mexicanista is recounted in chapter 4, "Legacy of Conquest."

12. Benson Latin American Collection, University of Texas, "Clemente N. Idar Papers . . . Descriptive Summary," http://www.lib.utexas.edu/taro/utlac/00197/lac-00197.html (accessed 8/24/13); Cynthia Orozco, "Clemente Idar," *The Handbook of Texas Online*, http://www.tshaonline.org/handbook/online/articles/II/fid4.html (accessed 3/10/10); Tiffany Ten Eyck, "In New York City: Carpenters Embrace Immigrant," *Labor Notes*, December 26, 2007, http://www.labornotes.org/node/1489 (accessed 4/6/10).

13. *El Imparcial de Texas*, April 8, 1920; tombstone inscription, San Fernando Cemetery #2, San Antonio, 1977; Benson Latin American Collection, "Clemente N. Idar Papers"; Orozco, "Clemente Idar"; Gilbert González, *Mexican Consuls and Labor Organizing, Imperial Politics in the American Southwest* (Austin: University of Texas Press, 1999), 21; author interview with Ed Idar Jr., June 22, 1988, Austin; Benson Latin American Collection, "Federico Idar and Idar Family Papers," http://www.lib.utexas.edu/taro/utlac/00199/lac-00199.html; Juan R. García, *Mexicans in the Midwest, 1900–1932* (Tucson: University of Arizona, 1996), 43–45, 229, 237; LULAC, "Comprehensive Immigration Reform," http://lulac.org/programs/immigration/ (accessed 2/25/13).

14. Ralph Armbruster-Sandoval, *Globalization and Cross-border Labor Solidarity in the Americas* (New York: Routledge, 2004), 170, n. 4; Julie Leininger Pycior, "Vale Mas la Revolución Que Viene: Ernesto Galarza and Transnational Scholar Activism," in *Leaders of the Mexican Ameri-*

can Generation: Biographical Sketches, ed. Anthony Quiroz (Urbana: University of Colorado Press, forthcoming); Arturo Cano, "Baldemar Velásquez, integrante de comité de jornaleros, relata su pelea en campos de EU," *La Jornada*, January 1, 2009, http://www.jornada.unam. mx/2009/01/12/index.php?section=sociedad&article=034n1soc (accessed 4/7/10); "Moreno, Luisa," *American Home Front in World War II* (Detroit: The Gale Group, 2005), Encyclopedia. com (accessed 1/22/10); Richard García, *Rise of the Mexican American Middle Class: San Antonio, 1929–1941* (College Station: Texas A&M University Press, 1991), 104.

15. *TIME*, December 28, 1942 and January 25, 1943.

16. "Good Neighbor Daydream," *The Nation* (January 16, 1943), 77; *The New York Times*, December 12, 1942; *The New York Times*, January 12, 1943; *TIME*, December 28, 1942; *TIME*, January 25, 1943; Robert Jackson Alexander and Eldon M. Parker, *A History of Organized Labor in Bolivia* (Westport, CT: Greenwood Press, 2005), 45–48; Rafael Menjívar, *Reforma Agraria: Guatemala, Bolivia, Cuba* (San Salvador: Editorial Universitaria de El Salvador, 1969), 217.

17. Ernesto Galarza, "The Crisis of the Pan American Union," *Inter-American Reports*, no. 5 (1949); William Becker, interview with Gabrielle Morris, Governmental History Documentation Project (Berkeley: University of California, 1981), http://archive.org/stream/underedmundbrowoorowlrich/underedmundbrowoorowlrich_djvu.txt (accessed 8/24/13); Organization of American States, "Staff Association," http://www.oas.org/columbus/staffassociation.asp (accessed December 30, 2009); Ernesto Galarza, "Standardization of Armaments in the Western Hemisphere," *Inter-American Reports*, no. 1 (October 1947).

18. Arturo Cano, "Críticas a activista por organizer a los 'esclavos para liberarlos,'" *La Jornada*, January 12, 2009, http://www.jornada.unam.mx/2009/01/12/index.php?section=sociedad&article=034n1soc (accessed 8/25/13); Stephen J. Pitti, *The Devil in Silicon Valley: Northern California, Race, and Mexican Americans* (Princeton: Princeton University Press, 2003), 137–149; Stephen J. Pitti, "Ernesto Galarza Remembered," *JSRI Latino Studies Series*, no. 10 (1997), http://www.jsri. msu.edu/RandS/research/ops/oc10.pdf (accessed 3/1/10).

19. Pycior, "Vale Mas La Revolución Que Viene"; Building Bridges Radio, "Farm Labor Organizing Committee: Building on Victories," 2008, http://www.archive.org/details/BuildingBridgesRadioFarmLaborOrganizingCommittee-BuildingOnVictories; *La Prensa*, July 5, 1917, 7; July 9, 1917, 5; July 11, 1917, 1, 5; July 24, 1917, 5; July 13, 1917, 5; July 3, 1919, 8; July 4, 1919, 8.

20. Baldemar Velásquez, speech to Labor Notes conference, August 15, 2008, http://www. youtube.com/watch?v=ZRm1HFPgBto&feature=related (accessed 2/21/11); Vicki Ruiz, *From Out of the Shadows: Mexican Women in Twentieth-Century America* (New York: Oxford, 1998), 97; Vicki Ruiz, "Una Mujer Sin Fronteras: Luisa Moreno and Latina Labor Activism," *Pacific Historical Review* 73, no. 1 (2004), 1–20.

21. David Gutiérrez, *Walls and Mirrors: Mexican Americans, Mexican Immigrants, and the Politics of Ethnicity* (Berkeley: University of California Press, 1995), 191–192 and 271, n. 52.

22. "Bert Corona and His Vision," Bert Corona Leadership Institute, http://www.bcli.info/ profile.htm (accessed 2/26/11); Gutiérrez, *Walls and Mirrors*, 191–192 and 271, n. 52; Mario T. García, *Memories of Chicano History: The Life and Narrative of Bert Corona* (Berkeley: University of California Press, 1994), 291, 295.

23. Gutiérrez, *Walls and Mirrors*, 192–199; García, *Memories of Chicano History*, 238–244; Alatorre interview.

24. Daniel Tichenor, *Dividing Lines: The Politics of Immigration Control in America* (Princeton: Princeton University Press, 2002), 40–41, 204–205; Baldemar Velásquez, remarks at AFL-CIO convention, Pittsburgh, 2009, http://www.youtube.com/watch?v=z_IbmChlmdw (accessed 3/2/11); author interview with Ruben Navarrette, San Diego, January 8, 2010; Steven Greenhouse, "AFL-CIO Official to Step Down," *The New York Times*, September 12, 2007, http://query. nytimes.com/gst/fullpage.html?res=9E00E5DD1331F931A2575AC0A9619C8B63 (accessed 4/6/10); Randy Shaw, *Beyond the Fields* (Berkeley: University of California Press, 2008), chapter 7; Bill Fletcher Jr. and Fernando Gapasin, *Solidarity Divided: The Crisis in Organized Labor and a New Path toward Social Justice* (Berkeley: University of California Press, 2008), 102–104; Ruth Milkman: "Labor and the New Immigrant Rights Movement: Lessons from California," Social Science Research Council, 2006, http://borderbattles.ssrc.org/Milkman/index2.html (accessed

3/2/11); Gzech, paper for Wilson Center/Enlaces America Roundtable; Nancy Cleland, "AFL-CIO Calls for Amnesty for Illegal U.S. Workers," *Los Angeles Times,* February 17, 2000.

25. Miriam Ching Yoon Louie, *Sweatshop Warriors: Immigrant Women Workers Take on the Global Factory* (Cambridge: South End Press, 2001), 220.

26. Milkman, "Labor and the New Immigrant Rights Movement," Gzech, paper for Wilson Center/Enlaces America Roundtable.

27. Pawel, "Former Chavez Ally Took His Own Path," *Los Angeles Times,* January 11, 2006; Service Employees International Union, *Tribute to Eliseo Medina,* Lisa Duncan, producer, http://www.seiu.org/2008/12/award-winning-video-on-seiu-labor-leader-eliseo-medina-shows-evolu-tion-of-immigrant-rights-movement.php; Milkman, "Labor and the New Immigrant Rights Movement."

28. James Parks, "New York Times Hails Partnership between AFL-CIO, Day Laborers," AFL-CIO Now Blog, August 11, 2006, http://blog.aflcio.org/2006/08/11/new-york-times-hails-part-nership-between-afl-cio-day-laborers/; search results for the term "immigration" on the AFL-CIO Now Blog, http://blog.aflcio.org/?s=immigration&submit.x=0&submit.y=0&submit=submit (both accessed 3/30/10).

29. *The New Urban Immigrant Workforce,* eds. Saumathi Jayaraman and Immanuel Ness (Armonk, NY: M. E. Sharpe, 2005), 5–7, 78–79, 177, 179; Mutualista Obrera Mexicana, "Dance for the Benefit of Horn and Hardhart Strikers, Local 302," Broadsides SY1937, no. 133, New-York Historical Society; Julie Leininger Pycior, "Precursors: Mexicans in New York before 1960," New York Historical Association, July 2005.

30. Velásquez interview.

31. Farm Labor Organizing Committee, "Justice for Santiago Rafael Cruz"; WTVD (Raleigh, NC), "Murder in Mexico," November 16, 2007, http://www.smfws.com/articles2007/november2007/art11162007b.htm (accessed 4/2/13); Claudia Boyd-Barrett, "FLOC, Family Seek Justice in 2007 Death," *Toledo Blade,* September 8, 2011, http://www.toledoblade.com/local/2011/09/08/FLOC-family-seek-justice-in-2007-death.html (accessed 4/2/13).

32. Baldemar Velásquez, speech to Labor Notes conference, August 15, 2008; Velásquez interview.

33. "Board Members: Policy Matters Ohio," http://www.policymattersohio.org/board-biogra-phies (accessed 7/22/13); Ralph Armbruster-Sandoval, *Globalization and Cross-border Labor Soli-darity in the Americas* (New York: Routledge, 2004), 170, n. 4.

34. Andrew Leonard, "I Dreamed I Saw José Hill Last Night," http://www.salon.com/2007/01/22/jennifer_gordon/ (accessed 7/22/13).

35. Velásquez talk to Labor Notes conference.

36. ABA Online, "Conversation: Transcript of Lucas Benitez's March 2000 Talk, http://www.abanet.org/publiced/lawday/convo/00/beniteztalk.html (accessed 4/6/10); Benítez interview with author, and author notes observing the CIW office, Immokalee, FL, February 22, 2010; Armbruster-Sandoval, *Globalization and Cross-border Labor Solidarity in the Americas,* 170, n. 4; "Sodexo and Coalition of Immokalee Workers Sign Fair Food Agreement," http://ciw-online.org/2010/08/24/ciw_sodexo_joint_release/ (access 8/24/13).

37. Benítez interview.

38. Benítez interview; Velásquez interview.

39. Julie Leininger Pycior, "Past Promises Unkept" (letter), *The New York Times,* November 12, 1993; Ernesto Galarza, "Program for Action," *Common Ground* 10 (1949), cited in Gilbert G. González and Raul Fernández, "Empire and the Origins of Twentieth-Century Migration from Mexico to the United States," *Pacific Historical Review* 71, no. 1 (2002), 19.

40. The Sodexo company website seems to make no mention of the CIW issue, although the website has no "search" function, so that fact cannot be verified, http://www.sodexo.com/group_en/default2.asp (accessed 3/11/10); ABA Online, "Lucas Benitez," http://www.abanet.org/publiced/lawday/convo/00/benitezbio.html (accessed 12/2/09); Benítez interview; Farm Labor Organizing Committee/FLOC, AFL-CIO, "Changing the System," http://www.supportfloc.org/Pages/default.aspx (accessed 8/24/13).

Chapter 8

1. Author interview with Soledad "Chole" Alatorre, May 3, 2010, Pacoima, CA.

2. Calvin Trillin, "Some Elements of Power," *The New Yorker,* May 2, 1977; author interview with María Varela, April 30, 2010, Providence, RI; author interview with Ernesto Cortés Jr., May 19, 2010, New York; MacArthur Foundation, "MacArthur Fellows Program, 1981–2010," http://www.macfound.org/site/c.lkLXJ8MQKrH/b.1139453/k.B938/Search_All_Fellows.htm (accessed 3/2/11); Ralph David Johnson, John A. Booth, and Richard J. Harris, *The Politics of San Antonio: Community, Progress and Power* (Lincoln: University of Nebraska Press, 1983), 196; Peter Applebome, "Changing Texas Politics at its Roots," *The New York Times,* May 31, 1988; Roberto Suro, "Los Ojos Journal: Aiding the Poor Receives Its Reward," *The New York Times,* August 20, 1990.

3. Soledad Alatorre to author, telephone conversation, May 1, 2010; Industrial Areas Foundation, "Locate IAF Facilities," http://www.industrialareasfoundation.org/affiliate-members (accessed 8/24/13); author notes on Worker Mass and May Day commemoration, May 1, 2010, Pacoima, CA; Cortés interview; Harry C. Boyte, "Seeds of a Different Politics," *The Good Society* 19, no. 1 (2010), 70–73. Hezekiah Walker, "I Need You to Survive," http://www.youtube.com/watch?v=LUUHPDUsLJo (accessed 3/2/11); OneLA-IAF, "Agenda: OneLA Assembly" and "OneLA-IAF Foreclosure Prevention Plan," May 2, 2010, Los Angeles; author audio recording, OneLA-IAF assembly, May 2, 2010, Los Angeles.

4. Thomas Holler, presentation to the Social Justice Committee, Mary Immaculate parish, Los Angeles, May 1, 2010.

5. "Priest becomes Savior in Foreclosure Crisis," CNN, April 23, 2008, http://edition.cnn.com/2009/LIVING/04/22/foreclosure.priest/index.html?eref=rss_topstories (accessed 3/2/11).

6. Alatorre interview; Cortés interview.

7. Hezekiah Walker, "I Need You to Survive"; audio recording by the author of the OneLA-IAF accountability session; Cortés interview.

8. Martin Luther King Jr., *A Testament of Hope: The Essential Writings and Speeches of Martin Luther King Jr.,* ed. James Melvin Washington, (New York: HarperCollins, 1991), 207; OneLA-IAF, "Agenda"; audio recording by author, OneLA-IAF accountability session.

9. Ernesto Cortés Jr. "Reweaving the Fabric: The Iron Rule and the IAF Strategy for Power and Politics," http://www.cpn.org/topics/community/reweaving.html (accessed 7/24/13).

10. Rick Orlov and Tony Castro, "Homeowner Help Might Be on Way," *Los Angeles Daily News,* May 13, 2009; "OneLA-IAF Foreclosure Prevention Plan"; audio recording by author, OneLA-IAF assembly; Society of Saint Vincent de Paul, Council of Los Angeles, "Board of Directors," http://svdpla.org/index.php/about/contents/board_of_directors (accessed 3/2/11).

11. Audio recording by author, OneLA accountability session, follow-up section; Rabbi Stephen Julius Stein, "Tikkun Olam: Actions Speak Loudly—BUT SO DO WORDS," Wiltshire Boulevard Temple bulletin, March 15, 2009, http://www.wilshireboulevardtemple.org/content/pdf/bulletin_03_15_09_OE_6_1_5321.pdf (accessed 3/2/11); Bill Boyarsky, "Pursuit of Justice," *The Jewish Journal,* March 24, 2010.

12. Audio recording by author, OneLA accountability session, follow-up section.

13. Jim Wassermann, "Critics Call California Foreclosure Plan a Big Bank Bailout," *Sacramento Bee,* July 14, 2010, http://www.mcclatchydc.com/2010/07/14/97444/critics-call-california-foreclosure.html#ixzz150EFoWv8 (accessed 3/2/11); Isaiah Poole, "Address Unemployment Pain, or Make It Worse," http://www.ourfuture.org/blog-entry/2010072814/progressive-breakfast-address-unemployment-pain-or-make-it-worse (accessed 3/2/11); Alan Zibel, "Calif. Lawmakers Want Foreclosure Investigation," *Los Angeles Daily News,* October 5, 2010, http://www.dailynews.com/ci_16259291?IADID=Search-www.dailynews.com-www.dailynews.com; Alejandro Lazo and E. Scott Reckard, "California Foreclosure Aid Fund Swells, but Banks Hesitate," *Los Angeles Times,* November 10, 2010.

14. Mary Beth Rogers, *Cold Anger: A Story of Money and Politics* (Denton: University of North Texas Press, 1990), 23; Troy Anderson, "California Homeowners to Get 1.2 Billion in Help," *Daily News* (Los Angeles), September 16, 2010; Cheryl Dahle, "Social Justice: Ernesto Cortés, Jr.," *Fast Company* (November 1999), http://www.fastcompany.com/magazine/30/cortes.html; Cortés interview.

Chapter 9

1. It turns out that the title of this chapter, "Power to Protect What We Value," resembles a chapter title in the seminal study of Ernesto Cortés by Mary Beth Rogers, *Cold Anger: A Story of Money and Politics* (Denton: University of North Texas Press, 1990), in which chapter 3 is entitled "We Need the Power to Protect What We Value." *La Epoca*, July 21, 1918, 6; Viviana Cavada, interview by José Angel Gutiérrez, Corpus Christi, 1998, CMAS no. 66, Special Collections, University of Texas at Arlington, http://library.uta.edu/tejanovoices/xml/CMAS_066.xml (accessed 8/24/13); Julie Leininger Pycior, "La Raza Organizes: Mexican American Life in San Antonio, 1914–1930, as Reflected in Mutualista Activities," PhD diss., University of Notre Dame, 1979, 34.

2. For the *mutualista* occupational breakdown, see the membership rolls of the largest and one of the longest-lasting groups, Sociedad de la Unión. Membership rolls, Sociedad de la Unión, Libros de Actas, 1915–30, Sociedad de la Unión papers, Mexican American Collection, Our Lady of the Lake University, San Antonio (hereafter OLLU); Hudspeth Directory Company, *El Paso* (Hudspeth Directory Company, Inc., 1920), 50, and Hudspeth, *El Paso*, 1922, 173; Worley and Company, *El Paso City Directory*, 1900: 92; 1904: 98; 1912: 173, 145, 544.

3. Judith Berg Sobré, *San Antonio on Parade* (College Station: Texas A&M University Press, 2003), 85, 96; Johnson and Chapman, *San Antonio City Directory* (San Antonio: Johnson and Chapman, 1891); Jules Appler, *San Antonio City Directory, 1921–1922* (San Antonio: Tower Publications, 1923), 45, 213, 234, 257, 291, 400, 521; Sociedad de la Unión, Libros de Actas, 1929–31, MAC/OLLU, 82, 85; *La Prensa*, May 17, 1917, 5; 1917, 5; April 4, 1919, 5; March 27, 1921, 6; December 11, 1921, 5; April 2, 1922, 5; May 6, 1923, 6; author interviews with Lucas Garza, November 15, 23, and 25, 1976; Jules A. Appler, *San Antonio City Directory* (San Antonio: Jules Appler, 1892).

4. Cynthia Orozco, "Simón G. Domínguez," *The Handbook of Texas*, http://www.tshaonline.org/handbook/online/articles/DD/fdoqx.html (accessed 01/25/11); Carlos Blanton, *The Strange Career of Bilingual Education in Texas* (College Station: Texas A&M Press, 2007), 26; José Limón, "El Primer Congreso Mexicanista: A Precursor to Contemporary Chicanismo," in *Latino/a Thought: Culture Politics and Society*, eds. Francisco H. Vásquez and Fernando D. Torres (New York: Rowan and Littlefield, 2002), 222; correspondence, box 2D65, Domínguez Papers, Center for American History, University of Texas; Teresa Paloma Acosta, "Sara Estela Ramírez," *The Handbook of Texas*, http://www.tshaonline.org/handbook/online/articles/fra60 (accessed 3/5/11).

5. Worley, *El Paso City Directory*, 1912: 32, 434; 1913: 33, 384; 1916: 83, 554; Hudspeth: *El Paso City Directory*, 1918: 105, 225; 1920: 91; 1923: 164, 733; 1926: 20, 727, 795.

6. Recording secretary's report for every meeting in the Sociedad de la Unión Libros de Actas, 1914–29, OLLU; *El Imparcial de Texas*, January 27, 1921, 11.

7. David Beito, "Thy Brother's Keeper," *Policy Review*, 1994, www.unz.org/Pub/PolicyRev-1994/00055?view=PDF (accessed 8/19/13).

8. *La Prensa*, February 13, 1925, section 2, p. 8; Garza interview; Sociedad de la Unión, Libro de Actas, 1914–15: 291; 1916–19: 21–22; 1919–22: 10; 1922–26: 12, 50, 111–112; 1929–31: 491 (see also the report of the Collector in the first meeting of each month), OLLU; *La Epoca*, January 16, 1931; Sobré, *San Antonio on Parade*, 91–94, 149; Charles Arnold, "Folklore, Manners and Customs of the Mexicans in San Antonio, Texas," (San Francisco: R&E Publications, 1971), 6–7.

9. *La Epoca*, September 12, 1921; Benson Latin American Collection, "Galindo Family Papers," http://www.lib.utexas.edu/taro/utlac/00235/lac-00235.html (accessed 4/2/13).

10. Sociedad de la Unión, Libros de Actas, 1919–21, 373 and 1922–26, 207, OLLU; author interview with Herman Gallegos, February 10, 2010, San Francisco; "An Interview with Ernesto Cortes," *Religion and Ethics Newsweekly*, http://www.pbs.org/wnet/religionandethics/episodes/march-2-2001/an-interview-with-ernesto-cortes/3456/ (accessed 7/14/11).

11. Mario T. García, *Mexican Americans: Leadership, Ideology, and Identity, 1930–1960* (New Haven: Yale University Press, 1989), 72–82.

12. At that time the pecan shellers were organizing and holding job actions. García, *Mexican Americans: Leadership, Ideology, and Identity*, 72–82; Benson Latin American Collection, "Founding of La Liga Pro-Defensa Escolar," http://www.lib.utexas.edu/benson/escobar/escobar6.html (accessed 3/5/11); Cynthia Orozco, "School Improvement League," *Handbook of Texas Online*, http://www.tshaonline.org/handbook/online/articles/kaswm (accessed 3/5/11).

13. Riku Sen, *Stir It Up: Lessons in Community Organizing and Advocacy* (New York: John Wiley and Sons, 2003), xlvii.

14. Gallegos interview; OneLA-IAF, "History," http://onela-iaf.org/%E2%80%9Cnever-do-others-what-they-can-do-themselves%E2%80%9D-%E2%80%93-iron-rule (accessed 8/24/13).

15. Saul D. Alinsky, "The War on Poverty: Political Pornography," *The Journal of Social Issues* 21, no. 1 (1965), 41–47.

16. Cortés interview.

17. Gallegos interview; Cortés interview; Richard Lueckens, "Saul Alinsky: *Homo Ludens* for Urban Democracy," *Christian Century*, November 15, 1989, 1050; Rogers, *Cold Anger*, 68; US Conference of Catholic Bishops, "Catholic Campaign for Human Development," http://www.usccb.org/cchd/index.shtml (accessed 3/5/11).

18. Rogers, *Cold Anger: A Story of Faith and Power Politics*, 82, 83.

19. Cortés notes that the prominent Catholic philosopher Jacques Maritain considered the IAF a prime example of the subsidiarity principle, and Cortés pointed out that the Alinsky/Maritain correspondence was compiled in a book. Cortés interview; Ernesto Cortés Jr., "Reweaving the Fabric: The Iron Rule and the IAF Strategy for Power and Politics," http://www.cpn.org/topics/community/reweaving.html (accessed 7/24/13); Bernard Doering, *The Philosopher and the Provocateur: The Correspondence of Jacques Maritain and Saul Alinsky* (Notre Dame: University of Notre Dame Press, 1994); Ernesto Cortés Jr., "Faith, Charity and Justice," *The American Prospect*, April 22, 2007, http://prospect.org/article/faith-charity-and-justice (accessed 8/19/13); Daniel A. Corford, *Working People of California* (Berkeley: University of California Press, 1995), 379–381; Gallegos interview; Mark R. Warren, *Dry Bones Rattling: Community Building to Revitalize American Democracy* (Princeton: Princeton University Press, 2001), 74–75.Homero Vera, "Catholic Mutual Society" http://www.st-theresas.com/organizations/scm/index.html (accessed 3/5/11); "Sociedad Católica Mutualista," *El Mesteño*, 2008; "History of St. Theresa Parish, Premont, Texas" http://www.st-theresas.com/history/index.html (accessed 3/5/11).

20. Homero Vera, "Catholic Mutual Society," http://pulido123.com/mesteno/stories/0008mutualists.html (accessed 8/19/13); "Sociedad Católica Mutualista," *El Mesteño*, 2008; "History of St. Theresa Parish, Premont, Texas," http://pulido123.com/mesteno/stories/0008mutualists.html (accessed 8/19/13).

21. Michael E. Engh, "From the City of Angels to the Parishes of San Antonio: Catholic Organization, Women Activists, and Racial Intersections, 1900–1950," in *Catholicism in the American West: A Rosary of Hidden Voices*, eds. Roberto R. Treviño and Richard V. Francaviglia (Arlington: University of Texas at Arlington, 2007), 49; Vera, "Catholic Mutual Society"; Sociedad Católica Mutualista, *El Mesteño*, 2008; "History of St. Theresa Parish, Premont, Texas."

22. For more recent activities by the San Antonio IAF group COPS, see COPS/Metro Alliance, "Recent Activities," http://copsmetro.wordpress.com/accomplishments/recent-actions/ and John W. Gonzalez, "Advocates of Medicaid Expansion Seek Bexar Backing," *San Antonio Express-News*, February 24, 2013, http://www.mysanantonio.com/default/article/Advocates-of-Medicaid-expansion-seek-Bexar-backing-4304907.php (both accessed 7/24/13).

23. Pycior, "La Raza Organizes," 33.

24. Arizona Interfaith Network-IAF, "Concept Paper on Immigration Reform Border Security, Comprehensive Reform, and Economic Recovery," July 6, 2010, http://www.arizonainterfaith.org/imm_reform.php (accessed 3/5/11).

25. Cortés interview; Jonathan Fox and Xóchitl Bada, "Migrant Civic Engagement," Research Paper Series on Latino Immigrant Civic and Political Participation, no. 3 (2009), Wilson Center Mexico Institute, www.wilsoncenter.org/migrantparticipation (accessed 5/20/10); Julie Leininger Pycior, "Ahead of Their Time to No Avail: The American GI Forum and the Immigration Reform Act of 1965," American GI Forum/Texas A&M Corpus Christi History Conference, Corpus Christi, March 27, 2008; Industrial Areas Foundation, "Our Initiatives," http://www.industrialareasfoundation.org/press (accessed 8/24/13); José Alfredo Martínez Hernández, "DIF Tlalnepantla Participa en Conferencia Informativa sobre Ley Arizona SB1070," *Diario al Momento* (Gobierno del Estado de México), June 24, 2010, http://diarioalmomento.com/index.php?option=com_content&task=view&id=7881&Itemid=201 (accessed 3/5/11).

26. 1000 Peace Women, "Maria Varela," http://www.1000peacewomen.org/eng/friedens-frauen_biographien_gefunden.php?WomenID=883 (accessed 3/5/11); Author interview with María Varela, April 22, 2010, Providence, RI, and author telephone interview with María Varela, August 24, 2010.

27. Jon Christensen, "Heroes and Heroines: María Varela, an Authentic 'Milagro,'" *Mother Jones*, January 1989, 27–28; Varela interview.

28. Varela interview.

29. The VISTA offer to Varela came from the administration of President Jimmy Carter. Varela interview; Ganados del Valle, http://ganadosdelvalle.org/, and Tierra Wools, http://handweavers.com/ (accessed 4/2/13); Julia Moskin, "Lamb the Conquistadors Would Recognize," *The New York Times*, April 19, 2011; Kaye Briegal, "The Alianza Hispano Americana," PhD diss., University of Southern California, 1974, 114–115; Julie Leininger Pycior, "Important but Neglected: Midwest Latino/a Biography and Memoir," Julian Samora Research Institute, http://jsri.msu.edu/upload/events/20thAnniversary/Pycior.pdf (accessed 8/24/13); María Ochoa, "Cooperative Re/weavings: Artistic Expression and Economic Development in a Northern New Mexican Village," *Mexican American Women: Changing Images/Perspectives in Mexican American Studies* 5 (1995), 122, 144, n. 1; Sociedad Protección Mútua de Trabajadores Unidos, http://www.eljeferuben.com/spmdtu.html (accessed 3/5/11); María Varela, "If You Have Come to Help Us . . . Go Home!" *US Catholic Historian* 26, no. 1 (2008), 67–82; Ochoa, "Cooperative Re/weavings," 17, n. 28; Varela interview; Pycior, "La Raza Organizes," 198–204.

30. "Alinsky, Saul: Course to Diocesan Clergy," 1964, John J. Egan Papers, AJEG 10771 CT-10775 CT, University of Notre Dame Archives, http://www.archives.nd.edu/cgi-bin/thindex.pl?keyword=alinsky&searchonly=JEG (accessed 3/5/110); Margery Frisbie, *An Alley in Chicago: The Ministry of A City Priest*, chapter 8, "What Do You Think of the Rosenberg Case?" http://archives.nd.edu/findaids/html/etext/alley008.htm (accessed 3/5/11).

31. Varela interview; Jay Dolan, "Catholics in the Midwest," http://www3.nd.edu/~jdolan/midwest.html (accessed 7/24/13); Christian Family Movement, "History," http://www.cfm.org/history.html (accessed 3/5/11).

32. Varela, "If You Have Come to Help Us . . . Go Home!"; Varela interview.

33. "YCSer Maria Varela, YCS Formation Day, 12–21–08," http://www.youtube.com/results?search_query=maria+varela+ycs&aq=f (accessed 3/5/11); Varela, "If You Have Come to Help Us . . . Go Home!"; Joseph Martin Palacios, *The Catholic Social Imagination: Activism and the Just Society in Mexico and the United States* (Chicago: University of Chicago Press, 2007), 25, 234; Roberto Suro, "Los Ojos Journal: Aiding the Poor Receives Its Reward," *The New York Times*, August 20, 1990; Cortés interview.

34. Tom Hayden, in his memoir, refers to Varela as "a fair-complexioned Mexican-American with deep brown eyes." Tom Hayden, *Reunion: A Memoir* (New York: Random House, 1989), xii; 84, 95–96; "YCSer Maria Varela, YCS Formation Day, 12–21–08"; Varela, "If You Have Come to Help Us . . . Go Home!"; Varela interview.

35. Hayden, *Reunion: A Memoir*, xii, 84, 95–96; Tom Hayden and Dick Flacks, "The Port Huron Statement at 40," *The Nation*, July 18, 2002; "YCSer Maria Varela, YCS Formation Day, 12–21–08"; Varela, "If You Have Come to Help Us . . . Go Home!"; *Remembering SNCC: A Circle of Trust*, ed. Cheryl Lynn Greenburg (New Brunswick, NJ: Rutgers University Press, 1998), 197.

36. Otra Vuelta, according to its website, is "a full-service tire recycling firm. We pick up old tires from landfills and tire shops. We then wash, cut and punch them to make doormats, flower pots, custom-order trailer and bed liners among other things. There were an estimated 290,000,000 scrap tires in 2003. Thanks to tire management and recycling centers these numbers have gone down. . . . Green is the way to go! Do your part!" Otra Vuelta, "Where Do Your Tires Go?" http://www.otra-vuelta.com/ (accessed 9/10/10); 1000 Peace Women, "María Varela"; Varela, "If You Have Come to Help Us . . . Go Home!"; Varela interviews; Institución filantrópica to the Consul General, San Antonio, 1926, ASRE, IV-100-26, Archivo de la Secretaría de Relaciones Exteriores "Génaro Estrada" (Mexico).

Chapter 10

1. *La Prensa*, April 15, 1925, July 24, 1925, 1; July 29, 1925, 1; July 18, 1925, 7, 12; May 20, 1925, 1; May 25, 1925, 8; June 1, 1925, 1; September 20, 1925, 16; September 22, 1925, 10; August 31, 1925, 1; January 29, 1925, 1; May 5, 1925, 1; May 20, 1925, 12; October 4, 1925, 8; June 19, 1927, 5; April 22, 1928, 1; Norma Williams, "Changes in Funeral Patterns and Gender Roles among Mexican Americans," in *Women on the U.S.-Mexican Border*, eds. Vicki Ruiz and Susan Tiano (Boston: Allen and Unwin, 1987), 201–206; Douglas Foley et al., *From Peones to Políticos: Class and Ethnicity in a South Texas Town, 1900–1977* (Austin: University of Texas Press, 1977), 116–117; Sara Evans, "Women," *Encyclopedia of Southern History* (Baton Rouge: Louisiana State University Press, 1989), 1355.

2. Thirteen of the "Santa Mónica" charter members were married, with the marital status so often noted throughout history with regard to women, whatever their ethnic background. Sociedad Hispano-Americana de Benevolencia Mutua, entre Señoras, bajo el patricinio de Santa Mónica, "Constitución y Leyes" (San Francisco: Imprenta Cosmopolitana, 1875), MF 2 H4, Bancroft Library, University of California, Berkeley, 9–10, 13, 17–18.

3. As was typical with officially Catholic *mutualista* societies of both genders, a priest served as one of the leaders as well, although never as an officer. Sociedad Hispano-Americana de Benevolencia Mutua, entre Señoras, bajo el patricinio de Santa Mónica, "Constitución y Leyes" (San Francisco: Imprenta Cosmopolitana, 1875), MF 2 H4, Bancroft Library, University of California, Berkeley, 9–10, 13, 17–18.

4. Thus did this organization anticipate both the 1920 women's suffrage amendment to the US constitution and the women's rights provisions of the revolutionary 1917 Mexican constitution. Center for Big Bend Studies, "Hispanic History and Pioneers of El Barrio, Alpine, Texas, 1882–1910," http://ww2.sulross.edu/cbbs/basics-elbarrio.php (accessed 8/24/13); Vicki Ruiz, *From Out of the Shadows* (New York: Oxford University Press, 1989), 87; Joshua Heyman, "The Oral History of the Mexican-American Community of Douglas, Arizona, 1901–1942," *Journal of the Southwest* 35, no. 2 (1993); Cynthia E. Orozco, "Mexican American Women," *Handbook of Texas Online*, http://www.tshaonline.org/handbook/online/articles/pwmly (accessed 1/20/12).

5. The "third space" concept was developed by historian David Gutiérrez. For more on this as it applied to Sociedades Guadalupanas, see Gina Marie Pitti, "The Sociedades Guadalupanas in the San Francisco Archdiocese, 1942–1962," *U.S. Catholic Historian* 21, no. 1 (2003), 83–98. Author interview with María Varela, April 30, 2010, Providence, RI; Bradford Smith et al., *Philanthropy in Communities of Color* (Bloomington: Indiana University Press, 1999), 45; Teresa Paloma Acosta, "Sociedades Guadalupanas," *Handbook of Texas Online*, http://www.tshaonline.org/handbook/online/articles/ics10 (accessed 4/3/13).

6. Emma Pérez, *The Decolonial Imaginary: Writing Chicanas into History* (Bloomington: Indiana University Press, 1999), 96.

7. Richard Goodwin, *Remembering America: A Voice from the Sixties* (New York: Harper & Row, 1988), 109; Arnoldo De León and Richard Griswold del Castillo, *North From Aztlán: A History of Mexican Americans in the United States* (New York: Twayne, 1996), 55, 78.

8. Juan Gómez Quiñones, *Chicano Politics: Reality and Promise, 1940–1990* (Albuquerque: University of New Mexico Press, 1990), 362–364; Julie Leininger Pycior, "Mexican American Organizations," *The Handbook of Texas*, http://www.tshaonline.org/handbook/online/articles/vzmvj (accessed 3/7/11); *San Antonio City Directory, 1921–1922* (Tower Publications, 1923), 45, 291, 400; *La Prensa*, May 22, 1917, 5; April 4, 1919, 5; May 1, 1922, 5; November 26, 1922, 5; February 13, 1925, section 2, p. 8; May 31, 1926, 8; Julie Leininger Pycior, "Tejanas Navigating the 1920s," in *Tejano Epic: Essays in Honor of Félix Almaráz, Jr.*, ed. Arnoldo De León (Austin: Texas State Historical Association, 2005), 71–80; *Organo de la Alianza* XXII, no. 6 (1929), 2, in file 32, "ORGANO DE LA ALIANZA" and *Alianza*, October 1932, 20, in file 33, "ORGANO DE LA ALIANZA," both files in box 33, AHA Collection, Arizona Collection, Arizona State University Archives, Tempe, AZ; Kaye Briegal, "The Alianza Hispano Americana," PhD diss., University of Southern California, 1973, 65; Teresa Palomo Acosta, "Alianza Hispano Americana," *Handbook of Texas*, http://www.tshaonline.org/handbook/online/articles/vnao2 (accessed 3/9/13).

9. Julie Leininger Pycior, "Tejana Activism, 1910–1930: An Overview," De León Symposium Lecture, Victoria, TX, April 30, 2005; Varela interview; *La Prensa*, May 22, 1917, 5; April 4, 1919,

5; May 1, 1922, 5; November 26, 1922, 5; Theda Skocpol, *Diminished Democracy: From Membership to Management in American Civic Life* (Norman: University of Oklahoma Press, 2004), 79–78.

10. Ruiz, *From Out of the Shadows*, 88.

11. Cynthia Orozco, "Origins of the League of United Latin American Citizens (LULAC) and the Mexican American Civil Rights Movement in Texas with an Analysis of Women's Political Participation in a Gendered Context, 1910–1929," PhD diss., University of California, Los Angeles, 1992, 228, 265, 302–303, 322.

12. In 1917 Jovita Idar married Bartolo Juárez, and after the revolution ended in 1920, they lived in San Antonio, where she set up a free kindergarten and was an editor for the Methodist newspaper *El Heraldo Mexicano*. Orozco, "Origins of the League of United Latin American Citizens (LULAC) and the Mexican American Civil Rights Movement in Texas with an Analysis of Women's Political Participation in a Gendered Context, 1910–1929," 228, 265, 302–303, 322; *La Epoca*, August 10, 1919, 4 and February 9, 1919, 3; *La Prensa*, December 23, 1917, 5; Pycior, "Tejana Activism, 1910–1930"; Omar S. Valerio-Jiménez, "New Avenues for Domestic Dispute and Divorce Lawsuits along the U.S.-Mexico Border, 1832–1893," *Journal of Women's History* 21, no. 1 (2009), 10–33.

13. Better known as a founder of the School Improvement League/Liga Pro-defensa Escolar is Eluterio Escobar, who was a proud product of one of the "escuelitas": a community-based school network that was operated in many cases by women. In Escobar's town of Pearsall, Texas, and in much of the region, these "escuelitas" acted as alternatives to separate and unequal public schools. As such, they had been a top priority of the Liga Femenil Mexicanista headed by Jovita Idar. Cynthia Orozco, "School Improvement League," *The Handbook of Texas*, http://www.tshaonline.org/handbook/online/articles/kaswm (accessed 3/12/11); Elizabeth Sutherland Martínez, *500 Years of Chicana Women's History* (New Brunswick: Rutgers University Press), 88; Cynthia Orozco, "María L. de Hernández," *The Handbook of Texas Online*, http://www.tshaonline.org/handbook/online/articles/fhe75 (accessed 3/12/11); Carlos Kevin Blanton, *The Strange Career of Bilingual Education in Texas, 1836–1981* (College Station: Texas A&M University Press, 2004), 26–27; Larry Ferlazzo and Lorie A. Hammond, *Building Parent Engagement in Schools* (Columbus: Linworth Books/Libraries Unlimited, 2009), 67–68; Pycior, "Tejana Activism, 1910–1930."

14. Author interview with Soledad "Chole" Alatorre, May 2, 2010, Pacoima, CA.

15. Mary S. Pardo, *Mexican American Women Activists* (Philadelphia: Temple University Press, 1998), 27–29.

16. Pardo, *Mexican American Women Activists*, 27–29; Vicki Ruiz and Virginia Sánchez-Korrol, *Latinas in the United States: A Historical Encyclopedia* (Bloomington: Indiana University, 2006), 171–172; Mario T. García, *Memories of Chicano History: The Life and Narrative of Bert Corona* (Berkeley: University of California Press, 1994), 166; University of California Television, *Organize! The Lessons of the Community Service Organization*, http://www.youtube.com/watch?v=hzMaRofspdk (accessed 3/7/11); Pycior, *LBJ and Mexican Americans*, 118.

17. Varela interview; Sarah Deutsch, *No Separate Refuge: Culture, Class and Gender on an Anglo-Hispanic Frontier, 1880–1940* (New York: Oxford University Press, 1989), introduction, 45.

18. María Ochoa, "Cooperative Re/weavings: Artistic Expression and Economic Development in a Northern New Mexican Village," *Mexican American Women: Changing Images/Perspectives in Mexican American Studies* 5 (1995), 123, 144; author telephone interview with María Varela, August 24, 2010.

Chapter 11

1. Jonathan Fox and Xóchitl Bada, "Migrant Civic Engagement," Research Paper Series on Latino Immigrant Civic and Political Participation, no. 3 (2009), Woodrow Wilson Center www.wilsoncenter.org/migrantparticipation (accessed 5/30/10).

2. Ruben Navarrette Jr., author interview, January 8, 2010, San Diego; Antonia Hernández, telephone interview with author, March 1, 2010; Juan Gómez-Quiñones, *Chicano Politics: Reality and Promise, 1940–1990* (Albuquerque: University of New Mexico Press, 1990), 111; Media Matters for America, "Limbaugh: Mexican immigrants who illegally enter the U.S. are 'unwilling to work,'" http://mediamatters.org/research/200603280009 (accessed 12/28/10); Soledad "Chloe"

Alatorre, author interview, May 2, 2010, Pacioma, CA; Mario T. García, *Memories of Chicano History: The Life and Narrative of Bert Corona* (Berkeley; University of California Press, 1994), 303.

3. Juan García, *Mexicans in the Midwest, 1900–1932* (Tucson: University of Arizona, 1996), 151; Navarrette interview; Ruben Navarrette Jr., "Spicing Up the World of Commentary," http://rubennavarrette.com/wordpress/ (accessed 12/29/10); "Columnist Navarrette Laid Off in San Diego," http://mije.org/richardprince/columnist-ruben-navarrette-laid-san-diego#Navarrette, Maynard Institute, June 18, 2010 (accessed 12/29/10); National Association for Hispanic Journalists, http://www.nahj.org/category/for-professionals/ (accessed 1/5/10); BurrellsLuce, "2009 Top Media Outlets," http://www.burrellesluce.com/top100/2009_Top_100List.pdf; Hernández interview; California Community Foundation, https://www.calfund.org/page.aspx?pid=711 (accessed 8/24/13), and "CCF Biographies," http://www.calfund.org/learn/staffbios.php#AHernandez (accessed 12/29/10).

4. Hernández interview.

5. Hernández interview; Marisela Chávez, "Mónica Lozano," in *Latinas in the United States: A Historical Encyclopedia*, volume 1, eds. Vicki Ruiz and Virginia Sánchez Korrol (Bloomington: Indiana University Press, 2006), 412–413; Cindy Y. Rodríguez, "Latino Vote Key to Obama's Re-election," http://www.cnn.com/2012/11/09/politics/latino-vote-key-election (accessed 3/13/13).

6. Eileen Truax, "Zacatecanos en LA Lamentan Pugna," *La Opinión*, May 19, 2009; Dick Morris, "GOP Backs New Immigration Bill," http://thehill.com/opinion/columnists/dick-morris/286395-gop-backs-immigration-bill (accessed 3/13/13); Marisela Chávez, "Mónica Lozano," in *Latinas in the United States: A Historical Encyclopedia*, volume 1, eds. Vicki Ruiz and Virginia Sánchez Korrol (Bloomington: Indiana University Press, 2006), 412–413.

7. Richard A. García, *Rise of the Mexican American Middle Class: San Antonio, 1929–1941* (College Station: Texas A&M University Press, 1991), 224–225.

8. Julie Leininger Pycior, "Tejanas Navigating the 1920s," in *Tejano Epic: Essays in Honor of Félix Almaráz, Jr.*, ed. Arnoldo De León (Austin: Texas State Historical Association, 2005).

9. The indefatigable Garza also published several novels and presided over a family of eight children. Juanita Luna Lawhn, "María Luisa Garza," in *Double Crossings/Entre Cruzamientos*, eds. Mario Martín Flores and Carlos von Son (n.p., NJ: Ediciones Nuevo Espacio, 2001), 83–96; Federico A. Subervi-Vélez, Marc Brindel, Juandalynn Taylor, and Renée Espinoza, "Spanish-language Daily Newspapers and Presidential Elections," in *The Mass Media and Latino Politics*, ed. Federico Subervi-Velez (New York: Routledge, 2008), 86; Xóchitl Bada, Jonathan Fox, Robert Donnelly, and Andrew Selee, *Context Matters: Latino Immigrant Civic Engagement in Nine U.S. Cities* (Washington: Reports on Latino Immigrant Civic Engagement, Woodrow Wilson International Center for Scholars, 2010); Nicolás Kanellos, "Publishers and Publishing," in *Greenwood Encyclopedia of Latino Literature*, ed. Nicolás Kanellos (Westport, CT: Greenwood Press, 2002); Pycior, "Tejanas Navigating the 1920s"; George J. Sánchez, *Becoming Mexican American* (New York: Oxford University Press, 2003), 219–221.

10. Julie Leininger Pycior, "La Raza Organizes: Mexican American Life in San Antonio, as Reflected in *Mutualista* Activities, 1914–1930," PhD diss., University of Notre Dame, 1979, Appendix II; García, *Mexicans in the Midwest, 1900–1932*, 131–149, 156, 163, 174, 185.

11. For examples of *mutualista* coverage by exile publications, see "Mutualistas and the Barrio Press," 89 ff., in Pycior, "La Raza Organizes." Douglas Monroy, *Rebirth: Mexican Los Angeles from the Great Migration to the Great Depression* (Berkeley: University of California Press, 1999), 208; García, *Rise of the Mexican American Middle Class: San Antonio, 1929–1941*, 224–225.

12. Ricardo Flores-Magón, "En Defensa de Los Mexicanos," *Regeneración*, May 11, 1912; Teresa Paloma Acosta, "Partido Liberal Mexicano," *The Handbook of Texas Online*, http://www.tshaonline.org/handbook/online/articles/wapo4 (accessed 12/25/10).

13. Felipe Cortés García to Ricardo Flores Magón, April 29, 1907, Archivo Electrónico Ricardo Flores Magón, http://www.archivomagon.net/ObrasCompletas/Correspondencia/Cor160.html (accessed 1/2/10).

14. Práxedis Guerrero's *mutualista* activities in Morenci, Arizona also attracted the attention of agents from the Mexican government of dictator Porfirio Díaz, who considered them subversive. Isidro Fabela and Josefina A. de Fabela, *Documentos Históricos de la Revolución Mexicana: Precursores de la Revolución Mexicana, 1906–1910*, volume 11 (Mexico City: Fondo de la Cultura Económica, 1966), 76; Rodolfo Acuña, *Corridos of Migration* (Tucson: University of Arizona

Press, 2007), 131, 137; Municipio de Práxedis Guerrero, "Práxedis Guerrero: Benemérito del Estado de Chihuahua," http://www.mpiopraxedisguerrero.gob.mx/Contenido/plantilla5.asp?cve_canal=5710&Portal=mpiopraxedisguerrero (accessed 3/13/13).

15. Other radical periodicals founded by women at this time included *Mujer Moderna* in San Antonio and *Pluma Roja* in Los Angeles. Pycior, "Tejana Activitism"; "Publishers and Publishing," ed. Kanellos, 444–445; Teresa Palomo Acosta, "Ramírez, Sara Estela," *Handbook of Texas Online*, http://www.tshaonline.org/handbook/online/articles/fra60 (accessed 12/29/10); Acuña, *Corridors of Migration*, 131–137; Teresa Paloma Acosta and Ruthe Winegarten, *Las Tejanas: 300 Years of History* (Austin: University of Texas Press, 2003), 74; Pycior, "La Raza Organizes," 190, 198, 202.

16. Pycior, "Tejana Activism."

17. Kanellos, "Publishers and Publishing"; Francisco Lomelí, *Handbook of Hispanic Cultures in the United States* (Houston: Arte Público Press, 1993), 76–78; Ana Luisa R. Martínez, "The Voice of the People: Pablo Cruz, *El Regidor*, and Mexican Americans Identity in San Antonio, Texas, 1888–1910," PhD diss., Texas Tech, 2003, 1, 85–85, 118, 211; García, *Rise of the Mexican American Middle Class*, 292; Ernesto Chávez, "Mutualista Organizations," http://www.jrank.org/cultures/pages/4230/Mutualista-Organizations.html (accessed 1/2/11); Pycior, "La Raza Organizes," chapter 4; John A. Adams, *Conflict and Commerce on the Rio Grande: Laredo, 1755–1955* (College Station: Texas A&M University Press, 2008), 102; *Rowell's American Newspaper Directory* (Berkeley: University of California, 1887), 625; F. Arturo Rosales, *Pobre Raza: Violence, Justice, and Mobilization among México Lindo Immigrants, 1900–1936* (Austin: University of Texas Press, 1999), 30.

18. Elliot Young, *Catarino Garza's Revolution on the Texas-Mexican Border* (Durham, NC: Duke University Press, 2004), 56.

19. Kanellos, "Publishers and Publishing"; David Romo, "Ringside Seat to a Revolution," *The Texas Observer*, January 13, 2006, 26–27; Martínez, "Voice of the People"; http://www.texasobserver.org/article.php?aid=2114; Nicolás Kanellos, *Hispanic Periodicals in the United States: Origins to 1960* (Houston: Arte Público Press, 2000), n. 52, 125–126.

20. Stan Steiner, *La Raza* (New York: Harper, 1970), photos after p. 114 and quote on p. 389.

21. The Crusade for Justice, for its part, had its own alternative newspaper, *El Gallo*. Gómez-Quiñones, *Chicano Politics*, 113; "María Varela," *Dictionary of Latino Civil Rights History*, ed. Francisco Arturo Rosales (Houston: Arte Público Press, 2006), 433; "María Varela," *Take Stock: Images of Change*, http://www.takestockphotos.com/pages/varela.html.

22. Gómez-Quiñones, *Chicano Politics*, 113; Elizabeth "Betita" Martínez, "A View from New Mexico: Recollections of the *Movimiento* Left," *Monthly Review* 54, no. 3 (2002), http://monthlyreview.org/0702martinez.htm; Elizabeth Sutherland Martínez, *500 Years of Chicana Women's History* (New Brunswick: Rutgers University Press, 2008), 62–63.

23. Hernández interview; Alexandra Starr, "Voice of América: The Spanish-language DJs behind the new wave of Latino activism," *Slate*, May 3, 2006, http://www.slate.com/id/2141008/ (accessed 1/9/11).

24. Adrián Félix, Carmen González, and Ricardo Ramírez, "Political Protest, Ethnic Media and Latino Naturalization," *American Behavioral Scientist* 52 (2008), 618–634; "Rebelión," http://www.rebelion.org/noticias/2006/4/30005.pdf (accessed 1/7/11).

25. Teresa Wantanabe and Héctor Becerra, "The Immigration Debate: How DJ's Put 500,000 Marchers in Motion," *Los Angeles Times*, March 28, 2006; "Piolín por la Mañana," http://piolin.univision.com/ (accessed 1/10/11).

26. At the same time that *Sin Fronteras* was doing its path-breaking reports, Rubén Salazar was making history at the *Los Angeles Times* as virtually the lone Mexican-heritage reporter, and he subsequently left the newspaper to head a Spanish-language television station. Chole Alatorre and Bert Corona were with Salazar in 1969 a few hours before he died from a sheriff's projectile on the day of the Chicano Moratorium against the Vietnam War. García, *Memories of Chicano History*, 277–283; "Rebelión," http://www.rebelion.org/noticias/2006/4/30005.pdf (accessed 1/7/11); Hernández, Ernesto Cortéz, Jr., author interview, May 19, 2010, New York City; Herman Gallegos, author interview, Feb. 10, 2010, San Francisco; Bada, Fox, Donnelly, and Selee, *Context Matters*, 7; Javier Rodríguez, "The Story of José Rodríguez," December 1, 2010, http://groups.yahoo.com/group/NetworkAztlan_News/message/43556 (accessed 1/7/11); Alberto Najar, "La Radio Latina en EEUU, Clave de la Resistencia," *La Jornada*, April 16, 2006; author interviews with Hernández, Cortés, and Gallegos; Javier Salas, univision.com, February 19, 2009 (accessed 1/7/11); Starr,

"Voice of América"; Ed Morales, "The Media is the Mensaje," *The Nation*, May 15, 2006, http:// www.edmorales.net/articles/mediaismessage.html (accessed 1/7/11).

27. Najar, "La Radio Latina en EEUU, Clave de la Resistencia."

28. Roberto Lovato, "Voices of a New Movimiento," *The Nation*, June 19, 2006, http://www. thenation.com/article/voices-new-movimiento?page=0,1 (accessed 4/21/13).

29. Lucas Benítez, interview by author, Immokalee, FL, February 22, 2010; author notes on the radio program "Radio Conciencia/Voice of the People," Coalition of Immokalee Workers, Immokalee, FL, 2/22/10; James E. García, "Spanish-language Radio," in *Encyclopedia of Latino Popular Culture*, eds. Cordelia Candelaria, Peter J. García, and Arturo J. Aldama (Westport, CT: Greenwood Publishing, 2004), 788–791; Morales, "The Media is the Mensaje"; Félix et al., "Political Protest, Ethnic Media and Latino Naturalization"; Jesús Rangel, "Story of a Mexican Immigrant 'Hero,'" *The New York Times*, January 7, 1985, http://query.nytimes.com/gst/fullpage. html?res=9A0DE1D81F38F934A35752C0A963948260 (accessed 1/9/11); María-Cristina García, "Morales, Félix Hessbrook," *Handbook of Texas Online*, http://www.tshaonline.org/handbook/ online/articles/fmobk (accessed 1/9/11); Cynthia Orozco, "Hernández, María L. de," *The Handbook of Texas*, http://www.tshaonline.org/handbook/online/articles/fhe75 (accessed 3/12/11); Cynthia Orozco, "School Improvement League," *The Handbook of Texas*, http://www.tshaonline. org/handbook/online/articles/kaswm (accessed 3/12/11).

30. "Univision Beats All the English-language Broadcast Nets in Monday Ratings," *TV Week*, http://www.tvweek.com/blogs/tvbizwire/2010/12/univision-beats-all-the-englis.php (accessed 1/10/11); Brian Seltzer, "TV Viewing Continues to Edge Up," *The New York Times*, January 2, 2010, http://www.nytimes.com/2011/01/03/business/media/03ratings.html?_r=1&scp=1&sq= univision+ratings+monday+night&st=nyt (accessed 1/10/11); Bada et al., *Context Matters;* "The ImpreMedia Executive Team"; Félix et al., "Political Protest, Ethnic Media and Latino Naturaliza- tion," ImpreMedia, http://impremedia.com/about/executive.html (accessed 1/10/11); KSOL (98.9 FM) San Francisco, KSQL (99.1 FM) Santa Cruz, CA, KVVF (105.7 FM) Santa Clara, CA, KVVZ (100.7 FM) San Rafael, CA, KBRG (100.3 FM) San Jose, CA, "Annual EEO Public File Report Form," 2010, http://u.univision.com/contentroot/uol/10portada/sp/pdf/local/2010_EEO_ Annual_Public_File_Report_SFR.pdf (accessed 3/9/11).

31. "The ImpreMedia Executive Team"; "Obama Names Outside Economic Advisory Board," http://www.npr.org/templates/story/story.php?storyId=100335758 (accessed 1/11/11).

32. Federación de Clubes Zacatecanos del Sur de California, http://www.federacionzacatecana. org/index.php?sectionName=home&subSection=news (accessed 1/10/11); COFEM: Consejo de Federaciones Mexicanas de Norteamérica, http://www.cofem.org/home.html (accessed 1/10/11); Red Mexicana de Líderes y Organizaciones Migrantes, http://redmexicanamigrante.org/ (accessed May 28, 2013).

33. See also the extensive, bilingual website of CIW, the Coalition of Immokalee Workers, http://www.ciw-online.org/. United Farm Workers/AFL-CIO, http://www.ufw.org/; Farm Labor Organizing Committee, AFL-CIO, http://www.supportfloc.org/Pages/default.aspx (accessed 8/24/13); AFL-CIO, http://aflcio.org/index.cfm; "West and Southwest," Industrial Areas Founda- tion, http://www.swiaf.org/ (accessed 8/24/13).

34. A December 2009 survey by the Pew Research Center concluded that "most of what the public learns about Hispanics comes not through focused coverage of the life and times of this population group but through event-driven news stories in which Hispanics are one of many elements." Pew Hispanic Center, "Hispanics in the News: An Event-Driven Narrative," December 7, 2009, http://pewhispanic.org/reports/report.php?ReportID=116; NCLR/National Council of La Raza, http://www.nclr.org/ (accessed 1/11/10); Raúl Yzaguirre, address to the NCLR national convention, July 27, 2009, http://www.youtube.com/watch?v=FbUS0Z2aCPc (accessed 4/10/10); Basta Dobbs, http://bastadobbs.com/ (accessed 1/11/11).

35. *La Opinión*, "History of La Opinión"; "Impremedia Partners with LAT Careers," http:// www.reuters.com/article/2010/08/17/idUS137441+17-Aug-2010+BW20100817 (accessed 8/25/13); "Univisión Ya Encontró Comprador," http://www.univision.com/content/content. jhtml?cid=900813 (accessed 1/12/11).

36. National Hispanic Media Coalition, "NHMC Advocates for More Diversity, Competition and Localism in Broadcast Media," http://www.nhmc.org/content/media-ownership (accessed 1/12/11).

37. National Hispanic Media Coalition, "NHMC Advocates for More Diversity, Competition and Localism in Broadcast Media"; Lovato, "Voices of a New Movimiento."

Chapter 12

1. Katherine Fulton and Andrew Blau, "Mutualismo Not Filantropolía" (Global Business Network/Monitor Institute, 2005), 41–42, http://www.monitorinstitute.com/downloads/what-we-think/looking-out-for-the-future/Looking_Out_for_the_Future.pdf (accessed 4/21/13).

2. Fulton and Blau, "Mutualismo Not Filantropolía."

3. Author interview with Herman Gallegos, February 2010, San Francisco.

4. Hispanics in Philanthropy, "Our Story," http://www.hiponline.org/about/our-story (accessed 8/24/13); Gallegos interview.

5. Herman Gallegos and Michael O'Neill, *Hispanics and the Non-profit Sector* (New York: the Foundation Center, 1991), 6, 22, 31.

6. Linda Gordon, *The Great Arizona Orphan Abduction* (Cambridge: Harvard University Press, 1999), 135–185; Juan García, *Mexicans in the Midwest, 1900–1932* (Tucson: University of Arizona, 1996), 163, 180–181, 184–185, 188–189; Julie Leininger Pycior, "La Raza Organizes: Mexican American Life in San Antonio, as Reflected in Mutualista Activities, 1914–1930" PhD diss., University of Notre Dame, 1979, 44, 54; Jonathan Fox and Xóchitl Bada, "Migrant Civic Engagement," Research Paper Series on Latino Immigrant Civic and Political Participation, no. 3 (2009), Woodrow Wilson Center Mexico Institute, www.wilsoncenter.org/migrantparticipation (accessed 5/30/10); Journal of "La Unión" library, Sociedad de la Unión papers, Mexican American Collection, Our Lady of the Lake University, San Antonio; San Francisco Foundation, "Board of Trustees," http://www.sff.org/about/who-we-are/board-of-trustees/?searchterm=gallegos (accessed 1/20/11).

7. Gallegos interview; Thomas Erlich, *Philanthropy and the Non-Profit Sector in a Changing America* (Bloomington, IN: Indiana University Press, 2001), 261.

8. Charles Clotfelter and Lisa Durán, "Caring for Each Other: Philanthropy in Communities of Color," Custom Development Solutions, http://www.cdsfunds.com/caring_for_each_other_philanthropy_in_communities_of_color.html (accessed 1/20/11); Katherine Fulton, Gabriel Kaspar, and Barbara Kibbee, "What's Next for Philanthropy," Monitor Institute, 2010, http://www.monitorinstitute.com/downloads/Whats_Next_for_Philanthropy.pdf (accessed 1/16/11); Mark Hugo López and Paul Taylor, "The 2010 Congressional Reapportionment and Latinos," Pew Hispanic Center/Pew Research Center, 2011, http://pewhispanic.org/files/reports/132.pdf (accessed 1/18/11); Gallegos interview; author interview with Lucas Benítez, February 22, 2010, Immokalee, FL; Louis Gerard Mendoza, *Historia: The Literary Making of Chicana and Chicano History* (College Station: Texas A&M University Press, 2001), 71, 103.

9. For more on women's charitable activities, see chapter 10. One of the few professional studies to take note of Latina organized giving, past and present, is "Latino Philanthropy Literature Review," Donor Research Project, Center on Philanthropy and Civil Society, CUNY Graduate Center, 2003; http://www.philanthropy.org/programs/literature_reviews/latino_lit_review.pdf (accessed 1/20/10); Hispanics in Philanthropy, "Our Story"; Antonia Hernández, author interview, March 1, 2010; "An Interview with Civil Rights Activist Antonia Hernández," *Harvard Latino Law Review* 11 (2008), https://litigation-essentials.lexisnexis.com/webcd/ (accessed 8/24/13); "Featured Contribution Susan U. Arnold," http://onphilanthropy.org/2007/featured-contribution-susan-raymond-phd (accessed 1/1/11).

10. "Globalization of Philanthropy: Immigrants at the Forefront" is listed in "Featured Contributor: Susan Raymond, Ph.D.," Fox and Bada, "Migrant Civic Engagement"; Manuel Gamio, *Mexican Immigration to the United States* (Chicago: University of Chicago Press, 1930; New York: Dover Press reissue, 1971), iii, 1–12, Appendix VIII, "Mexican Societies in the United States," and Appendix IX, "Supplementary Note on the Number and Distribution of Mexican Immigrants."

11. Andy Goodman and Linsey Pollak, "HIP to the Gap," Monitor Institute, 2005, http://www.futureofphilanthropy.org/files/usPhil_goodman_4hip_gap.pdf (accessed 7/28/13).

12. Hispanics in Philanthropy, "Our Story"; Gallegos interview; Florencia Torche, "Mexico's Fragile Middle Class," *Americas Quarterly* (Spring 2009); David Harvey, *A Brief History of Neo-*

liberalism (New York: Oxford University Press, 2007), 34–35; 143–145; Douglas S. Massey, Frank Kalter, and Karen A. Pren, "Structural Economic Change and International Migration from Mexico and Poland," in *Migration und Integration,* ed. Frank Kalter (Wiesbaden: VS Verlag, 2008), 143–145; *Forbes,* "The World's Billionaires," http://www.forbes.com/billionaires/list/ (accessed 7/28/13); Nacha Cattan and Carlos Manuel Rodríguez, "Carlos Slim's America Movil May Face Breakup Pressure in New Law," http://www.bloomberg.com/news/2013-03-11/mexico-proposal-would-allow-breakup-of-phone-tv-companies-1-.html (accessed 3/11/13); Grace Lee Boggs, "Thinking Dialectically about Solidarity," http://www.commondreams.org/view/2010/12/20–0, December 20, 2010 (accessed 1/18/11).

13. Maria Varela, "Ganados del Valle," *La Jicarita News,* January 2000.

14. Tyche Hendricks, "Three Questions for Herman Gallegos," *San Francisco Chronicle,* March 29, 2009, http://www.sfgate.com/cgi-bin/article.cgi?f=/c/a/2009/03/28/BAG716NLC9.DTL; National Council of La Raza, *NCLR Annual Report, 2009* (May 18, 2010), http://www.nclr.org/index.php/publications/nclr_2009_annual_report/ (accessed 1/18/11); National Council of La Raza, "Southwest Council of La Raza," http://www.nclr.org/index.php/about_us/history/formation_of_the_southwest_council_of_la_raza/ (accessed 1/18/11); David Moberg, "Labor's Turnaround: The AFL-CIO Has a Plan to Turn around the Movement," *In These Times,* March 3, 2013, http://inthesetimes.com/article/14678/labors_creaky_turnaround/ (accessed 3/9/13); NCLR, "Chapter 4: The Erosion of Job Quality," http://www.nclr.org/images/uploads/publications/Ch4_The_Erosion_of_Job_Quality.pdf (accessed 1/18/11); Ernesto Cortés Jr., "Justice at the Gates of the City: A Model for Shared Prosperity," in *Back to Shared Prosperity: Growing Inequality of Wealth and Income in America,* ed. Ray Marshall (New York: M. E. Sharpe, 2000), 361; author interview with Ernesto Cortés Jr., May 19, 2010, New York; AMOS/A Mid-Iowa Organizing Strategy, "Creating a Community Where We All Can Succeed!" http://amosiowa.org/ (accessed 8/24/13); "Grassley, Boswell, Attend AMOS Summit," *Des Moines Register,* http://blogs.desmoinesregister.com/dmr/index.php/2009/11/01/grassley-boswell-attend-amos-summit/.

15. Baldemar Velásquez, interview by author, March 21, 2010, Toledo, OH; Baldemar Velásquez, speech to Labor Notes Conference, 2008, Detroit, http://www.youtube.com/watch?v=ZRm1HFPgBto (accessed 7/20/13).

16. Cortés interview; Cortés, "Justice at the Gates of the City"; Antonia Hernández, author telephone interview, March 1, 2010; Lucas Benítez author interview, Feb. 22, 2010, Immokalee, FL; Public Citizen, "12 Months After: The Effects of *Citizens United* on Elections and the Integrity of the Legislative Process," January 18, 2011, http://www.citizen.org/12-months-after (accessed 1/23/11); Create Real Democracy, "Legalize Democracy: Abolish Corporate Personhood," http://createrealdemocracy.blogspot.com/2010/01/move-to-amend-legalize-democracyabolish.html (accessed 1/23/11); http://www.duhc.org/profiles/blogs/citizens-united-v-fec-supreme; National Voting Rights Institute, "Our Work/Public Interest Advocacy Organizations," http://www.nvri.org/resources/index.shtml (accessed 1/23/11); Gary Langer, "In Campaign Ruling on Campaign Finance, the Public Dissents," ABC News, http://blogs.abcnews.com/thenumbers/2010/02/in-supreme-court-ruling-on-campaign-finance-the-public-dissents.html; "Divided Court Strikes Down Money Restrictions," Stephen Dinan, *Washington Times,* January 2, 2010; Julie Leininger Pycior, *LBJ and Mexican Americans: The Paradox of Power* (Austin: University of Texas Press, 1997), 241–245; John H. Adams, "Rally Supports Migrant Workers, Boycott of N.C. Pickle Company," *The Layman Online,* November 15, 2000, http://www.layman.org/news5702/ (accessed 8/24/13); Mary Beth Rogers, *Cold Anger: A Story of Faith and Politics* (Denton, TX: University of North Texas Press, 1990), 28; Fox and Bada, "Migrant Civic Engagement."

17. University of California Television, *Organize! The Lessons of the Community Service Organization,* http://www.youtube.com/watch?v=hzMaRofspdk (accessed 3/7/11); Randy Shaw, "Lessons of the UNITE-HERE/SEIU Deal," *LA Progressive,* July 29, 2010, http://www.beyondchron.org/news/index.php?itemid=8361 (accessed 8/24/13); "Rutgers to Confer Four Degrees at 245th Commencement," http://news.rutgers.edu/medrel/news-releases/2011/04/rutgers-to-confer-fo-20110404 (accessed 7/28/13).

18. "An Interview with Ernesto Cortés," *Religion and Ethics Newsweekly,* March 1, 2001, http://www.pbs.org/wnet/religionandethics/episodes/march-2-2001/an-interview-with-ernesto-cortes/3456/ (accessed 3/13/11); Cortés interview.

Bibliography

Archival Collections

Archivo General de la Nación (Mexico City)
Archivo de la Secretaría de Relaciones Exteriores "Génaro Estrada" (Mexico City)
Archives and Special Collections, Arizona State University
Bancroft Library, University of California, Berkeley
Benson Latin American Collection, University of Texas
C. L. Sonnichsen Special Collections Department, University of Texas at El Paso
Daughters of the Republic of Texas Library
Department of State Papers, National Archives
Dolph Briscoe Center for American History, University of Texas
Institute of Texan Cultures (San Antonio)
Jesús Gamboa personal papers, San Antonio, Texas
Lyndon Baines Johnson Library
New-York Historical Society
Occidental College Special Collections and College Archives
Our Lady of the Lake University Mexican American Collection (San Antonio)
Smithsonian Institution Archives
Stanford University Department of Special Collections
Texas A&M University-Corpus Christi Special Collections
Texas State Library and Archives Commission
University of Arizona Special Collections
University of New Mexico Special Collections
University of Notre Dame Archives
Victoria Regional History Center, University of Houston-Victoria/Victoria College
Walter P. Reuther Labor History Archives, Wayne State University
Webb County (Texas) Heritage Foundation

Newspapers

Arizona Daily Star (Tucson)
The Boston Globe
The Catholic Worker (New York)
Chicago Tribune
Daily News (Los Angeles)
The Des Moines Register
El Conquistador (Milwaukee)
El Eco (Kingsville, Texas)
El Grito del Norte (Española, New Mexico)

El Heraldo Mexicano (San Antonio)
El Paso Herald
El Sol de San Luis (San Luis Potosí, Mexico)
The Guardian (Manchester, England)
The Jewish Journal (Los Angeles)
La Epoca (San Antonio)
La Jicarita News (New Mexico)
La Jornada (Universidad Autónoma Nacional de México)
La Mañana (Nuevo Laredo, Mexico)
La Prensa (San Antonio, founded 1913)
La Prensa (San Antonio, founded 1989)
La Voz (Phoenix)
La Voz Nueva (Denver)
Las Vegas Sun
Los Angeles Times
New York Daily News
The New York Times
The Pueblo Chieftain
Regeneración (various US sites)
The Sacramento Bee
San Antonio Express
San Fernando Valley Sun
San Marcos Daily Record
Sin Fronteras (Los Angeles)
Southern Messenger (San Antonio)
The Texas Observer (Los Angeles)
The Tidings (Los Angeles)
The Toledo Blade
Tri-City Herald (Kennewick, Washington)
Washington Post
The Washington Times

Oral History Interviews

Allatorre Soledad, interview by author, May 3, 2010, Pacoima, CA, and telephone interview, May 10, 2010.
Arroyo, Tomás, interview by Rebecca Sharpless Jiménez, June 2, 1983, Waco, Texas. Transcript, Baylor University Institute for Oral History, 1995.
Benítez, Lucas, interview by author, February 22, 2010, Immokalee, Florida.
Calderón, Ernesto, interview by José Angel Gutiérrez, October 25, 1997, Austin, Texas. No. 66, Center for Mexican American Studies, University of Texas at Arlington.
Cavada, Viviana, interview by José Angel Gutiérrez, June 16, 1998, Corpus Christi, Texas. Number 66, Center for Mexican American Studies, University of Texas at Arlington.
Cook, Gertrude, interview by author, May 5, 1977, San Antonio, Texas.
Cortés, Ernesto, Jr., interview by author, May 19, 2010, New York, New York.
Domínguez, Efraín, interview by author, November 18 and 19, 1976, San Antonio, Texas.
Gallegos, Herman, interview by author, February 10, 2010, San Francisco, California.

Gamboa, Clara, interview by author, May 10, 1977, San Antonio, Texas.

Gamboa, Jesús, interview by author, May 10, 1977, San Antonio, Texas.

Garza, Lucas, interview by author, November 15, 23, and 25, 1976, San Antonio, Texas.

Garza, María Luisa, interview by Juanita Luis Lawhn. Published in *Double Crossings/ Entre Cruzamientos,* eds. Mario Martín Flores and Carlos von Son, 83–96. Fair Haven, NJ: Ediciones Nuevo Espacio, 2001.

Gutiérrez, Gustavo, interview by author, November 19, 1976, San Antonio, Texas.

Hernández, Antonia, telephone interview by author, March 1, 2010.

Hernández, Elena, interview by author, November 19, 1976, San Antonio, Texas.

Hernández, Enríque, interview by author, November 19, 1976, San Antonio, Texas.

Idar, Eduardo, Jr., interview by author, June 22, 1983, Austin, Texas.

Labra, Armando, interview by Sherry Linkon, Center for Working Class Studies, Youngstown State University, June 24, 2009, Youngstown, Ohio.

Navarrette, Ruben, Jr., interview by author, January 8, 2010, San Diego, California.

Porras, Charles V., interview by Oscar J. Martínez, November 18, 1975, transcribed by Rhonda Hartman, March 18, 1976. El Paso, Texas. Institute of Oral History, University of Texas at El Paso.

Varela, María, interview by author, April 22, 2010, Providence, Rhode Island, and telephone interview, August 24, 2010.

Velásquez, Baldemar, interview by author, March 21, 2010, Toledo, Ohio.

Yzaguirre, Raúl, telephone interview by author, August 24, 1992.

Books, Articles, and Other Publications

Acosta, Teresa Paloma. "Alianza Hispano Americana." *The Handbook of Texas.* Austin: Texas State Historical Association, 20. http://www.tsha.utexas.edu/handbook/online/articles/view/AA/vna2.html (accessed April 11, 2010).

———. "Chapa, Francisco A." *The Handbook of Texas.* http://www.tshaonline.org/handbook/online/articles/CC/fch50.html (accessed January 25, 2011).

———. "Idar, Nicasio." *The Handbook of Texas.* http://www.tshaonline.org/handbook/online/articles/II/fid2.html (accessed January 25, 2011).

———. "In Re: Rodríguez." *The Handbook of Texas.* http://www.tshaonline.org/handbook/online/articles/II/pqitw.html (accessed January 25, 2011).

———. "Ochoa, Víctor." *The Handbook of Texas.* http://www.tshaonline.org/handbook/online/articles/foco5 (accessed January 25, 2011).

———. "Partido Liberal Mexicano." *The Handbook of Texas.* http://www.tshaonline.org/handbook/online/articles/PP/wap4.html (accessed January 25, 2011).

———. "Primer Congreso Mexicanista." *The Handbook of Texas.* http://www.tshaonline.org/handbook/online/articles/CC/vecyk.html (accessed January 25, 2011).

———. "Ramírez, Sara Estela." *The Handbook of Texas.* http://www.tshaonline.org/handbook/online/articles/fra60 (accessed March 5, 2011).

———. "Sociedades Guadalupanas." *The Handbook of Texas.* http://www.tshaonline.org/handbook/online/articles/SS/ics10.html (accessed January 25, 2011).

Acosta, Teresa Paloma and Ruthe Winegarten. *Las Tejanas: 300 Years of History.* Austin: University of Texas Press, 2003.

Acuña, Rodolfo. *Corridors of Migration.* Tucson: University of Arizona Press, 2007.

———. Reviewed work: *Los Mineros,* by Héctor Galán. *The Journal of American History* 79, no. 3 (1992): 1295–1296.

Adams, John A. *Conflict and Commerce on the Rio Grande: Laredo, 1755–1955.* College Station: Texas A&M University Press, 2008.

Alarcón, Rafael. "The Development of Hometown Associations in the United States." In *Sending Money Home: Hispanic Remittances and Community Development,* eds. Rodolfo de la Garza and Briant Lindsey Lowell, 1–34. Lanham, MD: Rowan and Littlefield, 2002.

Alinsky, Saul D. "The War on Poverty: Political Pornography." *The Journal of Social Issues* 21, no. 1 (1965): 41–47.

Almaráz, Félix D. *Knight without Armor: Carlos Eduardo Castañeda, 1896–1958.* College Station: Texas A&M University Press, 1999.

Alperovitz, Gar. *America beyond Capitalism: Reclaiming Our Wealth, Our Liberty, and Our Democracy.* New York: Wiley, 2005.

Alvarado, Rudolph Valier, and Sonya Yvette Alvarado. *Mexicans and Mexican Americans in Michigan.* East Lansing: Michigan State University Press, 2003.

Anders, Evan. "Canales, José Tomás." *The Handbook of Texas.* http://www.tsha.utexas .edu/handbook/online/articles/CC/fcaag.html (accessed February 2, 2010).

Anderson, Rodney D. *Outcasts in Their Own Land.* DeKalb: University of Northern Illinois Press, 1976.

Appler, Jules. *City Directory.* San Antonio: Tower Publications, 10 volumes: 1914–1915, 1916–1917, 1917–1918, 1922, 1922–1923, 1924–1925, 1926, 1927, 1928, 1931–1932.

Archdiocese of Los Angeles. "Historical Order of Bishops." http://www.archdiocese .la/about/heritage/bishops.html#amat (accessed April 19, 2010).

Armbruster-Sandoval, Ralph. *Globalization and Cross-border Labor Solidarity in the Americas.* New York: Routledge, 2004.

Arreola, Daniel D. "Plaza Towns of South Texas." *Geographical Review* 82, no. 1 (1992): 56–73.

———. *Tejano South Texas: A Mexican American Cultural Province.* Austin: University of Texas Press, 2002.

Arrieta, Olivia. "The Mexicano Community of the Clifton-Morenci Mining District: Organizational Life in the Context of Change." In *Community Empowerment and Chicano Scholarship,* eds. Mary Romero and Cordelia Candelaria, 127–142. Los Angeles: National Association of Chicano Studies, 1992.

Aufderheide, Pat. "An Actor Turns Activist." *Mother Jones Magazine* VIII, no. IX, (1983): 60.

Bada, Xóchitl, Jonathan Fox, Robert Donnelly, and Andrew Selee. *Context Matters: Latino Immigrant Civic Engagement in Nine U.S. Cities.* Reports on Latino Immigrant Civic Engagement, National Report. Washington: Woodrow Wilson International Center for Scholars, 2010.

Badillo, David A. *Latinos and the New Immigrant Church.* Baltimore: Johns Hopkins University Press, 2006.

Bailey, Richard. "Sheppard, John Morris." *The Handbook of Texas.* http://www.tsha online.org/handbook/online/articles/SS/fsh24.html (accessed January 25, 2011).

Balderrama, Francisco E., and Raymond Rodríguez. *Decade of Betrayal: Mexican Repatriation in the 1930s.* Albuquerque: University of New Mexico, 1995.

Bardacke, Frank. "Cesar's Ghost: Decline and Fall of the U.F.W." *The Nation,* July 26, 1993.

Barger, W. K., and Ernesto Reza. *The Farm Labor Movement in the Midwest.* Austin: University of Texas Press, 1994.

Barkley, Mary Starr. "History of Travis County and Austin, 1839–1899." Austin: Austin Printing Co., 1981.

Barragán, Leticia, Rina Ortiz, and Amanda Rosales. "El mutualismo en México: Siglo XIX." *Historia Obrera* 10 (1977). http://www.antorcha.net/biblioteca_virtual/historia/mutualismo/mutualismo.html (accessed August 19, 2013).

Barton, Paul. *Hispanic Methodists, Presbyterians and Baptists in Texas.* Austin: University of Texas Press, 2006.

Baulch, Joe. "Garza War." *The Handbook of Texas.* http://www.tsha.utexas.edu/handbook/online/articles/GG/jcgwk.html (accessed February 9, 2010).

Beito, David T. "Thy Brother's Keeper." *Policy Review.* 1994. http://www.unz.org/Pub/PolicyRev-1994q4-00055?View=PDF (accessed August 19, 2013).

———. *From Mutual Aid to the Welfare State.* Chapel Hill: University of North Carolina Press, 2000.

Benson, Susan Porter. *Household Accounts: Working-class family Economies in the Interwar United States.* Ithaca: Cornell University Press, 2009.

Berry, Kate A., and Martha L. Henderson. *Geographic Identities of Ethnic America.* Reno: University of Nevada Press, 2002.

Editors. *Black Issues in Higher Education. The Unfinished Agenda of the Selma-Montgomery Voting Rights March.* Hoboken: John Wiley and Son, 2005.

Bigott, Joseph C. "Lake County, Indiana." *Encyclopedia of Chicago.* http://encyclopedia.chicagohistory.org/pages/707.html (accessed May 5, 2010).

Blanton, Carlos Kevin. *The Strange Career of Bilingual Education in Texas, 1836–1981.* College Station: Texas A&M University Press, 2004.

Border Crossings: Mexican and Mexican-American Workers. Hart, John Mason, ed. Wilmington, DE: Scholarly Resources, 1998.

Borkman, Thomas. *Understanding Self-Help/Mutual Aid.* New Brunswick, NJ: Rutgers University Press, 1999.

Bortz, Jeffrey. *Revolution within the Revolution: Cotton Textile Workers and the Mexican Labor Regime, 1910–1923.* Stanford: Stanford University Press, 2008.

Boyte, Harry C. *Everyday Politics: Reconnecting Citizens and the Public Life.* Philadelphia: University of Pennsylvania Press, 2004.

———. "Seeds of a Different Politics." *The Good Society* 19, no. 1 (2010): 70–73.

Branch, Brian. "The Credit Union Difference." *World Council of Credit Unions.* March 7, 2005. www.woccu.org/functions/view_document.php?id=The_CU_Difference (accessed January 25, 2011).

Calderón, Roberto R. *Mexican Coal Mining Labor in Texas and Coahuila, 1880–1930.* College Station: Texas A&M University Press, 2000.

———. "Tejano Politics." *The Handbook of Texas.* http://www.tshaonline.org/handbook/online/articles/TT/wmtkn.html (accessed January 25, 2011).

———. "Unión, Trabajo, y Progreso: Laredo's Mexican Mutual Aid Societies, 1890s." In *Mexican Americans in Texas History,* eds. Emilio Zamora, Cynthia Orozco, and Rodolfo Rocha, 63–77. Austin: Texas State Historical Commission, 2000.

Calleros, Cleofas, in collaboration with Marjorie F. Graham. *El Paso Then and Now.* El Paso: American Printing Co., 1954.

Calvert, Robert A., and Arnoldo De León. *The History of Texas.* Arlington Heights, IL: Harlan Davidson, 1990.

Camarillo, Albert. *Chicanos in a Changing Society: From Mexican Pueblos to American*

Barrios in Santa Barbara and Southern California, 1848–1930. Cambridge: Harvard University Press, 1979.

Cano, Gustavo, and Alexandra Délano. "The Institute of Mexicans Abroad: The Day after . . . After 156 Years." American Political Science Association, September 2–5, 2004. http://ccis.ucsd.edu/2006/04/the-mexican-government-and-organised-mexican-immigrants-in-the-united-states-a-historical-analysis-of-political-trans nationalism-1848-2005-working-paper-148/ (accessed August 24, 2013).

Carrigan, William D. and Clive Webb. "The Lynching of Persons of Mexican Origin or Descent in the United States, 1848 to 1928." *Journal of Social History* 37, no. 2 (2003): 411–438.

Castañeda, Carlos E. *Our Catholic Heritage in Texas, 1517–1936.* 7 vols. Austin: Von Boeckmann-Jones Co., 1936–1958.

Cavazos Garza, Israel. *Mariano Escobedo.* Monterrey: Gobierno del Estado de Nuevo León, 1949.

Chabot, Frederick. *With the Makers of San Antonio.* San Antonio: Yanagua Press, 1939.

Chambers, Edward T., with Michael A. Cowan. *Roots for Radicals: Organizing for Power, Action, Justice.* New York: Continuum Press, 2008.

Christensen, Jon. "Heroes and Heroines: María Varela, an Authentic 'Milagro.'" *Mother Jones,* January 1989, 27–28.

Christianson, Scott. *The Last Gasp: The Rise and Fall of the American Gas Chamber.* Berkeley: University of California, 2010.

Clawson, Mary Ann. *Constructing Brotherhood: Class, Gender, and Fraternalism.* Princeton: Princeton University Press, 1989.

Clotfelter, Charles T., and Thomas Ehrlich. *Philanthropy and the Non-Profit Sector in a Changing America.* Bloomington: Indiana University Press, 2001.

Collins, Chuck, and Felice Yeskel. *Economic Apartheid in America: A Primer on Economic Inequality & Insecurity.* New York: The New Press, 2011.

Community Empowerment and Chicano Scholarship. Romero, Mary, and Cordelia Candelaria, eds. Los Angeles: National Association of Chicano Studies, 1992.

Corford, Daniel. *Working People of California.* Berkeley: University of California Press, 1995.

Cortés, Ernesto, Jr. "Faith, Charity and Justice." *The American Prospect.* April 22, 2007. http://prospect.org/article/faith-charity-and-justice (accessed August 19, 2013).

———. "Justice at the Gates of the City: A Model for Shared Prosperity." In *Back to Shared Prosperity: Growing Inequality of Wealth and Income in America,* ed. Ray Marshall. New York: M. E. Sharpe, 2000. http://www.swiaf.org/wp-content/uploads/2012/07/Cortes-Justice-at-the-Gates-English.pdf (accessed August 19, 2013).

Crimm, Ana Carolina Castillo. *De León: A Tejano Family History.* Austin: University of Texas Press, 1997.

Crimm, Ana Carolina Castillo, and Sara R. Massey. *Turn-of-the-Century Photographs from San Diego, Texas.* Austin: University of Texas Press, 2003.

Crutchfield, Leslie R., and Heather McLeod Grant. *Forces for Good: The Six Practices of Six High-Impact Nonprofits.* New York: Jossey-Bass, 2007.

Cuthbertson, Gilbert M. "Garza, Catarino Erasmo." *The Handbook of Texas.* http://www.tsha.utexas.edu/handbook/online/articles/GG/fga38.html (accessed March 4, 2010).

De Aragón, Ray John. *Padre Martínez and Bishop Lamy.* Santa Fe: Sunstone Press, 2006.

De La Garza, Beatriz. *A Law for the Lion: A Tale of Crime and Injustice in the Border-lands*. Austin: University of Texas Press, 2003.

De la Garza, Rodolfo, and Briant Lindsey Lowell, ed. *Sending Money Home: Hispanic Remittances and Community Development*. Lanham, MD: Rowan and Littlefield, 2002.

De León, Arnoldo. *A Social History of Mexican Americans in Nineteenth-Century Duval County*. San Diego: Duval County Commissioners Court, n.d.

———. *Ethnicity in the Sunbelt: Mexican Americans in Houston*. Houston: University of Houston Series in Mexican American Studies, no. 4, 2001.

———. *In Re: Ricardo Rodriguez: An Attempt at Chicano Disenfranchisement in Texas, 1896–1897*. San Antonio: Caravel Press, 1979.

———. *Mexican Americans in Texas*. Wheeling, IL: Harlan-Davidson, 1993.

———. *San Angelenos: Mexican Americans in San Angelo, Texas*. San Angelo: Fort Concho Museum Press, 1985.

———. *They Called Them Greasers: Anglo Attitudes toward Mexicans in Texas, 1821–1900*. Austin: University of Texas Press, 1983.

———. *The Tejano Community, 1836–1900*. Albuquerque: University of New Mexico Press, 1982.

De Sipio, Louis. "Sending Money Home . . . for Now: Remittances and Immigrant Adaptation in the United States." In *Sending Money Home: Hispanic Remittances and Community Development*, eds. Rodolfo de la Garza and Briant Lindsey Lowell, 1–24. Lanham, MD: Rowan and Littlefield, 2002.

Delgado, Héctor. *New Immigrants, Old Unions*. Philadelphia: Temple University Press, 1993.

Deutsch, Sarah. *No Separate Refuge: Culture, Class and Gender on an Anglo-Hispanic Frontier, 1880–1940*. New York: Oxford University Press, 1989.

Dictionary of Latino Civil Rights History. Rosales, F. Arturo, ed. Houston: Arte Público Press, 2006.

Doering, Bernard. *The Philosopher and the Provocateur: The Correspondence of Jacques Maritain and Saul Alinsky*. Notre Dame: University of Notre Dame Press, 1994.

Doyle, J. Kaaz. "Callaghan, Bryan V., Jr." *Handbook of Texas*. http://www.tsha.utexas.edu/handbook/online/articles/view/CC/fcadw.html (accessed April 5, 2010).

Driscoll, Barbara. *The Tracks North: The Railroad Bracero Program of World War II*. Austin: University of Texas Press, 1999.

Dyer, Thomas G. *Theodore Roosevelt and the Idea of Race*. Baton Rouge: LSU Press, 1980.

Engh, Michael. "From the City of Angels to the Parishes of San Antonio: Catholic Organization, Women Activists, and Racial Intersections, 1900–1950." *Catholicism in the American West: A Rosary of Hidden Voices*, eds. Roberto R. Treviño and Richard V. Francaviglia, 42–71. Arlington: University of Texas at Arlington, 2007.

Espinosa, Gastón. "Today We Act, Tomorrow We Vote: Latino Religions, Politics and Activism in Contemporary U.S. Civil Society." *Annals, American Academy of Political and Social Science* 612 (2007). http://www.jstor.org/discover/10.2307/25097934?uid=3739256&uid=2129&uid=2&uid=70&uid=4&sid=21102566295427 (accessed August 19, 2013).

Etulian, Richard W. *César Chávez: A Brief Biography with Documents*. Boston: Bedford/St. Martin's, 2002.

Fabela, Isidro, and Josefina A. de Fabela. *Documentos Históricos de la Revolucción Mexicana: Precursores de la Revolución Mexicana, 1906–1910*: Vol. 11. Mexico City: Fondo de la Cultura Económica, 1966.

Félix, Adrian, Carmen González, and Ricardo Ramírez. "Political Protest, Ethnic Media and Latino Naturalization." *American Behavioral Scientist* 52, no. 618 (2008). http://www.rebelion.org/noticias/2006/4/30005.pdf (accessed January 7, 2011).

Ferlazzo, Larry, and Lorie A. Hammond. *Building Parent Engagement in Schools.* Columbus: Linworth Books/Libraries Unlimited, 2009.

Ferguson, Charles M. *Fifty Million Brothers: A Panorama of American Lodges and Clubs.* New York: Farrar and Rinehart, 1937.

Fernández, José María. *The Biography of Casimiro Barela.* Albuquerque: University of New Mexico Press, 2003.

Fernández, Valeria. "Phoenix: Una Historia Muy Hispana." *La Voz,* September 27, 2006. http://www.azcentral.com/lavoz/front/articles/092606historiaphx-CR.html (accessed August 19, 2013).

Fink, Leonard. "American Labor History." Washington: American Historical Association, 1990.

Fisher, James T. *Communion of Immigrants: A History of Catholics in America.* New York: Oxford University Press, 2000; revised, 2007.

Fletcher, Bill, Jr., and Fernando Gapasin. *Solidarity Divided: The Crisis in Organized Labor and a New Path toward Social Justice.* Berkeley: University of California Press, 2008.

Flores, John. "Bert Corona." *Encyclopedia of U.S. Labor and Working-Class History,* ed. Eric Arnesen, 324–326. New York: Routledge, 2007.

Flores, Richard R. *Remembering the Alamo.* Austin: University of Texas Press, 2002.

Foner, Nancy. *In a New Land: A Comparative View of Immigration.* New York: New York University, 2005.

Fox, Jonathan. "Reframing Mexican Migration as a Multi-ethnic Process." *Latino Studies* 4, nos. 1–2 (2006): 39–61.

Franklin, V. P. "'A Way Out of No Way': The Bible and Catholic Evangelization in the United States." In *African Americans and the Bible: Sacred Texts and Social Textures,* eds. Vincent Wimbush and Rosamind Rodman, 650–660. London: Continuum International Publishing, 2000.

Frente de Trabajadores de la Energia. "2006, Cien años de la huelga minera de Cananea (México)." *Frente de Los Trabajadores de la Energia* 6, no. 8 (2006). http://www.fte-energia.org/E80/e80-01.html (accessed January 25, 2011).

Frisbie, Marjorie. *An Alley in Chicago: The Ministry of a City Priest.* New York: Sheed and Ward, 1991.

Galarza, Ernesto. The Crisis of the Pan American Union." *Inter-American Reports,* no. 5 (1949).

———. "Standardization of Armaments in the Western Hemisphere." *Inter-American Reports,* no. 1 (1947).

Gallego, B. J. "Get Acquainted with Big Bend History and Archeology." *La Vista de la Frontera* 16, no. 1. http://ww2.sulross.edu/cbbs/basics.php (accessed August 19, 2013).

Gallegos, Herman, and Michael O'Neill. *Hispanics and the Non-profit Sector.* New York: The Foundation Center, 1991.

Gamio, Manuel. *Mexican Immigration to the United States.* New York: Dover Press, 1971.

Ganz, Marshall. *Why David Sometimes Wins: Leadership, Organization, and Strategy in the Farmworkers Movement.* New York: Oxford University Press, 2009.

García, Arnoldo. "Toward a Left without Borders: The Story of the Center for Autonomous Social Action-General Brotherhood of Workers." *Monthly Review* (2002). http://www.solidarity-us.org/pdfs/cadreschool/fws.garcia.pdf (accessed August 19, 2013).

García, James E. "Spanish-language Radio." In *Encyclopedia of Latino Popular Culture*, eds. Cordelia Candelaria, Peter J. García, and Arturo J. Aldama, 510–511. Westport, CT: Greenwood Publishing, 2004.

García, Juan Ramón. *Mexicans in the Midwest, 1900–1932*. Tucson: University of Arizona Press, 1996.

García, Juan Ramón, and Thomas Gelsinon, eds. *Mexican American Women: Changing Images/Perspectives in Mexican American Studies*. Vol. 5. Tucson: MASRC, University of Arizona, 1995.

García, María-Cristina. "Gomez, Refugio." *The Handbook of Texas*. http://www.tsha .utexas.edu/handbook/online/articles/GG/fgo62_print.html (accessed April 3, 2010).

———. "Morales, Félix Hessbrook." *The Handbook of Texas*. http://www.tshaonline .org/handbook/online/articles/fmobk (accessed January 9, 2011).

García, Mario T. *Católicos: Resistance and Affirmation in Chicano Catholic History*. Austin: University of Texas Press, 2008.

———. *Desert Immigrants: Mexicans in El Paso, 1880–1920*. New Haven: Yale University Press, 1982.

———. *A Dolores Huerta Reader*. Albuquerque: University of New Mexico Press, 2008.

———. *Memories of Chicano History: The Life and Narrative of Bert Corona*. Berkeley: University of California Press, 1994.

———. *Mexican Americans: Leadership, Ideology, and Identity, 1930–1960*. New Haven: Yale University Press, 1989.

Garcia, Richard. *Rise of the Mexican American Middle Class: San Antonio, 1929–1941*. College Station: Texas A&M University Press, 1991.

Garcilazo, Jeffrey M. "McCarthyism, Mexican Americans, and the Los Angeles Committee for Protection of the Foreign-Born." *Western Historical Quarterly* 32, no. 3 (2001): 273–295.

Garza, Alicia A. "Rio Grande City Riots of 1888." *The Handbook of Texas*. http://www .tshaonline.org/handbook/online/articles/RR/jcr3.html (accessed April 20, 2010).

Giffords, Gloria Fraser. *Sanctuaries of Earth, Stone and Light: The Churches of Northern New Spain*. Tucson: University of Arizona Press, 2007.

Gilly, Adolfo. *La Revolución Interrumpida*. Mexico City: Ediciones ERA, 2007.

Goldring, Luin. "The Mexican State and Transmigrant Organizations: Negotiating the Boundaries of Membership and Participation." *Latin American Research Review* 37, no. 3 (2002): 55–99.

Gómez, Laura. *Manifest Destinies: The Making of the Mexican American Race*. New York: NYU Press, 2007.

Gómez-Quiñones, Juan. *Chicano Politics: Reality and Promise, 1940–1990*. Albuquerque: University of New Mexico Press, 1990.

———. *Roots of Chicano Politics: 1600–1940*. Albuquerque: University of New Mexico Press, 1994.

Gonzales, Manuel G. "Carlos I. Velasco and the Defense of Mexican Rights in Territorial Arizona." In *En Aquel Entonces: Readings in Mexican-American History*, eds. Manuel G. Gonzalez and Cynthia M. Gonzales, 96–107. Bloomington: Indiana University Press, 2000.

Gonzales, Michael J. "U.S. Copper Companies, the Mine Workers' Movement, and the Mexican Revolution." *The Hispanic American Historical Review* 76, no. 3 (1996): 503–534.

González, Aníbal A. "Southern Messenger." *The Handbook of Texas*. http://www.tsha online.org/handbook/online/articles/SS/ees19.html (accessed January 25, 2011).

González, Jovita. *Life along the Border*. María Eugenia Cotera, ed. College Station: Texas A&M Press, 2006.

González, Gilbert G. "Company Unions, the Mexican Consulate, and the Imperial Valley Agricultural Strikes, 1928–1934." *The Western Historical Quarterly* 27, no. 1 (1996): 53–73.

———. *Mexican Consuls and Labor Organizing: Imperial Politics in the American Southwest*. Austin: University of Texas Press, 1999.

———. Gilbert G. González and Raul Fernández. "Empire and the Origins of Twentieth-Century Migration from Mexico to the United States." *Pacific Historical Review* 71, no. 1 (2002): 19–57.

González Salas, Carlos. *Los Trabajadores de Tampico y Ciudad Madero*. Ciudad Victoria: Universidad Autónoma de Tamaulipas, Instituto de Investigaciones Históricas, 1993.

Goodwin, Richard. *Remembering America: A Voice from the Sixties*. NY: Harper and Row, 1988.

Gordon, Linda. *The Great Arizona Orphan Abduction*. Cambridge: Harvard University Press, 1999.

Gould, Louis L. *Progressives and Prohibitionists: Texas Democrats in the Wilson Era*. Austin: University of Texas Press, 1973.

———. "Progressive Era." *The Handbook of Texas*. http://www.tshaonline.org/handbook/online/articles/PP/npp1.html (accessed January 25, 2011).

Graham, Hugh Otis. *Collision Course: The Strange Conversion of Affirmative Action and Immigration in America*. New York: Oxford University Press, 2002.

Greenbaum, Susan D. "A Comparison of African American and Euro-American Mutual Aid Societies in 19th Century America." *Journal of Ethnic Studies* 19, no. 3 (1991): 95–119.

Greenberg, Sanford N. "White Primary." *The Handbook of Texas*. http://www.tsha online.org/handbook/online/articles/WW/wdw1.html (accessed January 25, 2011).

Greider, William. *Who Will Tell the People: The Betrayal of American Democracy*. New York: Simon and Schuster, 1992.

Griswold del Castillo, Richard. *La Familia: Chicano Families in the Urban Southwest, 1848 to the Present*. Notre Dame, IN: University of Notre Dame Press, 1984.

———. *The Los Angeles Barrio, 1850–1890: A Social History*. Berkeley: University of California Press, 1979.

Gross, Ariela, "Texan Mexicans and the Politics of Whiteness." *Law and History Review* 21, no. 1 (2003). http://weblaw.usc.edu/assets/docs/Texas_Mexicans.pdf (accessed August 19, 2013).

Guerín-González, Camille. *Mexican Workers and American Dreams*. New Brunswick: Rutgers, 1994.

Gutiérrez, David. "Migration, Emergent Ethnicity, and the 'Third Space': The Shifting Politics of Nationalism in Greater Mexico." *Journal of American History* 86, no. 24 (1999): 481–517.

———. *Walls and Mirrors: Mexican Americans, Mexican Immigrants, and the Politics of Ethnicity*. Berkeley: University of California Press, 1995.

Haney-López, Ian. *Racism on Trial: The Chicano Fight for Justice.* Cambridge, MA: Harvard University Press, 2004.

Hart, John Mason. "The Evolution of the Mexican and Mexican-American Working Class." *Border Crossings: Mexican and Mexican-American Workers,* 1–22. Wilmington, DE: Scholarly Resources, 1998.

Harvey, David. *A History of Neoliberalism.* New York: Oxford University Press, 2007.

L. P. Hartley. *The Go-Between.* New York: New York Review of Books Classics, 2011.

Hayden, Tom. *Reunion: A Memoir.* New York: Crowell-Collier, 1989.

Hayden, Tom, and Dick Flacks. "The Port Huron Statement at 40." *The Nation,* July 18, 2002.

Hernández, José Amaro. *Mutual Aid for Survival: The Case of the Mexican American.* Malabar, FL: Robert Krieger Publishing Company, 1983.

Hernández, Rubén. "A Legacy Once Lost." *Latino Perspectives,* October 2007, 4–7.

Hernandez-Truyol, Berta, and Matthew Hawk. "Traveling the Boundaries of Statelessness: Global Passports and Citizenship." *Immigration and Nationality Review* 27 (2006): 97–117.

Herring, Hubert. Review of Manuel Carrera Estampa, *Los Gremios Mexicanos: La Organización Gremial en Nueva España. American Historical Review* 62, no. 1. (1956): 169–170.

Heyman, Joshua. "The Oral History of the Mexican-American Community of Douglas, Arizona, 1901–1942." *Journal of the Southwest* 35, no. 2 (1993).

———. *Working People on the Border: Life and Labor in Sonora, 1886–1986.* Tucson: University of Arizona, 1991.

Hollinger, David. *Cosmopolitanism and Solidarity: Studies in Ethnoracial, Religious, and Professional Affiliation in the United States.* Madison: University of Wisconsin Press, 2006.

Hudspeth Directory Company. *Big Spring City Directory.* El Paso: Hudspeth Directory Company, Inc. 1929.

———. *El Paso City Directory.* 1918, 1919, 1920, 1922, 1923, 1924, 1925, 1926, 1927, 1929, 1930.

Imaz Bayona, Cecilia. "Las Organizaciones Sociales de Migrantes en Los Estados 4Unidos: El Caso del Club Social De Jala, Nayarit, en California y Su Gestión para La Co-existencia de Tradiciones Populares." In *Nuevas tendencias y desafíos de la migración internacional México-Estados Unidos,* ed. Raúl Delgado Wise, 47–67. Mexico City: UNAM, 2004.

Jackson, Robert Alexander, and Eldon M. Parker. *A History of Organized Labor in Bolivia.* Westport, CT: Greenwood Press, 2005.

Jayaraman, Saumathi, and Immanuel Ness. *The New Urban Immigrant Workforce.* Armonk, NY: M. E. Sharpe, 2005.

"Jesse Díaz and Javier Rodríguez: Undocumented in America." *New Left Review* 47 (2007). http://www.newleftreview.org/?view=2689 (accessed January 7, 2011).

Johnson, Ralph David, John A. Booth, and Richard J. Harris. *The Politics of San Antonio: Community, Progress and Power.* Lincoln: University of Nebraska Press, 1983.

Jones, Nancy Baker. "Leonor Villegas de Magnón." *The Handbook of Texas.* http://www.tshaonline.org/handbook/online/articles/VV/fvi19.html (accessed January 25, 2011).

———. "Jovita Idar." *The Handbook of Texas.* http://www.tshaonline.org/handbook/online/articles/fid03 (accessed February 28, 2011).

Justice, Glenn. "Buena Vista, Texas (Pecos County)." *The Handbook of Texas.* http://www
.tshaonline.org/handbook/online/articles/BB/hnb94.html (accessed January 25, 2011).

Kanellos, Nicolás. *Hispanic Periodicals in the United States: Origins to 1960.* Houston:
Arte Público Press, 2000.

———. *A History of Hispanic Theatre in the United States: Origins to 1940.* Austin: University of Texas Press, 1990.

———. "Publishers and Publishing." In *Greenwood Encyclopedia of Latino Literature,*
ed. Nicolás Kanellos, 910–935. Westport, CT: Greenwood Press, 2002.

Katz, Alfred H. "Self-help and Mutual Aid: An Emerging Social Movement?" *Annual
Review of Sociology* 7 (1981): 129–155.

Katz, Friederick. *The Life and Times of Pancho Villa.* Palo Alto, CA: Stanford University
Press, 1998.

Katz, Friederick, Jane-Dale Lloyd, and Luz Elena Galván de Terrazas, eds. Porfino
Díaz frente aldiscon-tento popular regional, 1891–1893. Mexico: Universidad
Iberoamerica, 1986.

Kheel Center for Labor, Management Documentation and Archives. *Trade Union Publications . . . 1850–1941.* Ithaca: Cornell University, 2007.

King, Martin Luther, Jr. *A Testament of Hope: The Essential Writings and Speeches of
Martin Luther King, Jr.* James Melvin Washington, ed. New York: HarperCollins,
1991.

Koenig, Rebecca Anne Todd. "Antonio Rodríguez." *The Handbook of Texas.* http://
www.tshaonline.org/handbook/online/articles/RR/fro99.html (accessed January
25, 2011).

———. "Fiestas Patrias." *The Handbook of Texas.* http://www.tshaonline.org/
handbook/online/articles/FF/lkf6.html (accessed January 25, 2011).

Knapp, Frank A., Jr. "A Note on General Mariano Escobedo." *Southwestern Historical
Quarterly* 55, no. 3 (1952): 394–401.

Kreneck, Thomas H. *Mexican American Odyssey: Felix Tijerina, Entrepreneur and Civic
Leader, 1905–1965.* College Station: Texas A&M University Press, 2001.

———. *Pueblo: History of Houston's Mexican American Community.* Houston: Houston
International University, 1989.

LaMothe, Louise. "Oral History of Antonia Herández." ABA Commission on Women
in the Profession/Women Trailblazers in the Law. January 20, 2006. http://www
.americanbar.org/content/dam/aba/directories/women_trailblazers/hernandez_
interview_3.authcheckdam.pdf (accessed August 19, 2013).

Larralde, Carlos, and Richard Griswold del Castillo. "San Diego's Ku Klux Klan,
1920–1980." *San Diego History* 46, nos. 2 and 3. http://www.sandiegohistory.org/
journal/2000-2/klan.htm (accessed February 21, 2011).

Lasater, Dale. *Falfurrias: Ed C. Lasater and the Development of South Texas.* College Station: Texas A&M University Press, 1985.

Leininger, Julie. *Chicanos in South Bend: Some Historical Narratives.* Notre Dame: Centro de Estudios Chicanos e Investigaciones Sociales, 1976.

Lernoux, Penny. *Cry of the People.* New York: Doubleday, 1980.

Limerick, Patricia Nelson. *The Legacy of Conquest: The Unbroken Past of the American
West.* New York: Norton, 1987.

Limón, José. "El Primer Congreso Mexicanista: A Precursor to Contemporary Chicanismo." In *Latino/a Thought: Culture Politics and Society,* eds. Francisco H. Vásquez
and Fernando D. Torres, 169–192. New York: Rowan and Littlefield, 2002.

López, José Timoteo. *La Historia de la Sociedad Protección Mutua de Trabajadores Unidos.* New York: Comet Press Books, 1958.

Lorey, David E. *The U.S.-Mexico Border in the Twentieth Century.* Wilmington, DE: Scholarly Resources, 1999.

Louie, Miriam Ching Yoon. *Sweatshop Warriors: Immigrant Women Workers Take on the Global Factory.* Cambridge: South End Press, 2001.

Lovato, Roberto. "Voices of a New Movimiento." *The Nation,* June 19, 2006. http://www.thenation.com/article/voices-new-movimiento?page=0,1 (accessed April 21, 2013).

Lowell, Briant Lindsey, and Rodolfo O. de la Garza. "A New Phase in the Story of Remittances." *Sending Money Home: Hispanic Remittances and Community Development,* 3–28. Lanham, MD: Rowan and Littlefield, 2002.

Lueckens, Richard. "Saul Alinsky: *Homo Ludens* for Urban Democracy." *Christian Century,* November 15, 1989, 1050.

Márquez, Benjamin, and James Jennings. "Representation by Other Means: Mexican American and Puerto Rican Social Movement Organizations." *PS: Political Science and Politics* 33, no. 3 (2000): 541–546.

Martínez, Elizabeth "Betita" Sutherland. "A View from New Mexico: Recollections of the *Movimiento* Left." *Monthly Review* 54, no. 3 (2002). http://monthlyreview.org/0702martinez.htm (accessed January 25, 2011).

———. *500 Years of Chicana Women's History.* New Brunswick: Rutgers University Press, 2008.

Martínez, Rubén. "Chicano/a Land Ethics and a Sense of Place." *Culture and Agriculture* 29, no. 2 (2007): 113–120.

Mason, Kenneth. *African Americans and Race Relations in San Antonio, Texas, 1867–1937.* New York: Garland Publishers, 1998.

Massey, Douglas S., Jorge Durand, and Nolan J. Malone. *Beyond Smoke and Mirrors: Immigration in an Era of Economic Integration.* New York: Russell Sage Foundation, 2003.

Massey, Douglas S., Frank Kalter, and Karen A. Pren. "Structural Economic Change and International Migration from Mexico and Poland." In *Migration und Integration,* ed. Frank Kalter, 134–161. Wiesbaden: VS Verlag, 2008.

Matovina, Timothy. *Guadalupe and Her Faithful: Latino Catholics in San Antonio. Colonial Origins to the Present.* Baltimore: Johns Hopkins University Press, 2005.

McBride, James. "The Liga Protectora Latina: A Mexican American Benevolent Society in Arizona." *Journal of the West* XIV (1975): 83–85.

McKenzie, Phyllis. *The Mexican-Texans.* College Station: Texas A&M University Press, 2004.

McMillan, Nora E. Ríos. "Nemesio García Naranjo." *The Handbook of Texas.* http://www.tshaonline.org/handbook/online/articles/GG/fga94.html (accessed January 25, 2011).

Meier, August. *Negro Thought in America: 1860–1915.* Ann Arbor: University of Michigan Press, 1963.

Meier, Matt S., and Margo Gutiérrez. *Encyclopedia of the Mexican American Civil Rights Movement.* Westport, CT: Greenwood Press, 2000.

Mellinger, Philip. *Race and Labor in Western Copper: The Fight for Equality.* Tucson: University of Arizona Press, 1995.

———. "The Men Have Become Organizers: Labor Conflict and Unionization in the

Mexican Mining Camps of Arizona, 1900–1915." *Western Historical Quarterly* 23, no. 3 (1992): 323–347.

Menchaca, Martha. *The Mexican Outsiders: A Community History of Marginalization and Discrimination in California*. Austin: University of Texas Press, 1995.

Mendoza, Louis Gerard. *Historia: The Literary Making of Chicana and Chicano History*. College Station: Texas A&M University Press, 2001.

"Migrating from Exploitation to Dignity: Immigrant Women Workers and the Struggle for Justice. An Interview with Miriam Ching Yoon Louie." *Multinational Monitor* 22, no. 10 (2001). http://multinationalmonitor.org/mm2001/01october/octo1 interviewlouie.html (accessed August 18, 2013).

Miller, Ernest H. *Corpus Christi, Texas City Directory*. Asheville, North Carolina: Miller Press, 1929.

Moberg, David. "Labor's Turnaround: The AFL-CIO Has a Plan to Turn around the Movement." *In These Times*, March 3, 2013.

Monroy, Douglas. *Rebirth: Mexican Los Angeles from the Great Migration to the Great Depression*. Berkeley: University of California Press, 1999.

Montejano, David. *Anglos and Mexicans in the Making of Texas, 1836–1986*. Austin: University of Texas Press, 1987.

Montgomery, David. "Workers' Movements in the United States Confront Imperialism: The Progressive Experience." *Journal of the Gilded Age and Progressive Era* 7, no. 1 (2008): 84–92.

Moore, James Talmadge. *Acts of Faith: The Catholic Church in Texas, 1900–1950*. College Station: Texas A&M University Press, 2002.

Morrison and Fourmy Directory Co. *City of Austin*. Galveston: Morrison and Fourmy Directory Co., 1903, 1909, 1910.

———. *Directory of the City of Houston*. Houston: Morrison and Fourmy Directory Co., 1910–1911, 1915, 1920–1921,1929.

Nathan, Debby. "Pocahontas on the Rio Grande." *The Texas Observer*, March 5, 1999. http://www.texasobserver.org/article.php?aid=968 (accessed January 25, 2011).

Navarro, Armando. *Mexicano Political Experience in Occupied Aztlán*. Lanham, MD: Rowman Altimira Press, 2005.

———. *The Immigration Crisis*. Lanham, MD: Rowman and Littlefield, 2009.

Ness, Immanuel. *Immigrants, Unions, and the New U.S. Labor Market*. Pittsburgh: Temple University Press, 2005.

Noriega, Rick. "Bill Analysis, H.C.R.111." May 7, 1999. http://www.legis.state.tx.us/ tlodocs/76R/analysis/doc/HC001111.doc (accessed January 25, 2011).

Ochoa, María. "Cooperative Re/weavings: Artistic Expression and Economic Development in a Northern New Mexican Village." *Perspectives in Mexican American Studies* 5 (1995): 121–149.

Ornelas, Michael R. *Beyond 1848: Readings in the Modern Chicano Historical Experience*. Dubuque, IA: Kendall-Hunt, 1993.

Orozco, Cynthia. "Beyond Machismo, La Familia and Ladies Auxiliaries: A Historiography of Mexican-Origin Women's Participation in Voluntary Associations and Politics in the United States, 1870–1990." *Renato Rosaldo Lecture Series* 10 (1992–1993): 37–78. Tucson: Mexican American Studies and Research Center, University of Arizona, 1994.

———. "American Council of Spanish-speaking People." http://www.tshaonline.org/ handbook/online/articles/AA/pqa1.html (accessed January 25, 2011).

———. "Domínguez, Simón G." *The Handbook of Texas*. http://www.tshaonline.org/handbook/online/articles/DD/fdoqx.html (accessed January 25, 2011).

———. "Cortez, Gregorio." *The Handbook of Texas*. http://www.tshaonline.org/handbook/online/articles/CC/fco94.html (accessed January 25, 2011).

———. "Garza, Higinio, Jr." *The Handbook of Texas*. http://www.tshaonline.org/handbook/online/articles/GG/fgaxx.html (accessed January 25, 2011).

———. "Gonzales, Manuel C." *The Handbook of Texas*. http://www.tshaonline.org/handbook/online/articles/GG/fgo57.html (accessed January 25, 2011).

———. "Hernández, María L. de." *The Handbook of Texas*. http://www.tshaonline.org/handbook/online/articles/fhe75 (accessed March 12, 2011).

———. "Idar, Clemente N." *The Handbook of Texas*. http://www.tshaonline.org/handbook/online/articles/fid04 (accessed February 28, 2011).

———. "Idar, Eduardo." *The Handbook of Texas*. http://www.tsha.utexas.edu/handbook/online/articles/II/fid5.html (accessed February 2, 2010).

———. "League of United Latin American Citizens." *The Handbook of Texas*. http://www.tshaonline.org/handbook/online/articles/LL/we11.html (accessed January 25, 2011).

———. "Mexican American Women." *The Handbook of Texas*. http://www.tshaonline.org/handbook/online/articles/pwmly (accessed January 20, 2012).

———. *"No Mexicans, Women or Dogs Allowed: The Rise of the Mexican American Civil Rights Movement*. Austin: University of Texas Press, 2009.

———. "Pérez, Lino, Sr." *The Handbook of Texas*. http://www.tshaonline.org/handbook/online/articles/PP/fpeew.html (accessed January 25, 2011).

———. "School Improvement League." *The Handbook of Texas*. http://www.tshaonline.org/handbook/online/articles/kaswm (accessed January 25, 2011).

Orozco, Manuel. "Latino Hometown Associations as Agents of Development in Latin America." In *Sending Money Home: Hispanic Remittances and Community Development,* eds. Rodolfo de la Garza and Briant Lindsey Lowell, 85–105. Lanham, MD: Rowan and Littlefield, 2002.

Oviedo, Joaquin. *Morenci Memories: True Tales of Copper Town*. Bloomington, IN: iUniverse, 2004.

Padilla, Génaro. *My History, Not Yours: The Formation of Mexican American Autobiography*. Madison: University of Wisconsin Press, 1993.

Palacios, Joseph Martin. *The Catholic Social Imagination: Activism and the Just Society in Mexico and the United States*. Chicago: University of Chicago Press, 2007.

Pantoja, Adrian D., Cecilia Menjívar, and Lisa Magaña. "The Spring Marches of 2006: Latinos, Immigration, and Political Mobilization in the 21st Century." *American Behavioral Scientist*, no. 499 (2008). http://abs.sagepub.com/cgi/reprint/52/4/499 (accessed August 24, 2013).

Paredes, Américo. *A Texas-Mexican Cancionero: Folksongs of the Lower Border*. Austin: University of Texas Press, 1995.

Park, Robert E., and H. A. Miller. *Old World Traits Transplanted*. New York: Harper Bros., 1921.

Parrillo, Vincent N. *Diversity in America*. Thousand Oaks, CA: Pine Forge Press, 2008.

Payne, F. B. *1911 City Directory of Laredo, Texas*. Laredo: F. B. Payne and Company, 1912.

Pawel, Miriam. *A Union of Their Dreams: Power, Hope, and Struggle in Cesar Chavez's Farm Worker Movement*. New York: Bloomsbury Press, 2009.

Peña, Manuel H. *Música Tejana: The Cultural Economy of Artistic Transformation*.

University of Houston Series in Mexican American Studies, no 1. College Station: Texas A&M University Press, 1999.

Pérez, Emma. *The Decolonial Imaginary: Writing Chicanas into History.* Bloomington: Indiana University Press, 1999.

Pitti, Gina Marie. "The Sociedades Guadalupanas in the San Francisco Archdiocese, 1942–1962." *US Catholic Historian* 21, no. 1 (2003): 83–98.

Pitti, Stephen J. *The Devil in the Silicon Valley: Northern California, Race, and Mexican Americans.* Princeton: Princeton University Press, 2003.

Pluecker, John. "Introduction to Conrado Espinosa." *Under the Texas Sun/El Sol de Texas,* 115–130. Translated by Ethriam Cash Brammer de González. Houston: Arte Público Press, 2007.

Polk, R. L., and Co. *Polk's Morrison & Fourmy Austin City Directory.* Houston: Morrison and Fourmy Directory Co., 1916, 1918, 1920, 1922, 1924, 1927.

Pycior, Julie Leininger. *LBJ and Mexican Americans: The Paradox of Power.* Austin: University of Texas Press, 1997.

———. "Tejanas Navigating the 1920s." In *Tejano Epic: Essays in Honor of Félix Almaráz, Jr.,* ed. Arnoldo De León, 71–81. Austin: Texas State Historical Association, 2005.

———. "Vale Mas La Revolución Que Viene: Ernesto Galarza and Transnational Scholar Activism." In *Leaders of the Mexican American Generation: Biographical Sketches,* ed. Anthony Quiroz. Urbana: University of Colorado Press [forthcoming].

Quiroga, Miguel González. "Mexicanos in Texas During the Civil War." In *Mexican Americans in Texas History,* eds. Emilio Zamora, Cynthia Orozco, and Rodolfo Rocha, 51–62. Austin: Texas State Historical Society, 2000.

Quiroz, Anthony. *Claiming Citizenship: Mexican Americans in Victoria, Texas.* College Station: Texas A&M University Press, 2005.

Raftery, Judith Rosenberg. *Land of Fair Promise: Politics and Reform in Los Angeles Schools, 1885–1941.* Stanford: Stanford University Press, 1992.

Reisler, Mark. *By the Sweat of Their Brow: Mexican Immigrant Labor in the United States, 1900–1940.* Westport, CT: Greenwood Press, 1976.

Remembering SNCC: A Circle of Trust. Greenburg, Cheryl Lynn, ed. New Brunswick, NJ: Rutgers University Press, 1998.

Rhodes, Alice J. "Lampasas, Texas." *The Handbook of Texas.* http://www.tshaonline.org/handbook/online/articles/hf101 (accessed February 28, 2011).

Ríos, Herminio, and Lupe Castillo. "Mexican American Newspapers, 1841–1942." *El Grito* 3, no. 4 (1972): 31–38.

Rivera-Salgado, Gaspar, and Luis Escala Rabadán. "Collective Identity and Organizational Strategies of Indigenous and Mestizo Mexican Migrants." In *Indigenous Mexican Migrants in the United States,* eds. Jonathan Fox and Gaspar Rivera-Salgado, 145–178. La Jolla: Center for U.S.-Mexican Studies, University of California, San Diego, 2004.

Rogers, Mary Beth. *Cold Anger: A Story of Faith and Power Politics.* Denton: University of North Texas Press, 1990.

Rojas Coria, Rosendo. *Tratado de Cooperativismo Mexicano.* Mexico City: Fondo de la Cultura Económica, 1952.

Romo, David Dorado. *Ringside Seat to Revolution: An Underground Cultural History of El Paso and Juárez, 1883–1923.* El Paso: Cinco Puntos Press, 2005.

————. "Ringside Seat to a Revolution." *The Texas Observer,* January 13, 2006, 26–27. http://www.texasobserver.org/article.php?aid=2114 (accessed January 25, 2011).

Romo, Ricardo. *East Los Angeles: History of a Barrio.* Austin: University of Texas Press, 1983.

————. "The Urbanization of Chicanos." In *Beyond 1848,* ed. Michael R. Ornelas. Dubuque, IA: Kendall-Hunt Publishing Co., 1993.

Rosales, F. Arturo. *Pobre Raza: Violence, Justice, and Mobilization among México Lindo Immigrants, 1900–1936.* Austin: University of Texas Press, 1999.

————. *Testimonio: A Documentary History of the Mexican American Struggle for Civil Rights.* Houston: Arte Público Press, 2000.

Rosales, Rodolfo. *The Illusion of Inclusion: The Untold Political Story of San Antonio.* Austin: University of Texas Press, 2000.

Rosenbaum, Robert J. "El Partido del Pueblo Unido." In *Beyond 1848: Readings in the Chicano Historical Experience,* ed. Manuel R. Ornelas. Dubuque, IA: Kendall-Hunt, 1993.

Rowell's American Newspaper Directory. Berkeley: University of California, 1887.

Ruiz, Vicki. *From Out of the Shadows: Mexican Women in Twentieth Century America.* New York: Oxford University Press, 1998.

————. "Una Mujer Sin Fronteras: Luisa Moreno and Latina Labor Activism." *Pacific Historical Review* 73, no. 1 (2004): 1–20.

Ryan, S. J., Steven P. "Jesuits." *The Handbook of Texas.* http://www.tshaonline.org/handbook/online/articles/JJ/ixj2.html (accessed January 25, 2011).

Sáenz, Andrés. *Early Tejano Ranching: Daily Life at Ranchos San José and El Fresnillo.* Andrés Tijerina, ed. College Station: Texas A&M University Press, 2001.

Salas, Carlos. "The impact of NAFTA on wages and incomes in Mexico." *In NAFTA at Seven: Its Impact On Workers In All Three Nations, Briefing Paper 106,* eds. Robert Scott, Carlos Salas, and Bruce Campbell. Washington: Economic Policy Institute, 2001.

San Antonio City Directory, 1892. San Antonio: Jules A. Appler, 1892.

San Miguel, Guadalupe, Jr. *Brown, Not White: School Integration and the Chicano Movement in Houston.* College Station, Texas: A&M University Press, 2001.

Sánchez, George J. *Becoming Mexican American: Ethnicity, Culture and Identity in Chicano Los Angeles, 1900–1945.* New York: Oxford University Press, 1993.

Santillán, Richard. "Midwestern Mexican American Women and Their Struggle for Gender Equality: A Historical Overview, 1920s–1960s." *Perspectives in Mexican American Studies* 5 (1995).

Santos, John Phillip. *Places Left Unfinished at the Time of Creation.* New York: Viking, 1999.

Sen, Rikyu. *Stir It Up: Lessons in Community Organizing and Advocacy.* New York: John Wiley and Sons, 2003.

Serbi-Vélez, Federico A., Marc Brindel, Juandalynn Taylor, and Renée Espinoza. "Spanish-language Daily Newspapers and Presidential Elections." In *The Mass Media and Latino Politics,* edited Federico Serbi-Velez, New York: Routledge, 2008.

Servín, Manuel P. *An Awakened Minority: The Mexican-Americans.* Beverly Hills: Glencoe Press, 1974.

Shaw, Randy. *Beyond the Fields: Cesar Chavez, the UFW, and the Struggle for Justice in the Twenty-first Century.* Berkeley: University of California Press, 2008.

Sheridan, Thomas. "Race and Class in a Southwestern City: The Mexican Community of Tucson, 1854–1941." In *Beyond 1848: Readings in the Modern Chicano Historical Experience,* ed. Michael R. Ornelas. Dubuque, IA: Kendall-Hunt Publishing, 1993.

Siegal, Larry J. *Criminology.* Florence, KY: Cengage, 2008.

Sierra, Christine M. "Chicano Political Development: Historical Considerations." In *Beyond 1848: Readings in the Modern Chicano Historical Experience,* ed. Michael R. Ornelas. Dubuque, IA: Kendall-Hunt Publishing Co., 1993.

Skocpol, Theda. *Diminished Democracy: From Membership to Management in American Civic Life.* Norman: University of Oklahoma Press, 2004.

Slate, John H. "Film Industry." *The Handbook of Texas.* http://www.tshaonline.org/handbook/online/articles/ecf01 (accessed August 19, 2013).

Smith, Bradford, and Others. *Philanthropy in Communities of Color.* Bloomington: Indiana University Press, 1999.

Smith, Robert Courtney. *Mexicans in New York City: Transnational Lives of New Immigrants.* Berkeley: University of California Press, 2006.

Sobré, Judith Berg. *San Antonio on Parade.* College Station, TX: Texas A&M University Press, 2003.

Sociedad de Obreros. *Reglamento: General Reforma.* Laredo: Gate City Printing Office, 1891.

Sociedad de Socorros Mutuos "Sociedad Matamoros." *Reglamento General.* Morelos: Francisco Pizarro, 1884.

Sociedad Hispano-Americana de Benevolencia Mutua entre Señoras. "Constitución y Leyes." San Francisco: Imprenta Cosmopolitana, 1875.

Sociedad Mutualista de Obreros "Ignacio Zaragoza." "Constitución y Regalmento." Ciudad Juárez: Imprenta Hernández, 1907.

Sociedad Mutualista "Hijos de Juárez." *Reglamento General.* Laredo: Bravo's Mexican Publishing Co., 1916.

Sociedad Mutualista Mexicana. *Pro-Mexico.* New York, 1927.

Sociedad Mutualista "Nicolas Bravo" de Panaderos. "Reglamento." Chihuahua: Tipografía de 'El Correo,' 1907.

Stein, Stephen Julius. "Tikkun Olam: Actions Speak Loudly—BUT SO DO WORDS." Wiltshire Boulevard Temple bulletin, March 15, 2009. http://www.wbtla.org/document.doc?id=100 (accessed August 19, 2013).

Stephenson, J. B. *City Directory of Austin.* Austin: J.B. Stephenson, 1905–1906, 1907, 1909–1910.

Steen, Ralph W. "Ferguson, James Edward." *The Handbook of Texas.* http://www.tshaonline.org/handbook/online/articles/FF/ffe5.html (accessed January 25, 2011).

Steiner, Stan. *La Raza: The Mexican Americans.* New York: Harper and Row, 1969.

Stern, Alexandra. *Eugenic Nation: Faults and Frontiers of Better Breeding in America.* Berkeley: University of California Press, 2005.

Stoddard, Lothrop. *The Rising Tide of Color against White World Supremacy.* New York: Scribner, 1920.

Suárez-Orozco, Marcelo. *Crossings: Mexican Immigration in Interdisciplinary Perspectives.* Cambridge: Harvard University David Rockefeller Center for Latin American Studies, 1998.

Subervi-Vélez, Federico A., Marc Brindel, Juandalynn Taylor, and Renée Espinoza. "Spanish-language Daily Newspapers and Presidential Elections." In *The Mass Media and Latino Politics,* ed. Federico Subervi-Velez. New York: Routledge, 2008.

Texas Department of State. *Official List of Notaries Public of the State of Texas*. Austin: Department of State, 1922.

Thompson, Jerry. *Warm Weather and Bad Whiskey: The 1886 Laredo Election Riot*. El Paso: University of El Paso Press, 1991.

———. *A Wild and Vivid Land: An Illustrated History of the South Texas Border*. Austin: Texas State Historical Association.

Tichnor, Daniel. *Dividing Lines: The Politics of Immigration Control in America*. Princeton: Princeton University Press, 2002.

Tilly, Charles, and José Luis Alvarez Galván. "Lousy Jobs, Invisible Unions: The Mexican Retail Sector in the Age of Globalization." *International Labor and Working-class History*, no. 7 (2006).

Torche, Florencia. "Mexico's Fragile Middle Class." *Americas Quarterly*. 2009. http://www.americasquarterly.org/mexican-middle-class (accessed January 25, 2011).

Ueda, Reed. *Postwar Immigrant America: A Social History*. New York: Bedford, 1989.

Ulloa, Berta. *Revolución Mexicana*. Mexico City: Tallares de la nación, 1963.

Valdéz, Dennis Nodín. *Al Norte Agricultural Workers in the Great Lakes Region, 1917–1970*. Austin: University of Texas Press, 1991.

Valdés, Dionicio Nodín. *Barrios Norteños: St. Paul and Midwestern Mexican Communities in the Twentieth Century*. Austin: University of Texas Press, 2000.

Valerio-Jiménez, Omar S. "New Avenues for Domestic Dispute and Divorce Lawsuits along the U.S.-Mexico Border, 1832–1893." *Journal of Women's History* 21, no. 1 (2009): 10–33.

Van der Linden, Marcel. "Transnationalizing American Labor History." *Journal of American History* 86, no. 3 (1999): 1078–1092.

Varela, María. "If You Have Come to Help Us . . . Go Home!" *US Catholic Historian* 26, no. 1 (2008): 67–82.

Vargas, Zaragosa. *Labor Rights Are Civil Rights: Mexican American Workers in Twentieth-Century America*. Princeton: Princeton University Press, 2004.

———. "Armies in the Fields and Factories: The Mexican Working Classes in the Midwest in the 1920s." *Mexican Studies/Estudios Mexicanos* 7, no. 1 (1991): 47–71.

Vera, Homero S. "Catarino Garza." *El Mesteño: A Magazine about Mexican American Heritage and Culture in South Texas and Mexico*. http://groups.yahoo.com/group/losbexarenos/message/1395 (accessed August 19, 2013).

———. "The Catholic Mutual Society" and "Father Juan Zavala." *El Mesteño* 3, no. 5 (2000). http://groups.yahoo.com/group/losbexarenos/message/1395 (accessed August 19, 2013).

Victor Rose's History of Victoria. Petty, J. W., Jr., ed. Victoria, Texas: Book Mart, 1961.

Waldrep, Christopher. *Lynching in America: A History in Documents*. New York: NYU University Press, 2006.

Walker, David. "Porfirian Labor Politics: Working Class Organizations in Mexico and Porfirio Díaz, 1876–1902." *The Americas* (1981): 247–298.

Warren, Mark R. *Dry Bones Rattling: Community Building to Revitalize American Democracy*. Princeton: Princeton University Press, 2001.

Wasserman, Mark. *Everyday Life and Politics in Nineteenth Century Mexico: Men Women, and War*. Albuquerque: University of New Mexico Press, 2000.

Williams, Charles B., Jr., and Hilda H. B. Williams. "Mutual Aid Societies and Economic Development: Survival Efforts." In *African Americans in the South: Issues of*

Race, Class, and Gender, ed. Hans A. Baer and Yvonne Jones. Athens: University of Georgia Press, 1992.

Witt, Laura Gutiérrez de, Martha Enna Rodríguez Melo, and María Elena Santoscoy. *Breve Historia de Coahuila*. Mexico City: El Colegio de México, 2005.

Worley, John F., and Company. *Dallas City Directory*. Dallas: John F. Worley Directory Company, 1925, 1929.

———. *El Paso City Directory*. El Paso: Press of John F. Worley, 1900, 1901, 1902, 1904, 1905, 1910, 1911, 1912, 1915, 1917.

Young, Elliot. *Catarino Garza's Revolution on the Texas-Mexican Border*. Durham: Duke University Press, 2004.

———. "Nemesio García." *The Handbook of Texas*. http://www.tshaonline.org/ handbook/online/articles/GG/fgajl.html (accessed January 25, 2011).

Yzaguirre, Raúl. "Liberty and Justice for All." In *Latinos and the Nation's Future*, ed. Henry Cisneros and John Rosales. Houston: Arte Público Press, 2009.

———. "Ready to Rumble: Civil Rights Heavyweight Raul Yzaguirre on Life, the Evolution of the NCLR, and giving Latinos a Fighting Chance." *Latino Leaders*. 2001. http://law-journals-books.vlex.com/vid/rumble-heavyweight-raul-yzaguirre-nclr-56471996 (accessed August 19, 2013)

Zabin, Carol, and Luis Escala. "From Civic Association to Political Participation: Mexican Hometown Associations and Mexican Immigrant Political Empowerment in Los Angeles." *Frontera Norte* 14, no. 27 (2002) 7–42. http://www.redalyc.org/pdf/136/13602701.pdf (accessed August 19, 2013).

Zamora, Emilio. *World of the Mexican Worker in Texas*. College Station: Texas A&M University, 1995.

———. "Labor Formation, Community, and Politics: The Mexican Working Class in Texas, 1900–1945." In *Border Crossings: Mexican and Mexican-American Workers*, ed. John Mason Hart. Wilmington, DE: Scholarly Resources, 1998.

Zuñiga, Víctor, and Rubén Hernández-León. *New Destinations: Mexican Immigration to the United States*. New York: Russell Sage Foundation, 2005.

Sources Only Available Online

Adams, John H. "Rally Supports Migrant Workers, Boycott of N.C. Pickle Company." *The Layman Online*. November 15, 2000. http://www.layman.org/news5702/ (accessed August 19, 2013).

American Bar Association. "Conversation: Transcript of Lucas Benitez's March 2000 Talk." http://www.abanet.org/publiced/lawday/convo/00/beniteztalk.html (accessed April 6, 2010).

AMOS (A Mid-Iowa Organizing Strategy). "Creating a Community Where All Can Succeed." http://amosiowa.org/ (accessed August 19, 2013).

Anti-Defamation League. "Ku Klux Klan: Recent Developments." http://www. adl.org/learn/ext_us/kkk/changes.asp?LEARN_Cat=Extremism&LEARN_ SubCat=Extremism_in_America&xpicked=4&item=kkk (accessed February 21, 2011).

Arizona Interfaith Network-IAF. "Concept Paper on Immigration Reform Border Security, Comprehensive Reform, and Economic Recovery." July 6, 2010. http:// www.arizonainterfaith.org/imm_reform.php (accessed February 2, 2010).

Arizona State University Archives. "Chicana/Chicano Experience in Arizona." http://www.asu.edu/lib/archives/website/organiza.htm (accessed February 21, 2011).

Banda, Magda, and Martha Zurita. "Latino Immigrant Engagement in the Chicago Region." Institute for Latino Studies, University of Notre Dame. http://latinostudies.nd.edu/assets/95265/original/ (accessed July 16, 2013).

Basta Dobbs. http://bastadobbs.com/ (accessed January 11, 2011).

Baytown Public Library. "La Sociedad Mutualista Parade Festivities, Orchestra. . . ." http://www.baytownlibrary.org/gallery/index.php/Street-Scenes/baypic828 (accessed August 19, 2013).

"Bert Corona and His Vision." Bert Corona Leadership Institute. http://www.bcli.info/profile.htm (accessed February 26, 2011).

Boggs, Grace Lee. "Thinking Dialectically about Solidarity." December 10, 2010. http://www.commondreams.org (accessed January 18, 2011).

Building Bridges Radio. "Farm Labor Organizing Committee—Building on Victories." Internet Archive. 2008. http://www.archive.org/details/BuildingBridgesRadioFarmLaborOrganizingCommittee-BuildingOnVictories (accessed March 10, 2010).

Burrelles*Luce*. "2009 Top Media Outlets." http://www.burrellesluce.com/top100/2009_Top_100List.pdf (accessed January 3, 2010).

California Community Foundation. http://www.calfund.org/index.php (accessed December 29, 2010).

———. "CCF Biographies." http://www.calfund.org/learn/staffbios.php#AHernandez (accessed December 29, 2010).

Castañeda, Oscar Rosales, and Maria Quintana. Timeline: Farm Worker Organizing in Washington State." http://depts.washington.edu/civilr/farmwk_timeline.htm (accessed August 19, 2013).

Cattan, Nacha, and Carlos Manuel Rodríguez. "Carlos Slim's America Movil May Face Breakup Pressure in New Law." http://www.bloomberg.com/news/2013–03–11/mexico-proposal-would-allow-breakup-of-phone-tv-companies-1-.html (accessed March 11, 2013).

Center for Big Bend Studies. "Hispanic History and Pioneers of El Barrio, Alpine, Texas, 1882–1910." http://www.sulross.edu/cbbs/basics-elbarrio.php (accessed January 20, 2012).

Center on Philanthropy and Civil Society, Graduate Center, City University of New York. "Latino Philanthropy Literature Review." http://www.philanthropy.org/programs/literature_reviews/latino_lit_review.pdf (accessed August 19, 2013).

Centro de los Derechos del Migrante, Inc. http://www.cdmigrante.org/ (accessed August 19, 2013).

Cervantes-Gautschi, Peter. "Wall Street and Immigration: Financial Services Giants Have Profited from the Beginning." Americas Program. December 4, 2007. http://www.cipamericas.org/archives/881 (accessed August 19, 2013).

Chávez, Ernesto. "Mutualista Organizations." http://www.jrank.org/cultures/pages/4230/Mutualista-Organizations.html (accessed January 2, 2011).

Christian Family Movement. "History." http://www.cfm.org/history.html (accessed November 15, 2010).

Club Barrio del Gpe. Mezquitillo, San Francisco del Rincón, Gto. http://francorrinconenses.blogspot.com/ (accessed January 11, 2011).

CNN "Mexico's President Praises Obama's Immigration Shift." http://www.cnn.
com/2012/06/18/politics/immigration/index.html (accessed January 7, 2013).
Coalition of Immokalee Workers. "About CIW." http://ciw-online.org/about.html
(accessed April 1 2010).
———. "Sodexo and Coalition of Immokalee Workers Sign Fair Food Agreement."
http://www.ciw-online.org/ciw_sodexo_joint_release.html (accessed January 18,
2012).
COFEM/Confederación de Federaciones Mexicanas en Norteamérica. "Clubs/Organi-
zations." http://www.cofem.org/clubs.html (accessed January 25, 2011).
———. "Historic Landmark." http://www.cofem.org/about/historic.html (accessed
January 25, 2011).
Colorado State Archives. "History FAQs." http://www.colorado.gov/dpa/doit/archives/
history/histfaqs.htm (accessed April 19, 2010).
Compeán, Mario. "Mexican Americans in the Columbia Basin: A Historical Over-
view." Columbia River Basin Ethnic History Archive. http://www.vancouver.wsu.
edu/crbeha/ma/ma.htm (accessed January 25, 2011).
CONFEMEX (Confederación de Federaciones Mexicanas). "Celebran Miembros de
CONFEMEX Su 6to Aniversario." http://www.confemexusa.com/archive/sexto_
aniveresario_confemex.html (accessed January 25, 2011).
———. "Quienes Somos." http://www.confemexusa.com/quienes_somos.html
(accessed January 25, 2011).
Cortés, Ernesto, Jr. "Ernesto Cortés, Jr." http://www.swiaf.org/readings/ernesto-
cortes/ (accessed August 19, 2013).
———. "Reweaving the Fabric: The Iron Rule and the IAF Strategy for Power and
Politics." http://www.cpn.org/topics/community/reweaving.html (accessed July 24,
2013).
Coyne, Kevin. "Pushing Boundaries: A History of the Knights of Columbus." http://
www.kofc.org/un/eb/en/anniversary/historical/index4.html (accessed January 25,
2011).
Create Real Democracy. "Legalize Democracy: Abolish Corporate Personhood." http://
createrealdemocracy.blogspot.com/2010/01/move-to-amend-legalize-democracy-
abolish.html (accessed January 23, 2011).
Cripps, Thomas. "'Art [and History] by Lightning Flash': The Birth of a Nation and
Black Protest." Center for History and New Media. http://chnm.gmu.edu/episodes/
the-birth-of-a-nation-and-black-protest/ (accessed April 30, 2010).
Dahle, Cheryl. "Social Justice: Ernesto Cortés, Jr." Fast Company. November 1999.
http://www.fastcompany.com/magazine/30/cortes.html (accessed January 25,
2011).
Das, William A. "For Whom and for What? The Contributions of the Non-Profit Sector." The Aspen Institute. http://www.aspeninstitute.org/policy-work/nonprofit-
philanthropy/archives/whom-what-contributions-t (accessed August 19, 2013).
De Los Santos, Nancy. The Bronze Screen. http://www.kqed.org/tv/programs/index.
jsp?pgmid=14764 (accessed August 19, 2013).
Delgado-Wise, Raúl, and Luis Eduardo Guarnizo. "Migration and Development:
Lessons from the Mexican Experience." Migration Information Service. February 2007. http://www.migrationinformation.org/Feature/display.cfm?ID=581
(accessed January 25, 2011).

"Director of Immigrant Rights Organization Latino Movement USA." Democratic Underground. http://www.democraticunderground.com/discuss/duboard. php?az=show_mesg&forum=364&topic_id=1130201&mesg_id=1132461 (accessed January 27, 2011).

Diocese of Las Cruces. "The Tradition of Stewardship in the U.S. Hispanic Communities." http://www.dioceseoflascruces.org/assets/bp_sp_02.pdf (accessed August 19, 2013).

Dolan, Jay. "Catholics in the Midwest." http://www.nd.edu/~jdolan/midwest.html (accessed January 25, 2011).

Donor Research Project, Center for Philanthropy and Civil Society. "Latino Philanthropy Literature Review." City University of New York Graduate Center. 2003. http://www.philanthropy.org/programs/literature_reviews/latino_lit_review.pdf (accessed January 20, 2011).

Durán, Lisa. "Caring for Each Other: Philanthropy in Communities of Color." Custom Development Solutions, Inc. http://www.cdsfunds.com/caring_for_each_other_philanthropy_in_communities_of_color.html (accessed January 20, 2011).

Embassy of the United States—Dominican Republic. "President Obama Announces Nomination of Raul H. Yzaguirre, Sr., to Become U.S. Ambassador to the Dominican Republic." http://santodomingo.usembassy.gov/pr-091130.html (accessed May 12, 2010).

Evangelista, James. "Penitente Morada, Abiquiu, New Mexico." http://evangelista-photography.blogspot.com/2010/05/penitente-morada-abiquiu-nm.html (accessed January 10, 2013).

Farm Labor Organizing Committee, FLOC, AFL-CIO. http://supportfloc.org (accessed April 1, 2010).

———. "Changing the System." http://supportfloc.org/solution.aspx (accessed January 18, 2012).

Federación de Clubes Zacatecanos. "Historia de la Federación." http://www.federacionzacatecana.org/ (accessed January 6, 2013).

Federación Jaliscence. "Patrocinador." http://fedjalisco.org/category/patrocinadores/ (accessed August 19, 2013)

Federación Oaxaqueña de Comunidades y Organizaciones Indígenas en California (FOCOICA). "Bienvenidos a La Pagina Web. . . ." http://www.angelfire.com/or2/focoica/pagina.htm (accessed June 2, 2010).

Fernández, Ticia, and Santos V. Canales. "Brownsville City Cemetery." http://www.cemeteries-of-tx.com/Etx/Cameron/Cemetery/brownsvillecity.htm (accessed January 25, 2011).

Forbes. "The World's Billionaires." http://www.forbes.com/billionaires/list/ (accessed July 28, 2013).

Fox, Jonathan, and Xóchitl Bada, "Migrant Civic Engagement." Research Paper Series on Latino Immigrant Civic and Political Participation, no. 3, June 2009. Woodrow Wilson Center Mexico Institute. www.wilsoncenter.org/migrantparticipation (accessed May 30, 2010).

Fulton, Katherine, Gabriel Kaspar, and Barbara Kibbee. "What's Next for Philanthropy." Monitor Institute (2010). http://www.monitorinstitute.com/downloads/Whats_Next_for_Philanthropy.pdf (accessed January 16, 2011).

Galán, Héctor. Los Mineros. Espinosa Productions. http://espinosa.siteutopia.net/productions/mineros.htm (accessed January 14, 2013).

García Zamora, Rodolfo. "Collective Remittances and the 3x1 Program as a Transnational Social Learning Process." http://www.wilsoncenter.org/sites/default/files/ Garcia%20Zamora%20-%20Collective%20Remittances%203x1.pdf (accessed August 19, 2013).

———. "The 3x1 Program in Mexico: Achievements and Challenges." *Focal Point.* Canadian Foundation for the Americas (May–June 2007). http://www.focal.ca/ pdf/focalpoint_se_may-june2007.pdf (accessed August 19, 2013).

Garza, Raúl G. "Leñeros (Woodmen) Burial Customs." *Tricounties Geneology and History,* December 11, 2001. http://www.joycetice.com/flaghold/flag081.htm (accessed January 25, 2011).

Geo-Mexico. "Mexican Home Town Associations (HTAs) and their Considerable Effectiveness. http://geo-mexico.com/?p=5589 (accessed January 7, 2013).

Goodman, Andy, and Linsey Pollak. "HIP to the Gap." Monitor Institute. 2005. http:// www.futureofphilanthropy.org/files/usPhil_goodman_4hip_gap.pdf (accessed July 28, 2013).

Greater Houston Preservation Alliance. "Endangered Buildings." http://issuu.com/ ghpa/docs/2004_summer (accessed August 19, 2013).

Guerra, Guillermo. "Founding Families of Reynosa, Tamaulipas, Mexico." http:// www.vsalgs.org/stnemgenealogy/reynosa.html (accessed August 19, 2013).

Guzmán, Betsy. "The Hispanic Population: Census 2000 Brief." US Census Bureau, 2001, Table 2, "Hispanic Population by Type for Regions, States and Puerto Rico." http://www.census.gov/prod/2001pubs/c2kbr01-3.pdf (accessed January 30, 2011).

"An Interview with Civil Rights Activist Antonia Hernández." *Harvard Latino Law Review* 11 (2008). http://www.law.harvard.edu/students/orgs/llr/vo111/321–332.pdf (accessed January 20, 2011).

Hispanic Lifestyle. "2012 COFEM Annual Conference and Expo." http://www.hispaniclifestyle.com/blog/articles/community/2012-cofem-annual-conference-expo/ (accessed January 9, 2013).

Hispanics in Philanthropy. "About Us." http://www.hiponline.org/about/our-story (accessed August 19, 2013).

"Illinois Voting History." http://www.270towin.com/states/Illinois (accessed January 9, 2013).

Imaz B., Cecilia. "Las organizaciones sociales de migrantes mexicanos en Estados Unidos: el caso del Club Social de Jala, Nayarit, en California y su gestión para la coexistencia de tradiciones populares." http://meme.phpwebhosting. com/~migracion/modules/libro_nuevas_tendencias_de_la_migracion/5.pdf (accessed January 25, 2011).

Immanuel Presbyterian Church. "Snapshots: OneLA-IAF, 1.30.11." http:// immanuelpresblog.org/tag/one-la/ (accessed July 8, 2011).

IMPLU Corporation. "Confedración Mutualista Mexicana e Hispano Americana." http://www.implu.com/nonprofit/840260776 (accessed May 14, 2010).

ImpreMedia. "The ImpreMedia Executive Team." http://impremedia.com/about/ executive.html (accessed January 10, 2011).

Improved Order of Redmen. http://www.redmen.org/ (accessed January 25, 2011).

Industrial Areas Foundation. "Locate IAF Affiliates." http://industrialareasfoundation. org/locate.html (accessed January 25, 2011).

Instituto de Antropología e Historia. "Los Gremios y Cofradías en Nueva España."

http://www.gobiernodigital.inah.gob.mx/Exposiciones/gremios_cofradias/index.html (accessed January 10, 2013).

Instituto de las Mujeres del Distrito Federal. "Elisa Acuña." http://www.inmujer.df.gob.mx/muj_destacadas/elisaacuna.html (accessed February 3, 2010).

Instituto de los Mexicanos en el exterior, *Directorio de Organizaciones y Clubes de Oriundos*. http://www.ime.gob.mx/DirectorioOrganizaciones/busqueda.aspx (accessed April 10, 2010).

Instituto de Antropología e Historia. "Los Gremios y Cofradías en Nueva España." http://www.gobiernodigital.inah.gob.mx/Exposiciones/gremios_cofradias/index.html (accessed January 10, 2013).

Javien, Ana Lau. "La Participación de las Mujeres en La Revolución Mexicana: Juana Belén Gutiérrez de Mendoza (1875–1942)." http://dialogos-ojs.historia.ucr.ac.cr/index.php/Dialogos/article/view/115/114 (accessed August 19, 2013).

Jones-Correa, Michael. "Mexican Migrants and Their Relation to U.S. Civil Society." http://www.wilsoncenter.org/news/docs/MJC%20MX%20Migrant%20US%20Civ%20Soc.pdf (accessed February 6, 2011).

KCET. "Local Hero: Antonia Hernández." http://www.kcet.org/socal/local_heroes/hhm/local-hero-antonia-hernandez.html (accessed January 29, 2011).

KSOL (98.9 FM) San Francisco, CA; KSQL (99.1 FM) Santa Cruz, CA; KVVF (105.7 FM) Santa Clara, CA; KVVZ (100.7 FM) San Rafael, CA; KBRG (100.3 FM) San Jose, CA. "Annual EEO Public File Report Form." 2010. http://u.univision.com/contentroot/uol/10portada/sp/pdf/local/2010_EEO_Annual_Public_File_Report_SFR.pdf (accessed March 9, 2011).

La Opinión. "History of *La Opinión*." http://www.laopinion.com/mediakit/about/history/page_05.html (accessed January 12, 2011).

Lappé, Frances Moore. "Lucas Benítez: Dignity in the Fields." *Yes!* January 3, 2012. http://www.yesmagazine.org/issues/the-yes-breakthrough-15/lucas-benitez-dignity-in-the-fields (accessed August 19, 2013).

"Las Guadalupanas." St. Theresa's Parish, Premont, Texas. http://www.st-theresas.com/organizations/guadalupanas/index.html (accessed January 25, 2011).

League of United Latin American Citizens. "Civil Rights." http://lulac.org/programs/rights/ (accessed May 10, 2010).

———. League of United Latin American Citizens. "Historic Latino Voter Turnout Helps Elect Barack Obama." http://lulac.org/news/pr/historic_turnout/ (accessed May 10, 2010).

Leonard, Andrew. "I Dreamed I saw José Hill Last Night." www.salon.com/2007/01/22 jennifer_gordon (accessed July 22, 2013).

"Leonor Villegas de Magnón." *Great Texas Women*. http://www.utexas.edu/gtw/villegas.php (accessed January 25, 2011).

Library of Congress. "Progressive Era to New Era: 1900–1929." *The Learning Page*. http://lcweb2.10c.gov/learn/features/timeline/progress/immigrnt/immigrnt.html (accessed January 25, 2011).

Lomax, John Nova. "Lomax on Lomax." *Houston Press* blog. June 14, 2007. http://blogs.houstonpress.com/rocks/2007/06/lomax_on_lomax.php (accessed January 25, 2011).

López, Mark Hugo, and Paul Taylor. "The 2010 Congressional Reapportionment and Latinos." Pew Hispanic Center/Pew Research Center. 2011. http://pewhispanic.org/files/reports/132.pdf (accessed January 18, 2011).

Los Alegres de Terán. "Gregorio Cortez." http://www.youtube.com/watch?v=jj4–
    6ZCc7i4 (accessed August 19, 2013).
"Los Penitentes." http://www.eljeferuben.com/lospenitentes.html (accessed January
    10, 2013).
MacArthur Foundation. "MacArthur Fellows Program, 1981–2010." http://www
    .macfound.org/site/c.lkLXJ8MQKrH/b.1139453/k.B938/Search_All_Fellows.htm
    (accessed January 25, 2011).
Malatin, Jeff. "Women in Arizona Politics: From Suffrage to Governing." http://www
    .ic.arizona.edu/ic/mcbride/ws200/jeff.html#2 (accessed March 10, 2013).
"Mariano Escobedo." *Personajes de la Historia de México.* Arámbula, Jesús Gallegos, ed.
    http://redescolar.ilce.edu.mx/redescolar/publicaciones/publi_quepaso/marian
    oesco.htm (accessed January 25, 2011).
Martínez, George A. "The Legal Construction of Race: Mexican Americans and White-
    ness." www.jsri.msu.edu/upload/occasionalpapers/oc54.pdf (accessed August 19,
    2013).
Martínez, Hernández, and José Alfredo. "DIF Tlalnepantla Participa en Conferencia
    Informativa sobre Ley Arizona SB1070." *Diario al Momento* (Gobierno del Estado
    de México). June 24, 2010. http://diarioalmomento.com/index.php?option=com_
    content&task=view&id=7881&Itemid=201 (accessed January 25, 2011).
Maynard Institute. "Columnist Navarrette Laid Off in San Diego." http://mije.org/
    richardprince/columnist-ruben-navarrette-laid-san-diego#Navarrette. June 18, 2010
    (accessed December 29, 2010).
McCain, John. Address to National Council of La Raza. July 14, 2008. http://www.
    mccain.senate.gov/public/index.cfm?FuseAction=PressOffice
    .Speeches&ContentRecord_id=0378B4AD-377F-4064-B50D-B6394B966DCD
    (accessed August 19, 2013).
Méndez, Rita. Speech to the 12th meeting of the CCIME, November 10–11, 2009.
    http://www.ime.gob.mx/images/stories/ime/CCIME/reuniones_ordinarias/
    xii/12_dis_rm.pdf (accessed January 7, 2013).
Media Matters for America. "Limbaugh: Mexican immigrants who illegally enter the
    U.S. are 'unwilling to work.'" http://mediamatters.org/research/200603280009
    (accessed December 28, 2010).
Metropolitan Museum of Art. "Thomas Cole." http://metmuseum.org/Collections/
    search-the-collections/20010582#fullscreen (accessed January 9, 2013).
Mexico, Government of. "Práxedis G. Guerrero." *Enciclopedia de Municipios de México:
    Estado de Chihuahua.* http://www.inafed.gob.mx/work/enciclopedia/EMM08
    chihuahua/index.html (accessed August 19, 2013).
"Mexico: Migrants, Remittances, 3x1." *Migration News* 16, no. 4 (2009). http://
    migration.ucdavis.edu/mn/comments.php?id=3548_0_2_0 (accessed January 25,
    2011).
Mexico Institute. Woodrow Wilson International Center for Scholars. "2006 Presiden-
    tial Election Votes by State and Party."
http://www.wilsoncenter.org/news/docs/MexicoGovernmentStats1.pdf (accessed Janu-
    ary 25, 2011).
Migration Policy Institute. "Illinois: Social and Demographic Characteristics." http://
    www.migrationinformation.org/datahub/state.cfm?ID=IL (accessed January 25,
    2011).

Milkman, Ruth. "Labor and the New Immigrant Rights Movement: Lessons from California." Social Science Research Council. 2006. http://borderbattles.ssrc.org/Milkman/index2.html (accessed March 2, 2011).

Morales, Ed. "The Media is the *Mensaje*." *The Nation.* May 15, 2006. http://www.edmorales.net/articles/mediaismessage.html (accessed January 7, 2011).

Municipio de Práxedis Guerrero. "Práxedis Guerrero: Benemérito del Estado de Chihuahua." http://www.mpiopraxedisguerrero.gob.mx/Plantilla5.asp?cve_Noticia=1605&Portal=mpiopraxedisguerrero (accessed August 19, 2013).

National Association of Hispanic Journalists. http://www.nahj12.com/ (accessed August 19, 2013).

National Council of La Raza. *NCLR Annual Report, 2009.* May 18, 2010. http://www.nclr.org/index.php/publications/nclr_2009_annual_report/ (accessed January 18, 2011).

———. "NCLR Affiliate Network." http://www.nclr.org/index.php/nclr_affiliates/affiliate_network/ (accessed August 19, 2013).

National Day Labor Organizing Committee. "Program Areas." http://www.ndlon.org/en/program-areas (accessed August 19, 2013).

National Hispanic Media Coalition. "NHMC Advocates for More Diversity, Competition and Localism in Broadcast Media." http://www.nhmc.org/content/media-ownership (accessed January 12, 2011).

National Humanities Center. "Toolbox Library: Primary Resources in U.S. History and Literature—The Making of African American Identity, Volume I." http://nationalhumanitiescenter.org/pds/maai/community/text5/text5read.htm (accessed February 14, 2011).

National Register of Historic Places. "National Register System." http://nrhp.focus.nps.gov/natregsearchresult.do?fullresult=true&recordid=5 (accessed August 19, 2013).

Navarrette, Ruben. http://rubennavarrette.com/wordpress/ (accessed December 29, 2010).

New Americans Initiative. "Governor Quinn Joins ICIRR to Celebrate 50,000 New Citizens." 2011. http://icirr.org/content/governor-quinn-joins-icirr-celebrate-50000-new-citizens-1 (accessed August 19, 2013).

New Mexico Office of the State Historian. "Ortero, Miguel A." http://www.newmexicohistory.org/filedetails.php?fileID=4783 (accessed April 21, 2010).

New-York Historical Society. "Nature and the American Vision: The Hudson River School." http://www.nyhistory.org/node/569/gallery (accessed January 9, 2013).

Obama, Barack. Address to National Council of La Raza. July 13, 2008. http://www.whitehouse.gov/photos-and-video/video/2011/07/25/president-obama-addresses-council-la-raza (accessed August 19, 2013).

———. Speech to the League of United Latin American Citizens. July 8, 2008. http://www.youtube.com/watch?v=fx8-h1WdEbg&feature=related (accessed May 10, 2010).

———. Speech to the League of United Latin American Citizens (transcript). http://www.realclearpolitics.com/articles/2008/07/obamas_speech_to_lulac.html (accessed February 13, 2011).

Olmos, Lizette Janness. "Profile: Jaime Martínez." *LULAC News.* May/June 2007. http://www.lulac.net/publications/lulacnews/2007mayjun.pdf (accessed January 25, 2011).

Ortiz Alvarado, Tereso. "Historia (Casa Guanajuato de Dallas)." http://www.
    redesmexico.mx/index.php?option=com_content&view=article&id=991:Dal
    las%20/%20Dallas%20-%20M%C3%A9xico%20Casa%20Guanajuato.%20
    &catid=97:estados-unidos&Itemid=125 (accessed August 19, 2013).

Otra Vuelta. "Where Do Your Tires Go?" http://www.otra-vuelta.com/ (accessed
    November 22, 2010.

Patterson, Kent. "Cananea Mine Battle Reveals Anti-labor Offensive in Mexico, United
    States." Americas Program, Center for International Policy. http://www.axisoflogic
    .com/artman/publish/Article_58834.shtml (accessed August 19, 2013).

Pew Hispanic Center. "Hispanics in the News: An Event-Driven Narrative." December
    7, 2009. http://pewhispanic.org/reports/report.php?ReportID=116 (accessed Janu-
    ary 11, 2011).

Phoenix Hispanic Historic Property Survey. "Migration, Marginalization and Com-
    munity Development, 1900–1939." http://phoenix.gov/HISTORIC/hhps2a.pdf
    (accessed February 21, 2011).

"Piolín por la Mañana." http://piolin.univision.com/ (accessed January 10, 2011).

Pitti, José, Antonia Castañeda, and Carlos Cortés. "A History of Mexican Americans
    in California." http://www.cr.nps.gov/history/online_books/5views/5views5.htm
    (accessed August 19, 2013).

Public Citizen. "12 Months After: The Effects of *Citizens United* on Elections and the
    Integrity of the Legislative Process." January 18, 2011. http://www.citizen.org/
    12-months-after (accessed January 23, 2011).

Pycior, Julie Leininger. "Important but Neglected: Midwest Latino Biography and
    Memoir." Julian Samora Research Institute, Michigan State University. http://
    www.jsri.msu.edu/pdfs/20th/Pycior.pdf (accessed January 3, 2013).

Ramos, Henry A. J., and Gabriel Kasper. "Building a Tradition of Latino Philanthropy:
    Hispanics as Donors, Grantees, Grantmakers, and Volunteers." Center for Philan-
    thropy and Public Policy, University of Southern California. Research paper no. 4.
    2000. http://cppp.usc.edu/doc/RP4.pdf (accessed January 20, 2011).

Religion and Ethics Newsweekly. "An Interview with Ernesto Cortes." March 1, 2001.
    http://www.pbs.org/wnet/religionandethics/episodes/march-2–2001/an-interview-
    with-ernesto-cortes/3456/ (accessed January 3, 2013).

Reynolds, John. *San Antonio Bibliography Matrix.* http://www.colfa.utsa.edu/users/
    jreynolds/NEH/WWI/WWIPOL.htm (accessed January 25, 2011).

"Rita Mendez Signed the Petition: Stand with President Obama: Pass the DREAM
    Act." http://www.change.org/petitions/stand-with-president-obama-pass-the-
    dream-act (accessed January 7, 2013).

Romero Hicks, and Juan Carlos. "Comisión Estatal de Apoyo Integral a Los Migrantes
    y Sús Familias." http://www.guanajuato.gob.mx/gestiones/romerohicks/cuarto/
    social/sdsh2.pdf (accessed January 25, 2011).

Saenz, Rogelio. "Latinos in America 2010." *Population Bulletin Update,* http://www.
    prb.org/pdf10/latinos-update2010.pdf (accessed January 6, 2010).

St. Anthony Messenger Press/Franciscan Communications. "Saint Isidore the Farmer."
    http://www.americancatholic.org/features/saints/saint.aspx?id=1384 (accessed
    April 19, 2010).

Saint Theresa Parish. "History of St. Theresa Parish, Premont, Texas." http://www.
    st-theresas.com/history/index.html (accessed March 3, 2011).

San Antonio Geological and Historical Society. "Wildflower Memorial Park." http://

www.rootsweb.ancestry.com/˜txsaghs2/Pages/Links-Cemetery-Bexar-N-Z.htm (accessed August 19, 2013).

San Francisco Foundation "Board of Trustees." www.sff.ora/about-tssf/who-we-are/board-of-trustees/ (accessed August 19, 2013).

Serrano Díaz, Mónica. "El movimiento anarquista en México." http://www.mono grafias.com/trabajos14/anarquismo/anarquismo.shtml (accessed January 25, 2011).

Service Employees International Union. *Tribute to Eliseo Medina*. Lisa Duncan, producer. http://www.seiu.org/2008/12/award-winning-video-on-seiu-labor-leader-eliseo-medina-shows-evolution-of-immigrant-rights-movement.php (accessed January 25, 2011).

Shaw, Randy. "Lessons of the UNITE-HERE/SEIU Deal." *LA Progressive*. July 29, 2010. http://www.beyondchron.org/news/index.php?itemid=8361 (accessed August 19, 2013).

Skocpol, Theda. "What a Mighty Power We Can Be: African American Fraternal Groups and the Struggle for Equal Rights." http://www.slideshare.net/jsucus/african-american-fraternal-groups-talk-presentation (accessed April 22, 2010).

Smithsonian People, Places, Topics. "Inventor and Revolutionary Victor Ochoa." http://www.smithsonianeducation.org/scitech/impacto/graphic/victor/revolutionary_price.html (accessed January 25, 2011).

Sociedad Mutualista Mexicano de Jornaleros (Waco, Texas). "Mutualista Hall." http://www.mutualistahall.webs.com/ (accessed January 30, 2011).

Society of Saint Vincent de Paul, Council of Los Angeles. "Board of Directors." http://svdpla.org/index.php/about/contents/board_of_directors (accessed January 25, 2011).

Sodexo USA. "Sodexo and Coalition of Immokalee Workers Sign Fair Food Agreement." http://www.sodexousa.com/usen/newsroom/press/press10/ciwfairfood agreement.asp (accessed January 18, 2012).

South Texas College. "A Hundred Years of Civil Rights: Celebrating El Primer Congreso Mexicanista." http://offtheshelf.southtexascollege.edu/wp-content/uploads/2011/11/Flyer_PrimerCongreso.jpg (accessed January 12, 2013).

"SPMDTU." http://www.spmdtu.org/ (accessed August 19, 2013).

Starr, Alexandra. "Voice of América: The Spanish-language DJs behind the new wave of Latino activism." Slate. May 3, 2006. http://www.slate.com/id/2141008/ (accessed January 9, 2011).

Stephenson, Pam. "Santa Maria Cemetery." http://impactnews.com/austin-metro/round-rock-pflugerville-hutto/santa-maria-cemetery/ (accessed August 19, 2013).

Take Stock: Images of Change. http://www.takestockphotos.com/pages/varela.html (accessed January 25, 2011).

Ten Eyck, Tiffany. "In New York City: Carpenters Embrace Immigrant." *Labor Notes*. December 26, 2007. http://www.labornotes.org/node/1489 (accessed April 6, 2010).

Texas Department of Insurance. "About Workers' Compensation." http://www.tdi .state.tx.us/wc/dwc/index.html (accessed January 25, 2011).

"The Tradition of Stewardship in the U.S. Hispanic Communities." http://www .dioceseoflascruces.org/includes/tinymce/jscripts/tiny_mce/plugins/filemanager/files/spch/bp_sp_02.pdf (accessed January 25, 2010).

Turner Classic Movies. "Overview of Heart of the Sunset—Full Synopsis" http://www.tcm.com/tcmdb/title.jsp?stid=497836 (accessed January 25, 2011).

"United Farm Workers of America, AFL-CIO Premiere." April 16, 1975. http://www
    .farmworkermovement.us/ufwarchives/elmalcriado/Scott/Brochure_001.pdf
    (accessed February 23, 2011).

University of California Television. *Organize! The Lessons of the Community Service
    Organization.* http://www.youtube.com/watch?v=hzMaRofspdk (accessed March 7,
    2011).

US Conference of Catholic Bishops. "Catholic Campaign for Human Development."
    http://www.usccb.org/cchd/index.shtml (accessed January 25, 2011).

Velásquez, Baldemar. Speech to Labor Notes conference. August 15, 2008. http://
    www.youtube.com/watch?v=ZRm1HFPgBto&feature=related (accessed January 25,
    2011).

"Victor Ochoa." Smithsonian Institution. http://www.smithsonianeducation.org/
    scitech/impacto/graphic/victor/index.html (accessed January 31, 2011).

Waco Convention and Visitors Bureau. "Waco's Multicultural Heritage." http://www
    .wacocvb.com/waco-culture.html (accessed January 25, 2011).

Walker, Hezekiah. "I Need You to Survive." http://www.youtube.com/
    watch?v=LUUHPDUsLJo (accessed January 25, 2011).

Washington's Birthday Celebration Association. http://www.wbcalaredo.org/home/
    contact-us/3455-faq-s.html (accessed August 19, 2013).

Webb County Historical Commission. "Laredo's Historic Landmarks." 2000. http://
    www.ci.laredo.tx.us/city-planning/Departments/Historic/Landmarks.pdf (accessed
    August 19, 2013).

Wrothe, William H. "Lamy, Jean-Baptiste." New Mexico Office of the State Historian.
    http://www.newmexicohistory.org/filedetails.php?fileID=501 (accessed April 19,
    2010).

"YCSer Maria Varela, YCS Formation Day, 12–21–08." http://www.youtube.com/
    results?search_query=maria+varela+ycs&aq=f (accessed November 13, 2010).

Yzaguirre, Raúl. Address to the convention of National Council of La Raza, July 27,
    2009. http://www.youtube.com/watch?v=FbUSoZ2aCPc (accessed April 10,
    2010).

———. "Comments of Raúl Yzaguirre." EEOC History: 35th Anniversary. http://www
    .eeoc.gov/eeoc/history/35th/voices/yzaguirre-text.html (accessed January 25, 2011).

———. "Civil Rights and the Hispanic Voter: The Legacy of Willie Velásquez." June
    19, 2008. http://www.youtube.com/watch?v=dTqIq2qb1Vo (accessed April 14,
    2010).

Zolberg, Aristide. "A Century of Informality on the United States-Mexico Border."
    Social Science Research Council. In *Border Battles: The U.S. Immigration Debate.*
    http://borderbattles.ssrc.org/Zolberg/index1.html (accessed January 25, 2011).

Other Unpublished Sources

Almaráz, Félix, Jr. "Francisco I. Madero and the Texas Prelude to the Mexican Revolu-
    tion." Bexar County Precinct 4 Newsletter, 1986, 1–2.

Arnold, Charles. "Folklore, Manners and Customs of the Mexicans in San Antonio,
    Texas." Master's thesis, University of Texas, 1928.

Ayala, Adriana. "Negotiating Race Relations through Activism: Women Activists and Women's Organizations in San Antonio, Texas, during the 1920s." PhD diss., University of Texas, 2005.

Briegal, Kay. "The Alianza Hispano-Americana." PhD diss., University of Southern California, 1974.

Calderón, Roberto. Presentation to the Texas State Historical Association, Austin, March 3, 1993.

Cano, Gustavo, and Alexandra Délano. "The Mexican Government and Organised Mexican Immigrants in the United States: A Historical Analysis of Political Transnationalism, 1848–2005." Mexico-North Research Network, Washington, D.C., and Center for Comparative Immigration Studies, University of California, San Diego and St. Antony's College, Oxford University, Working Paper 148 (June 2007).

Castañeda, Antonia. Remarks presented at "Las Tejanas: 300 Years of History, A Symposium," University of Texas at Austin, October 17, 2003.

Gomilla, Michelle. "*Los Refugiados y Los Comerciantes:* Mexican Refugees and Businessmen in Downtown El Paso: 1910–1920." Master's thesis, University of Texas at El Paso, 1990.

OneLA-IAF. "Agenda—One LA Assembly." Los Angeles, May 2, 2010.

———. "OneLA-IAF Foreclosure Prevention Plan." Los Angeles, May 2, 2010.

———. "Plan de Prevención de Ejecuciones Hipotecarias." Los Angeles, May 2, 2010.

Orozco, Cynthia E. "The Origins of the League of United Latin American Citizens (LULAC) and the Mexican American Civil Rights Movement in Texas with an Analysis of Women's Political Participation in a Gendered Context, 1910–1929." PhD diss., University of California, Los Angeles, 1992.

Pycior, Julie Leininger. "Ahead of Their Time to No Avail: The American GI Forum and the Immigration Reform Act of 1965." American GI Forum/Texas A&M Corpus Christi History Conference, Corpus Christi, TX, March 27, 2008.

———. "The Mexican Community in New York City: Precursors." New York State Historical Association, Fordham University, Bronx, NY, June 12, 2000.

———. "Tejana Activism, 1910–1930: An Overview." De León Symposium Lecture, Victoria, TX, April 30, 2005.

———. "Transnational Labor Organizing: Lessons from the Mexican-heritage Community." Lecture, Julian Samora Research Institute, Michigan State University, East Lansing, March 17, 2010.

Rivera, Alex, producer. *The Sixth Section. POV,* PBS. 2003. http://sixthsection.com/img-stadium-hires.jpg (accessed January 25, 2011).

Rogers, T. Guy. "The Housing Situation of Mexicans in San Antonio." Master's thesis, University of Texas, 1927.

San Fernando Cemetery #1 and #2, San Antonio. Gravestone markers.app?action=DocumentDisplay&crawlid=1&doctype=cite&docid=11+Harv.+Latino+L.+Rev.+321&srctype=smi&srcid=3B15&key=fd922919ac5dde15fc629c26142bc507 (accessed 8/24/13); "Featured Contributor: Susan U. Arnold," http://onphilanthropy.com/2007/featured-contributor-susan-raymond-phd/ (accessed 1/17/11).

Index